Audi at Le Mans

Lars Krone / Alexander von Wegner

Delius Klasing Verlag

Contents

About the good fortune of being in the right place at the right time

---

Those who can claim that they were in the right place at the right time can, no doubt, count themselves lucky.

The creation of this book involved an almost astonishing chain of lucky events. Back in 1999, the then young Speedpool Multimedia Service GmbH based in Hamburg was already working for Motorsport Communications of AUDI AG and has been enjoying its trust ever since.

Alexander von Wegner was at Le Mans for Audi as early as in the 2000s. We both had the opportunity to support and represent Audi not only at Le Mans but in the entire FIA World Endurance Championship (WEC) since 2012. When Audi Tradition awarded this book project to Speedpool, the subject of Le Mans came full circle. That our employer readily agreed to provide us with year-long resources for this historic review was certainly a boon, too.

A well-managed and digitally available archive maintained by Speedpool afforded us quick and systematic access to all press releases, press kits, booklets, magazines, audio recordings and other documents created on behalf of Audi from 1999 to 2016. We focused our attention mainly on Le Mans but considered other notable events as well.

National and international daily papers, special-interest magazines and books from our private possession provided further input. AUDI AG's corporate archive containing additional special-interest magazines for the general public and academia, detailed press reviews, corporate press releases, various monographs, slides from the initial Le Mans years and other photographic material and provided valuable advice.

Interviews with contemporary witnesses had to be closely matched with existing written sources. Without any claim to scientific quality, we wished to share those sources with our readers and therefore worked with notes and references.

To this day, all the interviewees – from former mechanics to engineers to race drivers to Heads of Sport to the former Chairman of the Management Board – continue to show great passion for and close ties to their brand. Without hesitation, they all agreed to assist us by sharing their recollections. The decades-long trusting collaboration with the officials at Motorsport Communications provided an important basis for this work as well. Finally, as well as the perfect support provided by our employers, independent journalists and their observations have enhanced this volume.

Stéphane Barbé, Ulrich Baretzky, Dieter Basche, Thomas Bauch, Eva-Maria Becker, Christian Borel, Dindo Capello, Carole Capitaine, Christof Caspar, Andrew Cotton, Pierre Dieudonné, Marcel Fässler, Ralf Friese, Leena Gade, Graham Goodwin, Ralf Jüttner, Andreas Köppen, Siegfried Krause, Tom Kristensen, Axel Löffler, Stefan Moser, Peter Oberndorfer, Petra van Oyen, Dr. Franz-Josef Paefgen, Stefan Pajung, Dr. Mathias Pfaffel, Jürgen Pippig, Torsten Robbens, Mark Schneider, Thomas Stebich, Stefan Trauf, Dr. Wolfgang Ullrich, Thomas Voigt, Gary Watkins, Timo Witt.

Our thanks go to all of them. It is our hope that browsing, reading and marveling at the content of this book will give you, our esteemed readers, equal pleasure as creating it did to us.

Lars Krone, Alexander von Wegner

Dear readers,

The 24-hour race at Le Mans and Audi are inextricably linked. From 1999 to 2016, the brand with the four rings competed in the world's biggest endurance race on 18 occasions – scoring 13 victories during that period. No brand was equally successful in such a short time. I'm happy that I had the opportunity to experience most of those exciting years. In 1994, I signed my first contract as a factory driver, and in 1998, a special honor was bestowed on me: I was the first driver to be allowed to test an Audi LMP sports car. Finally, in 2012, I contested my last race at Le Mans. I have really taken Audi into my heart in all those years. While thinking about my future following my active career, it was clear for me that I wanted to stay connected to Audi. That's why I took over the Audi Zentrum Alessandria, where I can contribute a lot of what I learned at Audi Sport. Team spirit, for instance, is very important to me. I'm proud of Audi Italy having recognized us as the best Audi dealership in 2022. For me, Audi has always been a step ahead of the competition, both in motorsport and with production cars. That's why I want to turn every customer into an Audi ambassador. For Vorsprung durch Technik, Le Mans was the ideal stage.

I hope you'll enjoy the read and am handing over to Tom Kristensen now!

Dindo Capello

Dindo and I were racing together with Audi at Le Mans for many years. I can't even remember how many times he handed over an R8, R10, R15 or R18 to me during a driver change. But now we're celebrating a premiere: we're taking turns in writing a foreword. The first time we shared a car was in 2001, in the ALMS. It was my first full season with Audi. I'd joined the brand with the four rings the year before. When Dr. Wolfgang Ullrich showed me the first sketches of the Audi R8 in 1999 I knew: that's where my future lies. I remained loyal to Audi up until the end of my career in 2014, and afterwards as a brand ambassador. We won Le Mans together seven times. The secret of success? I'm not going to reveal it here yet but you're going to read about it in this exciting book. Our successes were awesome and also attracted huge attention in my native Denmark. When I raced at Le Mans for the first time in 1997 there may have been 500 Danish fans on site.

Later, there were 25,000 of them who created an incredible atmosphere at the Danish camp. The visits to the marquee there together with my teammates were absolute highlights every year. I hope you're going to enjoy this book that looks back on 18 years of Le Mans – years that have shaped the history of the world's major sports car race.

And now Marcel Fässler is taking over!

Tom Kristensen

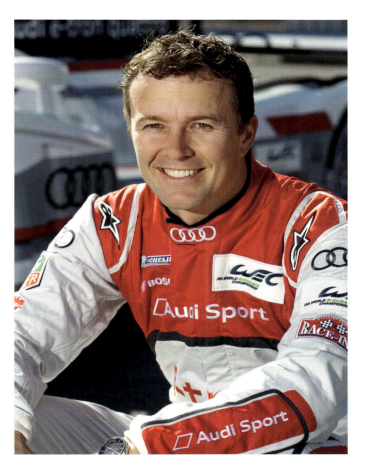

Of course, a dream came true for me when Audi selected me for the Le Mans project in 2010! What racer wouldn't want to be driving for a brand that stands so much for technology, progress, innovation, power and speed as Audi? And, of course, I was hoping for success. My expectations were not disappointed. Audi, with Dr. Wolfgang Ullrich at the helm, was focused, hard-working, simply a hugely powerful team. That's why my seven seasons with André Lotterer and Benoît Tréluyer as teammates and with Leena Gade as our race engineer were unique. We were a really cool team, always in an upbeat mood, not only on but also off the track. In the iconic 24-hour race, we triumphed together, we celebrated together and we also went through setbacks together, but that only bound us together more closely. The emotions of standing on the top step of the podium, cheered by 100,000 people, are unforgettable. Although only our three names appear on the winners' lists, the victories belong to our entire team in which every single member was indispensable. I feel honored to have the opportunity of being one of three drivers to write the foreword in this exciting book. And, as a Swiss, I'm delighted that, together with Audi, I've had the opportunity to be the first to have given my small but race-loving country legendary Le Mans victories.

Enjoy this fantastic book.

Marcel Fässler

The Ferris wheel in Le Mans
is one of the most popular
photography backdrops

Pioneer of progress

Le Mans is a city that has many facets. Movie buffs love its filming locations, its arts and crafts scene is versatile and architectural historians rave about the Old Town. In addition, the city looks back on 150 years of pioneering technical progress.

Authorities block off the 13.6-kilometer Circuit des 24 Heures only for the test day and the race

Intercontinental progress

At the end of the 19th century, not only automobiles accelerate progress. The first airplanes make an old dream of humanity come true. The pioneers of motorized flight include the brothers Wilbur and Orville Wright from America. In 1908, they meet with the Bollée family of inventors in Le Mans. Léon Bollée, who is President of Aéro-Club de la Sarthe, offers logistical support for the flights. They take off from the horse racing track Hunaudières – the area after which the longest straight of the race track will be named. On August 8, 1908, Wilbur Wright proves that he has mastered the feat of controlled motorized flight. [5]

Biotope of creativity

France is the country in which automobile racing has its roots. Starting with the first city-to-city race Paris–Rouen in 1894, initial international competitions soon emerge. [6] Around the turn of the century, James Gordon Bennett, publisher of the New York

Saturday, May 26, 1923, 4 pm: The first edition of the Le Mans 24 Hours, the Grand Prix d'Endurance de 24 Heures "Coupe Rudge-Whitworth" is started. Production touring cars are supposed to compete against each other in a 24-hour Grand Prix. The French importer of the same-named manufacturer of detachable rims led by Emile Coquille donates the cup. Changeable rims are not the norm in those days. [1] Rain and hail make it difficult to travel on unpaved roads and the crews have to perform repairs themselves. Even so, 30 of the 33 entrants finish the race. This arrival rate of 90.9 percent has remained the highest to this day. [2] The winners are André Lagache and René Léonard in a Chenard & Walcker. [3]

Half a century earlier, the city on the Sarthe attracts attention due to some remarkable inventions. In 1873, a steam-powered automobile travels through Le Mans: Amedée Bollée's "L'Obéissante" (the one that obeys) already has four independently suspended wheels, a steam engine and single-wheel steering. [4]

1906 is the first year in which Le Mans appears as a race track in chronicles. Ferenc Szisz wins the Grand Prix de l'ACF

The winged B of the Bentley brand is found five times on the winners' lists up until 1930 (left).
Frank Clement, Walt Owen Bentley and John Duff with the 1924 winning car, a 3-liter-Bentley (below)

Herald, initiates the eponymous races. Each participating country may enter a maximum of three race cars. The victorious nation will host the following competition. [7] However, the Automobile Club de France (ACF) as the 1905 winner suspends the series in 1906, staging the first Grand Prix de France instead. In that way, France circumvents the national limitation of participants. In fact, 26 French automobiles meet with only six from Italy and two from Germany. The venue is a 103-kilometer circuit near Le Mans. To implement the project locally, the Automobile Club de la Sarthe (ACS), a predecessor of the Automobile Club de l'Ouest (ACO), is established. [8] Hungarian Ferenc Szisz wins in a Renault achieving an average speed of more than 100 km/h. [9]

In 1922, the ACO committee issues a formidable task to Georges Durand, its Secretary General from 1906 to 1941: He is supposed to create a competition serving to enhance the quality of touring cars. Together with journalist Charles Faroux, the subsequent Race Director of the Le Mans 24 Hours between 1923 and 1956, and Emil Coquille from the Rudge-Whitworth rim manufacturer, Durand creates the basic elements of a set of regulations. [10]

[1] Christian Moity, Jean-Marc Teissedre: 24 Heures du Mans 1923–1992, Tome 1. Besançon/Le Mans: Editions d'Art J. P. Barthelemy/Automobile Club de l'Ouest, 1992, p. 11 et seq

[2] https://assets.lemans.org/explorer/pdf/courses/2018/24-heures-du-mans/press-kit/fr/statistiques-historiques-fr.pdf, last retrieved on May 12, 2022

[3] Ibid

[4] Exhibition catalog: Sarthe, terre des pionniers. Centenaire des vols de Wilbur Wright au Mans 1908–2008, Le Mans: Archives départementales de la Sarthe, 2008, p. 21 et seq

[5] Ibid, p. 23 et seq

[6] Peter Higham: The Guinness Book of International Motor Racing, London: Guinness World Records Limited/Motorbooks International, 1995, p. 192

[7] Carlo Demand, Paul Simsa: Die Gordon-Bennett-Rennen 1900–1905, Stuttgart: Motorbuch-Verlag, 1987, p. 17

[8] Christian Moity, Jean-Marc Teissedre: 24 Heures du Mans 1923–1992, Tome 1. Besançon/Le Mans: Editions d'Art J. P. Barthelemy/Automobile Club de l'Ouest, 1992, p. 9. The ACO itself names 1906 as the date of its foundation, see www.lemans.org/fr/page/qui-est-laco/2334 last retrieved on June 15, 2022

[9] Mark Hughes: Kings of the Wild Frontier, in Autosport, February 16, 2006, p. 68

[10] Christian Moity, Jean-Marc Teissedre: 24 Heures du Mans 1923–1992, Tome 1. Besançon/Le Mans: Editions d'Art J. P. Barthelemy/Automobile Club de l'Ouest, 1992, p. 11 et seq

Jaguar with the C-Type of Peter Whitehead/Peter Walker wins Le Mans in 1951

A storied track

Its unusual track is one of the special characteristics of this race. From 1923 to date, the ACO has counted 15 versions. [11] It is still not a permanent circuit. The major portion of it consists of public roads that are blocked off only for qualifying and the race. Consequently, unlike permanent race tracks, the Circuit des 24 Heures cannot be practiced outside of the races. In view of of many other street tracks that is not a unique characteristic, but Le Mans, with more than 13 kilometers per lap, is by far the longest track of this kind.

Le Mans remains unusual also in other respects. When a world sports car championship is created for the first time in 1953 it includes the Sebring 12 Hours in Florida, the Mille Miglia in Northern Italy, the Le Mans 24 Hours, the Spa-Francorchamps 24 Hours in Belgium, the ADAC Nürburgring 1000-Kilometer Race, the Tourist Trophy in Dundrod, Northern Ireland, and the Carrera Panamericana in Mexico. Two years later, the Targa Florio in Sicily joins the championship as well. [12] With the venues in Northern Ireland, Mexico, the two Italian ones plus the one in France, five competitions at that time are held on non-permanent race tracks. Le Mans is the only one of them that still exists today. [13]

Ferrari enters its name on the winners' lists nine times, here with Olivier Gendebien/Phil Hill in 1962

The Hunaudières straight (also known as Mulsanne straight) is special as well. Up until 1989, it runs in a straight line for about five kilometers; since 1990, two chicanes have been slowing the racers down. The French privateer team W. M. uses it to achieve the highest top speed. [14] At 405 km/h, Roger Dorchy sets this eternal record in 1988, before the chicanes are built. [15] Race cars run this fast neither in Formula One nor in the oval at Indianapolis.

The legend of Le Mans

What are the elements of the legend of Le Mans? What are its origins? Individual indicators serve to track it down. The number of worldwide 24-hour races is long. An international foursome forms its core group: Daytona (USA), Le Mans (France), Nürburgring (Germany) and Spa-Francorchamps (Belgium). In this group Le Mans is the only non-per-

The race track primarily uses blocked off public roads like the Arnage section shown here

manent track. It looks back on the greatest tradition (90 races from 1923 to 2022) and enables the longest distances within 24 hours as the result of a unique combination: the fastest race track is driven by the most advanced race cars.

Above and beyond those prosaic statistics, every race makes its own history. The Bentley brand established in 1919 delivers its first automobile in 1921 and is on the Le Mans grid as early as in 1923. Between 1924 and 1930, the British win five times, and once more in 2003. The race drivers of the past century – Sir "Tim" Birkin, Sammy Davis, Glen Kidston, "Benjy" Benjafield, John Duff and Woolf Barnato – shape the image of the legendary Bentley Boys as a group of "extraordinary playboys, racers and adventurers." [16]

[11] https://assets.lemans.org/explorer/pdf/courses/2020/ 24-heures-du-mans/press-kit/statistiques-historiques-fr.pdf, last retrieved on June 7, 2022. The Circuit des 24 Heures is not to be confused with the Circuit Bugatti, a modern permanent race track that shares only a few kilometers of the road from the pit lane entrance to an area behind the Dunlop Chicane with the endurance race track

[12] Peter Higham: The Guinness Book of International Motor Racing, London: Guinness World Records Limited/ Motorbooks International, 1995, p. 262 and 264

[13] About the history of the Targa Florio, the Carrera Panamericana and the Mille Miglia see Mike Cotton: Great Road Races, in Le Mans Series & Sportscar Racer 11/1999, p. 38 et seq. The name Targa Florio has been living on in a round of the Italian Rally Championship since 1978: www.acisport.it/it/CIAR/calendario-e-risultati/2022, last retrieved on June 10, 2022

[14] Gary Watkins: Straight fighters, in Motor Sport, October 2001, p. 46

[15] https://assets.lemans.org/explorer/pdf/courses/2020/24-heures-du-mans/press-kit/statistiques-historiques-fr.pdf, last retrieved on June 7, 2022

[16] www.bentleymotors.com/en/world-of-bentley/the-bentley-story/history-and-heritage/historic-people/original-bentley-boys.html, last retrieved on June 9, 2022. Bentley press information: City of Le Mans renames Street "Rue des Bentley Boys" as Bentley Centenary celebrations continue at 24 Hours of Le Mans, June 13, 2019

The 14 track versions before and during Audi's time at Le Mans

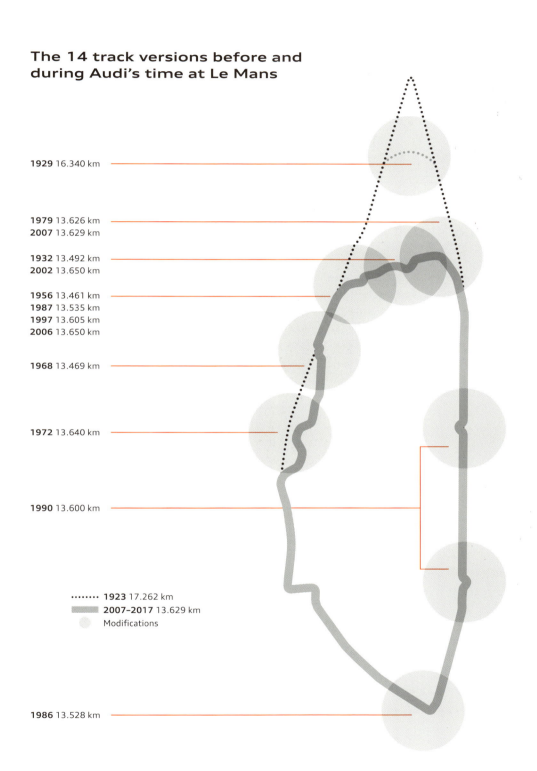

1929 16.340 km

1979 13.626 km
2007 13.629 km

1932 13.492 km
2002 13.650 km

1956 13.461 km
1987 13.535 km
1997 13.605 km
2006 13.650 km

1968 13.469 km

1972 13.640 km

1990 13.600 km

········ **1923** 17.262 km
▬▬▬ **2007–2017** 13.629 km
⚪ Modifications

1986 13.528 km

In 1970, Porsche achieves its first overall victory with the 917. The style of the poster inspires subsequent Chairman of Audi's Management Board Franz-Josef Paefgen

In 1950, Louis Rosier wins together with his son, Jean-Louis. The father drives the Talbot-Lago for almost 24 hours and turns the wheel over to his son for only two laps. [17] Two years later, Pierre Levegh, also in a Talbot, achieves a solo drive until, while leading the race, he retires with a defect in the last hour. [18]

Maximum suspense in 1969: The gap between the victorious Ford GT40 and its pursuer, Porsche, after 24 hours amounts to merely 120 meters. [19] At the start, the subsequent winner, Jacky Ickx, leisurely walks toward his race car. For safety reasons, the Belgian protests against the Le Mans start in which the drivers run to their cars, pull away quickly and often do not buckle up immediately. Ickx puts on his safety belts and accepts the resulting deficit. Subsequently, the ACO abolishes the traditional starting procedure. [20]

The appeal of the Le Mans 24 Hours captures celebrities and automotive marques from all over the world. 23 Formula One World Champions race at La Sarthe. Particularly attractive are the multiple awards such as the "Double Crown" for winners of the Le Mans 24 Hours and the Formula One World Championship that, to date, has gone to five drivers. Two drivers have won the Le Mans 24 Hours and the Indianapolis 500-Mile Race. The "Triple Crown" made up of Formula One, Indianapolis and Le Mans is the top-level award. [21] To date, only the Briton Graham Hill, the 1962 and 1968 F1 World Champion, 1966 Indy and 1972 Le Mans winner, has achieved it. [22] More recently, Jacques Villeneuve, in 2007, travels to Le Mans as F1 World Champion and Indy 500 winner. However, the Canadian misses claiming the "Triple Crown" and as the runner-up in 2008 clinches his best result. [23]

Almost all major automotive brands have succumbed to the temptation of Le Mans. Be it the "big three" from America, Chrysler, Ford and GM, the European manufacturers from the automotive nations Germany (Audi, BMW, Mercedes, Porsche), France (Peugeot and Renault), Great Britain (Aston Martin and Jaguar) and Italy (Ferrari, Alfa Romeo) or the Japanese marques Toyota, Nissan and Mazda – Le Mans attracts them all. [24]

At least two cultural facets make another contribution to the legend. The movie "Le Mans," and particularly its main man Steve McQueen, continue enjoying cult status more than half a century following its release in 1971. [25] Even though a range of competing movies, for instance about Formula One, are produced over the course of the decades, "Le Mans" is regarded as an epitome of racing movies. [26] Le Mans owes an unusual association with the world of art to BMW. In 1975, French race driver and art lover Hervé Poulain together with BMW Motorsport Director

Under the heading Garage 56, the ACO encourages teams and manufacturers to pursue unusual concepts such as the Nissan DeltaWing

In the 2000s, ACO President Jean-Claude Plassart opens the race for new technologies, FIA President Jean Todt supports the relaunch of a world championship

Jacky Ickx wins the 24-hour race six times between 1969 and 1982, Tom Kristensen nine times between 1997 and 2013. They are the two most successful participants

[17] https://assets.lemans.org/explorer/pdf/courses/2018/24-heures-du-mans/press-kit/fr/statistiques-historiques-fr.pdf, last retrieved on May 12, 2022

[18] Gordon Cruickshank: Pierre Levegh's 23 Hours of Le Mans, in Motor Sport, June 1997, p. 70 et seq

[19] https://assets.lemans.org/explorer/pdf/courses/2020/24-heures-du-mans/press-kit/statistiques-historiques-fr.pdf, last retrieved on June 7, 2022. Three years earlier the distance – of 20 meters – is even shorter, but is based on an artificially caused gap between two cars of the brand resulting from a team order issued by Ford

[20] https://assets.lemans.org/explorer/pdf/courses/2018/24-heures-du-mans/press-kit/fr/statistiques-historiques-fr.pdf, last retrieved on May 12, 2022

[21] Ibid

[22] Motorsport, March 2002, p. 21–42

[23] Gary Watkins: Villeneuve: I want to rewrite record books, in Autosport, January 18, 2007, p. 22

[24] The ACO systematically records the participation of the 60 most frequently represented brands from a total group of more than 240 manufacturers, see https://assets.lemans.org/explorer/pdf/courses/2018/24-heures-du-mans/press-kit/fr/statistiques-historiques-fr.pdf, last retrieved on May 12, 2022

[25] Helmut Luckner: Hochspannung, in auto motor und sport Edition 70 Jahre auto motor und sport, 2016, p. 78–83. Leben am Limit, in auto motor und sport Edition Helden, 2019, p. 22–29. Adam Smith: King of Cool, in Edgar Middle East Magazine, No. 20 November 2013, p. 68–72

[26] Richard Heseltine: Wheel to Reel, in Motor Sport, June 2005, p. 78 et seq, evaluates no fewer than 20 films of this type, spread across five decades

In 1991, Mazda achieves the first and only victory with a rotary engine

The Mazda 787 B uses a four-rotor engine (both pictures)

Jochen Neerpasch initiates the first Art Car created by artist Alexander Calder. Many other great artists from Andy Warhol to Jeff Koons follow suit. [27] Arguably, no other race cars make it from the pit lane to the Louvre.

Serving innovation

Today, Le Mans claims playing a leading role in the areas of powertrain technology, renewable fuels and corporate social responsibility. [28] These ideas follow a remarkable tradition. As early as in 1959, the

ACO introduces an Indice au rendement énergétique (energy efficiency index). [29] In 1982, the fuel tank capacity is limited to 100 liters for the first time, and refueling permitted only 24 times. In 1985, the permissible amount of fuel drops by another 15 percent. [30] The introduction of fundamentally energy-based regulations in 2014 marks another milestone achievement.

Many standalone technical solutions or systems are related to Le Mans as well. In 1953, winner Jaguar makes history with the first disc brake system. [31] Michelin, in 1967, launches the first slick

for racing. [32] In 1980, a gasoline-ethanol mixture is the first alternative fuel. [33] In 2006, Audi, on clinching the first victory of a diesel engine, relies on a gas-to-liquid fuel. [34] In 2012, the manufacturer with the four rings is also the first winner to use a hybrid powertrain.

Clearly more difficult to assess are two types of propulsion that never become widely accepted in automobile production. In 1963, a turbine-powered Rover-BRM celebrates its racing debut at Le Mans. Generally, the low efficiency of a turbine opposes its application in automobiles. In 1991, Mazda is the first and only overall winner to use a Wankel engine. The rotary engine achieves no such success in any other motorsport discipline. [35] However, despite 32 licensees and various applications worldwide, the technology never gains traction on an industrial scale and experiences its demise as early as in the seventies. [36] The application of the rotary engine as a range extender that Audi tests in the A1 e-tron starting in 2011 does not progress beyond the trial stage. [37]

The Art Cars' origin is at Le Mans. Head of BMW Motorsport Jochen Neerpasch and auctioneer Hervé Poulain (above) convince artists like Andy Warhol (right) to use the surfaces of race cars as canvases

Race Director Daniel Poissenot is receptive to technological innovations (above).
Jaguar returns in the Group C era of the race and wins again, here in 1988 (bottom)

[27] BMW Group Corporate Communications: The BMW Art Cars go digital, July 21, 2021, and press kit: BMW Art Car Collection (undated), www.press.bmwgroup.com/deutschland/article/detail/T0005913DE/bmw-art-car-collection?language=de, last retrieved on June 13, 2022

[28] https://assets.lemans.org/explorer/pdf/courses/2022/24-heures-du-mans/presse/press-kit-24-heures-du-mans-2022.pdf, last retrieved on June 13, 2022

[29] https://assets.lemans.org/explorer/pdf/courses/2018/24-heures-du-mans/press-kit/uk/statistiques-historiques-en.pdf, last retrieved on February 9, 2023. The ACO no longer reports the exact calculation bases today. Generally, this and subsequent indices put fuel consumption in relation to distance driven, which is why race cars from smaller displacement classes featuring more favorable aerodynamic shapes frequently win these classifications

[30] Ibid, Formula One emphasizes fuel restrictions during those days as well, albeit primarily to reduce the excessive power output of turbo engines

[31] Keith Howard: Disc Brakes, in Motor Sport, May 2000, p. 52–53

[32] Michelin Formel 1 & Motorsport News No. 3, July 2001, p. 12

[33] https://assets.lemans.org/explorer/pdf/courses/2018/24-heures-du-mans/press-kit/uk/statistiques-historiques-en.pdf, last retrieved on February 9, 2023

[34] Markus Gärtner: Optimising the formula, in Audi 2006 Annual Report, p. 12–15; William Whey: From terra firma to top of the podium, in Ibid, p. 16–17

[35] https://assets.lemans.org/explorer/pdf/courses/2018/24-heures-du-mans/press-kit/uk/statistiques-historiques-en.pdf, last retrieved on February 9, 2023. Not to be ignored is the fact that Mazda with a Wankel engine achieved overall victory at Spa in 1981, www.totalenergies24hours.com/winners, last retrieved on June 15, 2022, as well as various class wins at the Daytona 24 Hours since 1979, s. Connie Goudinoff: Mazda Motorsports, Osceola: Motorbooks International, 1992, p. 152 et seq. In addition, the NSU Wankel Spider won the German Rally Championship for Grand Tourisme cars in 1966 with Karl-Heinz Panowitz/Rainer Strunz and the German Hill Climb Championship in 1967 and 1968 with Siegfried Spiess

[36] A detailed description of the background driven by industrial policy and economic aspects in Mathias Pfaffel: Vom selbständigen Unternehmen zum integrierten Konzernstandort. Die AUDI NSU AUTO UNION AG in Neckarsulm 1969–1984, Stuttgart: Franz Steiner Verlag, 2019, p. 65 et seq, p. 368 et seq and 665 et seq

[37] Johannes Köbler: High voltage! in Encounter. The Audi Technology Magazine 01/2011, p. 106–117. Daniel Schuster: Powered Up, in Encounter. The Audi Technology Magazine 01/2012, p. 44–51

In 2012, Audi starts electrifying its race cars at Le Mans. At a PR event, Tom Kristensen uses an Audi A1 e-tron test vehicle with a rotary engine as a range extender

The introduction of Garage 56 for concepts outside the current regulations proves to be a virtually visionary move. They are intended to provide impetus based on their performance capacity and reliability. In 2012, the 475-kilogram Nissan DeltaWing setting lap times on LMP2 level while requiring 30 percent less power, 40 percent less fuel and 50 percent less tires to do so is the first in a range of such concepts. Not every year is focused on energy efficiency. In 2016, a specially modified Morgan-Nissan enables Frédéric Sausset to contest the race despite a quadruple amputation of his arms and legs. [38]

The driver parade and (for many years) the scrutineering take place in the shadow of the cathedral in Le Mans

Famous and infamous

Unfortunately, not all the facets of Le Mans have a positive connotation. When Pierre Levegh in 1955 collides with another car at the start and finish line his Mercedes flies into the bleachers. 84 people die, including the ill-fated driver. Le Mans acquires sad worldwide fame due to what has remained the most serious accident in motorsport history to date. [39]

Only few motorsport enthusiasts associate another, completely cheerful, tradition with Le Mans. In 1967, American race driver Dan Gurney whimsically invents the champagne shower during a podium ceremony at La Sarthe. [40]

Although trackside scrutineering of the technology and documents would be more convenient the ACO still extends an invitation to witness it in the downtown area. As a result, Le Mans remains a sporting event in close touch with its fans. [41]

The sprint toward the race cars that after 1969 was abolished for safety reasons can be witnessed only symbolically in the more recent past (above). The twelve-meter-tall Audi Tower has been standing in the Village since 2007 (right)

Eight aircraft traditionally paint the French tricolor flag against the backdrop of the sky shortly before the start

[38] https://assets.lemans.org/explorer/pdf/courses/2020/24-heures-du-mans/press-kit/statistiques-historiques-fr.pdf, last retrieved on February 9, 2023

[39] Wilfried Feldenkirchen: Unternehmenspolitische Aspekte in der Geschichte des Motorsports bei der Daimler-Benz AG, in Wilfried Feldenkirchen, Armin Herrmann, Harry Niemann: Wissenschaftliche Schriftenreihe des DaimlerChrysler Konzernarchivs Band 5 – Geschichte des Rennsports, Bielefeld: Delius Klasing, 2002, p. 142

[40] British journalist Simon Arron discusses the background during the lifetime of the late race driver who neither planned nor practiced this procedure in 1967. Simon Arron: Mover and shaker, in Autosport, December 20/27, 2001, p. 60–61

[41] www.24h-lemans.com/fr/actualites/le-programme-des-verifications-administratives-et-techniques-des-24-heures-du-mans-2022-56273, last retrieved on June 15, 2022

A powerful past

Audi's sporting history begins more than a century ago. Following many major changes, the year of 1978 marks a new beginning in motorsport for the brand with the four rings. Le Mans evolves into Audi Sport's heyday.

In the advert on the left, Audi proudly promotes an early success: In 1911, two years after the company has been founded, the Type B wins the Austrian Alpine Rally. With the Type C, Audi, between 1912 and 1914, even wins the Team Award at that event across a more than 1,000-kilometer mountainous distance three times in a row. [1] Following Auto Union's unforgotten wins in Grand Prix racing before the Second World War, the company, in the post-war era, is represented besides numerous successes in motorcycle races in touring car racing and rallying, for instance by DKW and NSU.

Debut at Le Mans

The days shortly before Auto Union ceases its active participation in racing at the end of the 1958 season are still seeing a premiere. [2] Heinz Meier, who in 1954 wins the 1.3-liter touring car class in the Mille Miglia in Italy in a DKW F91, ventures a participation in the Le Mans 24 Hours in a DKW Monza in 1957. The privateer driver from Düsseldorf has the car entered in the French competition via Porsche driver Wolfgang Seidel. During the 24 hours the air filter repeatedly forces the team to clean it. Finally, on Sunday morning, the mechanics remove the filter. Shortly afterwards, the three-cylinder two-stroke engine that has been enlarged from 896 to 994 cubic centimeters fails. [3]

Six years later, André Guilhaudin, a race driver and car dealer in Chambéry, is on the grid also under the banner of the four rings. He has won the Index of Performance the year before together with his teammate Alain Bertaut and is sharing the cockpit with him again. Decades later, Bertaut, a trade journalist for L'Action d'Automobile back then, is an ACO

[1] Audi Communications: Press kit Audi. Vorsprung. 100. Mut, 2009, p. 23

[2] Thomas Erdmann, Ralf Friese, Peter Kirchberg, Ralph Plagmann: Vier Ringe: Die Audi Geschichte, Bielefeld: Delius Klasing, 2009, p. 162 et seq

[3] Quentin Spurring: Le Mans. The official history of the world's greatest Motor race 1949–59, Haynes Publishing, Sparkford 2011, p. 297

official with responsibility for the regulations. From 1997 on, Audi engages in exchanges with him concerning LMP regulatory questions. Following Panhard's withdrawal, Guilhaudin and Charles Deutsch's sports car company CD must find a technical replacement for the 1963 Le Mans commitment. [4] They opt for the mechanical system of the new DKW F12. Auto Union is delighted and gets involved in the project, DKW's trial department takes care of the chassis and suspension. [5] The streamlined bodywork is manufactured by coachbuilder Chalmette in Grenoble, an acquaintance of Guilhaudin. The cd value of the drop-shaped bodyshell is supposed to be 0.17. [6] Tuner Dieter Mantzel achieves around 72 horsepower with the 702-cc three-cylinder two-stroke engine. Despite a gentle driving style the race car sets a new class record lap of 5m04.2s in the second practice session, accelerating to 215 km/h while class rival René-Bonnet achieves only 192 km/h and the Abarth GT 184 km/h. Mantzel notes that even after 750 practice kilometers there is "practically zero" tire wear on the 577-kilogram car. Guilhaudin crashes right at the beginning of the race through no fault of his own when spinning on a fuel spill in the Arnage Corner. He tries to return to the track on his own and warns the spectators not to help him. They do so anyhow, so the penalty of a disqualification provided for by the regulations is imposed. [7]

Johann Abt and Hans-Joachim Nowak, here at Spa, are among the privateer drivers who in the seventies with the Audi 80 are starting to shape the brand's sporting profile in touring car racing

Hannu Mikkola clinched the first quattro victory in the World Rally Championship in 1981 and became World Champion in 1983, Michèle Mouton narrowly missed out on the title in 1982, and Stig Blomqvist, a second quattro driver, won the WRC in 1984. Walter Röhrl wins the 1984 Monte Carlo Rally with Audi, among others (from left)

Privateers and factory racing

While the four rings return to La Sarthe only 36 years later, the relaunch of the Audi brand after the Second World War falls into the year of 1965. [8] From 1972 on, the Audi 80 is not only a top seller at the brand's dealerships. [9] Starting in 1973, a factory cup supports the activities of privateer race drivers. They contest circuit races ranging from club racing events all the way to the Spa 24 Hours. In later years, Willi Bergmeister/Hans-Joachim Nowak even win the European Touring Car Championship. In 1978, the factory starts a commitment with a 160-hp Audi 80 in the German Rally Championship. The newly formed motorsport department gathers experience for the upcoming participation in the world championship with the Audi quattro. [10] The successes of the car with all-wheel drive are legendary: Michèle Mouton/Fabrizia Pons are the first female crew to win world championship rounds starting in 1981. The 1982 and 1984 manufacturers' titles and the drivers' titles of Hannu Mikkola/Arne Hertz in 1983 and Stig Blomqvist/Björn Cederberg in 1984 spawn Audi's growth into an international name in motorsport. In the next stage, the company demonstrates the superiority of its all-wheel drive system also in circuit events – initially in 1988 by winning the American Trans-Am

series with an Audi 200 quattro. In 1989, the 720-hp Audi 90 quattro celebrates victories in the IMSA GTO category; in 1990 and 1991, the championship wins in the DTM go to the Audi V8 quattro.

Chairman with a penchant for racing

For the 1993 season, Audi, under the leadership of then Head of Sport Dieter Basche, turns to Super Touring Cars before Wolfgang Ullrich assumes Basche's role in November 1993. Although the naturally aspirated two-liter engines deliver only around 300 horsepower und all-wheel-drive race cars must run with higher weight, quattro again proves its superiority – from 1993 on with the Audi 80 quattro in France and from 1995 on with the A4 quattro in worldwide racing series. The year of 1996 marks the pinnacle of success. Audi wins Super Touring Car championships in the United Kingdom, Germany, Belgium, Spain, Italy, South Africa and Australia. [11]

Ferdinand Piëch drives innovations like quattro and TDI at Audi and as the "father" of the Porsche 917 has special ties with Le Mans

With the Audi 80 – here at the Sachs Rallye Baltic in 1979 – the brand prepares for the World Rally Championship

The Audi quattro revolutionizes rallying, here with Michèle Mouton/Fabrizia Pons

4 Patrice Vergès: Des DB aux Matra. Drivers, 2005, p. 85 et seq
5 Karl-Friedrich Trübsbach: Vorbericht Les 24 Heures du Mans am 15./16. Juni 1963, internal document of the Sport Support Department VI-35 dated June 7, 1963
6 Patrice Vergès: Des DB aux Matra. Drivers, 2005, p. 86
7 A. S. Mantzel: Rennbericht über Rennen Le Mans am 15./16. Juni 1963, correspondence dated June 18, 1963
8 Thomas Erdmann, Ralf Friese, Peter Kirchberg, Ralph Plagmann: Vier Ringe: Die Audi Geschichte, Bielefeld: Delius Klasing, 2009, p. 212
9 www.audi-mediacenter.com/en/press-releases/audi-captures-the-zeitgeist-with-this-car-first-audi-80-unveiled-50-years-ago-14739, last retrieved on January 26, 2023
10 Thomas Erdmann, Ralf Friese, Peter Kirchberg, Ralph Plagmann: Vier Ringe: Die Audi Geschichte, Bielefeld: Delius Klasing, 2009, p. 238
11 Concerning the entire history, see Alexander von Wegner: 30 years of Audi Sport, Ingolstadt: AUDI AG, 2010

Following its deployment in rallying, all-wheel drive also prevails in circuit racing, for instance with the Audi 90 quattro in the 1989 IMSA GTO championship

Before Le Mans, Audi is successful in Super Touring Car racing, here with Frank Biela, John Bintcliffe, Yvan Muller, Tamara Vidali, Emanuele Pirro, Philipp Peter, Wolfgang Ullrich, Karl Wendlinger and Dindo Capello

An early concept of the Audi TT with a V8 mid-engine starts promoting the inspiration for GT racing in 1996 but is chanceless at Le Mans under the GT2 regulations at that time (both pictures)

"That was a humdinger," former Chairman of the Management Board Franz-Josef Paefgen still says approvingly. [12] Even so, for the sake of differentiation, he continues, "I once visited a Super Touring Car weekend at the Nürburgring. I had never seen so-called competitors deal with each other in such kind and friendly ways. That was a huge family. I didn't say anything but thought to myself if that is motorsport then this, somehow, is the wrong show. At the same time, BMW had a program with Williams in order to return to Formula One via a Le Mans commitment. And Mercedes had a bridge into Formula One as well. We wanted to finally pit ourselves against the big names. But you can't assert a claim to the luxury car class in the marketplace with a two-liter touring car."

There was yet another factor: Audi gets caught in a dead-end street. From 1998 on, all-wheel drive is banned in FIA circuit competition, and as early as in 1997, the A4 quattro has to race with so much additional ballast that it is chanceless. That urgently calls for a new field of activities. "Because Ferdinand Piëch did not want to enter Formula One under any circumstances the next bigger thing after touring cars was endurance racing with Le Mans at the top of the list," Paefgen adds.

The sources shedding light on the decision-making process at that stage are scarce: Management board decisions from those days are not available and neither are internal documents. Press releases exist from the time that the project was announced in 1998. In retrospect, a technical presentation from 2004 defines a timeline of key decisions. For the first time, the then Chairman of the Board and the Head of Sport divulge the background facts to the authors in extensive interviews, referring to their recollections, as do many other stakeholders.

English ties

An initial conceptual impetus can no longer be defined precisely. At least it was not the mid-engine Audi TT described by Othmar Wickenheiser in this context, according to the stakeholders' statements. [13] "The car had massive conceptual disadvantages. It would have been absurd to make that car competitive," says Franz-Josef Paefgen. The prototype depicted here merely shows how a mid-engine would be conceptually feasible. [14] The Audi CEO at that time has a good relationship with Richard Lloyd, who oversees Audi's BTCC touring car team and as both Team Principal and driver has been a Le Mans entrant for many years. The Brit suggests to the German to seriously pursue Le Mans. During a joint visit to the 24-hour race in 1997 both reach an oral agreement: "In two years, we're going to race here." [15] The formal decision follows, Audi's management board approves the plans. "During a winter drive I told Mr. Piëch the story before dinner," Paefgen recalls. "He responded, 'well, in that case, you've got to work hard, I know what I'm talking about.' Then he grinned and that was it."

A model from November 1997 shows what an open-cockpit Le Mans sports car could look like

The CEO's attempt to explain the new goal to Audi Sport produces mixed responses. While traveling to see Richard Lloyd in Norwich in the East Anglian County of Norfolk Paefgen introduces the project to leading employees. "He talked about how as a child he was at Le Mans with his father, watching the race behind the guard rail. And if he were ever in a position of making something like that a reality professionally that's what he would do. Now the time had come. He wanted a car with an engine not only for participating but for winning," Ulrich Baretzky, Head of Sports Engine Development, recalls. "After that we were sitting in my office, somewhat disconcerted.

We were still fully involved in Super Touring Cars. It was clear to me that this will be the first pedigreed racing engine since the Silver Arrows. I felt considerable responsibility." [16] Wolfgang Ullrich's response elicits no enthusiasm from the chairman to this day: "There was nothing," Paefgen recalls. [17] In defense of the Head of Sport, it should be said that he will go on to lead Audi to 13 victories in 18 Le Mans participations, help the brand shine brighter in racing than ever before, build an excellent network in the world of endurance racing and be recognized with the ACO's accolade "Spirit of Le Mans" as early as in 2007. [18] Now in retirement, he works for the club as

[12] Transcript of interview with Dr. Franz-Josef Paefgen on October 27, 2022
[13] Othmar Wickenheiser: Audi Design: Automobildesign von 1965 bis zur Gegenwart. Bielefeld: Delius Klasing, 2015
[14] Transcript of interview with Dr. Franz-Josef Paefgen on October 27, 2022
[15] Ibid
[16] Transcript of interview with Ulrich Baretzky on December 19, 2022
[17] Transcript of interview with Dr. Franz-Josef Paefgen on October 27, 2022
[18] www.audi-mediacenter.com/en/press-releases/seal-visits-audi-at-le-mans-8027, last retrieved on January 27, 2023

Audi tests the aerodynamics of the subsequent R8R on a model in the wind tunnel in the first half of 1998 (both pictures)

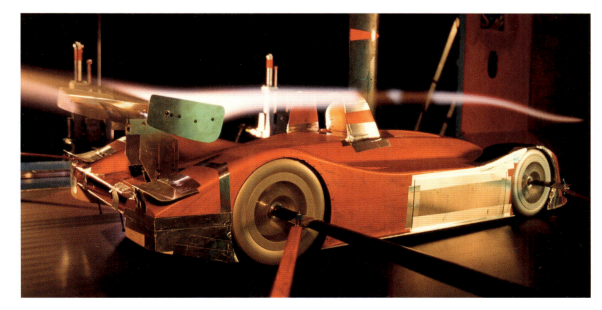

In summer of 1998, Dindo Capello drives the first rollout in Neustadt (left) in the presence of Wolfgang Ullrich and Chief Technology Officer Werner Mischke (pictured left).
The visual kinship of individual styling elements between the R8R and the Audi TT Roadster is intended (above)

Audi Sport model nomenclature

R1	Audi quattro (1980–1984)
R2	Audi Sport quattro (1984–1987)
R3	Audi 200 quattro (1987)
R4	Audi 200 quattro Trans-Am (1988)
R5	Audi 90 quattro IMSA GTO (1989)
R6	Audi V8 quattro DTM (1990–1992)
R7	Audi 80 quattro/A4 quattro (1993–1998)
R8	Audi R8R/R8 (1999–2006)
R9	Audi R8C (1999)
R10	Audi R10 TDI (2006–2008)
R11	Audi A4 DTM (2004)
R12	Audi A4 DTM (2005–2006)
R13	Audi A4 DTM (2007)
R14	Audi A4 DTM (2008–2011)
R15	Audi R15 TDI (2009–2010)
R16	Audi R8 LMS (2009–2015)
R17	Audi A5 DTM (2012)
R18	Audi R18 TDI (2011), RP1
	Audi R18 e-tron quattro/ultra (2012), RP2
	Audi R18 e-tron quattro (2013), RP3
	Audi R18 e-tron quattro (2014), RP4
	Audi R18 e-tron quattro (2015), RP5
	Audi R18 (2016), RP6

a consultant. Today, he admits, "I have to honestly say that, actually, this personal love of Le Mans arrived only with that project." [19]

Conceptual diversity

Richard Lloyd pursues the project a lot more actively. Among other things, he is the owner of a company called Protocar that handles projects for the automotive industry. For the previously mentioned appointment in Norwich, a seat buck for initial dimensioning is created. [20] Lloyd works together with industrial designers like Peter Stevens to develop the concept for a road-approved sports car as the basis for a Le Mans model. After an initial idea for a GT2 model at the end of 1996, [21] a concept for a GT1 race car soon emerges there. [22] The project is named "Aurora," an acronym for "Audi Road Racing." [23]

The regulations back then provide the rationale behind a road-approved vehicle. Up until the end of 1993, the Group C prototypes are the only race

Wolfgang Ullrich evolves into a great sports car enthusiast during the Le Mans program

cars in contention for overall victory at Le Mans, plus there are some IMSA cars featuring similar concepts. After the end of Group C, the development is split into three concepts, all of which score overall victories between 1994 and 2003 before the new LMP1 regulations come into effect in 2004: GT1 sports cars, later called LM-GTP (winners: 1994 Dauer Porsche 962, 1995 McLaren F1, 1998 Porsche 911 GT1, 2003 Bentley Speed 8), WSC prototypes (1996 and 1997 TWR Porsche) and LMP race cars (1999 BMW V12 LMR, Audi R8 from 2000 forward). Differences in regulations are intended to make for suspense among the concepts – until 1998, GT1 sports cars, for instance, can still have a rear diffusor, 20 liters more fuel tank capacity, an ABS system and traction control to compensate for other disadvantages. Even so, the rules remain moving targets for Audi because the adjustments for 1999, for instance with alignments of fuel tank capacities and diffusors, are beginning to shift in favor of the LMP race cars. [24]

Following a preliminary concept in August 1997, Audi Sport in Ingolstadt carefully reviews many options. [25] For example, legal counsel and regulatory expert Andreas Köppen checks with Alain Bertaut from the ACO whether an open version of a GT1 model without a windshield would be conceivable. Bertaut expresses skepticism. When the Frenchman finally asks about the lack of doors and Audi refers to the possibilities of entering the monocoque from the top he rejects the idea. [26]

Like competitors Porsche with the 911 GT1 and Mercedes with the CLK-GTR creating a systematic resemblance between their sports cars and their volume models, an elective affinity exists at Audi as well: The styling work of Luc Donckerwolke, who contributes ample creativity, feeds distinctive design elements of the Audi TT Roadster into the future sports prototype. In December 1997, an open-cockpit wind tunnel model is created in Ingolstadt, and the decision to build an LMP race car dates to February 1998. Roughly during that stage, the first pictures emerge of the rival Toyota GT-One featuring

The pictures taken at the oval in Neustadt in fall of 1998 remain the only PR photographs published by Audi for a long time

[19] Transcript of interview with Dr. Wolfgang Ullrich on December 7, 2022
[20] The authors owe this information to Andreas Köppen. Transcript of interview with Andreas Köppen on October 27, 2022
[21] www.facebook.com/PeterStevensDesign/posts/ pfbid02Uh2x2uKGWQXJXWrS1C9dWuBa8Y5wKeJdx1YU8ovFY5cNtobh1fmbuv5YPiB2CBQvl, last retrieved on January 27, 2023
[22] www.facebook.com/PeterStevensDesign/posts/audi-gt-part-2-the-gt1-road-and-race-carthe-next-logical-step-beyond-the-audi-tt/806185946081074/, last retrieved on January 27, 2023
[23] The authors owe this information to Andreas Köppen and former development engineer Romolo Liebchen
[24] Autosport, September 3, 1998, p. 19
[25] These and the following project dates have been extracted from Dr. Wolfgang Ullrich's presentation at ÖVK event: Audi – der Sieger von Le Mans, dated May 11, 2004
[26] Transcript of interview with Andreas Köppen on October 27, 2022

particularly radical styling. [27] That prompts Audi Sport's vehicle developer Norbert Weber, who has been experienced and respected ever since the rallying era, to provide new impetus to the direction of the project – departing from the highly aesthetic orientation of the Donckerwolke designs and moving toward a more uncompromising concept. [28] The public can subsequently see this transformation in the form of three different evolutions of the R8R. Just when this development is picking up pace Weber dies in a traffic accident in April 1998. [29]

Wolfgang Ullrich responds by appointing Wolfgang Appel to the vacancy and signing two consultants: Dieter Basche, Ullrich's predecessor from 1991 to 1993, and Tony Southgate from the UK. "Dieter Basche had an incredible technical background and as a former Head of Sport was highly respected by the team," Ullrich justifies his choice today. "I am still convinced that that was an important detail for everything having panned out so well in total." [30]

Initially, the drivers, here Dindo Capello watched by vehicle developer Wolfgang Appel, still use sequential shifters, pneumatic systems are introduced later. The side mirrors are motorcycle accessories

Franz-Josef Paefgen, here with Emanuele Pirro in 1999, initiates the Le Mans program and decisively drives it

Among other things, Basche's responsibilities include the definition of key topics. He carefully focuses on the sports car's drivability. [31] Tony Southgate comes on board because Franz-Josef Paefgen tasks his Head of Sport to sign a designer with sports prototype experience. [32] Richard Lloyd recommends Southgate, who has Formula One experience, participated in the Le Mans winning Jaguar designs and most recently designed the Nissan R390 for the 1997 and 1998 24-hour races. He is provided with an office in Ingolstadt where he is present every other week between commitments on race tracks and in wind tunnels. [33]

Volkswagen Chairman Ferdinand Piëch tries selling Audi and Bentley on the W12 engine in vain. The powerplant ultimately drives the VW W12 to setting records in Nardò

Many ideas, one engine

But basic decisions have to be made not only concerning the chassis. The regulations permit considerable diversity concerning the powertrain as well. Engine developer Ulrich Baretzky and his team approach the task analytically: Compared to naturally aspirated units, turbo engines have the advantage of being adaptable to circumstances, such as temperature differences of more than 20 degrees between day and night, and ambient air pressure. In addition, output can be dimmed via boost pressure when rain calls for gentler power development. Within the group of turbo engines at Le Mans, restrictor diameters and boost pressure limitations are defined according to cubic capacity. Based on calculations, the department in Neckarsulm opts for a 3.6-liter V8 unit with two turbochargers – not least because Audi offers this cubic capacity in a production engine. [34]

On July 21, 1998, the V8 runs on the dyno for the first time

Audi rejects the W12 engine (right). Ulrich Baretzky (below) initially uses a "bastard" V8 engine in the Konrad Porsche 962 (below right)

[27] Gary Watkins: One step beyond? in Autosport January 15, 1998, p. 76 et seq
[28] Transcript of interview with Dr. Wolfgang Ullrich on December 7, 2022
[29] Audi MediaInfo: Norbert Weber tödlich verunglückt, April 24, 1998
[30] Transcript of interview with Dr. Wolfgang Ullrich on December 7, 2022
[31] Transcript of interview with Dieter Basche on October 28, 2022
[32] Transcript of interview with Dr. Wolfgang Ullrich on December 7, 2022
[33] Tony Southgate: From drawing board to chequered flag, Croydon: Motor Racing Publications, 2010, p. 214
[34] Transcript of interview with Ulrich Baretzky on December 19, 2022

The Audi R8C does its first laps at Snetterton in April 1999

Franz-Josef Paefgen also fosters contacts with the chairmen of the management boards of other brands such as BMW's Bernd Pischetsrieder and Daimler's Jürgen Schrempp. During this era of racing at Le Mans, BMW always uses naturally aspirated V12 engines, Mercedes, in 1997, begins in GT racing with V12 and, in 1998, switches to naturally aspirated V8 units. Both chairmen rave about their characteristics and consumption in communications with the Audi manager. Paefgen develops doubts and repeatedly asks Baretzky to investigate the possibility of a large-volume aspirated powerplant. But the engine man sticks to his guns. "That, no doubt, strained our working relationship to some extent, but subsequently led to a relationship of mutual trust," Baretzky says today. [35] The former chairman concedes: "Mr. Baretzky was always an institution. We told him we're going to Le Mans and he checked everything together with the concept people. He just started working and didn't need to talk to anyone anymore. And the engines were there in time for the rollouts and were good, too." [36] History shows that, in 1999, BMW clinches the last victory by a naturally aspirated engine, and afterwards, the turbo engines dominate as gasoline or diesel units.

Ferdinand Piëch brings something else into play: the W12 engine. [37] "We investigated that, using a totally neutral approach, and the concept people said, no chance. We explained all that to Mr. Piëch in a carefully prepared meeting," Franz-Josef Paefgen recalls. [38] Another subsequent attempt to place the W12 with Bentley remains futile as well (see p. 86). Instead of achieving honors in racing, VW ultimately sets records with it in Nardò. [39]

Learning to walk

Audi still has not announced its sports car project but rumors are intensifying. AutoBild, for instance, in an article on May 26, 1998, spreads speculations about the Group's Audi and Volkswagen brands, as well as the Bentley brand that was up for sale and subsequently acquired by VW, regarding Le Mans, Formula One and touring car racing. [40] A day later, Audi

Richard Lloyd has major influence in the early stage of the Le Mans program and deploys the Audi R8C. In 2008, he dies in a plane crash

endeavors to clarify the situation, excludes Formula One and announces the development of a sports racing car for the 1999 season. [41] Already 24 days earlier, a delegation from Audi – technicians plus drivers Dindo Capello and Frank Biela – contests the pre-qualifying of the Le Mans 24 Hours with Team GTC alongside Thomas Bscher in preparation for next year. In the race, the McLaren drops out, now with Emanuele Pirro instead of Biela at the wheel.

Meanwhile the technology is learning to walk. On July 21, 1998, the first evolution of the V8 engine does its first revolutions on a dyno. Up to that point, Audi Sport has been using a production-based V8 engine, converted to biturbo operation, to enable the development of a boost pressure control unit. The engineers test this unit, internally dubbed "bastard engine," in a Porsche 962 of the Konrad Motorsport team before the first Audi sports prototype with Dindo Capello at the wheel does its initial laps on AUDI AG's test track in Neustadt in August 1998. [42]

England again

Even though Ingolstadt is working on an open-cockpit car a closed concept has by no means been abandoned. On July 1, Audi announces the acquisition of English racing factory TOM'S GB. [43] Since the brand is taking over Cosworth [44] and Lamborghini [45] during that time as well the brand's intentions initially remain unclear for the public. Then the project launch of a closed-cockpit Le Mans sports car, the subsequent R8C, dates to September 1998. It is created

Frank Biela tests at Most in September 1998, driving a body version for the first time that has been extended by panel sheets (above). By the beginning of 1999, the first evolution leads to the second one in preparation for the Sebring 12 Hours in March (left)

in England following the renaming of TOM'S GB in racing technology norfolk (rtn); the company's Managing Director is Siegfried Krause. "I had motivated the English to do something in difficult times and they worked very effectively and developed the car with a relatively small budget," Franz-Josef Paefgen says, justifying the decision today. "I was no longer able to tell any of them that it's over now." [46]

On October 19, 1998 – five months after the announcement of a sports car program – Audi publishes further details: the participation in the 1999 Le Mans 24 Hours, the first driver squad with Frank Biela, Dindo Capello, Emanuele Pirro and Yvan Muller as well as Joest Racing as the operational team. For the first time, the public is also informed of a project name, the subsequent name of the model is: R8. [47] It is based on a retroactive numbering of the projects since the rallying days. [48] Especially the

In January 1999, at Le Castellet, with Emanuele Pirro and Michele Alboreto, Audi Sport tests various body versions preceding the second evolution. A third one follows by the time of the Le Mans race in June 1999

[35] Transcript of interview with Ulrich Baretzky on December 19, 2022

[36] Transcript of interview with Dr. Franz-Josef Paefgen on October 27, 2022

[37] Audi hat kein Interesse am W12-Motor aus Wolfsburg: VW-Plan vertagt, in auto motor und sport, February 24, 1999, p. 214

[38] Transcript of interview with Dr. Franz-Josef Paefgen on October 27, 2022

[39] www.volkswagen-newsroom.com/en/publications/more/mission-maximum-180, last retrieved on January 27, 2023

[40] AutoBild, May 26, 1998

[41] Audi MediaInfo: Audi verstärkt internationales Motorsport-Engagement, May 27, 1998

[42] Transcript of interview with Ulrich Baretzky on December 19, 2022

[43] Audi MediaInfo: Audi übernimmt englische Rennsport-Firma, July 1, 1998

[44] Audi MediaInfo: Audi plant Erwerb von Cosworth, June 4, 1998

[45] Audi MediaInfo: Audi plant Erwerb von Lamborghini, June 12, 1998

[46] Transcript of interview with Dr. Franz-Josef Paefgen on October 27, 2022

[47] Audi MediaInfo: Audi startet bei den 24 Stunden von Le Mans, October 19, 1998

[48] Alexander von Wegner: 30 years of Audi Sport, Ingolstadt: AUDI AG 2010, p. 30 et seq. The authors obtain the list from long-standing vehicle developer Wolfgang-Dieter Appel. Not every project is retrospectively provided with its own number – all Super Touring Car generations, for instance, are grouped under the abbreviation R7, whereas the rally concept with a mid-engine or the Audi 80 for DTM class 1 have not been allocated a number

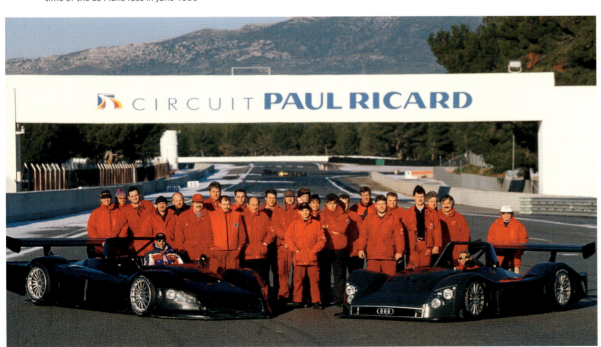

The model shown in Berlin is internally dubbed "wooden box" to distinguish it from the real race cars (above). Dindo Capello, Wolfgang Ullrich, Frank Biela, Franz-Josef Paefgen, Michele Alboreto, Emanuele Pirro and Laurent Aiello in Berlin in December 1998. Yvan Muller is missing due to a racing commitment in the Trophée Andros (right)

choice of team is a surprise and, retrospectively, a major gain up until the end of the LMP project. After Le Mans in 1998 and the end of Porsche's factory-backed program, Reinhold Joest gets in touch with Dieter Basche. No one in Ingolstadt expected the team owner from the Odenwald region and former race driver to abandon his ties to the Stuttgart-based brand. Within a matter of days, both parties meet for the first time. [49] Prior to that, the Head of Sport pursues initial discussions in a totally different direction: Peter Sauber is a preferred candidate for Ullrich. [50]

A message loud and clear

On December 13, 1998, Audi presents itself to a large audience at the Berlin Velodrom. Following the announcement of Le Mans winner and Formula One Championship runner-up Michele Alboreto as another driver, Laurent Aiello is joining the

lineup as a sixth racer. As an intriguing detail, the Frenchman, who has previously defeated Audi in the STW Cup and wins Le Mans in 1998 with Porsche, is racing in the 1999 British Touring Car Championship as a factory driver for Nissan and concurrently for Audi at Le Mans – and thus against Nissan. Audi also confirms former RTL presenter Petra van Oyen as the new sports press spokeswoman. However,

Former tennis pro and TV presenter Petra van Oyen assumes responsibility for sports PR at Audi at the beginning of the Le Mans program

there is one headline emanating from the Velodrom that also surprises many at Audi because it is not included in any speech manuscript: "We want to win the Le Mans 24 Hours as early as in 1999," Chairman Paefgen self-confidently announces in front of 400 guests. Wolfram Riedel, Editor-in-Chief of PS report, notes a "murmur going through the crowd." [51]

24 years later, the former CEO reveals that he is still unhappy about the spirit at Audi Sport half a year before the first Le Mans race: "First, [there was] this initial inertia of not wanting to get into that project. Plus, the thinking that still prevailed at that time: 'well, let's wait and see. We're going to submit an entry for a car, we stand no chance against the big names anyway, and race.' Like saying, a little in the first year and a little better in the second year. And I was terribly unhappy with that: no knife between the teeth, no fighting spirit. That's why I thought I really need to tell them why you race. You race to win and not to get some kind of booby prize." [52]

The year of 1998 ends in this call to arms. Just a few weeks later, the debut season with the sports prototypes marks the beginning of a new chapter in Audi's motorsport history.

[49] Transcript of interview with Ralf Jüttner on November 17, 2022
[50] Transcript of interview with Dr. Wolfgang Ullrich on December 7, 2022
[51] PS report 52, December 21, 1998
[52] Transcript of interview with Dr. Franz-Josef Paefgen on October 27, 2022

Hundreds of guests at the Velodrom hear the chairman's message of intending to win at Le Mans

Plunging in

In preparation for the race in 1999, there is considerable weight of expectations building up. At Audi's debut, the competition is not only particularly fierce but also extensive. Except for last year's winner, Porsche, all marques are returning, partly with models that have been designed from scratch.

When the authors asked former CEO Franz-Josef Paefgen whether he really felt that the claim for victory that was announced for the debut year was realistic, he responded with a gesture of holding his index finger barely above his thumb, saying, "That's about how big I felt." [1]

Fierce competition

There were several reasons for this skepticism. In 1999, the LMP classes for open-cockpit sports cars and LM-GTP for coupés are well-filled in Le Mans. 26 participants enter the race in total, minus a Nissan and a Mercedes that had been involved in pre-start accidents. The conceptual and brand-related variety are top-class: BMW replaces last year's V12 LM with the new LMR created by the Williams F1 team again.

[1] Transcript of interview with Dr. Franz-Josef Paefgen on October 27, 2022

The third evolution of the Audi R8R, here car number 8, ultimately scores a podium finish

It is powered by a naturally aspirated V12 engine. In addition to the two current cars, two last-generation models – fielded by David Price Racing and Team Goh – have been entered. Low-volume manufacturer Panoz builds two naturally aspirated roadsters based on the previous GT1 coupés. Nissan switches from partner TWR and the turbocharged coupé R390 to G-Force with consultant Nigel Stroud and the open-top R391 with naturally aspirated engines. In a partnership with Courage, Nissan also supplies the previous 3.5-liter turbo engines for the French roadster. Toyota, with the GT-One designed by André de Cortanze, is deemed to be one of the favorites. Entries for three of the red LM-GTP coupés with 3.6-liter V8 biturbo have been submitted. Mercedes-Benz, the dominant force in the 1997 and 1998 FIA GT Championship is building the CLR with radical aerodynamics and a V8 naturally aspirated engine for 1999. Here, three cars are in the pits as well when the race week kicks off.

At the beginning of the year, there is one thing that is still not publicly known even though rumors start intensifying in December 1998: Audi is doubling its entire lineup of cars, drivers and teams. [2] In addi-tion to two open-cockpit R8R cars, the brand is pre-paring two R8C for six additional drivers with Audi Sport UK.

Debut in Florida

Audi has selected a tough track for its sports car premiere: The circuit at Sebring in Florida leads across decades-old, poorly grouted concrete slabs. They are the runways of a former airfield. "It is so bumpy here that we've had to raise the ride height by 15mm," says an amazed Head of Sport Wolfgang Ullrich. [3] For Audi, the historically first round of the new American Le Mans Series evolves into an assessment of where the squad stands: In qualifying, Frank Biela/Emanuele Pirro/Perry McCarthy achieve eleventh place in front of Michele Alboreto/Dindo Capello/Stefan Johansson. The prototypes from Ingolstadt are three and a half seconds short of BMW's time. "Michele was an idol for me," Dindo Capello still admits today. "He achieved everything without having come from an affluent family. When I had the privilege of driving with Michele and Stefan that was

[2] Audi eyes dual enduro assault, in Autosport, December 3, 1998, p. 15
[3] Robin Shute: BMW steals Florida classic, in Le Mans and Sportscar Racer, April 1999, p. 27

In the debut at Sebring, Dindo Capello with his teammates Michele Alboreto and Stefan Johansson takes third position

Twin-pack

Despite their visual differences there is a kinship between the two R8R and R8C race cars. The roadster and the 10 centimeters flatter and 15 centimeters longer coupé share the engine, driveline, brakes and rear suspension. The monocoque, bodywork and front suspensions have been designed discretely. [4] The conceptual diversity derives its appeal also from details: In the open-cockpit car, 33.2-millimeter restrictors sit in front of the two turbochargers. In combination with boost pressure of 1.67 bar, the 3.6-liter V8 engine delivers 550 horsepower. The closed car's ratings: 33.9-millimeter restrictor, 1.87 bar boost pressure, 600 horsepower. On the roadster, the radiators sit in the front, on the coupé, they sit on the side. Common to both models are fuel tanks with a volume of 90 liters and and a base weight of 900 kilograms. The R8R is allowed to use tires with a maximum width of 16 inches. Michelin supplies 32/65-18 size tires for the front axle and 36/71-18 size tires for the rear wheels. For the R8C, 14-inch and thus 29/65-18 size tires are specified for the front and 31/71-18 for the rear. [5] While Audi Sport in Ingolstadt realizes the monocoque with Dallara and aerodynamics with Fondmetal, the coupé is created completely at rtn in Norwich where all the means required for CFRP processing

are available. In many areas, an intriguing competition between both concepts ensues: aerodynamics, tire wear, serviceability, duration of driver changes, windshield dirt accumulation and visibility as well as ventilation. Due to the late project launch, the coupé has however a development deficit that ultimately can no longer be recovered.

Comparison: the R8C Coupé (left) and the R8R Roadster

[4] Audi MediaInfo: Audi unveils ultra flat
coupe, April 12, 1999
[5] Audi Motorsport Communications:
press kit Le Mans 1999

Wolfgang Appel leads vehicle development

Reinhold Joest contributes valuable experience as a driver and victorious Team Principal

incredible for me because both of them were former Ferrari Formula One drivers. After practice, they decided that I should drive the qualifying, which was really a great honor." [6]

Both race cars survive the distance. Alboreto/Capello/Johansson achieve third position after 310 laps. Biela/Pirro/McCarthy finish two positions behind them after incurring a 15-minute time loss due to a clutch problem. Stefan Johansson analyzes the situation realistically: "The first endurance test under race conditions was extremely satisfactory. But for Le Mans, the first thing we need to work on, is increasing the speed." [7] Tom Kristensen in the new BMW V12 LMR saves victory with a 9.2-second advantage in front of an American Riley & Scott from Dyson Racing. Both race cars have a three-lap advantage over Audi.

John Wickham is Team Manager of Audi Sport UK

The Audi R8C is created at rtn under the leadership of designer Peter Elleray

The rapid development means that the first evolution of the R8R never gets to compete in a race. It is already history when the second evolution races at Sebring. By the time of the Le Mans race, a third version has emerged.

Premiere of the coupé

Three weeks after Sebring, Audi, on April 12, presents the R8C including a program and personnel. Richard Lloyd's Apex team supports the commitment under the name of Audi Sport UK, John Wickham is the Team Manager. The driver combinations: Brits Perry McCarthy and James Weaver share car number 10 with former winner Andy Wallace. Richard Lloyd decisively influences this combination. [8] For car number 9, Didier Theys and the two former winners Stefan Johansson and Stéphane Ortelli are initially planned. However, the elegant, only 98 centimeter tall coupé from England has a development deficit. It is created in just six months under the leadership of Peter Elleray at rtn in Norfolk. On April 1, it does its first laps at Snetterton, followed by the hurdle of the pre-qualifying session for Le Mans. This selection process on May 2 is split, each car is assigned to one of two groups. Dindo Capello achieves the third-best time in the Audi R8R in session 1, Stéphane Ortelli in the coupé takes eleventh place. In part 2, Emanuele Pirro claims seventh. [9] Up until two minutes before the end, Andy Wallace in car number 10 has not qualified for the race weekend. [10] A lost door and lack of spare parts mean that the team first has to look for the missing component along the track and quickly repair the R8C.

A new driver

Head of Sport Wolfgang Ullrich has to master an altogether different challenge in May. In selecting his drivers, he opts for Biela, Pirro, Capello and Muller as four known quantities from the brand's touring car program, augmented by Alboreto and Aiello. "It

Stefan Johansson, Andy Wallace, Stéphane Ortelli, James Weaver (concealed), Perry McCarthy and Didier Theys form the original lineup for the R8C before Theys switches to the roadster. Also pictured are Dieter Gass (fourth from left) as well as John Wickham, Hartmut Diel, Peter Elleray and Tony Southgate (far right)

was already important to me at that time to have race drivers with solid basic experience, who have raced in the world in a variety of cars, who have ties to the brand and with whom you can go through thick and thin because the first years will be difficult," he says today. [11] However, Yvan Muller chooses to give preference to touring cars. All of a sudden he no longer wants to race at Le Mans. "That came out of the clear blue and was really very late," says Ullrich, who is forced to change plans: Didier Theys, who joins the factory lineup based on a recommendation by Jean-Gilbert Mal-Voy from the Belgian Audi Club, switches from the coupé to the roadster. [12]

[6] Transcript of interview with Dindo Capello on November 24, 2022
[7] Audi MediaInfo: Audi Tests successful at 12 hours of Sebring/USA, March 21, 1999
[8] Transcript of interview with Dr. Wolfgang Ullrich on December 7, 2022
[9] Gary Watkins: First blood to Toyota, in Autosport, May 6, 1999, p. 71
[10] Audi MediaInfo: Audi enjoys successful Le Mans baptism, May 2, 1999
[11] Transcript of interview with Dr. Wolfgang Ullrich on December 7, 2022
[12] Charles-Henri Bonnet: Winning Spirit since 1980, Kortenberg: Motion Motorsports 2017, p. 239

Tony Southgate joins Audi Sport as a consultant. Easily detectible: the support bars that are still found on the engine in 1999 but disappear for the 2000 season

Laurent Aiello, Yvan Muller, Michele Alboreto, Dindo Capello, Frank Biela and Emanuele Pirro are planned to drive the R8R until Muller leaves the project in May

As a consultant, former Head of Sport Dieter Basche develops ideas for improving the drivability of the race cars across the long distance

Preparation of the R8R cars in Ingolstadt. In the background, development engineer Romolo Liebchen (black shirt)

Super touring car driver Christian Abt, who has already become involved in testing the R8, takes his place on short notice. [13]

On a grand stage for the first time

At the beginning of the Le Mans week, the mood at Audi has been dampened. On Monday, Dindo Capello learns about his father having succumbed to cancer at the age of merely 60. He travels to Italy for the funeral and returns on Tuesday evening. [14] "For him, my going to Le Mans was a dream but, unfortunately, he was no longer able to witness it," Capello recalls. [15] In terms of racing, Audi starts approaching its rivals on Wednesday. In the first qualifying session, Michele Alboreto with a time of 3m37.140s is four tenths of a second faster than in pre-qualifying. He is in tenth position, in front of Emanuele Pirro. Problems with the clutch and a defective sixth gear throw the coupés back to positions 22 and 23. [16] A day later, the roadsters improve their times by more than two seconds. Dindo Capello advances to ninth position, Frank Biela is in eleventh and thus "Rookie of Le Mans." Recurring transmission issues mean positions 20 and 23 for the two R8C. Toyota with two cars locks out the front row, in front of a BMW, a Mercedes and a Panoz.

A turbulent weekend

When the race starts at 4 pm Michele Alboreto, Emanuele Pirro, Andy Wallace and Stéphane Ortelli are sitting in the cockpits. After 20 minutes, Richard Lloyd's mechanics have to change the transmission on the number 10 coupé. Nearly 42 minutes are lost. "The problems with the gearbox have nothing to do with the transmission but with the link between the gearshift and the gearbox unit itself which is different from that on the R8R," says Ullrich. [17] Audi modifies a Mega-Line pneumatic shift actuator from motorcycle racing. The driver uses a steering-wheel-mounted paddle shifter. Its electrical signal controls the air pressure system that always evenly engages the gears. Only the two roadsters use this solution. Consultant Tony Southgate writes, "We could only get three pneumatic gearshift systems made in time for the race. We had decided to put two of them on the more developed R8Rs and keep one system as a spare. So both the R8Cs would have the normal manual gear linkage." [18]

The R8C driven by Abt/Ortelli/Johansson retires with differential failure shortly before 8 pm, the second coupé in the morning, at around 8.20 am, with a driveline defect." [19]

Joest Racing has long been working intensively with Audi Sport on the idea of a quick-change system for the transmission which Audi perfects on the R8 a year later. In a practice session on Thursday after qualifying, a change is accomplished in "less than six minutes," according to the Audi Express newspaper produced for the paddock. [20] In his biography, Southgate even records exactly 4m56s. [21] Then, in

Ferdinand Piëch (left) with his wife and Franz-Josef Paefgen in the pit lane of Le Mans. The picture was taken in 2001

[13] Audi MediaInfo: Le Mans entries close: Audi announces driver line-up, May 14, 1999
[14] Audi Express 1, June 10, 1999, p. 3
[15] Transcript of interview with Dindo Capello on November 24, 2022
[16] Audi MediaInfo: Audi R8R drivers optimistic, June 10, 1999
[17] Audi MediaInfo: Audi R8R records consistent lap times, June 12, 1999
[18] Tony Southgate: From drawing board to chequered flag, Croydon: Motor Racing Publications, 2010, p. 224
[19] Audi MediaInfo: Audi R8Rs still amongst the leaders, June 13, 1999
[20] Audi Express 3, June 12, 1999, p. 3
[21] Tony Southgate: From drawing board to chequered flag, Croydon: Motor Racing Publications, 2010, p. 224

From eleventh on the grid, Frank Biela/Emanuele Pirro/Didier Theys continously move toward the front of the field

The beginnings of the quick-change rear end can be proven as far back as in 1999 on the R8R

Christian Abt, Stefan Johansson and Stéphane Ortelli in the Audi R8C in front of rival Mercedes. In the background (on the right) a Toyota GT-One

Siegfried Krause is Managing Director of rtn in Norwich

racing conditions, the first change on car number 7 shortly after 8 pm takes nine minutes. [22] The number 8 roadster is continuously gaining ground. Frank Biela, Emanuele Pirro and Didier Theys are running in fourth position when in the early morning hours the brake discs need to be changed and later an exhaust pipe as well. On the other hand, Audi Sport Team Joest has to change the transmission three times in total on car number 7. [23] When the mechanics detect a damaged cable at 7.25 am, they install a manually shifted transmission on the last, 30-minute occasion of a change. [24]

At its Le Mans debut, Audi also benefits from partly spectacular retirements of its competitors. After Mark Webber's Mercedes lifts off in qualifying on Thursday and again in warm-up on Saturday, the same happens to his teammate Peter Dumbreck

while running in third position on the 76th race lap. Mercedes subsequently withdraws the sister car driven by Pedro Lamy, Franck Lagorce and Bernd Schneider. After transmission issues, the Toyota of Martin Brundle, Emmanuel Collard and Vincenzo Sospiri that had started from pole position retires five hours into the race after spinning and a puncture. Thierry Boutsen seriously crashes in another Toyota on lap 174 when a lapped GT participant touches him. One hour before the race ends, a puncture deprives the third Toyota with a Japanese crew of its chances. The clearly leading BMW retires with JJ Lehto when a mechanical defect jams the throttle linkage and the Finn crashes five and a half hours before the end of the race. [25] The second BMW with Yannick Dalmas, Pierluigi Martini and Joachim Winkelhock provides the Munich-based brand with its first and so far only victory at La Sarthe.

Biela/Pirro/Theys clinch third position at the Audi R8R's debut in front of the sister car driven by Aiello, Alboreto and Capello. Afterward Audi places an ad in major daily newspapers congratulating BMW and Toyota on having scored positions one and two, listing Audi's own third and fourth positions and announcing the brand's return the following year. Franz-Josef Paefgen stresses that he was inspired to do so by the Porsche posters from the seventies on which all the top positions were listed – including those of rivals. [26]

Head of Audi Sport Ullrich is relieved: "For a Le Mans newcomer, this is a very good result, and we are all extremely pleased. We had very ambitious goals and were highly motivated. For all those who have set their sights on winning at Le Mans, this result is a new encouragement to give everything once again." [27] With positions six and eight claimed at Charlotte as well as three and four at Silverstone, the career of the R8R ends in 2000 in the American Le Mans Series. Its successor, the R8, has long been ready to race.

Laurent Aiello, Michele Alboreto and Dindo Capello in the number 7 Audi R8R are setting better lap times than their sister car but finish behind it in fourth position after a triple transmission change

[22] Audi Express 4, June 13, 1999, p. 3
[23] Transcript of interview with Dindo Capello on November 24, 2022
[24] Audi MediaInfo: Audi R8Rs still amongst the leaders, June 13, 1999
[25] Gary Watkins: BMW restores Teutonic order, in Autosport, June 17, 1999, p. 66 et seq
[26] Transcript of interview with Dr. Franz-Josef Paefgen on October 27, 2022
[27] Audi MediaInfo: Post Race Summary Quotes, June 13, 1999

Car number 10 with Andy Wallace, James Weaver and Perry McCarthy drives into the morning hours until it retires

Rainer Kammergruber is the project leader for the R8R and the R8C in the year of their debut

R8 to the power of three

In just the second year of its LMP program, Audi triumphs at Le Mans, achieving an amazing one-two-three win with the new R8.

The location for the premiere of the race car is spectacular: On March 11, Allan McNish, in front of a crowd of hundreds of onlookers, presents the second generation of the Audi Sport prototype on the blocked off Ocean Drive in Miami Beach. The special atmosphere in Florida's metropolis also serves as the backdrop for various photo shoots of Audi's new driver squad. The nine drivers from six countries present themselves and their new equipment in front of the skyline or when the sun sets on the beach. Except for two of them, all the drivers are known from the previous year, but the two new signings are packing quite a punch: Scot Allan McNish, the 1998 Le Mans winner, and Tom Kristensen from Denmark, the 1997 Le Mans winner. The three R8 cars are provided with accentuating colors taking cues from the German flag to distinguish them from each other. The black car number 7 is driven at Le Mans by Christian Abt, Michele Alboreto and Dindo Capello, sitting behind the wheel in the red number 8 are Frank Biela, Emanuele Pirro and Tom Kristensen. The yellow number 9 R8 is taken over by Allan McNish, Laurent Aiello and Stéphane Ortelli. With the latter drivers, the 1998 winning Porsche crew is now forming a driver trio at Audi. Wolfgang Ullrich is convinced of the lineup as well as of the

Frank Biela (pictured) together with Tom Kristensen and Emanuele Pirro scores Audi's first Le Mans victory

Debut
of a winner

The beginning of the Audi R8's development takes place at a time when Audi is still busy with its Le Mans debut. The brand delves into the sports car theme in fast-forward mode: Concurrently with the R8R and R8C, the engineers are already laying the foundations for the successor model. "Our work on the new R8 began the Tuesday after the race [at Le Mans 1999]." Those are the words with which the Audi press kit quotes Project Leader Wolfgang Appel in 2000. [1] In a professional presentation, the project launch date is subsequently stated more precisely as having been in May of 1999. [2] The same year already sees the first prototype that has been produced in black carbon. Christmas arrives a day early when the R8 with chassis number 401 rolls out for the first time on the in-house test track at Neustadt on December 23 with Frank Biela at the wheel. [3]

Even though the name R8 is retained without the suffix "R" the sports car is a new design. Even the monocoque is clearly different. Instead of the voluminous rollover bar, a CFRP structure with a much smaller cross section is installed behind the driver. This results in an asymmetric body shape resembling the one previously featured in 1999 by the Le Mans winning BMW V12 LMR.

The monocoque includes many other improvements: The sidewalls have been pulled further toward the top and a brace splits the cell into two parts lengthwise. "The cockpit is now closed like in a Formula car – and just as tight too," explains Wolfgang Appel. Although that entails disadvantages during driver changes it increases the driver's safety. [4]

This strut in the center of the cockpit, which was not objected to during a concept approval at the end of 1999, displeased ACO regulations expert Alain

Bertaut at the beginning of 2000 with regard to the prescribed minimum opening. Legal counsel Andreas Köppen succeeds in getting the strut accepted as part of a new safety structure. [5]

With regard to splitting the airflow, Audi clearly departs from the previous concept. "In terms of the concept, our first roadster still resembled the Ferrari 333 SP," former Head of Sport Wolfgang Ullrich admits today. [6] The radiators, still lying flat at the front end in 1999, provide him with a rather

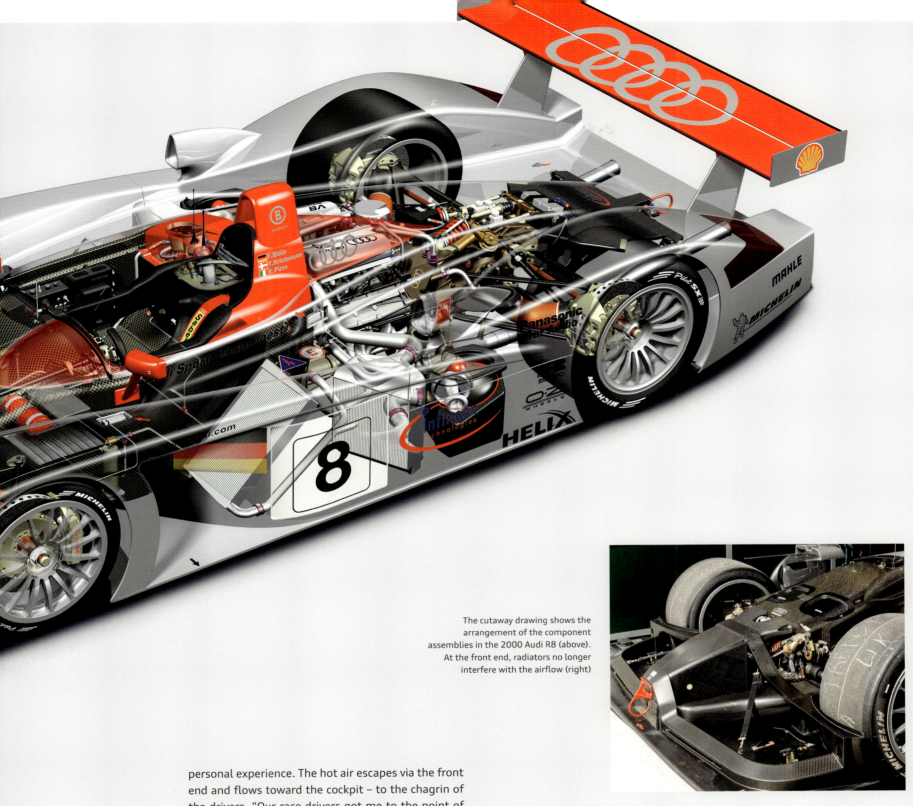

The cutaway drawing shows the arrangement of the component assemblies in the 2000 Audi R8 (above). At the front end, radiators no longer interfere with the airflow (right)

personal experience. The hot air escapes via the front end and flows toward the cockpit – to the chagrin of the drivers. "Our race drivers got me to the point of saying, 'You're going to drive the R8R at least once in the pit lane to feel the hot airflow. That's what I did and it was clearly noticeable.'" [7] For the new R8, the radiators migrate into the side pods.

The aerodynamics development proves to be very complex. Michael Pfadenhauer and his team design the concept. In the model wind tunnel at the Research

[1] Audi Motorsport Communications: Press kit Audi at Le Mans 2000
[2] Dr. Wolfgang Ullrich: Audi – der Sieger von Le Mans, presentation at ÖVK event, May 11, 2004
[3] Thomas Voigt: Audi R8. Born to win, Ingolstadt, AUDI AG 2006, p. 14
[4] Audi Motorsport Communications: Press kit Audi at Le Mans 2000
[5] Transcript of interview with Andreas Köppen on October 27, 2022
[6] Transcript of interview with Dr. Wolfgang Ullrich on December 8, 2022
[7] Ibid

The bodywork on the R8 is still truly a covering. On the R10, its successor, the monocoque is directly exposed to the airflow

Institute for Automotive Engineering and Powertrain Systems Stuttgart (FKFS) the body shell can be optimized on a 1-4-scale model. Fondmetal's larger-scale wind tunnel accommodates 40-percent models. They already contain all cooling units and, thanks to rotating wheels, provide conclusive information about real-world airflow. The main development takes place at Fondmetal. Finally, the real-world race cars are standing in AUDI AG's aeroacoustics wind tunnel for verification. [8] For the 2001 season, Audi Sport modifies airflow through the front end once again. The discharged air no longer exits directly behind the front wheels but flows a little further toward the rear. When the factory program ends in 2002 Audi stops

the development. However, in 2004, new regulations for the rear wing ring in the development of mail-box-like structures that can be seen on page 51.

The engineers focus special attention on investigating aerodynamic sensitivity. The Mercedes race cars at Le Mans in 1999 are not the only ones lifting off. [9] That is why Audi Sport closely examines the conditions during slipstreaming, resulting in the chart on page 50. Management derives several handling instructions from those findings: On straights or in cornering situations, there are no slipstreaming issues. Across humps the drivers are supposed to stay outside of the marked two-meter line and not supposed to enter or exit the slipstream in such track sections either. "Drivers from other manufacturers also approached me to ask if they could take a look at this chart," Ullrich says today. "And I said, sure why not? It's about safety and you mustn't make any differences there. That made the rounds very quickly." [10]

In addition, the engineers manage to lower the LMP sports car's center of gravity further and to reduce its base weight. As a result, ballast weight can be positioned optimally to set the car up for the relevant race track. [11]

In the area of the driveline, Audi makes spectacular strides. A significantly updated transmission supplied by Audi's partner Ricardo is only half the size of the one used in the R8R. [12] The real kicker, though, is a quick-change system for the transmission and the rear axle hinged to it. "Even on the Audi R8R, changing the rear end was not particularly complicated," says Wolfgang Ullrich. "But only on the R8 the concept was designed for really accomplishing that in a very short period. The idea had always existed. It arrived the moment we went to Le Mans. Wolfgang Appel performed a very extensive analysis at the time, investigating what the most frequent causes of failures were at Le Mans over the last 15 years. And the transmission was at the very top of the list. I promoted the quick-change idea because during my time at Porsche – even though I wasn't part of the motorsport department – I overheard that the conversation

Changing the rear end makes for short pit stops and spectacular scenes between 2000 and 2003 (right). Progress is visible also in the cockpit (below)

was repeatedly focused on a Porsche double-clutch (PDK) transmission for Le Mans. Then, an emergency decision to race without a PDK was made three weeks in advance each year because the transmission is the most vulnerable aspect at Le Mans." [13]

[8] Michael Pfadenhauer: Aerodynamikentwicklung im Rennsport am Beispiel des Audi R8, in Michael Bargende, Jochen Wiedemann: Kraftfahrwesen und Verbrennungsmotoren, Renningen: expert verlag 2001, p. 357
[9] Porsche driver Yannick Dalmas rolls over as early as in 1998 at Road Atlanta, see Autosport, October 15, 1998, p. 13
[10] Transcript of interview with Dr. Wolfgang Ullrich on December 8, 2022
[11] Audi Motorsport Communications: Press kit Audi at Le Mans 2000
[12] Ibid
[13] Transcript of interview with Dr. Wolfgang Ullrich on December 8, 2022

The pneumatic system from motorcycle racing that was integrated on the R8R on relatively short notice has become a reliable standard component on the R8. With the help of quick-release couplings, all lines can be closed and separated. Only a few screws connect the transmission with the engine. The change idea is originally conceived to enable fast responses to transmissions failures. However, in the subsequent years, the modular design proves useful for a totally different reason: in case of a crash, the entire rear end can be changed within just a few minutes as well.

Mechanic Thomas Bauch is involved in that more than once: "We permanently preheated the spare transmission. Otherwise, a cold transmission does not go together with a warm engine. The first thing we did to change the unit was to take off the wheels and the tailgate, remove the tailpipe and then the diffusor. A crane on the ceiling lifted the old transmission. The new transmission arrived with a motor crane. All we

did then was insert it, connect the fasteners, tighten all the screws and then reverse everything: tailpipe, diffusor, rear bonnet, tires and out again!" [14]

Until 2003, the teams keep changing rear ends in record time. Scenes of that can still be found today on YouTube. However, for the 2004 season, the regulations ban the idea. "That's when the ACO said that being able to change such extensive parts of the vehicle so quickly was not in keeping with the spirit of an endurance race," legal counsel Andreas Köppen recalls. "There are specific things you're not allowed to change, but at first the transmission was not one of them. Of course, that's debatable. The theoretically greatest endurance race is run without any external intervention. You try to do everything that's possible and we took advantage of the regulations." [15]

The familiar 3.6-liter V8 biturbo unit continues to power the mid-engine sports car. In 2001, Audi accomplishes a significant development step: direct

Slipstream optimization

Front downforce in the slipstream

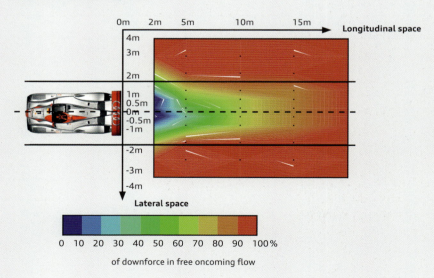

Rear downforce in the slipstream

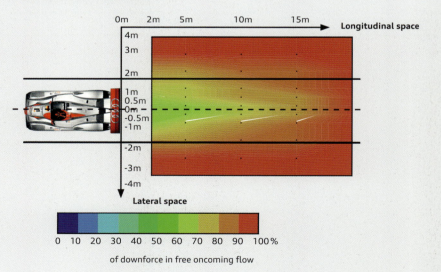

Audi investigates how downforce at the front end (left) and at the rear end (right) changes during slipstreaming and derives actions for the drivers from the findings

injection replaces multi-point injection (see page 62). Over the years, the regulations continue to reduce power output: 32.4-millimeter air restrictors initially permit 610 horsepower. In 2003, their cross section drops to 30.7 millimeters and output to 550 horsepower. With 29.9 millimeters, only 520 horsepower is possible in 2005.

"The R8 was a huge step forward when compared to the R8R," summarizes developer Wolfgang Appel. "Following our Le Mans debut in June 1999 we had a list of proposals that we worked through point by point. The aim was to achieve two goals simultaneously: to make the car faster and, at the same time, more maintenance friendly. We achieved both targets. The R8 was the quickest LM P1 from the very beginning. We also set new standards as far as user-friendliness was concerned. The highlight was without doubt the removable rear end. However, many other parts were quick and easy to change, so that after an accident we hardly ever had to retire a car." [16]

For the 2004 season, the developers compensate for the effects of the new rear wing regulations by using box-like body shapes

[14] Transcript of interview with Thomas Bauch on October 28, 2022
[15] Transcript of interview with Andreas Köppen on October 27, 2022
[16] Thomas Voigt: Audi R8. Born to win, AUDI AG, Ingolstadt 2006, p. 19

The rear end has a compact CFRP structure instead of the tubular frame on the R8R. The engine no longer has supports

new R8: "After our successful debut last year we have put together a team which is certainly able to bring home the first Le Mans victory for Audi," he says. [17]

Action-packed calendar instead of occasional test races

Unlike the year before with just a few commitments, Audi's agenda for the first time includes a full season. In addition to Le Mans, the brand with the four rings is also active in the American Le Mans Series, aka ALMS. Pharmaceutical entrepreneur and Le Mans enthusiast Don Panoz initiated the series he intends to run according to ACO regulations. Following the single inaugural event of the Petit Le Mans in October 1998, the ALMS celebrates a successful premiere in 1999. "The members of the management board obviously wanted to get as much as possible for their money. And we obviously wanted to contest not only one race per year with the R8 but compete internationally in order to also support the Audi brand globally with the project," says Ullrich, explaining the reasons that motivated the manufacturer to enter the series that, in 2000, alongside races in North America, is also run for the first time in Europe at the Nürburgring and Silver-

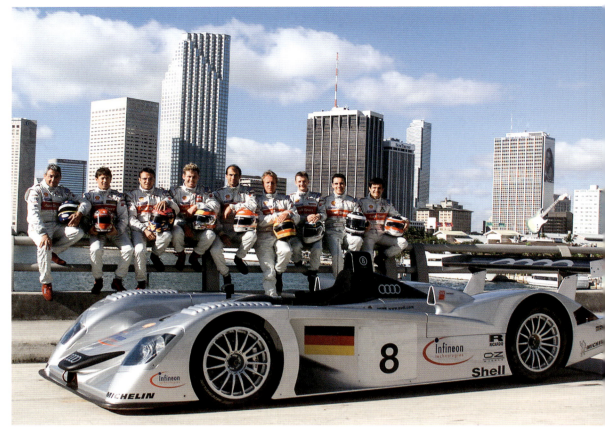

Michele Alboreto, Dindo Capello, Christian Abt, Tom Kristensen, Emanuele Pirro, Frank Biela, Allan McNish, Laurent Aiello and Stéphane Ortelli in front of the skyline at Miami Beach

stone as well as in Adelaide, Australia. "I soon established a good relationship with Dan Panoz and was convinced that whenever he does something he does it well. Audi of America with Len Hunt was thrilled by the program right away and supported it directly. But the collaboration with the ACO was important to us as well." [18]

Joest Racing continues to be the fielding team. The outfit based in the German Odenwald region with its long-standing experience in North American racing is perfectly suited for the ALMS program. In the 1980s and 1990s, with Porsche race cars, Reinhold Joest's squad scored several victories in the IMSA series, including in the iconic endurance events at Daytona and Sebring. In an interview in summer of 2000, Wolfgang Ullrich explains what the collaboration between Audi Sport and Joest looks like. "All the cars were developed at Audi Sport and that's from where the parts are supplied to the teams as well. The commitments that are part of the Le Mans series are entirely in the hands of the Joest team. For Le Mans itself, from the mechanic to the engineer, there was a 50-percent mix of Team Joest and of

Victorious premiere: The new Audi R8 scores Audi's first LMP victory at Sebring

Audi Sport, respectively. For America, the situation differs: there, Team Joest has sole responsibility for the commitment." [19]

Old vs. New World

Following the 1999 boom year, three manufacturers – Mercedes, Nissan and Toyota – completely withdraw from the sports prototype scene. BMW limits its involvement to the ALMS, so avoiding Audi at Le Mans. A potential newcomer stops its LMP project even before the first race: Porsche tests a new open-cockpit prototype, the LMP 2000, in 1999. But the management board, on short notice, does not approve its fielding. [20] Consequently, Audi's main competitors at La Sarthe are from the United States. Panoz again contests the race with its brawny front-engine roadster. Five of the slightly modified cars are distributed to Dave Price Racing's factory-backed team as well as to customer teams. The most important change at Panoz: in the Americans' top car, 60-year-old racing legend Mario Andretti, the 1978 Formula One World Champion, joins regular drivers David Brabham and Jan Magnussen. Cadillac, after 50 years, returns to Le Mans with four Northstar LMP cars developed by Riley & Scott. But even the accomplished driver crew cannot achieve a lot with the prototype that has not been fully

The Porsche LMP 2000, shown here with Bob Wollek at the wheel, does not get beyond the testing stage

[17] Audi MediaInfo: Audi Team Complete for Le Mans 2000, February 1, 2000
[18] Transcript of interview with Dr. Wolfgang Ullrich on December 8, 2022
[19] Peter Hartmann: Die Formel 1 ist kein Thema, in PS report, July 31, 2000
[20] https://newsroom.porsche.com/en/history/porsche-goodwood-festival-of-speed-speedster-festivalofspeedster-england-70-years-racecar-magic-moments-15867.html, last retrieved on January 24, 2023

Tom Kristensen switches to Audi for the 2000 season

Allan McNish, another newcomer to Audi's lineup, is the fastest driver in the prequalification in April and in qualifying

Reunion: The 1998 Le Mans winners Stéphane Ortelli, Allan McNish and Laurent Aiello (from left) celebrate the Scot's pole position during the driver parade (above).
On the black R8 the mechanics are changing the rear end during the race (above, right)

developed yet and is too slow. Chrysler competes as the third US manufacturer. Following major successes in the GT class, the company, together with the Oreca team, ventures stepping up to the LMP900 category. The chassis is supplied by Reynard, which Stefan Johansson's team relies on as well. In addition, there are two privately fielded Courage, a two-year old BMW V12 LM and two Lola cars. Especially the Lola entered by the Rafanelli team is regarded as a secret favorite after having clinched pole position in the ALMS race at Silverstone. However, at Le Mans, it does not finish due to engine failure.

First win at Sebring

Exactly one week after the presentation in Miami, the R8 makes its racing debut at Sebring, which is about a three-hour drive away. In qualifying, new signing Tom Kristensen crashes into the tire walls, in plain view of Ullrich, but in the race, there is no stopping the Dane and his partners Frank Biela and Emanuele Pirro as they claim the first victory of an Audi sports prototype. "In 1999, I had offers from practically all manufacturers but I knew right in my first race that the decision to switch to Audi was the right one," Kristensen relates later. [21] Michele Alboreto, Dindo Capello and Allan McNish as the runners-up round out the successful Le Mans "dress rehearsal." Since the R8 cars are subsequently prepared for Le Mans in Ingolstadt the Joest squad contests the following ALMS races at Charlotte and Silverstone with updated previous-generation R8R models. [22]

At the Le Mans pre-practice in late April, the second generation of the Audi sports prototype finally does its first laps on the Circuit de la Sarthe. And leaves a positive impression: Allan McNish sets the best time in car number 9, followed by the two sister cars. The

US manufacturers Panoz (front, shown here with Mario Andretti at the wheel) and Cadillac are among Audi's rivals in 2000

three silver-colored "flatfish" are within barely one second of each other.

Consequently, for the race in June, Audi is regarded as the number one candidate for victory. "Condemned to win," writes the German magazine mot and continues by saying that the brand from Ingolstadt, "can actually just beat itself." [23] Not only German media see Audi in the role of the favorite: "In recent years there has rarely been a team regarded as a stronger favourite than Audi is now," says the UK magazine Autosport. [24] The mood in the paddock of the four rings is optimistic as well: "We feel that we've done everything to race perfectly prepared," says CEO of AUDI AG Franz-Josef Paefgen. [25]

Consequently, in qualifying, the name of the game is R8 in front of R8 and R8 at the front of the 48-car field. Allan McNish in the yellow car clinches the first Le Mans pole for Audi at 3m36.124s; Tom Kristensen in the red sister model claims second position, just half a second short of the final best time. Curiously, at one point, the Scot and the Dane are the front runners clocked at identical times. Dindo Capello in the black R8 takes the third spot and is angry: "I was running on a lap that would have been enough for pole. But I was so excited that I made a braking mistake in the Ford chicane. 300 meters before the finish I lost pole like an idiot." [26] As the best non-Audi car, the Andretti-Panoz follows in fourth, in front of the Lola of the Rafanelli team.

Everything seems to be prepared for a triumphant race of the R8 cars. Yet there is a problem that the public is unaware of and that might have crucial consequences in the race: During qualifying the uniball joints repeatedly separate from the wishbones with which they are bolted to the wheel carrier and the chassis. "That caused a certain amount

Upbeat mood: Christian Abt (left) and Michele Alboreto looking forward to the Audi R8's first Le Mans race

The officials from Audi Sport and Joest Racing watching the race from the pit wall booths

[21] Transcript of interview with Tom Kristensen on December 6, 2022
[22] Audi MediaInfo: Audi starts as championship leader at Charlotte, March 24, 2000
[23] Markus Stier: Zum Siegen verurteilt, in mot, May 29, 2000
[24] Tim Scott and Gary Watkins: Tasty Entrées, in Autosport Le Mans Guide 2000, p. 10
[25] Interview with Dr. Franz-Josef Paefgen, Donaukurier, June 14, 2000
[26] Transcript of interview with Dindo Capello on November 24, 2022

Le Mans winners Emanuele Pirro, Tom Kristensen and Frank Biela giving three cheers
on the podium for Head of Sport Wolfgang Ullrich

of panic," Joest's chief engineer Ralf Jüttner recalls. "We then talked to Wolfgang Appel and during the night before the race sent our pilot to Ingolstadt to pick up bearings with a large overlap. When we were ready to install the bearings, we noticed that we didn't have the tool required for press-fitting them, so we dispatched the pilot again. Audi engineer Romolo Liebchen picked up the new bearings from the airport in Le Mans with his motocross bike and managed to squeeze through the dense public traffic. After the warm-up, we installed the parts and were finished just in time for the pre-starting procedure." [27] Wolfgang Ullrich recalls the events on that day as well: "That was a hot action. But it was the right thing to do and emphasized the cohesion of the team and showed what is possible when everyone wants something, when everyone first said that will never work. It worked." [28]

Triumphant drive

The three Audi cars subsequently also shape the 68th running of the 24-hour race. Remarkably, Ullrich refuses issuing a team order for the race: "I am convinced that I would have created a greater risk with a team order. Because I would have stripped the teams and drivers of a certain amount of their motivation and concentration. And that, in my opinion, is more dangerous than letting them drive their pace, obviously, without taking any unnecessary risks. But that was a watchword we had issued even earlier and everyone heeded that well." [29]

Audi in front of Audi in front of Audi: The R8 immediately achieves a one-two-three win at Le Mans

After the start, the R8 cars defend their lead but temporarily drop behind the Panoz due to an early safety car deployment. That means a front-engine model is leading again at Le Mans for the first time since 1963. [30] Just ten minutes after the race has been released, Allan McNish takes the top spot again, and Michele Alboreto bumps David Brabham from second position a little later. Three hours into

Legendary design: Allan McNish together with Dindo Capello wins the ALMS finale at Adelaide in the R8 sporting a crocodile look, so securing the drivers' title (above and right)

Head of Sport Wolfgang Ullrich watches events together with Wolfgang Appel, Head of Vehicle Engineering, Joest's Technical Director Ralf Jüttner and Martin Mühlmeier, Head of Test and Simulation (from left)

the race, the R8 cars are closing their ranks again as the front runners while Panoz, after encountering problems, drops out of the top ten. At 11 pm, car number 9 driven by Aiello/McNish/Ortelli pits and has the rear end changed within a few minutes. Once again, the bushings on the wishbones are causing trouble. [31] The team repeats the same procedure at 2.34 am for safety reasons on the black R8 of Abt/Alboreto/Capello after a slip and tire failure. "We didn't want to take any risk," says Ullrich, looking back. "And changing a rear end in more or less four minutes was often quicker than a complex check of the technology." [32] That clears the way for the red R8 of Frank Biela, Tom Kristensen and Emanuele Pirro, who, with a one-lap advantage, win the race in front of their teammates Laurent Aiello, Allan McNish and Stéphane Ortelli who had started from pole. Only two tire failures slow down the winning trio in the early stage. Ever since the eleventh hour, it has continuously been leading the race. Christian Abt, Michele Alboreto and Dindo Capello complete Audi's one-two-three win. In the final stage, the management board's task for a finishing photo showing all three R8 cars, which at that time are dispersed on the track, causes some discomfort. "I looked at several aghast engineers' eyes when I passed our boss's wish on to them. They all explained to me what

kind of a risk that entailed. That's when I told them, 'Friends, please let's not discuss that, just do it.' And that worked out." [33]

The gap between the third- and fourth-placed cars shows how dominant the R8 is: At the Le Mans debut of Henri Pescarolo's team, the Courage Peugeot completes 24 laps less. "Three R8 and nothing else for a long time," a pertinent headline says. [34] The Head of Sport understands the importance of that success: "This success carries a lot of weight in our company. It is of historic significance because such a victory at Le Mans is unique." [35]

Initial title wins

After Le Mans, the Joest squad contests the remaining ALMS races with two R8 cars. Allan McNish and Dindo Capello – augmented by Michele Alboreto at Petit Le Mans – win six of the remaining nine races. Twice Frank Biela and Emanuele Pirro are the front runners. The drivers' title goes to McNish, Audi clinches the chassis and engine classifications while the Joest team competing under Audi Sport North America's entry can celebrate winning the teams' title.

[27] Transcript of interview with Ralf Jüttner on November 17, 2022
[28] Transcript of interview with Dr. Wolfgang Ullrich on December 8, 2022
[29] Peter Wyss: Was ist der Sieg für Audi wert, in Motorsport aktuell, June 27, 2000
[30] Christian Moity, Jean-Marc Teissedre: 2000 Le Mans 24 Hours, Brussels: GSN Publishing 2000, p. 132
[31] Transcript of interview with Ralf Jüttner on November 17, 2022
[32] Audi MediaInfo: Flashback: Le Mans 2000 and the Audi idea of changing the rear end, March 12, 2015
[33] Transcript of interview with Dr. Wolfgang Ullrich on December 8, 2022
[34] Julius Eckert: Drei R8, dann lange nichts mehr, in Heilbronner Stimme, June 19, 2000
[35] Peter Hartmann: Die Formel 1 ist kein Thema, in PS report, July 31, 2000

A sad season

Michele Alboreto's fatal accident casts a shadow over the year of 2001. Audi clinches its second victory in a row at Le Mans, relying on a new technology, FSI direct injection.

Michele Alboreto, together with Laurent Aiello and Dindo Capello, wins the Sebring 12 Hours on March 17, 2001, scoring a one-two-three-four success for Audi. "It is really amazing: Every time I come to the United States, I win a race," says the Italian. "Now I'm looking forward very much to the rest of the season, especially Le Mans. After this success my goal is clear: Winning Sebring and Le Mans in a row is a great dream for me." [1] Five and a half weeks later, Michele Alboreto is dead. He dies on April 25, during tests at the Lausitzring. [2] In 45 years of Audi motorsport history since 1978 until the editorial deadline of this book he is the only factory driver to have lost his life in the cockpit of an Audi race car.

The routine at this test is to complete two high-speed laps on the oval track, two laps on the infield and to then return to the pits. After that follow the infield, the oval and the pits again. Following a tire change, Alboreto drives to the infield where he has a slow puncture that he does not notice. The tire blows out in the oval. [3] The Cottbus prosecutor's office

[1] Audi MediaInfo: Audi repeats last year's Sebring victory, March 18, 2001
[2] Audi MediaInfo: Michele Alboreto fatally injured during testing, April 25, 2001
[3] www.motorsportmagazine.com/archive/article/june-2014/86/lunch-dr-wolfgang-ullrich, last retrieved on January 26, 2023

Michele Alboreto loses his life in a test accident at the Lausitzring on April 25, 2001

On the test day, Audi remembers Michele Alboreto with a mourning ribbon, ten years later with a sticker

investigates the cause of the accident by working together with three DEKRA experts and three specialists from Audi and Michelin. A pointed object has acted on the tread of the left rear tire, initially causing minor damage. That leads to a gradual loss of inflation pressure and, at around 320 km/h, to the tire's mechanical destruction. As a result, the R8 hits the grassy area, loses grip, and is carried off toward the right across the guard rail. [4]

Wolfgang Ullrich finds moving words during his eulogy: "Caro Michele, your whole life was dedicated to motorsport, the love for your family and your close friends. I called you up for Audi in 1998 to share your experience and your energy in developing a racing sportscar for Le Mans. In the shortest time you won the hearts of the whole team and became one of us. Always open, helpful and always there – you were a wonderful person and an extraordinary personality. With impressive professionalism and conviction you were a perfect representative of Audi. With enthu-

siasm and dedication you made it possible for us to develop an extremely successful sportscar. You lost your life the day before yesterday, while undertaking your favourite work in the cockpit of our R8 in preparation for your great goal – the victory in Le Mans with Audi. Michele, you gave us so much, we will miss you terribly and you will always remain in our hearts." [5]

Audi Sport rigorously investigates the causes and takes action on many levels. On the sporting side, after consulting with the drivers, the decision is made to participate in the pre-test at Le Mans on May 6. [6] On the technical level, Audi doubles down on pursuing the project of a Tyre Pressure Monitoring System (TPMS) that had already been started. The TPMS is being tested but not available when Alboreto crashes. Following its rollout for Le Mans in 2001, it will be retained up until the end of the LMP program, detecting countless slow punctures in time.

Whether Audi would have raced at Le Mans if the system had not been ready for use on time cannot be clearly reconstructed. "I don't remember, but it would not have been clever to say that because it massively jeopardizes motivation. I think we systematically communicated that we would achieve that, then we can be sure that something like that cannot happen again," Wolfgang Ullrich says today. [7] Former CEO Franz-Josef Paefgen refers to the fact that he did not issue such a stipulation because he was able to fully rely on Audi Sport. [8] Legal counsel Andreas Köppen recalls, "It had to be clear that the accident was not attributeable to a defect of the vehicle." [9] An aspect that was validated by the experts.

On a regulatory level, Audi advocates making the new-generation LMP race cars as of 2004 clearly less aerodynamically sensitive. [10] On a manpower level, the sport department decides to sign Alboreto's fellow countryman Christian Pescatori as a new driver. [11] On a public relations level, Audi advocates maximum transparency and an appropriate culture of remembrance, publishes the press release of the prosecutor's office as well as the Head of Sport's eulogy, explicitly bids farewell to Michele Alboreto in the Le Mans media booklets and, during the 2011 pretest, in addition pays tribute to him with a sticker on the tenth anniversary of his death.

Audi R8 in the customer's hand

In addition to the factory-backed Audi Sport Team Joest, two customer teams, Champion Racing and Johansson Motorsport, are fielding the R8 for the first time. Looking back, Ullrich says, "There were

Christian Pescatori is signed by Audi for Le Mans on short notice (above). Rod Bymaster and Len Hunt from Audi of America are important supporters of Audi Sport's Le Mans program (right)

[4] Audi MediaInfo: Non official translation of the press release of the public prosecutor Cottbus, April 30, 2001
[5] Audi MediaInfo: Funeral for Michele Alboreto in Italy, April 27, 2001
[6] Audi MediaInfo: Cause of the accident clarified, April 30, 2001
[7] Transcript of interview with Dr. Wolfgang Ullrich on December 7, 2022
[8] Transcript of interview with Dr. Franz-Josef Paefgen on October 27, 2022
[9] Transcript of interview with Andreas Köppen on October 27, 2022
[10] Ibid
[11] Audi MediaInfo: Audi completes driver line-up for Le Mans, May 28, 2001

In 2001, Audi Sport Team Joest competes at Le Mans with two R8 cars

The direct-injection V8 engine debuts in 2001 (left). In 2007, it races for the last time at Le Mans with the technology – that has since been renamed TFSI – in the Swiss Spirit Lola (right)

Direct is better

The efficiency of an engine essentially consists of a mechanical and a thermal component. Audi's lightweight 175-kilogram biturbo engine with a 12.2:1 compression ratio enables a favorable power-to-weight ratio and delivers high efficiency even at low engine speeds. To make even better use of the energy contained in the fuel, the Fuel Straight Injection (FSI) technology is created. At Le Mans the full-throttle operation sums up to 71-percent. Following an analysis of the overall conditions, Audi decides against stratified charge operation in which an ignitable mixture is generated only in the vicinity of the spark plug with surplus air in the remainder of the combustion chamber. Instead, homogeneous charge operation is adopted. Carefully coordinated intake ports generate tumble, i.e., a rolling motion of the air. Together with targeted injection, a homogeneous mixture is generated. [12]

From a range of injectors with six and twelve jets and a swirl nozzle, Audi selects the multi-hole version with six holes. It sprays the conventional, unleaded fuel in two to six milliseconds. Following the launch of the project in January 2000, the FSI is running for the first time in November. The soot development at the first test at Most is so severe that the colleagues from Bentley ask whether Audi was driving a diesel. New maps produce a solution. Oil seals failing due to shift shocks jeopardize the debut. O-rings provide a last-minute solution. To be on the safe side,

Audi Sport had already prepared eight conventional multi-point injection engines in addition to the FSI versions for Le Mans. [13]

[12] Presentation by Ulrich Baretzky, Wolfgang Hatz, Dr. Wolfgang Ullrich: Rennsport bei Audi – Impulse für die Serienentwicklung am Beispiel FSI, p. 2 et seq
[13] Transcript of interview with Ulrich Baretzky on December 19, 2022

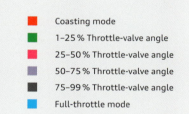

Coasting mode
1–25 % Throttle-valve angle
25–50 % Throttle-valve angle
50–75 % Throttle-valve angle
75–99 % Throttle-valve angle
Full-throttle mode

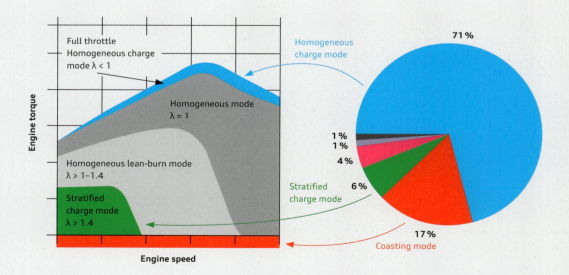

Operating ranges of the gasoline direct injection engine and load percentages during a Le Mans lap

importers that wanted to expand Audi's motorsport program. That's when the idea was born that the R8 could be fielded by supported customer teams." [14] However, for Audi it is important not to hand the cars over to just any team, as Andreas Köppen adds: "We never sold cars to a real privateer team. That was always done through the importer. The cars required a substantial amount of support, not least to ensure safety. That's why entries had to take place through the importers and a highly professional team related to them." [15] With that, Audi picks up an approach that had led to many successes as far back as in the rally years and the Super Touring Car era.

Champion Racing is the motorsport department of Champion Motors, one of the biggest Audi and Porsche dealers in the United States. Its founder, Dave Maraj, soon recognizes the marketing potential of motorsport for his business, and in 1993 starts entering Porsche cars in races in America. The motto is "Race what you sell." Champion Racing soon makes a name for itself. Starting in 1999, the Florida-based team competes in the ALMS. When a project with a Lola-Porsche prototype fails and Porsche's range does not include a vehicle with potential for overall victory, Maraj turns to Head of Audi Sport Wolfgang Ullrich, to acquire the R8 and use it in the ALMS and

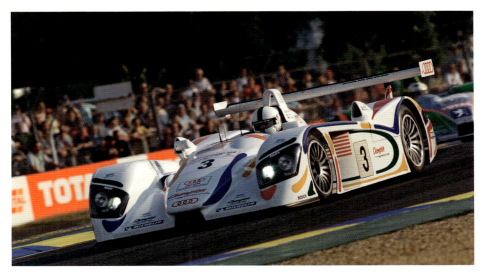

Champion Racing, while in third position, retires six and a half hours into the race due to clutch failure

at Le Mans. Both men already know each other well: since 2000, Champion, supported by Audi of America, has been fielding two Audi S4 Competition cars alongside the Porsche entries in the Speedvision GT series. Ullrich therefore does not have to think twice about the proposal and agrees. Drivers, among others, are the former Le Mans winners Andy Wallace and Johnny Herbert.

Johansson Motorsport is the second R8 customer team. The owner of the squad is ex-F1 driver Stefan Johansson, the 1997 overall Le Mans winner. Following programs in US single-seater racing, the Swede teams up with businessman Jim Matthews and switches to the ALMS in 2000. At the end of the year, the two go separate ways. [16] Over the winter months, Johansson re-establishes his outfit. The race car is the Audi R8. Arena International Motorsport led by seasoned racer Mike Earle assumes responsibility for technical support. The Englishman is an old friend of Johansson's: in 1989, The Swede races for Earle's former team, Onyx, in Formula One. [17] The main sponsor is the Gulf Oil Company that celebrates its 100th anniversary in 2001. [18] As a result, the Johansson R8 receives one of the best known liveries in motorsport because race cars sporting the iconic powder blue and orange Gulf look have been

In 2001, last year's winner Audi (center) meets with Corvette, Cadillac, MG Lola, Bentley, Chrysler, Courage Peugeot, Panoz, Saleen and others (from left)

[14] Transcript of interview with Dr. Wolfgang Ullrich on Dezember 8, 2022
[15] Transcript of interview with Andreas Köppen on October 27, 2022
[16] James Baker: American Le Mans Series Yearbook 2000. Teddington: Haymarket Autosport Publications, 2001, p. 99
[17] Teaminfo Johansson Motorsport, undated
[18] www.gulfoilltd.com/about-us/gulf-history, last retrieved on August 4, 2022

celebrating numerous victories since the end of the nineteen-sixties not only at Le Mans. The team's main activity is the new European Le Mans Series. Team Principal Johansson's fellow drivers are BAR Formula One test driver Patrick Lemarié and Tom Coronel, a former champion of Japanese Formula 3 and Formula Nippon.

In-house competition

In 2001, Audi meets with a new rival: Bentley, a sister brand in the Volkswagen Group. With five victories, in 1924 and 1927 until 1930, the British luxury brand has gone down in Le Mans history. The so-called Bentley Boys such as three-time race winner Woolf Barnato have become legends. In 1931, Bentley is acquired by Rolls Royce and in the subsequent decades disappears more and more in the shadow of the brand sporting the "Emily" on its radiator grille.

Johnny Herbert, Ralf Kelleners and Didier Theys (from left) form the driver crew in the Champion Audi

In 1998, the Volkswagen Group awakens Bentley from its deep slumber by acquiring the brand. The cultivation of its image includes a Le Mans program with two coupés for the GTP class. They use modified engines of the Audi R8 and in 2001 debut at La Sarthe with a strong driver lineup. On its return to racing there, Bentley immediately becomes "best of the rest" after Audi and claims a podium finish.

In the LMP900 category, Audi again meets with three US brands, Cadillac, Chrysler and Panoz. Cadillac updates last year's model and races with two cars fielded by DAMS. In the second year of the LMP program, Chrysler relies on the chassis from Dallara, the V8 engines have been completely updated. As the third brand from the land of the "Stars and Stripes," Panoz is in the field with its front-engine roadsters. For the first time, the team enters the LMP07 type that uses a four-liter V8 engine from Zytek instead of the Ford V8 powerplant. However, the new car that debuts in Adelaide at the end of 2000 has not been fully developed. During the course of the season, Panoz will return to the proven LMP-1 Roadster S.

Dome is a new rival at Le Mans. The Japanese contested the 24-hour race from 1979 to 1986. Now, two S101 Judd are fielded by customer teams, plus three Courage with Judd or Peugeot power. Two British Ascari Judd cars round out the LMP900 field. Concerning the competitors' chances vis-à-vis Audi, the German sport auto magazine writes: "Like last year, Audi was in a class of its own – which speaks both for the class of the Ingolstadt brand and against the quality of its pursuers." [19]

The Audi teams can prepare for Le Mans in 2001 with two races in the United States and two in Europe, plus the traditional pre-test – which they do with aplomb, ultimately scoring four victories. In the preliminary practice, Tom Kristensen sets the best time in front of the Champion R8. The two other R8 cars take fifth and sixth positions. Following Alboreto's accident, Audi Sport Team Joest deploys only four drivers: Kristensen/Capello and Biela/Pirro. Laurent Aiello races at a parallel DTM event.

The fans are struggling with wet conditions at Le Mans in 2001 as well

Pole for Capello

In qualifying for the race, the two Joest R8 cars are running in a different league. Capello, who is sharing the R8 with new signing Pescatori and Laurent Aiello, clinches pole position at 3m32.429s. Tom Kristensen, who is forming a trio again with Frank Biela and Emanuele Pirro, claims a spot on the front row as well, with a deficit of just 0.029 seconds. In third, Ralf Kelleners' gap in the Champion Audi amounts to 1.9 seconds; behind Jan Lammers' Dome, Stefan Johansson follows in fifth.

Rain, rain, rain

Now, if not earlier, it is clear that the factory-fielded R8 are going to decide victory among themselves. On 310 of the total of 321 laps completed in the race, the two cars are the leaders. Due to the torrential rain, that edition of the race will go down in history. "We were running on intermediates or rain tires for 19 hours," Tom Kristensen recalls. [20] Shortly after the start, an initial rain shower shakes up the field, also affecting three of the four R8: Aiello, the leader, has to have the rear bonnet and a tie rod replaced and drops back to 29th position, Johansson touches a guard rail – which, including the repair, costs him three laps – and Kelleners spins as well. Frank Biela takes the lead while Aiello fights back with fast lap times, running in second position overall again just two and a half hours into the race. Constant rain showers require maximum concentration of the drivers. For hours on end, they can only drive on the straights at part throttle, aquaplaning, fog and poor visibility are their constant companions up until the finish. Accidents cause several safety car periods. But even they do not provide any relief.

[19] Claus Mühlberger: Wet-Einsatz, in sport auto, 07/2001, p. 151
[20] Transcript of interview with Tom Kristensen on December 6, 2022

Trick fountains: Tom Kristensen in the subsequent winning car feels like he is sitting in a bathtub

The pole-sitting Audi of Aiello/Capello/Pescatori sees the checkered flag as the runner-up (above). Team Principal Stefan Johannson (pictured on the right) shares an Audi R8 with Patrick Lemarié and Tom Coronel (right)

"Because the pace was so slow, the cockpit of the open R8 filled up with water. It was like lying in a bath," [21] Kristensen recalls.

While the two customer R8 cars retire, the Joest cars dominate events. Paul Frère, a 1960 Le Mans winner and at 84 years of age still working as a journalist, is impressed: "Observing the cars also highlighted major handling differences among the cars and in this respect, the Audis seemed unbeatable. The ease with which they took the chicane after the Dunlop bridge whoever the driver, was a delight to watch. They outclassed all the other drivers." [22] The new FSI technology has a major part in the good-natured handling of the R8 cars: "The engine responds like a normally aspirated engine, this makes the car much easier to control on the wet surface," enthuses Pirro. [23] Audi announces the deployment of this technology only after having claimed victory.

Emanuele Pirro celebrates his second consecutive Le Mans triumph standing on the winning Audi

To the surprise of the engineers, the oil level rises as the race progresses. Driving behind the safety car during long periods causes the fuel to condense on the relatively cold surfaces of the combustion wall. This then mixes with the oil, resulting in decreased viscosity. This causes the cams to wear increasingly, metal shavings get into the oil lines and the engine performance declines. [24]

Following several slips and replacement of the rear end during the night, Capello and company temporarily drop back by three laps. At noon on Sunday, Kristensen, while leading the race, suddenly encounters problems with fourth gear. The entire rear end of the Dane's car is exchanged within just a few minutes as well. "Tom K.", Biela and Pirro subsequently score their second consecutive victory in front of their sister car – and remember Michele Alboreto. "My thoughts are with Michele. I wish he could have been here with us," Pirro says wistfully. [25]

In front in Europe and North America

After Le Mans, Audi continues to dominate the sports car scene both in Europe and North America. In the ELMS, Johansson Motorsport scores a victory in the remaining races at Most and with Stefan Johansson secures the drivers' title. In the teams' classification, the squad prevails as well. On the other side of the ocean, in the ALMS, the Joest duos of Dindo Capello/Tom Kristensen and Frank Biela/Emanuele Pirro are battling for the drivers' championship. In the finale of the season, at Road Atlanta, Biela, thanks to more bonus points for leading laps and fastest race laps, beats his partner Pirro by four points, followed by Capello and Kristensen. Champion Racing achieves several podium finishes in the first year with the R8.

[21] Tom Kristensen, Lars Krone: Tom Kristensen – The Book, no location, no publisher: 2015, p. 126.
[22] Paul Frère: Water, water, in Christian Moity, Jean-Marc Teissedre: 2001 Le Mans 24 Hours, Brussels: GSN Publishing 2001, p. 195
[23] Audi MediaInfo: Advantage through FSI Technology, November 6, 2001
[24] Transcript of interview with Ulrich Baretzky on December 19, 2022
[25] Audi MediaInfo: Audi repeats its Le Mans triumph, June 17, 2001

A perfect result for the Volkswagen Group: Audi scores a one-two win, Bentley finishes in third, and Volkswagen wins the LMP675 class for less powerful sports prototypes

In 2001, Audi clinches the second in a total of nine victories in the Petit Le Mans race at Road Atlanta

Mission: hat-trick

In 2002, Frank Biela, Tom Kristensen and Emanuele Pirro in an Audi R8 fielded by the Joest team win the world's biggest sports car race for the third consecutive time – a unique feat in the history of Le Mans.

A browse through the annals of the Le Mans 24 Hours will reveal that some drivers have won the French classic several times but three victories in a row are rare in the 100-year history of the event. By the time this book is published, merely nine drivers have achieved a Le Mans hat-trick: Woolf Barnato (1928–30), Olivier Gendebien (1960–62), Henri Pescarolo (1972–74), Jacky Ickx (1975–77), Kazuki Nakajima (2018–20) and four drivers who achieve that feat with Audi. Besides Marco Werner, who wins at La Sarthe from 2005 to 2007, Frank Biela, Emanuele Pirro and Tom Kristensen are those drivers. Following their victories in the two previous years, that hat-trick is the big goal for the trio in 2002 because the same driver combination winning three times in a row would be a novelty in the history of Le Mans. In a pre-race interview, Frank Biela admits that this potential success obviously plays a role before the event: "But there's no guarantee that we're going to be in front again this time. That's why I'd rather not even think about it. Although, of course, it keeps crossing my mind. A third victory in a row would definitely be great – for me and also for Audi." [1]

Four Audi at Le Mans

That is why there is never any question about Biela racing with Kristensen and Pirro again, the motto being "Never change a winning team." One third of the sister car's cockpit on the other hand is filled with a new driver. Italians Dindo Capello and Christian Pescatori are augmented by a teammate from the UK: Because Laurent Aiello is focused on the DTM project with ABT Sportsline – which pays off in the form of the title win – Wolfgang Ullrich signs three-time Grand Prix winner Johnny Herbert. The Englishman has clinched several ALMS podium finishes in the privately fielded Champion R8 and therefore knows the sports prototype well. [2] At the beginning of March, Audi announces the fielding of a third race car at Le Mans. [3] The announcement of its driver

[1] Oliver Konze: Audi-interner Konkurrenzkampf größer denn je, in Donaukurier, June 13, 2002
[2] Audi MediaInfo: Johnny Herbert strengthens Audi works team, January 22, 2002
[3] Audi MediaInfo: Audi tackles Le Mans with three "works" cars, March 7, 2002

Numerically perfect: The one-two-three result in 2002 sees car number 1 win in front of numbers 2 and 3

Like the year before, customers are again fielding the R8 in 2002. Champion Racing is involved exclusively in the ALMS, in which the Joest factory team competes as well with two cars. At Le Mans, the three Joest cars are joined by a last-generation R8 from Team Goh. Marketing expert Kazumichi Goh forms the Japanese team in 1996 and immediately wins the GT Championship in his country. From 1997 on, the team contests Le Mans four times, with McLaren, BMW, Panoz and Dome. Sixth position in the 2000 edition is the best result it achieves. In addition, in 1998, Goh officially starts handling Lola imports to Japan. [6] Now the squad, supported by Audi Japan, is fielding an R8 for the first time. "We had no chance to win in Le Mans as a private team to now, but with the R8 things look totally different," says the team owner, explaining why he switched to the brand with the four rings. [7] As drivers, he signs two fellow countrymen, Seiji Ara and Hiroki Katoh. Goh has been promoting Ara for several years. They have known each other from the Japanese VW Golf Cup in which Ara, in 1994, impresses his subsequent boss with his driving skills. [8] Thanks to two victories, Katoh, in 2001, finishes runner-up in the FIA Sportscar Championship (SCC). The third Goh driver is Frenchman Yannick Dalmas, the 1992 Sportscar World Champion and a four-time Le Mans winner who is intended to help the team with his experience at its R8 debut.

Audi kicks off the 2002 season with a one-two win in the Sebring 12 Hours, where its US rivals Panoz (left) and Cadillac (center) compete as well (above).
The traditional technical scrutineering at the beginning of the race week in Le Mans provides deep insights into the Audi R8's inner workings (below)

squad – consisting of Michael Krumm, Philipp Peter and Marco Werner – by the brand follows about two weeks later. [4] "Our bosses weren't really happy that Le Mans was not such a prominent topic in the German media," Ullrich recalls. "That's why I suggested to sign other German-speaking drivers besides Frank Biela. Plus, in Philipp Peter we had someone of interest to Austria." [5] Peter is an old acquaintance and belonged to the Audi driver squad as far back as in the Super Touring Car years. He is a Le Mans rookie – just like Marco Werner, the 1995 overall winner of the Daytona 24 Hours. On the other hand, Michael Krumm, a former Formula 3 and GT Champion in Japan, has two starts at La Sarthe under his belt.

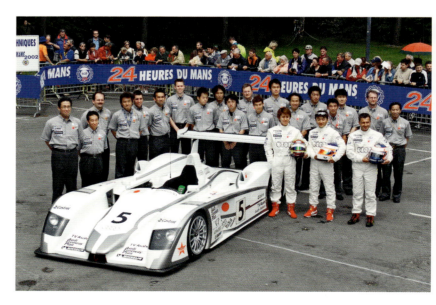

Audi Sport Japan Team Goh is fielding an Audi R8 for the first time in 2002

Bentley & company as underdogs

Thanks to this promising package, Audi is again regarded as an "overwhelming favourite" at Le Mans [9] – even though Ullrich cautions the squad not to underestimate its rivals. "Doing that is the first mistake." [10] The Bentley sister brand is regarded as one of the main competitors. The Brits in their second year are putting an updated EXP Speed 8 on the grid, whose V8 engine built by Audi now has four instead of 3.6 liters of displacement. Butch Leitzinger, Eric van de Poele and Andy Wallace, who at Bentley's debut in 2001 finished in third overall, see the checkered flag in fourth position this time, 13 laps behind the winners.

Other opponents come from the United States. Panoz returns to an Evo version of the original front-engine roadster while a privateer team takes care of the new, 2001 development LMP07 – now with Mugen powerplants. Cadillac is fielding an all-new car that, visually, is heavily reminiscent of the Audi R8. The originator of the concept is Nigel Stroud, the designer of the 1991 Le Mans winning Mazda. Celebrating its return after two years is the Courage factory team on whose products – powered again by Peugeot V6 turbo engines – Henri Pescarolo relies as well. The Frenchman has Toyota's former Technical Director André de Cortanze design a new body shell specifically developed for the fast sections at Le Mans. Several teams are relying on naturally aspirated 4-liter Judd V10 engines. The two Dallara cars of the Oreca squad that continues to operate on its own account after Chrysler's withdrawal are rated as strong rivals. "Exactly that car won the Daytona 24 Hours in January. Its engine, no doubt, will deliver 15 to 20 hp more than our 3.6-liter V8 biturbo in qualifying,"

[4] Audi MediaInfo: Audi driver line-up for Le Mans completed, March 22, 2002

[5] Transcript of interview with Dr. Wolfgang Ullrich on December 8, 2022

[6] Team Goh International press kit, undated

[7] Audi Motorsport Communications: Booklet Audi Press Information Le Mans 2002, p. 69

[8] One to watch: Seiji Ara, in Autosport, June 2, 2002, p. 29

[9] Tim Scott, Gary Watkins: The men and their machines, in Autosport Le Mans Guide 2002, p. 28

[10] Oliver Konze: Scheitern ist für Audi Sport am Wochenende in Le Mans ein Fremdwort, in Donaukurier, June 12, 2002

Successful quintet: Race engineer Joachim Hausner (left) and engine engineer Stefan Dreyer (right) posing with the subsequent race winners in the middle

Several punctures cause the number 2 Audi to lose ground in the battle for victory

says Wolfgang Ullrich. [11] The three Dome S101 from Racing for Holland and Kondo/Chamberlain Racing also rely on ex-race driver John Judd's V10. One Riley & Scott, one Ascari as well as one Panoz and one Lola that as camera cars for a Michel Vaillant film are contesting the race without ambitions for positions at the front round out the LMP900 field.

Pre-Le Mans commitments

While Biela/Kristensen/Pirro and Capello/Herbert/Pescatori contest their first race at the Sebring 12 Hours in mid-March – the latter squad wins – new signings Krumm/Peter/Werner can gather initial experience with the R8 in a 30-hour test in April. [12] On the first weekend in May, the pre-practice follows at Le Mans. Here the Sebring winners set the pace; second place goes to the best Oreca Dallara Judd in front of the other factory R8 cars reeling off 4,000 troublefree kilometers in total. Following a slip, Audi Sport Japan Team Goh has to quit practice early and only achieves 12th position. [13] At the second ALMS round in mid-May at Sears Point, Panoz in pouring rain prevails against the Champion and Joest R8 cars.

Before Le Mans, speculations keep appearing in the media whether Biela, Kristensen and Pirro are supposed to achieve the hat-trick by means of a team strategy. Audi's Head of Sport immediately rejects that idea: "I keep my fingers crossed for all the guys, the cars are equal." [14] Frank Biela adds, "I think that competitive thinking is much stronger than in the years before." However, the German is equally sure that "there will be no ego trip at Audi's expense." [15]

Pole number two for Capello

Capello underpins his claim to victory by clinching a pole position. Setting a best time of 3m29.905s, the Italian is the first Audi driver to break the 3.30-minute record at Le Mans. It is his second consecutive pole. Tom Kristensen is in second position, and Michael Krumm completes the Audi trio at the top. Due to an accident on Wednesday and elec-

Philipp Peter, Marco Werner and Michael Krumm drive the number 3 Audi R8 (above, from left).
In the race, they not only prevail against Jan Lammers' Dome but manage the leap onto the podium at their debut with Audi (below)

Heroes in the background: Joest's mechanics deserve much of the credit for achieving the one-two-three win (top left).
Audi's physician Dr. Christian John (with black cap) takes care of everyone's health (above).
Befitting the 2002 FIFA World Cup, the Audi drivers pose with the jerseys of their national teams (left)

Four-time Le Mans winner Yannick Dalmas races for Team Goh

tronics issues on Thursday, Team Goh loses valuable on-track time and does not make it beyond the 15th spot on the grid.

Hot and humid summer temperatures await the 50 entrants for the race. As early as on the formation lap, Michael Krumm has a puncture – a mishap that slows down the entire Audi squad several times during the one-day chase. Krumm has to change the tire and starts the race from the pit lane. At the very front of the field, Johnny Herbert in the pole-sitting R8 and Frank Biela are fighting a thrilling duel during which the lead changes several times. At the beginning of the third hour, there is a piece of bad news for Tom Kristensen, who takes over from Biela: "Suddenly, our race engineer, Jo Hausner, radioed me, saying, 'Tom, you're getting a stop-and-go penalty for overtaking under a yellow flag.' I responded,

I didn't see any flags but Jo, who doesn't like that over the radio at all, just said, 'Tom, stop-and-go, no discussion.' So I came in and served the two-minute penalty." [16]

Shortly before the end of the fourth hour of racing, Christian Pescatori suffers a tire blow-out as well. "Unfortunately, he had to complete almost a whole lap on three tires at 50, 60 km/h," his teammate Capello recalls. "We lost nearly one minute." [17] It would not be the last flat tire for the number 2 R8. Two more follow and ultimately cost the car all chances for victory. Even so, the causes remain unclear. Ralf Jüttner, Joest's Technical Director, looks

[11] Oliver Konze: Scheitern ist für Audi Sport am Wochenende in Le Mans ein Fremdwort, in Donaukurier, June 12, 2002
[12] Audi MediaInfo: Audi driver line-up for Le Mans completed, March 22, 2002
[13] Audi MediaInfo: Successful Le Mans dress rehearsal for Audi, May 5, 2002
[14] Oliver Konze: Scheitern ist für Audi Sport am Wochenende in Le Mans ein Fremdwort, in Donaukurier, June 12, 2002
[15] Oliver Konze: Audi-interner Konkurrenzkampf größer denn je, in Donaukurier, June 13, 2002
[16] Transcript of interview with Tom Kristensen on December 6, 2022
[17] Transcript of interview with Dindo Capello on November 24, 2022

New methodology

Except for the 1989 Audi 90 quattro IMSA GTO that is built on a tubular frame all of Audi's racing and rallying models up to 1998 are based on production cars. The development method typically used up until that time, depicted in the left-hand column on p. 75 (top), is as follows: First, the engineers design a race car and then they test it. If they are not satisfied with the results they may have to re-design parts or component assemblies in case of doubt. The beginning of the sports prototype era poses new challenges – for instance with the chassis. "The 1999 Audi R8R was our first concept with a stressed CFRP structure. This material exhibits a completely different behavior. While metallic materials bend or break in a crash, carbon fiber collapses. Consequently, the calculation methods used here are totally different," long-time Technical Director Martin Mühlmeier recalls. [18] In the early stages, Dallara assists with its experience. The Italian company has acquired its expertise in many years of designing single-seaters

and sports prototypes. "Audi Sport subsequently entered the field of CFRP on its own," says Mühlmeier. "We implemented this know-how, strengthened our resources by recruiting highly skilled personnel and developed proprietary calculation methods. This soon made it possible for us to calculate structures, strength and crash behavior in-house."

The methods, shown in the right-hand column, change accordingly. Audi extends this approach to various areas of the race car, as shown in the chart below. Initial lap time simulations exist as early as in 1996, and suspension kinematics simulation follows in 1997. 1999 marks the beginning of CFD (computational fluid dynamics) simulations of aerodynamics, FEM (finite elements method) calculation and work on an elastokinematics test bench. [19] Since then, instead of using costly full-vehicle prototypes and lengthy iterations – i.e., repetitions of necessary re-developments – the engineers have been

Testing effort 1997–2002

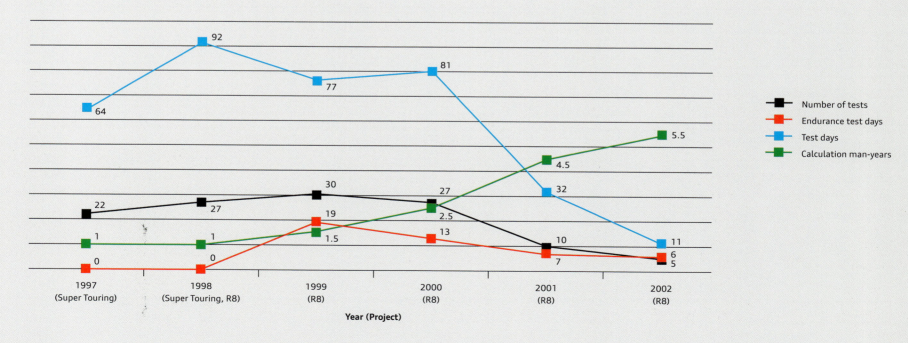

Legend:
- Number of tests (black)
- Endurance test days (red)
- Test days (blue)
- Calculation man-years (green)

Motorsport development process chain

```
                              Simulation
                                  ↓
              Design           Design
                ↓                 ↓
              Trial           Test bench
                                  ↓
                                Trial
```

Disadvantages:
· Costly total vehicle
  prototypes
· Lengthy iterations

Advantages:
· Iterations on virtual level
  (cost-efficient and fast)
· Validation on more cost-efficient
  component level
· Virtual total vehicle with validated
  components as basis for trials

◄──────────────────────────────────────►

Production-based race cars up until 1998   Sports prototypes from 1998 on

detecting deficits already on the computer or during component trials preceding actual race car testing operations. The time that the specialists initially spend working on computers increases accordingly. The green curve in the chart on p. 74 illustrates that: calculation man-years refers to how much time is devoted to design and simulation. From 1.5 years of cumulative working hours performed by all relevant employees in 1999, the number increases more than three-and-a half times by 2002. By contrast, the number of tests, test days and endurance test days (i.e., the up to 30-hour pre-Le Mans cycles) noticeably decreases after 2000. These statistical series clearly indicate the early maturity of the R8. While in the first year the engineers and drivers are still spending 81 days on testing, that number drops to just 32 in the subsequent period. For the next season, nearly a third of the 2001 level suffices to create the prerequisites for victory for the third time. This method that has fundamentally changed at that stage will subsequently benefit all Audi Sport projects such as the DTM race cars from 2004 on or customer racing in later years.

[18] Audi MediaInfo Magazine: Motorsport and Production. Audi Le Mans Prototypes 1999–2013, 2013, p. 8
[19] Entwicklungsprozess Audi Sport – Trends, working paper by Dr. Martin Mühlmeier (undated)

	Simulation	Test bench	Trial
Aerodynamics	CFD calculation	Model wind tunnel	
Chassis strength	FEM calculation	Torsion test bench	
Chassis crash	CFRP FEM calculation	Crash test	
Suspension strength	FEM calculation	Pulse test bench	
Suspension kinematics	ADAMS kinematics	Elastokinematics test bench	
Suspension setup	Vertical dynamics simulation	Hydropulse test bench	
Engine	FEM calculation	Engine dyno	
Drivetrain	FEM calculation	Powertrain dyno	
Total vehicle	Lap time simulation	Flat-belt type test bench	

Following commitments in the privateer Champion Audi, ex Grand Prix winner Johnny Herbert joins the factory squad in 2002

The Biela/Kristensen/ Pirro trio wins for the third consecutive time

back: "We and Audi suspected the gravel traps, some of which were newly filled. There were many discussions with the ACO at that time. After the race, we even collected gravel samples from several sections of the track on behalf of Audi. But to my knowledge, nothing came of that." [20]

Things go better for car number 1 that takes the lead four hours into the race. Its advantage amounts to two laps some of the time but at 11.36 pm, it suffers a puncture as well. "I barely managed to prevent crashing into the tire wall. Fortunately, the defect was on the left front, had it been on the right, I wouldn't have been able to catch the car," says Kristensen. [21] The Dane pits but, thanks to a quick repair job by chief mechanic Thomas Loitsch's crew, soon continues his race. Subsequently, Kristensen, Biela and Pirro go on to score their third victory in a row. It is the first and only time to date for a driver trio to have achieved that feat. Audi and the Joest squad can celebrate

Together with Wolfgang Ullrich and Reinhold Joest the nine Audi drivers celebrate their brand's one-two-three win

ALMS founder Don Panoz (left) presents Tom Kristensen with the trophy for the drivers' title, Dindo Capello misses it just barely

Champion Racing focuses on the ALMS in 2002

a hat-trick too. Audi can subsequently take the winner's trophy home to Ingolstadt. Although it is designed to be a floating trophy the regulations allow a team to keep it permanently after claiming a third triumph in a row.

In the end, the runner-up's spot is the best that Capello/Herbert/Pescatori can do, and Krumm/Peter/Werner produce the second Audi one-two-three result after 2000. Following their early puncture, they are in the last spot some of the time and afterwards show a strong comeback. Following a radiator change, the seventh spot goes to the "Japanese" Audi.

A special trio

"A one-two-three finish was a dream. But it was a dream that came true," Dr. Ullrich subsequently writes in a guest article, praising the winning crew. "This trio is very special. [...] Their main strengths are that they have a unique combination so when any of them set up the car, it is pretty well 100 percent perfect for the other two. They also have not

too different a seating position, so that needs little adjustments at stops. And finally each of them possesses great speed as a driver, and this, combined with their reliability on not making mistakes, makes them a very strong line-up." [22]

Le Mans is followed by eight races in the ALMS, in which Audi is the winner on eight occasions. The drivers' title ultimately goes to Tom Kristensen with just a two-point advantage over his partner at Joest, Dindo Capello. Audi again clinches the manufacturers' titles for chassis and engines, Joest defends the teams' classification.

[20] Information provided by Ralf Jüttner on January 26, 2023
[21] Transcript of interview with Tom Kristensen on December 6, 2022
[22] Dr. Wolfgang Ullrich: Hattrick is our racing pinnacle, in Autosport, June 20, 2002, p. 122

JJ Lehto in Champion Racing's Audi R8 on
course for third position

Private pleasure

For the first time, only Audi cars entered by customer teams are competing at Le Mans. Victory this time goes to the Bentley sister brand.

The 2003 season represents a turning point in Audi's motorsport program. The brand with the four rings does not engage in any factory commitments – which also has effects on the R8 racing program. The short-and-crisp announcement is made in a press release in November 2002: "After winning the Le Mans 24 Hours and the American Le Mans Series (ALMS) three times in a row, AUDI AG has restructured its motorsport programme for the 2003 season. The Audi R8, today's most successful sportscar, will continue to race next year and will be entered by customer teams supported by Audi importers." [1] Consequently, Audi Sport discontinues the development of the R8 and focuses on future projects. [2] They include both the development of an R8 successor that has been in progress since early April [3] and the design of a vehicle for the return to DTM racing in 2004 that is given the green light in August. [4]

[1] Audi Mediainfo: Customer racing programme for Audi in 2003, November 28, 2002
[2] Audi Motorsport Communications: Booklet Motorsport Media Info 2003, p. 2
[3] Oliver Konze: Audi baut schon mal einen neuen Rennwagen, entscheidet über Einsatz aber wieder später, in Donaukurier, June 25, 2003
[4] Thomas Voigt: Audi A4. DTM Champion 2004. Ingolstadt: AUDI AG, 2004, p. 28

At Sebring, Audi meets with the new Bentley for the first time and after 12 hours is the front runner

Support for four teams

At the beginning of February, Audi announces the teams for the R8 commitments. [5] Audi Sport makes the know-how of its customer racing department available to them.[6] Joest Racing, previously signed to run the factory-backed commitments in North America and at Le Mans, is involved with one R8 exclusively in the American Le Mans Series. At Le Mans, the team based in Germany's Odenwald region is involved in the Bentley project.

Champion Racing on the other hand competes both in the ALMS and at Le Mans. At La Sarthe, where the Americans are racing again after a one-year break, Dave Maraj's team relies on factory driver Emanuele Pirro and on Stefan Johansson, who has dissolved his team, plus on former BMW and Cadillac driver JJ Lehto, a 1995 Le Mans winner. Audi Sport Japan Team Goh is hoping for a better result in the iconic French race than seventh place at the team's debut the year before. Seiji Ara remains loyal to the team; his partners this time are factory driver Marco Werner and former Formula One driver Jan Magnussen, who, between 1999 and 2002, beat the R8 five times in the ALMS with the Panoz LMP1. Brian Willis, the designer of the 1999 Le Mans winning BMW V12 LMR, is the new Technical Director. [7]

For the first time since Audi's 1999 debut, Audi Sport UK is active again at Le Mans. The Britons sign Mike Earle's Arena Motorsport outfit as their fielding team. "The timing was perfect," says Team Manager David Ingram, looking back. "The Bentley programme was coming up to its third year and there were a lot of resources from the group going into that. One of the byproducts of this was that Audi decided not to run a works team in 2003 so this was our opportunity. I spoke to the people I knew in Audi Sport from touring car days. We came to an agreement whereby we could buy a car and I put together a programme. In normal circumstances we would have gone straight to Richard Lloyd but he was involved in the Bentley project. A suitable alternative was found in the person of Mike Earle who had run the Johansson R8. The logic was that his guys understood the R8." [8] Wolfgang Ullrich is happy with that lineup and sets the course of action: "Teams Arena, Champion, Goh and Joest, which are deploying the R8, have been time-tested partners for many years, whom we know very well. They will exploit the potential of the R8. Our goal is to win the ALMS again and to reach the podium at Le Mans." [9]

Audi Sport UK competes with one R8 at Le Mans. The drivers: Frank Biela, Mika Salo and Perry McCarthy (from left)

British Racing Green

Bentley competes with an all-new development of a coupé in the GTP class in 2003. On the drivers' side of the house, Audi's sister brand, which in 2003 is the only manufacturer to directly battle for overall victory at Le Mans, is augmented by Tom Kristensen and Dindo Capello, two aces from Ingolstadt. They share a Bentley Speed 8 with Guy Smith. Ex-Formula One racers Mark Blundell, David Brabham and Johnny Herbert drive the premium brand's second green prototype.

Victory at Sebring

The 12-hour race at Sebring in mid-March provides the Audi teams with the only opportunity for racing before Le Mans because the ALMS season does not continue until the end of June. Three of the four customer teams, Joest, Champion and Audi Sport UK, are contesting the race. Joest and Champion fight a nail-biting battle for victory that ultimately, with a 13.493-second advantage, goes to the German

Rivals this time: Joest employee Ralf Jüttner (left), the new Technical Director at Bentley, talking shop with Head of Audi Sport Wolfgang Ullrich

squad with its driver trio Frank Biela/Philipp Peter/ Marco Werner. JJ Lehto/Stefan Johansson/Emanuele Pirro finish as runners-up, and Audi Sport UK's R8 with Jonny Kane/Perry McCarthy/Mika Salo does so in sixth position. With deficits of four and five laps, respectively, the new Bentley Speed 8 cars claim positions three and four. Although Tom Kristensen achieves the fastest race lap the sports prototype, that has not yet been fully developed, is difficult to drive on the long runs. The drivers are struggling with cockpit temperatures of more than 60 degrees centigrade, plus the t res that are slimmer than those of the R8 degrade faster. [10]

In the following months, Bentley continuously optimizes the new race car [11] – which pays off: On the Le Mans test day on May 4, the Brits set the pace. Clocked at 3m34.482s, Tom Kristensen sets a superior best time. Jan Magnussen from Team Goh is the fastest driver of an R8. The Dane, at 3m38.385s, is

Ex-Formula One driver Jan Magnussen races for Audi Sport Japan Team Goh

[5] Audi MediaInfo: Strong Audi teams in Le Mans and America, February 4, 2003

[6] Audi Motorsport Communications: Booklet Motorsport Media Info 2003, p. 3

[7] Press release Audi Sport Japan Team Goh: Audi Sport Japan Team Goh Announces Participation Set Up in Le Mans 24-Hour Race for 2003, April 25, 2003

[8] Ian Wagstaff: Audi R8, Dorchester: Veloce Publishing, 2011, p. 57

[9] Audi Motorsport Communications: Booklet Motorsport Media Info 2003, p. 2 et seq

[10] Nils Finderup: Tom K & Le Mans. Forlaget Finsen, no location 2003, p. 105

[11] Ibid, p. 106

the runner-up. After the second Bentley, Frank Biela follows in the British Audi, whose squad after the modest appearance at Sebring now does a clearly better job of handling the R8. "We got a bit lost at Sebring," says Mika Salo. "The car didn't understeer and it didn't oversteer, but it was slow. I didn't know what to do. Frank drove it before Test Day and suddenly we found two seconds." [12] Fifth place goes to the Champion Audi that primarily reels off long runs.

Bentley dominates

Despite Bentley's clear advantage the Audi teams in the duel of the "competing subsidiaries" [13] of the Volkswagen Group have hopes of clinching the fourth consecutive Le Mans victory for the R8. "Our competitors first have to finish as easily as in the previous years," says Frank Biela. [14] Fellow Audi driver JJ Lehto adds, "I don't believe that we will be the fastest car in qualifying or at certain times in the

Light show in the pit lane: Two Audi R8 waiting for the night-time qualifying to start

The R8 cars from Audi Sport UK and Champion Racing fighting with one of the three Japanese Dome

race but that doesn't mean we cannot win. We have a proven race winning car that has an engine offering fantastic fuel economy combined with exceptional reliability." [15]

Consequently, it comes as no surprise that Bentley captures the front row in qualifying. With a 2.9-second deficit, Frank Biela, in third place, is the best R8 driver, Jan Magnussen is fifth, JJ Lehto sixth. But in the race Bentley again sets the benchmark, clinching a dominant one-two victory. For Autosport, it is "one of the most dominant displays at the world's biggest sportscar race. Ever." [16] The three Audi are battling for the remaining podium position because Bentley is showing no weakness: "The Speed 8 were driven flat out for the best part of 24 hours, yet experienced not a single major mechanical problem between them. [...] What's more, the hopes of the three customer Audi teams of being able to keep up with the faster British Racing Green coupés – courtesy of better tyre wear and fuel consumption – went out of the window almost immediately. The Speed 8 drivers were able to triple-stint their narrow tyres and, if they so desired, could make a 90 litre tank of fuel last for 14 laps – just one fewer than the German cars." [17]

The best R8 in the race, in third overall, is the Champion Racing car that, as a result, clinches LMP900 class victory. Fourth place goes to the Goh Audi. Time losses of 20 minutes in total due to a change of the right front suspension and for eliminating misfiring cost the podium. For the R8 of Audi Sport UK, the race takes an extremely unfortunate turn. Two hours into the race, Frank Biela, while running in third position, coasts down without fuel. "I am just so upset for the team," says the disconsolate German after his mishap. "I found myself baulked by another car beside me and I couldn't turn into the pit-lane which

The Champion R8 in third position clinches the best Audi result

Former F1 drivers Mika Salo, Stefan Johansson and JJ Lehto (from left) compete for the privateer Audi teams in 2003

Goh's Team Manager Torsten Robbens (right) asks Jan Magnussen about his impressions of the track

[12] Gary Watkins: Quick, quick, Salo, in Autosport, Le Mans Guide 2003, p. 9
[13] Konkurrierende Töchter, in Kölnische Rundschau, June 13, 2003
[14] Dieter Christof Serowy: Wiederholungstäter, in Auto Zeitung 10/2003
[15] Press release Champion Racing: American team takes on world's best in classic enduro, June 2003
[16] Gary Watkins: Time machine, in Autosport, June 19, 2003, p. 66
[17] Ibid

JJ Lehto, Emanuele Pirro and Stefan Johansson (from left) finish in third place overall and win the LMP900 class

meant I had to start another lap. I knew immediately that I would not have enough fuel to do so. When the engine died, I tried to get back to the pits using the starter but it was impossible." [18]

At the end of the race, Wolfgang Ullrich presents himself as a fair loser: "The Audi customer teams have done a great job and proven how good the Audi R8 is as a year old 'used car.' You should not forget the basic concept of the R8 is now four years old. Bentley has developed a completely new car for this year's race and has earned the victory." [19]

Kazumichi Goh (left) celebrates victory in the 1,000-kilometer race at Le Mans together with his drivers Tom Kristensen and Seiji Ara

Joest Racing wins the ALMS with Frank Biela and Marco Werner, pictured here at Trois-Rivières

Despite the praise expressed by the Head of Audi Sport the outcome of the race is painful for Champion Racing's owner Dave Maraj: "I was very disappointed I didn't beat the Bentleys," Maraj says later. "I wasn't even aware we had won LMP900 until about six months after! I said 'We won our class?' I didn't even know. I was just really upset that we lost the big win. During all the years we raced I would say that was my biggest disappointment." [20]

Four other titles

After Le Mans, Joest and Champion contest the remaining eight ALMS races. 14 days after the race in France, Johnny Herbert and JJ Lehto clinch Champion Racing's long awaited first victory with the R8 at Road Atlanta; three others follow, including the one at Petit Le Mans. But despite the strong season Champion falls slightly short of winning the championship. In the end, the Joest duo of Marco Werner/ Frank Biela that clinches four victories during the season, scoring 170 points, has seven points more than Champion's driver Lehto; his teammate Johnny Herbert trails him with 160 points. Joest also secures the teams' classification, and Audi clearly wins the chassis and engine manufacturers' championships for the fourth time in a row. After the Le Mans 24 Hours, Team Goh contests two more 1,000-kilometer races. At the request of and with support by Audi Belgium, Seiji Ara and Tom Kristensen race at Spa, a round of the FIA Sportscar Championship, where they clinch victory. The duo achieves another win in early November, at Le Mans, where the ACO on the Circuit Bugatti is holding a test race for the new Le Mans Endurance Series that is planned for 2004. Consequently, the first year of the R8 in which customer teams exclusively race ends in ten victories in twelve races.

[18] Audi MediaInfo: Audi drivers on the podium for the fifth time in a row at Le Mans, June 15, 2003

[19] Ibid

[20] David Tremayne: Champion Racing. A little bit of Magic. Phoenix: David Bull Publishing, 2014, p. 232. All statements taken from previously published sources. Dave Maraj died in a fatal boating accident in July 2018: https://thecoastalstar.com/profiles/blogs/obituary-devinder-dave-maraj, last retrieved on August 22, 2022

Two peas in a pod?

On February 4, 2003, Bentley publishes a press release that says, "It is no exaggeration to describe the Bentley Speed 8 Le Mans GT prototype that will race at both Sebring and Le Mans as a new car. Though the previous two generations of Speed 8 performed spectacularly well [...], it was felt that for the final year of the three-year programme, a fresh approach was required. [...] The concept driving the design was to ensure much better exploitation of the airflow over the body and particularly to the rear wing. To achieve this, the external cockpit area has been much reduced [...] making a smaller hole in the air and allowing the car to use a much smaller, more aerodynamic engine cover. In addition, the air-intake that had sat on top of the car in previous generation Speed 8s has been deleted in favour of 'snorkel'-type intakes on the sides of the car. This not only further increases the efficiency of the air-flow over the car, it also lowers the height of the car." [21]

What at first glance seems to be a purely technical development step reflects complex corporate policy interests. In 1998, the Volkswagen Group acquires the tradition-steeped Bentley brand. Since 2001, Bentley has been competing against its Volkswagen sister brand, Audi, with a closed-cockpit GTP prototype and celebrates third place at its debut. In spring of 2002, Franz-Josef Paefgen switches from the role of Chairman of the Management Board of AUDI AG to that of Chairman and Chief Executive Officer at Bentley. He obtains detailed explanations of the vehicle – the coupé developed by Peter Elleray at rtn and fielded by Richard Lloyd's team, which means that exactly those parties that in 1999 still attended to the Audi R8C are on board now. "The first Bentley was an offspring from those days," Paefgen says two decades later. [22] "The intake scoop above the roof is typical for naturally aspirated engines. However, in the case of a turbo engine, the intake scoops sit on the outside, as close as possible to the turbochargers." But the Bentley always had a V8 biturbo engine. So why the roof-mounted air scoop? This is another case where Ferdinand Piëch at an early stage of the concept is trying to deploy the W12 engine to Le Mans. The managers however recognize the futility of that effort and instead use a 3.6-liter V8 biturbo from Audi Sport's engine department in Neckarsulm.

Euphoria is huge after the podium finish in 2001. "In England, they thought we are going to win now," Paefgen comments about his first weeks and months. "But I told our employees: you cannot win with that car, so we went to Le Mans with only one car in 2002." [23] Instead, a new race car that is heavily focused on aerodynamics is created. In more than 1,000 work steps the engineers fine-tune airflow in the 40-percent wind tunnel in Emmen. [24] Likewise, Neckarsulm, to distinguish it from Audi's 3.6-liter V8, has been building a four-liter powerplant since 2002. "Dr. Paefgen insisted on four liters of displacement. But that could not be achieved by just enlarging bore and stroke. The entire combustion

[21] Press release Team Bentley, February 4, 2003
[22] Transcript of interview with Franz-Josef Paefgen on October 27, 2022
[23] Ibid
[24] Brian Gush, Dr. Franz-Josef Paefgen: Der Bentley Speed 8 für das 24-Stunden-Rennen in Le Mans 2003, in ATZ 4/2004, p. 282

Mark Blundell, Johnny Herbert, David Brabham, Team Director John Wickham, PR Manager Sarah Parris, Dindo Capello, Guy Smith and Tom Kristensen alongside the two Bentley Speed 8 cars. The faces shown here also include employees of Joest Racing and Audi Sport from Germany

Following their victory for Bentley, Tom Kristensen and Dindo Capello return to Audi and go on to celebrate many other sports car victories

process no longer worked and we had to develop the injection system with the nozzle geometry from scratch," says Ulrich Baretzky. [25]

Following Audi's hat-trick at Le Mans, the weights also shift politically. Ten years after the victory, Peter Elleray writes, "The full resources of the group will be placed behind the Bentley campaign." [26] Consequently, the rumor about Bentley being an "Audi with a roof" soon makes the rounds. That is something reputable publications do not publish and is clearly rejected by designer Elleray as well. [27] Franz-Josef Paefgen comments on the issue, "Once again to establish the truth: The car was created entirely in Norwich, the engine, of course, by Ulrich Baretzky. Wolfgang Ullrich looked at the concept, because I always had him around a bit. But all the decisions were made by Peter Elleray." [28]

An agreement is reached concerning Audi and Bentley's fielding and strategy: "The continued development of the successful Audi R8 will cease." [29] "Dr. Ullrich said that he could live with that and even felt that the car would remain competitive," says Paefgen. "For me, that meant: I'll take that risk. If we finished shortly behind a fast Audi as the runner-up then I would have been out of luck, but I can live with that. But racing against an Audi that is not racing is terrible, you cannot do that." [30] Irrespective of that, Wolfgang Ullrich provides the same answer in 2013: "The truth is that there was an open competition. If our customer teams had been faster, then Bentley would have been out of luck." [31]

The agreement also includes two Audi drivers and staff from Joest Racing supporting the Bentley team. "At first we thought that we could mix the drivers and the teams," says Paefgen. "We invested a lot of effort in writing lists and schedules together with Head of Motorsport Brian Gush and Team Director John Wickham. Not even two weeks passed before one of the cars had only English drivers, and the team was an all-English team, and the other one was the international one with the Joest team." [32] The squad of the English car, number 8, consists of Brits Mark Blundell and Johnny Herbert with Australian David Brabham led by race engineer Paul Thomas. Dindo Capello, Tom Kristensen and Brit Guy Smith directed by engineer Joachim Hausner drive car number 7. 73 years after Bentley's last Le Mans victory, they win in front of the sister car with a two-lap advantage. Afterward, the Bentley program is history.

[25] Transcript of interview with Ulrich Baretzky on December 19, 2022
[26] Peter Elleray: Minutes from disaster, in Race Tech International No. 152, June 2013, p. 33
[27] Ibid and Autosport Le Mans Guide 2003, p. 15
[28] Transcript of interview with Franz-Josef Paefgen on October 27, 2022
[29] Audi Motorsport Communications: Booklet Motorsport Media Info 2003, p. 2
[30] Transcript of interview with Franz-Josef Paefgen on October 27, 2022
[31] www.motorsport-total.com/24-stunden-von-le-mans/news/grosses-jubilaeum-ullrich-20-jahre-audi-sportchef-13113001, last retrieved on January 23, 2023. He confirms that view today, Transcript of interview with Dr. Wolfgang Ullrich on December 7, 2022
[32] Transcript of interview with Franz-Josef Paefgen on October 27, 2022

Bentley relies on a four-liter V8 engine from Neckarsulm. For each of the brand's five Le Mans victories between 1924 and 1930, a laurel wreath has been attached to the front splitter. The place for the sixth one has already been selected

Let's Goh

In its fifth year of racing, the Audi R8 continues to be the benchmark at Le Mans. A riveting race sees privateer Audi Sport Japan Team Goh prevail against its rivals.

It's Saturday, 4.25 pm. Not even 30 minutes into the 72nd edition of the Le Mans 24 Hours all hopes for victory seem to be lost for the Audi R8 of Seiji Ara, Dindo Capello and Tom Kristensen. After the Italian has spun, the white sports prototype with the elegant red-and-black stripes is standing in the gravel trap of the Dunlop chicane. Several minutes pass before the Audi is back on track. Capello has dropped to 24th position and is one lap behind. "I thought everything was over," he recalls. [1] Yet what follows is a sensational comeback producing one of the closest decisions in the history of the iconic endurance race.

Following Bentley's end of program, Audi is again regarded as the top favorite at Le Mans. Once more Head of Sport Wolfgang Ullrich relies on importer teams supported by factory drivers, deploying as many as seven of them: Frank Biela, Dindo Capello, new signing Pierre Kaffer, Tom Kristensen, Allan

[1] Transcript of interview with Dindo Capello, November 24, 2022

Audi Sport Japan Team Goh is the first privateer Audi outfit to win at Le Mans

Strong debut: On making its debut with Audi, the Veloqx squad wins at Sebring (top).
Successful quartet: Kazumichi Goh (pictured right) with his drivers Dindo Capello,
Tom Kristensen and Seiji Ara (below)

McNish, Emanuele Pirro and Marco Werner. Together with privateer drivers Johnny Herbert, JJ Lehto and Guy Smith, a total of eight Le Mans winners belong to the lineups of the privateer outfits Champion Racing, Team Goh and Veloqx Motorsport.

Powerful Audi customer teams

As before, Champion races in the ALMS, deploying Lehto and title defender Werner as its driver squad. Pirro complements the team at Sebring and Le Mans. Audi Sport Japan Team Goh competes with an R8 as well. Team Principal Kazumichi Goh wants to quit following the squad's retirement the year before. But when his team wins the 1,000-kilometer races at

Spa and Le Mans in 2003 and Tom Kristensen manages to dissuade the principal from withdrawing, he continues the commitment. [2] In terms of drivers, Goh relies on his protégé Seiji Ara and Capello in the ACO's new Le Mans Endurance Series (LMES), complemented by Kristensen at selected races such as Le Mans. Team Goh intensively prepares for the season's highlight, using its own weather radar station for accurate forecasts. Strategy is the responsibility of a six-member team including Jo Hausner from Audi Sport, who has taken care of the winning race car every year since 2000. Another ace up the squad's sleeve is a high-tech tire warmer from Tyre Technology Limited in the UK. "As a test customer, we already tested the various evolutions of the system," recalls Goh's Team Manager Torsten Robbens. "In 2004, we were the only ones to use the latest version." [3] It has the advantage of heating the tires up to operating temperatures clearly faster and more evenly than conventional heating blankets. [4]

New to the Audi ranks is Audi Sport UK Team Veloqx that prepares two R8 cars. Sam Li, a Hong Kong businessman, has founded the fielding team Veloqx Motorsport at the end of 2001. It wins the British GT Championship right in its debut season. The following year Veloqx competes in the Sebring 12 Hours as well as at Le Mans in the 24 Hours and in the 1,000-kilometer race, scoring two class victories. The driver squad is mainly made up of British racers. They include Allan McNish, who has returned from Formula One, three-time Grand Prix winner Johnny Herbert, last year's winner Guy Smith, plus the Germans Frank Biela and Pierre Kaffer.

Competitors as underdogs

Nearly all the competitors rely on modified cars in the top category that has been renamed LMP1. Pescarolo has made major changes, using V10 engines from Judd for the first time. In addition, chief engineer André de Cortanze updates the car's aerodynamics. Because the cars have seen a clear departure from Courage's original base, they are homologated for the first time as Pescarolo cars. In terms of drivers, the team again relies on an all-French lineup including subsequent Audi factory driver Benoît Tréluyer. However, judged to be Audi's fiercest rivals are the three Dome S101 that won the 2002 and 2003 FIA Sportscar Cup. Especially the two cars from Racing for Holland are regarded as secret favorites. Team Principal Jan Lammers, Justin Wilson and Ralph Firman Jr. are three former Formula One racers in the squad. Zytek from the UK, a company previously known primarily as an electronics supplier and engine tuner, is putting a car of its own on the grid for the first time. [5] Zytek is staffed with strong professionals: Bentley's former Team Director John Wickham is Team Manager, the drivers include Andy Wallace (1988 winner) and last year's runner-up David Brabham, among others. A privateer Lola equipped with a turbodiesel engine based on the VW Touareg is among the entrants too. The LMP1 field of 18 vehicles is completed by three other Lola cars, one Dallara, one Panoz, one Lister, one Reynard and one Nasamax using bioethanol fuel.

The ALMS and the LMES each hold one race before Le Mans between which the official Le Mans test day takes place. In North America, the Sebring 12 Hours ring in the season. Champion and Veloqx race there with three Audi R8 cars, and the UK squad claims an Audi one-two-three win with Biela, Kaffer and McNish in front of Lehto/Pirro/Werner and Davies/Herbert/Smith.

On April 25, the official Le Mans test day follows, which ends with the Audi quartet claiming the top four positions. Allan McNish in the Veloqx R8 takes the top spot after a 3m32.615s lap, making him twelve thousandths of a second faster than Johnny Herbert in the sister car. Champion Racing and Team Goh, respectively, follow barely one and a half and 1.7 seconds later. During the test day, a story also occurred that Dindo Capello recalls with a smile:

[2] Gary Watkins: Give it another Goh, in Autosport Le Mans Guide 2009, p. 15
[3] Transcript of interview with Torsten Robbens, August 23, 2022
[4] www.dailysportscar.com/archive/subscribers/technical/tyrewarmers.htm, last retrieved on August 24, 2022
[5] www.gibsontech.co.uk/our-history, last retrieved on August 23, 2022

Seiji Ara crosses the finish line in first position, amidst Team Goh's cheers

Barely beaten: Jamie Davies (pictured), Johnny Herbert and Guy Smith finish runners-up at Le Mans

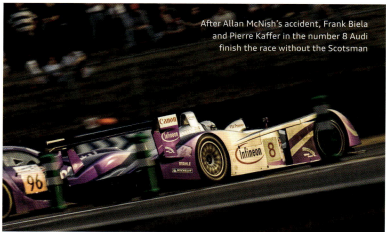

After Allan McNish's accident, Frank Biela and Pierre Kaffer in the number 8 Audi finish the race without the Scotsman

"We were having a meeting in one of the lounges above the pits when Kazumichi Goh came in and proudly said, 'Our car is on the poster for the race.' Tom Kristensen and I looked at each other, because we knew it was bad luck to be on the poster. We then went to Mr. Goh and said, 'We know it's a superstition, but the car featured on the poster has never won at Le Mans.' Even though he had already agreed with the ACO and already paid for it, Mr. Goh had the car removed from the poster again." [6]

Audi's dominance continues in the LMES opener at Monza in early May. Once again, the R8 controls the action, clinching a one-two-three triumph. This time, victory goes to Johnny Herbert/Jamie Davies in front of Pierre Kaffer/Allan McNish and Seiji Ara/Dindo Capello/Tom Kristensen.

Role of the favorite for Audi

Following those results, Audi is regarded as a big favorite at Le Mans. For Autosport it is clear: "Audi looks a dead-cert to continue VW's monopoly of the podium position in the new millenium. [...] There is, however, one weapon missing from the Audi armoury this year: The ability to change the entire rear end in double quick time has been removed courtesy

Guy Smith (left) describes his impressions of the track to David Ingram (right), one of the driving forces of Audi UK's motorsport program

of a new rule demanding that the same gearbox casing is retained right through the race." [7] However, a riveting race is expected among the R8 cars. "It has been years since the race at the top has been so wide open, at least insofar as teams. There is likely to be an intense contest across many hours between the three Audi entrants." [8]

Consequently, pole position going to the R8 comes as no surprise. More surprising may be the fact that it's clinched not by an Audi factory driver but by Johnny Herbert. 3m32.838s is the best time set by the Briton. His teammate Allan McNish, still the fastest driver on Wednesday, ultimately takes second position at 3m33.233s. The Scotsman is forced to cancel his plan for a late attack to claim the top spot: due to problems with the injection system, the Veloqx team changes the V8 engine of car number 88 to be on the

safe side. Following initial damper issues, Champion Racing focuses on the setup for the race and starts to the classic one-day event from sixth on the grid.

Suspense up until the end

When the race begins at 4 pm the two Veloqx R8 cars use their good starting base and defend their top spots with Jamie Davies and Allan McNish. It takes the four Audi cars barely half a lap to be in the top four. But just a few minutes later, the Goh Audi that has entered the race from fourth on the grid encounters problems. "There was something wrong with the brakes already at an early stage," says Capello. "The brake balance would sometimes shift toward the front and then toward the rear. That's why I ended up in the gravel trap of the Dunlop chicane. In

Race Director Daniel Poissenot, Wolfgang Ullrich and ACO President Jean-Claude Plassart (from left) answer questions at Audi's press conference

[6] Transcript of interview with Dindo Capello on November 24, 2022
[7] Gary Watkins: Who can match Audi? in Autosport Le Mans Guide 2004, p. 20
[8] http://archive.dailysportscar.com/subscribers/ lemans/2004/2004race/car_by_car.htm, last retrieved on August 23, 2022

Veloqx Team Principal Sam Li (center) dominates the LMES inaugural season with Johnny Herbert, Allan McNish, Pierre Kaffer and Jamie Davies

Tom Kristensen (blue cap) is the focus of media attention after scoring his fifth consecutive Le Mans victory

the pits it turned out that a spring for adjusting the balance was defective. After the repair, our comeback began." [9]

Up until Sunday morning the number 88 Veloqx Audi is leading the race while its brand colleagues are struggling. Following Capello's spin, misfortune strikes as many as two R8 cars shortly before 6 pm. While running in positions two and three, McNish and Lehto hit an oil spill in the Porsche corners causing them to get off track and crashing into the track barrier. "As soon as I braked I lost grip," says McNish, describing the situation. "And I turned into the corner and was just sliding [...] I knew I was going off the circuit, I tried to go into the tyre wall at the best angle possible." [10] Both Audi cars are damaged but make it back to the pits. Particularly the TV footage showing McNish dragging his R8 without the front hood, with bent wheels and a heavily deformed left side leaves indelible memories with viewers. At first glance, it's hardly imaginable that the cars will continue the race, but in the pits the Veloqx and Champion crews, after assessing the damage, immediate-

ly start repairing the cars. Both teams, as usual for Audi at Le Mans, have their garages at the end of the pit lane, whereas the Goh team has opted for the very first garage. Timo Witt, engine engineer from Audi Sport with Team Goh, recalls, "At Le Mans, it was known that the upper end or the lower end of the pit lane is always the most promising position because you have more room toward the front or rear and can move around the car more freely. When we arrived, we saw that the upper end of the pit lane was already occupied by the other Audi teams, so we decided to just move downward." [11]

Following an initial examination by Audi's team physician Christian John, McNish, the unlucky driver, is admitted to the trackside hospital where doctors diagnose a brain concussion. McNish has to retire from the race. The mechanics virtually perform miracles. After 31 minutes, the Champion R8 is back on track. After one hour and seven minutes, the Veloqx Audi resumes racing after having lost a lot of ground. At that time, Ara/Capello/Kristensen are already back in second position behind the front runners Davies/

Herbert/Smith, who defend their lead up until shortly after seven o'clock on Sunday morning. At that time, the mechanics change the pushrod on the left rear wheel suspension and the previous leader, with a one-lap deficit, drops back to second position behind the Team Goh car. Following a puncture on the "Japanese" R8 shortly afterwards, the advantage of that car now amounts to only one minute. When its closest rival, Jamie Davies, makes an off-track excursion into the gravel trap in the Dunlop chicane at noon, the race seems to have been decided. But about three and a half hours before the checkered flag falls Capello experiences another moment of shock when gasoline spilled during a refueling stop ignites. "Apparently, the valve of the quick release didn't close properly," Timo Witt recalls. "The engine hood had vent slots directly next to the tank, into which gasoline ran and ignited on the hot exhaust manifolds." [12] Team members and track marshals quickly extinguish the flames and Capello continues racing without a major time loss. In the final stage, Johnny Herbert goes for broke, trying to still intercept the race leader, Seiji Ara. When the Briton careens through the gravel trap eight minutes before the race ends the decision has been made. Ara crosses the finish line with an advantage of 41.354s over Herbert, marking the fourth-closest finish in the iconic 24-hour race to date. [13] At 5,169.970 kilometers, no other Audi R8 has ever covered such a long distance at Le Mans. [14] For Tom Kristensen, it's the fifth consecutive Le Mans victory. However, "Tom K" knows that this time a bit of luck lent a helping hand: "Had Dindo not had his accident, he would likely have fallen victim to this unforeseen oil as well." [15] For Capello, it takes a load off his mind: "Finally, I also won at Le Mans with Audi, even though we didn't really expect to have big chances. We were struggling at the races before Le Mans, our car wasn't easy to drive. Technically, we weren't in as good a position as the other Audi teams. That changed with Jo Hausner, who joined us at Le Mans. We also had the smallest budget of the Audi teams." [16] Team Principal Kazumichi Goh particularly praises the team spirit of his squad: "Today is the happiest day of my life. [...] We clearly proved that a multi-cultural crew can achieve a lot. " [17]

Champion Racing is the third Audi team that can celebrate a podium finish. JJ Lehto, Emanuele Pirro and

Champion Racing clinches third position like the year before

Champion as champions: ALMS President Scott Atherton (center) presents the champions' trophies to JJ Lehto and Marco Werner (above).
During scrutineering in the center of Le Mans spectators turn out in droves to see Champion Racing's Audi (below)

Marco Werner in third position clinch the second podium in a row for the US team. Frank Biela and Pierre Kaffer in the second Veloqx Audi see the checkered flag in fifth position.

Title rain for Audi teams

After Le Mans, Goh and Veloqx contest the three remaining LMES rounds. Veloqx remains unbeaten there. Herbert/Davies win the season's finale at Spa – marking the 50th victory of an Audi R8 in just five years and in merely 60 races contested – plus the title after Kaffer/McNish retire due to an accident. For both race teams, that closes the R8 chapter. Whereas Veloqx quits racing altogether, Team Goh appears again at La Sarthe with a Porsche RS Spyder in 2009. Champion Racing wins seven of the remaining eight races in the ALMS and scores its first title wins with the R8, including the drivers' title for JJ Lehto and Marco Werner.

9 Transcript of interview with Dindo Capello, November 24, 2022
10 https://au.motorsport.com/lemans/news/allan-mcnish-interview/1144224/, last retrieved on August 22, 2022
11 Transcript of interview with Timo Witt, October 27, 2022
12 Ibid
13 https://assets.lemans.org/explorer/pdf/courses/2018/24-heures-du-mans/press-kit/uk/statistiques-historiques-en.pdf, last retrieved on February 8, 2023
14 Ibid
15 Finderup, Nils: Tom Kristensen. We are the Champions, Forlaget Finsen, no location, 2005, p. 97
16 Transcript of interview with Dindo Capello, November 24, 2022
17 Audi MediaInfo: "Japanese" Audi R8 wins Le Mans, June 13, 2004. In 2004, Team Goh takes care of another car in the LMES and at Le Mans, the Porsche 996 GT3 RSR of the Japanese ChoroQ Racing Team. Thanks to the runner-up's spot in the LM-GT class the Goh squad celebrates another podium at La Sarthe

Good morning, America

Audi's customer team Champion is the first American racing team since 1967 to win the 24-hour race, although the Audi R8 is only a long shot in the competition.

2005 is a year of transition for Audi Sport. In terms of factory commitments in racing, the brand from Ingolstadt is again focused on the DTM while intensive work on a new LMP1 sports prototype is progressing behind the scenes. As before, fielding the proven Audi R8 cars is in the hands of importer teams. In the meantime, the Audi managers are discussing whether to continue supporting customer teams at all due to further changes of the regulations issued by the ACO like more weight and smaller restrictors. "But we remembered the Super Touring Car days that used to impose restrictions on us nearly every year as well and we'd always come up with a solution that would put us in contention," Wolfgang Ullrich recalls. "The R8 simply had such great potential, not only in terms of lap performance per se but also in terms of handling, in terms of reliability, that we be-

lieved that podium finishes were definitely possible if everything worked perfectly." [1] Champion Racing is again part of the program. Dave Maraj's outfit doubles its entry: in 2005, it competes at Le Mans with two cars for the first time. The US R8 cars have strong driver squads, made up of five Audi factory drivers: Frank Biela, Allan McNish, and Emanuele Pirro as well as Tom Kristensen and Marco Werner in the sister car – all of them, except for the latter, are previous winners at Le Mans. Champion's regular driver JJ Lehto, another former winner at La Sarthe, completes the lineup. To make the dream of victory at Le Mans come true, Maraj, for the first time, prescribes a regular fitness regimen for his team. Dedicated trackside hospitality serves special, healthy food. In addition, Maraj introduces the first regular pit stop practice for his squad including the replace-

[1] Transcript of interview with Dr. Wolfgang Ullrich on December 7, 2022

Tom Kristensen, JJ Lehto, and Marco
Werner (pictured) clinch victory in
the number 3 Champion R8

ment of vehicle components such as suspension parts, body elements, and even hot turbochargers. Furthermore, Champion develops specialty tools for every type of repair enabling the crew to work even more effectively. [2] The team delivers an optimal start to the season. At the ALMS opener, the Sebring 12 Hours, the two R8 cars clinch a one-two victory: Kristensen/Lehto/Werner win with just a 6.3-second advantage over Biela/McNish/Pirro. Another victory follows at Road Atlanta.

A French Audi

Alongside Champion Racing another privateer team relies on Audi: The French outfit Oreca (Organisation & Exploitation Courses Automobiles). The company founded by Hugues de Chaunac has been clinching numerous successes in single-seater, rally, and touring car racing since 1972. Oreca has left its mark also at Le Mans. The squad celebrates its debut in 1977 with a privately entered Renault Alpine. [3] Following a brief interlude with a BMW M1 in 1981, Oreca returns ten years later – as the fielding team for Mazda. [4] The project is a success: Mazda is the first Japanese manufacturer to win at Le Mans – and with a Wankel engine to boot. Oreca subsequently enters the Chrysler Viper in the iconic endurance race and from 1998 to 2000 achieves the victory hat-trick in the GTS category. 2000 sees the squad's promotion to the prototype category. With a Dallara LMP01 it claims two results in the top five. [5]

However, de Chaunac has even bigger dreams – so, what kind of entry would better serve his purposes than that of an Audi R8? In August 2004, the Frenchman proposes his idea to Head of Audi Motorsport

Head of Audi Sport Wolfgang Ullrich celebrates on the podium with the victorious drivers, JJ Lehto, Tom Kristensen, Marco Werner, and Champion's boss Dave Maraj (above).
At the start the two Pescarolo cars are still the front runners (below)

[2] David Tremayne: Champion Racing. A little bit of magic, Phoenix: David Bull Publishing 2014, p. 283 et seq
[3] François Hurel: Alpine au Mans, Nîmes: Editions du Palmier 2002, p. 123 et seq
[4] Pierre Dieudonné: Never stop Challenging! Mazda's Conquest of Le Mans, Waterloo: Apach 2011, p. 233 et seq
[5] Oreca press kit, 2002
[6] Autosport February 17, 2005, p. 18 and Autosport March 17, 2005, p. 21
[7] Michael Cotton, Alfredo Filippone, Oliver Loisy: Le Mans Endurance Series Yearbook 2005, St. Cyr-au-Mont: Apollo Publishing, undated, p. 38 et seq

Wolfgang Ullrich. At a meeting in Ingolstadt, the parties soon reach an agreement. At the end of November, the team officially announces its project that Audi France, led by Director Patrice Franke, supports. Audi offers factory drivers but de Chaunac rejects the offer: He wants to win the most important race in his native land with an all-francophone crew and signs Jean-Marc Gounon, Stéphane Ortelli, and Formula One test driver Franck Montagny. [6] At a first test race, the 1,000 Kilometers of Spa in mid-April, the R8 is on course for a podium finish, but does not finish after an accident. [7]

ACO issues further restrictions

The new technical regulations are reflected in the lap times – which is evident as early as on the Le Mans test day on June 5. That's when Henri Pescarolo's squad particularly impresses, clearly outperforming the R8 cars. The Pescarolo C60H driven by Emmanuel Collard, Jean-Christophe Boullion, and Erik Comas clocked at 3m32.468s achieves the absolute best time. It is followed in second place by its sister car in which the Le Mans debut of World Rally Champion Sébastien Loeb causes a sensation. The fastest Audi in the pre-test, the number 3 Champion R8 driven by JJ Lehto and Marco Werner – Tom Kristensen, like Allan McNish, is racing in parallel in the DTM at

For Champion's Team Principal Dave Maraj (left, with Frank Biela), the Le Mans victory makes a dream come true

Le Mans record entrant Henri Pescarolo (left) congratulates Tom Kristensen on his seventh win at La Sarthe

The close battle between Audi and Pescarolo remains a thriller up until the end

Briefing: The Champion team discusses the race strategy with Emanuele Pirro, Graham Taylor, Brad Kettler, Marco Werner, JJ Lehto, Tom Kristensen, Jo Hausner, Lee Willard, Bret Faler (obscured from view, both Michelin), Richard Lane (obscured from view), Marcus Haselgrove, Allan McNish, Mike Peters, and Frank Biela (clockwise, from left)

Brno –, finishes fourth after 3m38.719s. The two other R8 cars achieve positions seven (Oreca) and eight (Champion number 2).

That the Pescarolo cars are so much faster is not only attributable to the handicaps imposed on the sports prototypes from Ingolstadt because Pescarolo has invested a lot of work in his car over the winter. While the monocoque has remained the same the aerodynamic shell is completely new. Team Principal Pescarolo even drives the car in the first tests himself. [8] "My goal is to try to beat the Audis, not to be the first behind them," the Frenchman confidently says before the race. "[..] The new rules don't mean an Audi can't win any more, but at least they won't fight between themselves alone." [9]

Instead of on fast lap times, the Audi teams focus on other fortes for the 73rd edition of the iconic race. "I see the most potential in the Audi R8 is its consistency", says Marco Werner. „Although we will not have the quickest car, we certainly have the best." His teammate Kristensen specifies the strategy: "With team work, no mistakes and low fuel consumption we must be able to work our way slowly towards the front in the race." [10] Many observers expect the other LMP1 competitors to have no more than underdog chances. Despite third place in the pre-test, they include the two updated factory-fielded Courage C60H cars, plus two Dome S101 and two Dallara cars as well as one DBA and one Zytek.

Pescarolo qualifies for pole

The week of the race starts barely one week after the test. Yet even before the cars do their first laps Peugeot hits the headlines: The French announce their return to Le Mans in 2007 – with an LMP1 sports prototype to be powered by a diesel engine. [11] With that, the French brand confirms rumors that have been circulating for months that it might be using compression-ignition engines for its comeback. [12]

After a wet qualifying on Wednesday, Pescarolo driver Emmanuel Collard beats the sister car to pole position on Thursday after 3m34.715s. Because the Audi teams do not expect having a chance for the front row they focus on the setup for the race. With an all-or-nothing lap Allan McNish in the fastest R8 clinches the third spot. "I honestly didn't expect to be that high up on the grid," says the Scot who was short 3.080 seconds of clinching pole. "Critically we're ahead of some cars that, if we'd started behind them, could have compromised the early stages of the race for us." [13] The Oreca Audi qualifies in fifth place, the second Champion Audi of Kristensen/Lehto/Werner in eighth.

Hot, hotter, Le Mans

When on Saturday at 4 pm the race starts in front of 230,000 spectators the sun is burning in the sky. Temperatures above 30 degrees centigrade make for a heat battle. The two Pescarolo cars dominate the first stage of the race with lap times that are about five seconds better than Audi's. One hour into the race, the best-placed sports prototype from Ingolstadt driven by Biela/McNish/Pirro follows with a 1.15-minute deficit in third place, with the French R8 on its heels, Kristensen/Lehto/Werner are sixth. "Right from the outset the Audis could only count on their legendary reliability to best the French car," writes Paul Frère. "[...] One little advantage they still had was their direct injection engine's excellent fuel consumption that allowed them to do an extra lap between refuelling stops in relation to their rivals." [14]

But Pescarolo's joy about their one-two lead is short-lived. Two hours into the race, car number 17 running in second position collides with a GT2 Panoz and has to pit for a five-minute repair, causing the car to drop back to seventh place. Further problems later force the car to end its race. At 6 pm, the three Audi cars are running in positions two, three, and four with deficits between two and a half and barely three minutes. Just half an hour later, the leading Pescarolo is struck by misfortune as well: Erik Comas pits with transmission problems. Following a quick repair job, he goes out again. But the car is still not running smoothly, forcing the former Formula One driver to pit again. In total, the Pescarolo loses 27 minutes and drops back to 21st position. Audi takes the lead for the first time.

But the squad soon suffers its first setback too: At 7.12 pm, Emanuele Pirro in the leading R8 slips into the tire wall in the Arnage section, requiring the front hood to be changed and costing three positions. The second Champion car takes the lead – and will not relinquish it before crossing the finish line. But the race is not a walk in the park for the subsequent winners. Halfway into the race, the advantage of Kristensen/Lehto/Werner over Biela/McNish/Pirro plateaus at barely one lap, the Oreca Audi trails them with a six-lap deficit after a wishbone had to be changed twice. In the early morning hours, McNish reduces his deficit to less than one minute. Is a duel

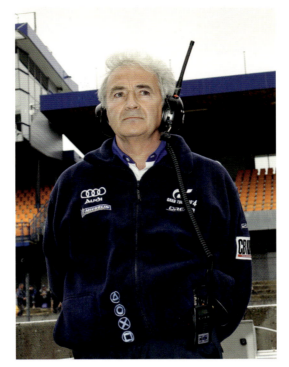

Oreca boss Hugues de Chaunac with his seasoned squad puts an Audi R8 on the grid

De Chaunac relies on a francophone driver trio: Stéphane Ortelli, Jean-Marc Gounon and Franck Montagny (from left)

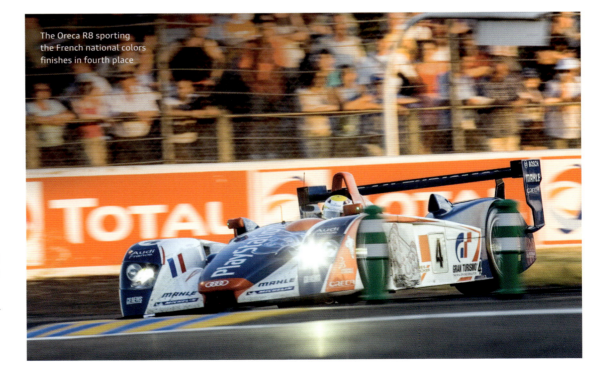

The Oreca R8 sporting the French national colors finishes in fourth place

[8] Christian Moity, Jean-Marc Teissedre: 2005 Le Mans 24 hours, Waterloo: Apach Publishing 2015, p. 40
[9] www.dailysportscar.com/archive/subscribers/news/lemans/ 2004lemans/lemans520.htm, last retrieved on August 15, 2022
[10] Audi MediaInfo: Audi Teams face tough task at Le Mans, June 9, 2005
[11] Peugeot press release: Peugeot bringt den HDi-Diesel mit FAP in die Pole Position, June 15, 2005
[12] Peugeot debates Le Mans Return, in Autosport, Feb 3, 2005, p. 21
[13] www.audi-mediacenter.com/en/press-releases/audi-on-second-row-at-le-mans-8528, last retrieved on August 15, 2022
[14] Paul Frère: A year of transition, in Christian Moity, Jean-Marc Teissedre: 2005 Le Mans 24 hours, Waterloo: Apach Publishing 2015, p. 218

The number 2 Champion Audi is the fastest R8 in qualifying and finishes the race in third position

Champion's long-term mechanic Keith Bransford is waiting for the winning car to pit

within the Champion squad looming? A preliminary decision is produced at 6.45 am: In the Indianapolis corner, the tread comes off the right front tire of McNish's R8, the Scot slips off track. Recovery and repair cost about 20 minutes and cause number 2 to drop back to third position. As a result, the remaining Pescarolo is running in position two again. It is clearly the fastest car in the field. Because the R8 cars are five to six seconds slower on average Collard/Comas/Boullion can reduce their deficit from three to one lap and continue dreaming of victory. At this point, anything is still possible. When the advantage melts down to less than one lap Champion reacts and keeps brilliantly fighting Tom Kristensen in the cockpit for the last three and a half hours of the race to save the time for another driver change. 90 minutes before the end, Pescarolo finally stops fighting: the V10 engine threatens to die from overheating and the driver squad subsequently merely manages to finish the race for number 16.[15] As a result, the number 3 Champion R8 claims victory, which is a very special one: For the first time in 38 years, an American team is the winner again. Tom Kristensen claims his seventh victory, breaking Jacky Ickx's record. The first person to congratulate the Dane is no other than Ickx, who leaves a message on "Tom K.'s" mailbox after he crossed the finish line. For JJ Lehto, it is the second win after 1995 and for Marco Werner it is the first.

Consistency is crucial

"For us, this win is everything," rejoices Dave Maraj. [16] Race engineer Brad Kettler recalls that, "We were hopelessly too slow. [...] The whole

race was a battle of nerves. After the pit stops, we were running in front and then our rivals caught us again – this went on for the whole 24 hours." [17] Henri Pescarolo and his team have to settle for second position. Behind them Biela, McNish, and Pirro in third place round out the success for Champion. Jean-Marc Gounon, Franck Montagny, and Stéphane Ortelli in the R8 of Audi PlayStation Team Oreca cross the finish line in fourth. "We got very close to zero fault which is our credo but we did not obtain the result we were hoping for," Hugues de Chaunac says for the record. "I feel both frustrated and surprised by the two suspension breakages. It's never happened on an Audi before." [18]

A look at the total pit stop times shows why the number 3 Audi ultimately is the front runner. Kristensen/ Lehto/Werner pit for 33m53s in total whereas the second-placed Pescarolo pitting for 1h13m08s does so twice as long. [19] That the Pescarolo sets an average lap time which is 5.2 seconds better than that of the winners can no longer make a difference due to the many time losses on account of incidents. [20] Autosport states: "Kristensen and his team-mates in the best-placed of the two Champion Racing Audis, JJ Lehto and Marco Werner, didn't have the fastest car in the race [...] It could even be argued that theirs wasn't the fastest of the R8s last weekend. What they did have was an incredible consistency, coupled with flawless reliability in temperatures in excess of 35C, and that set them apart from the rest." [21]

The end of an era

That marks the end of the impressive era of the Audi R8 at La Sarthe. However, it keeps racing in events other than Le Mans – continuing all the way into 2006. Champion Racing wins seven of ten ALMS races in total, earning them the top spot in

Confident: Champion drivers Tom Kristensen, JJ Lehto, Marco Werner, Emanuele Pirro, Frank Biela, and Allan McNish (above, from left to right).
In the traditional driver parade, Wolfgang Ullrich chauffeurs factory drivers Biela, Pirro, and McNish in a Horch from Audi Tradition (below)

the teams' classification and, with Frank Biela and Emanuele Pirro, in the drivers' championship. In addition, the manufacturers' classification goes to Audi. Oreca puts their R8 on the grid in two races of the Le Mans Endurance Series (LMES). In the 1,000-km race at Silverstone, Stéphane Ortelli and Allan McNish clinch victory. In 2006, in the ALMS, the racing oldie triumphs even two more times.

[15] www.dailysportscar.com/archive/subscribers/news/lemans/2005lemans/lemans694.htm, last retrieved on August 15, 2022

[16] www.championracing.net/2010/history/audi_r8/2005/Le_Mans_American_team_make_history.htm, last retrieved on August 15, 2022

[17] Audi MediaInfo: Flashback: Le Mans 2005 and an Audi victory that seemed impossible, April 16, 2015

[18] Oreca Press release: Hugues de Chaunac: Well done Audi, June 19, 2005

[19] Christian Moity, Jean-Marc Teissedre: 2005 Le Mans 24 hours, Waterloo: Apach Publishing 2015, p. 227 et seq

[20] http://archive.dailysportscar.com/subscribers/lemans/2005/race/race_lmp1conclusions.htm, last retrieved on August 15, 2022

[21] Gary Watkins: Tom cruises into history, in Autosport, June 23, 2005, p. 66

From race car to icon

The world of sports cars is full of logos such as the horses from Maranello or Stuttgart, the three-pointed star or the winged "B." The four rings have long been part of this lineup as well, having begun with the Audi R8.

When it comes to a Le Mans sports car with timeless qualities, the conversation will soon turn to Porsche models 956 and 962. Can the R8 with a total of 63 victories in 80 races stand comparison with this Group C model? Motorsport journalist Gary Watkins says, "Comparison is always invited with the Porsche 956 and [...] the 962, partly because both German machines enjoyed such long careers. An allegation often levelled against the R8 was that it didn't face the same kind of opposition as the 956/962. Those who make such suggestions appear to be looking back at the early days of Group C through rose-tinted spectacles. In terms of factory opposition, the Porsche had to beat only the Ford C100 and the Lancia LC2, great-looking cars rather than

For the farewell in 2006, a special livery is created listing all the successes

World Class

2

Winner
24h Le Mans
2000, 2001, 2002, 2004, 2005
ALMS
2000, 2001, 2002, 2003, 2004, 2005
ELMS
2001
LMES
2004

FSI P

MAHLE

MICHELIN

great racing cars. By the time Jaguar and then Mercedes-engined Saubers started beating 962s with any regularity, the Porsche design was already in its sixth year of competition. The R8 triumphed over factory rivals from Cadillac, Chrysler, Panoz, Bentley, MG, and, briefly in America, BMW [...]. It is fair to say that the R8 beat opposition of a comparable level to that faced by the Porsche in its pomp." [1]

Looking back, former Head of Sport Wolfgang Ullrich says, "The R8 was indeed the car that grew on me more than any other one. Maybe because it was the first one with which we ventured out into the big world of endurance racing. Because with the

R8R before it, we only contested two, three races. On the other hand, the car from 2016 was a concept I liked a lot as well because, for me, it had awesome potential and I personally felt sorry that it could never show its true capabilities. But I believe that the R8 will remain the first successful son when you group it into a family and because it was a very special one. It will, no doubt, remain my favorite car." [2]

The drivers love the R8 too. Five-time Le Mans winner Frank Biela, who previously clinched touring car titles in DTM and Super Touring Car racing with Audi, arrives at this conclusion: "The new car was an enormous step in the right direction. All the small issues that we had with the R8R in 1999 were analysed and resolved. I felt much more comfortable in the R8 from the very beginning than in the R8R. [...] The R8 was definitely the most important car in my career." [3] His long-time teammate Emanuele Pirro agrees, "I've been off the track, for sure. But I'm sure I had not one spin with the R8. You never had to fight the car. You braked, turned in and put the power down. The corner was finished for you. It was such a driver-friendly car that it never stressed you." [4] Tom Kristensen is still fascinated by the versatility of this model: "The R8 is a unique car. Not only because it was competitive for so long, despite the regulation changes [...] but also because it was so successful on such different tracks like Le Mans, which is extremely fast, tight street circuits in the USA or bumpy tracks like Sebring." [5]

Allan McNish, who drove the R8 before and after his Formula One career, draws a comparison: "It didn't matter if it was raining like hell at Silverstone or scorching hot at Le Mans, you could always make the car work. The 2000 car was a bit tricky to drive, but by the time I came back to the R8 in 2004, it was quick in every situation, and that's what really impressed me." [6] The teams are equally enthusiastic about the race car from Ingolstadt. Dave Maraj, Champion Racing's Team Principal who died in 2018, even admitted, "The Audi R8 was the car that elevated our team from amateur to professional status.

In its last race at Lime Rock on July 1, 2006, the Audi R8 in the hands of Dindo Capello/ Allan McNish remains unbeaten

On the occasion of the Audi R8's 50th victory in 2004, Audi assembles the race car and trophies in a studio

Thanks to the R8 we have become one of the most successful American sportscar teams. I sold our former Lola immediately after I'd seen the R8 racing for the first time. I flew to Ingolstadt and managed to convince Dr Ullrich to sell us an R8 and to train our guys. From there on things improved rapidly." [7]

Ullrich sees the car's strength in the sum of various aspects: "Consistent care over the years and an extremely good base. One of the strengths was the fact that the car was very good in terms of its concept, that it had a good aerodynamic base and that the 'keep it simple' principle was still strictly adhered to at that time. That's why it could be put in the hands of customer teams with relatively little concern. After an accident, it could even be repaired in a very short time." [8]

[1] Gary Watkins: Farewell to an icon, in Autosport, November 23, 2006, p. 47 et seq
[2] Transcript of interview with Dr. Wolfgang Ullrich on December 7, 2022
[3] Thomas Voigt: Audi R8. Born to win, Ingolstadt: AUDI AG, 2006, p. 23
[4] Gary Watkins: Farewell to an icon, in Autosport, November 23, 2006, p. 47
[5] Tom Kristensen, Lars Krone: Tom Kristensen – The Book, no location, no publisher, 2015, p. 257
[6] Gary Watkins: Farewell to an icon, in Autosport, November 23, 2006, p. 47
[7] Thomas Voigt: Audi R8. Born to win, Ingolstadt: AUDI AG, 2006, p. 93
[8] Transcript of interview with Dr. Wolfgang Ullrich on December 7, 2022

The premiere of the R10 TDI on
December 13, 2005 generates
strong media response

In the lion's den

Paris is a worthy location for the presentation of the Audi R10 TDI. Audi's diesel campaign kicks off in the French capital – in direct view of the future rival Peugeot.

The symbolism of Paris can hardly be overestimated: Even on a gray December day, the Eiffel Tower including the Audi R10 TDI, Tom Kristensen, Audi's return to Le Mans as a factory and the message announcing diesel power that has been successfully kept under wraps are fit for generating a flood of headlines: "This is the Audi R10: The most important new Le Mans car for six years – and it's a Diesel" (Autosport), "Audi with a technology revolution" (Magdeburger Volkszeitung), "Diesel sensation" (Bild Zeitung), "The fastest Audi of all time ... running on diesel" (Express Düsseldorf), "Winning alternatively" (Auto Zeitung), "Winning without knocking" (Focus), "Audi wants to shine with a diesel at Le Mans" (Heilbronner Stimme). What those headlines do not say is that, as early as on June 15, 2005, in other words almost exactly half a year before Audi, Peugeot is the first manufacturer to announce a diesel-powered sports prototype for Le Mans – albeit not to be fielded until the 2007 season. [1] As a result, the appearance at the Trocadéro is a first major PR victory for Audi. The brand celebrates its first success in racing not even three months later at the Sebring 12 Hours, and its second one another three months later at the Le Mans 24 Hours. That that is exactly where in June 2006 Peugeot presents its V12 diesel engine – sans race car – for the following year remains a rather marginal journalistic note. Although, in retrospect, the historic first diesel victory at Le Mans reads like a triumphant feat, it seems like a natural one, considering the rather small competition by privateer Pescarolo sports cars. Yet it is anything but natural. The audacity to design the first LMP1 model with a diesel engine for racing is a project packed with challenges.

[1] Peugeot press release: Peugeot bringt den HDi-Diesel mit FAP in die Pole Position, June 15, 2005

Audi TDI Power

A long journey

The channels in a corporation can be like winding roads. As early as in October 1997 – Audi's first Le Mans race is still 20 months away – then Chairman of the VW Management Board Ferdinand Piëch in response to a question by special-interest magazine mot about diesel at Le Mans says, "It all depends on the regulations. There used to be a minimum-range regulation at Le Mans. With that, the diesel could immediately become relevant." [2] Three years later, he suggests that idea to Team Principal Reinhold Joest, who points out the absence of a relevant regulation. [3] Another year later, in 2001, Audi engineers discuss the chance of creating such regulations for the first time with ACO representatives Daniel Poissenot and Daniel Perdrix. "While we hadn't even been on the Le Mans grid yet with gasoline direct injection engines, we were talking in Ingolstadt about the potential for diesel engines. At first, I wasn't convinced but then I saw the opportunity," Ulrich

Baretzky recalls. [4] When managers up to and including the first executive board members indicate their support, the engine developers in Neckarsulm start working on the first concepts and engineering designs. In 2002, the ACO announces the incorporation of diesel engines into its regulations for 2004. [5] That paves the regulatory way but the in-house marching orders are still lacking.

"You should do that"

The top-level decision comes about in a memorable way. The Lola-Caterpillar prototype with a VW TDI powerplant that was unsuccessfully fielded privately and independently in 2004 fuels the pursuit of the diesel theme in a factory-backed project. On Race Saturday, June 12, Audi Chairman of the Management Board Martin Winterkorn and Ulrich

Baretzky are given the opportunity to talk to Ferdinand Piëch in the VIP lounge. Following a few questions on his part, the executive – now Chairman of VW's Supervisory Board since 2002 – responds with usual brevity: "You should do that." Those are the marching orders for engineering the racing TDI. They are followed by initial pre-trials of a modified V8 production TDI (internally dubbed "bastard engine") at the turn of the year 2004/2005. One-cylinder racing engine trials in 2005 provide initial conclusions about injection, combustion process and durability. The V12 TDI's dyno debut falls into May 2005, the first test at Misano into the month of November. [6]

Baretzky and engineering designer Hartmut Diel distribute the maximum permissible displacement of 5.5 liters, combined with a boost pressure limit of 2,940 millibar and thus a lower level than with smaller volumes, to twelve cylinders. That keeps the loads per unit as low as possible. A 90-degree bank angle is the best compromise between torsional stiffness, design height and center of gravity position. The hydraulic system initially operates with pressure of 2,000 bar – a level that is clearly above mass-produced units and keeps increasing in the following years. The common-rail system is adopted from production. [7]

Challenging combination

Just in terms of the powerplant per se, a diesel racing engine entails major challenges. Even more challenging is the combination of the chassis and the engine because the R10 that has been in development since 2003 has initially been designed for a gasoline engine. The plan calls for a direct-injection V8 unit with three injectors per combustion chamber in order to achieve anti-knock properties depending on engine speed and load despite higher compression. [8]

[2] Interview with Ferdinand Piëch: Überall grüne Männchen, in mot, October 11, 1997
[3] Audi Express 1, June 16, 2006, p. 3
[4] Transcript of interview with Ulrich Baretzky on December 19, 2022
[5] Transcript of interview with Andreas Köppen on October 27, 2022
[6] Transcript of interview with Ulrich Baretzky on December 19, 2022
[7] Michael Hackethal: Nagelprobe, in Motorsport-Guide 04, January-February 2009, p. 21 et seq
[8] Transcript of interview with Ulrich Baretzky on December 19, 2022

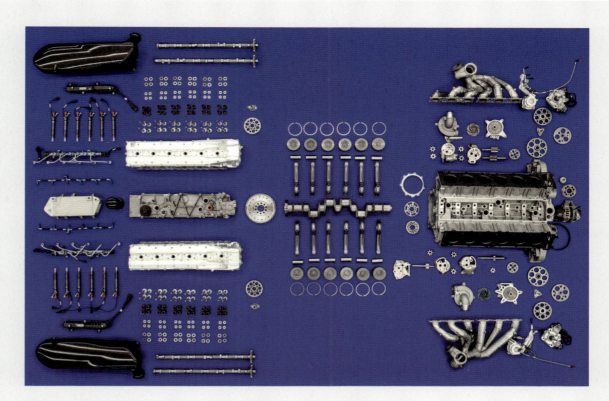

Audi includes single parts in its public presentation of the V12 TDI right from the beginning

Engine developer Ulrich Baretzky, engine designer Hartmut Diel and Wolfgang Appel, Head of Vehicle Engineering, come up with good compromises for the design of the R10 TDI

The huge body parts require good transportation logistics

The new monocoque is initially created in anticipation of a gasoline engine

Wolfgang Appel, Head of Vehicle Engineering, and his team successfully accomplish the integration of the V12 TDI. In view of a permissible vehicle length of 4.65 meters, the installed length of the engine forces the designers to create a clearly longer wheelbase along with accepting other compromises. For the first time, a part of the rear chassis is hinged to the engine. The transmission has only five instead of six speeds to reduce its installed length. It is supplied by Xtrac and has a torque-reducing input gear ratio. Even so, the engineers must limit the engine's capacity to roughly 1,100 to 1,200 Newton meters of torque at slightly more than 650 horsepower to keep from overloading the driveline. Since the combustion principle requires about 30 percent more cooling area compared to a gasoline unit, the aerodynamicists are challenged as well.

Finally, the weight of the engine and the mass concentrated far at the rear end pose a major task – not only for the designers. "It took many laps, even days, to get used to the R10 and early upshifting in the diesel," Dindo Capello recalls. "Even so, it was one of the cars, if not the car, that I liked the most. Naturally, it wasn't as agile as the R15 and didn't have as much downforce as the R18 but I often won. The R10 was a beast." [9] The smoothness of the TDI engine that is quieter than the wind noise, confuses the drivers at first because they are used to shifting according to the acoustics. The optimal engine speed is between 3,000 and 5,000 revolutions.

While the R8 still uses a classic chassis with composite bodywork most of the CFRP parts of the R10 monocoque are exposed directly to the airflow.

The R10 TDI has aluminum pistons with 12-percent silicon content and laser-welded oil ducts

A diesel tank truck is still an unusual sight at Le Mans. Shell converts its international marketing campaigns from the Formula One theme with Ferrari and Michael Schumacher to Le Mans, Audi and V-Power diesel

Sitting on the high-strength aluminum crankcase are two one-piece cylinder heads (pictured at right). Their milled hoods (pictured at left) are attached to the rear wall of the cell and enable the transmission of forces from the chassis and the monocoque

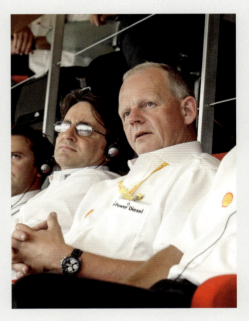

With GTL and BTL fuels, Wolfgang Warnecke from Shell helps promote public awareness of the TDI as an alternative powerplant

Dispensing with an additional bodywork saves weight. The R10 is also the first race car conforming to the new LMP1 regulations. The double rollhoop structure enhances safety. A step in the front splitter and the underfloor rising toward the side are intended to defuse the car's aerodynamic sensitivity. Although the new regulations pursue the objective of a 15-percent reduction of downforce Audi manages to make up a large part of the lost aerodynamic efficiency through intensive work in the wind tunnel. [10]

Complementing an engine that in 2006 requires almost five liters less fuel per 100 kilometers than the R8 to clinch victory, Shell, in 2006, introduces its gas-based GTL (gas-to-liquids) diesel fuel also in motorsport. It is colorless and odorless, burns clean and contains no sulfur. [11] In 2008, BTL (biomass-to-liquids) components are added to the mixture. [12]

In its three-year cycle, the R10 TDI passes through a process of systematic facelifting. In 2007, the regulations require the fuel tank volume to drop from 90 to 81 liters. Attention is also focused on efficiency, consumption, durability and drivability. Partner Bosch optimizes the electronics. The bodywork is subjected to minor modifications, the powertrain is friction- and weight-optimized and the engine's weight is reduced from 2008 on. Upgrades are also found in the chassis and dampers. Tire partner Michelin helps optimize the balance between the front and rear axles with new compounds and designs. [13]

[9] Transcript of interview with Dindo Capello on November 24, 2022
[10] Audi Motorsport Communications: Booklet Le Mans 2006, p. 12
[11] Audi 2006 Annual Report, p. 13
[12] Audi Motorsport Communications: Booklet 24h Le Mans 2008, p. 7
[13] Audi Motorsport Communications: Booklet 24h Le Mans 2007, p. 16 et seq

Audi's biggest rival in 2006 is Pescarolo Judd

Peugeot, in 2006, presents the HDi diesel engine for 2007 at Le Mans. Pictured from left to right: Departing Sport Director Jean-Pierre Nicolas, engine developer Claude Guillois, Brand Director Frédéric Saint-Geours, test driver Eric Hélary, the new Sport Director Michel Barge, Technical Director Bruno Famin and Christian Peugeot

doubt on the rating even before the race: "I'm really worried about the equivalency. If their [Audi's] reliability is good, we have no chance." [14] The differences in range between gasoline and diesel engines are an additional factor.

Audi in terms of the team and drivers returns to Le Mans as a manufacturer after three years without any fundamental surprises – even so, some things are new. The two Audi R10 TDI have been entered by Audi Sport Team Joest. Reinhold Joest's squad has not been in France officially for three years although some of its team members have been involved in other programs. None of the six Audi drivers is new either but their combination inspires headlines in some media: "Kristensen and McNish form Audi 'superteam,'" writes Autosport. Dindo Capello completes the lineup. 16 years later, Kristensen judges the trio that was to last until 2012 in these words: "When Allan, Dindo and I were racing together we were closer to each other, had a similar level of experience and were similarly successful. We were more united, somewhat closer to each other in all areas of life. But I must also say that Le Mans was fun with every one of my 16 teammates, that it was challenging sometimes and that they would probably say the same about me as well." [15] Frank Biela

Limited competition

2006 marks a gradual rise from the bottom of a valley in terms of the field at Le Mans. While twelve entrants in the LMP1 class are in a field of 50 race cars, a look at the results speaks volumes: Behind an Audi, a Pescarolo and the second Audi, fourth position goes to a Corvette – a production-based GT1 sports car with a 25-lap deficit. The two Pescarolo Judd – the, ultimately, best one driven by Eric Hélary, Franck Montagny and World Rally Champion Sébastien Loeb – prove to be the fiercest rivals. The individual prototypes from Courage, Creation and Dome, respectively, rely on John Judd's engine as well. A Zytek with its own engine, two Courage Mugen, a Lister Storm and a Lola Aer complete the fastest dozen. Le Mans legend Henri Pescarolo casts

"The diesel engine, a deplorable shame. [...] A great danger for the Le Mans 24 Hours [...]": The arrival of the compression-ignition engine does not find favor with all fans

and Emanuele Pirro, the 2000 to 2002 joint winners with Kristensen, are now sharing the cockpit with last year's winner Marco Werner.

A bumpy beginning

It is not an easy victory that Dindo Capello, Tom Kristensen and Allan McNish score on the R10 TDI's debut at Sebring. "At Sebring, we changed eleven engines on both cars in the space of one week. Those were exceptional circumstances," engine engineer Timo Witt recalls. [16] The riser tube in the oil reservoir for measuring the oil level is the root cause. Instead

[14] Gary Watkins: Can this car beat Audi's diesel? in Autosport, June 15, 2006, p. 70
[15] Transcript of interview with Tom Kristensen on December 6, 2022
[16] Transcript of interview with Timo Witt on October 28, 2022

Joest employee Michael Werner puts diesel in the tank from now on

In spite of all the obstacles, the R10 TDI of Dindo Capello/Tom Kristensen/Allan McNish claims its debut victory at Sebring with race engineer Jo Hausner (in the white shirt on the pit wall)

Car number 7 drops back to third position with problems at Le Mans

of being permanently bonded it is attached with a tape that keeps separating when the oil gets hot and clogs the filter in front of the oil pump. That repeatedly causes the oil pressure to drop. As late as in the morning before the race, the technical crew is forced to change the V12 on the car of the subsequent winners. An incorrectly installed plug on the oil-water heat exchanger causes the oil temperature to rise

rapidly. The team has to separate the engine from the monocoque. "Take the airboxes off, take the inner V plate off, take the heat exchanger off. Water has run into the oil; oil has run into the water. 'Yikes! I dropped a nut into the combustion chamber' – got it out with a magnet again, and so on," Witt recalls this hectic phase. [17] Car number 2 is ready at the last moment. Capello starts behind the field from the pit lane and with his teammates goes on to score victory with a four-lap advantage. But: when the vacuum in the crankcase suddenly drops, and that happens again twice during the race, the engineers are worried. They later find out that only nine of the twelve cylinders are functioning. That is caused by a problem with the cable harness resulting in failure of a top dead center sensor that defines ignition timing. Consequently, the engine fires randomly instead of being precisely timed. Pressures rise massively and

Christoph Mayer – always dubbed "Gummi Mayer" [Rubber Mayer] on the radio – is one of many diligent mechanics. He takes care of tires for Audi Sport Team Joest

Frank Biela, Marco Werner, Emanuele Pirro, Dindo Capello, Allan McNish and Tom Kristensen are facing a row of photographers during scrutineering on June 13

three pistons break in a place of a cooling duct with imperfect dimensional stability, causing combustion gases to flow into the engine's interior.

Audi retires the sister car shortly before the race's midpoint because tire wear particles are clogging the radiators. Due to telemetry failure shortly after the start, the engineers have no readings telling them how long the engine was running at excessive temperatures. [18]

Saving kilometers

On the test day at Le Mans, Audi reels off 164 laps in total with both prototypes. A hydraulic issue on Biela/Pirro/Werner's car and shifting issues on the sister car show that the teething troubles have not been eliminated yet. [19] During the race week, rain sets in right in time for qualifying on Wednesday night. Since the race engines have already been installed, Audi only drives the mandatory laps. The reason is that engine changes at the beginning of the project take so many hours that the typical switching from practice to racing engines before the final qualifying cannot be reliably accomplished. That is why the engine department wants to minimize pre-race driving time. [20] Both Pescarolo cars are the front runners on Wednesday, Kristensen and his colleagues are in third position in front of their sister car. Capello aquaplanes off track in the S corner in front of Tertre Rouge, damaging the right rear suspension in the process. [21] In dry conditions on Thursday, Capello, after 2001 and 2002, secures pole position for the third time. Marco Werner is only 0.118 seconds slower. About two seconds behind him, both Pescarolo are on the second row of the grid.

Pre-start time pressure

Before Le Mans, Audi Sport completes 30,000 test kilometers, and the V12 TDI runs another 1,500 hours on engine dynos. [22] Even so, the Race Saturday, exactly 200 days after the first rollout, sees an unexpected beginning: Allan McNish in car

Tom Kristensen, Allan McNish and Dindo Capello at the press conference on Friday express confidence in conversation with host Thomas Voigt (above).
The fans marvel at the R10 TDI on its arrival at Le Mans during Technical Scrutineering (below)

[17] Transcript of interview with Timo Witt on October 28, 2022
[18] Audi MediaInfo: Audi triumphs with Diesel power at Sebring, March 19, 2006
[19] Audi MediaInfo: Audi R10 TDI makes strong impression, June 4, 2006
[20] Transcript of interview with Ralf Jüttner on November 17, 2022
[21] Audi MediaInfo: Audi R10 TDI cars provisionally on second row, June 15, 2006
[22] Audi MediaInfo: Facts about Audi's historical Le Mans victory, June 20, 2006

Frank Biela looks back on three victories with the R8. In 2006, he achieves his fourth Le Mans success and first one with a diesel

Emanuele Pirro in conversation with his chief mechanic, long-standing Joest employee Roberto Tavaglione

Marco Werner in 2006 celebrates his second win in a row

number 7 does not get very far in the warm-up session. Following damage to a spline that connects the differential with the tripods for the drive shafts, race engineer Joachim Hausner decides to have the alternatively available rigid axle – aka spool – installed. When the cars are already on the pre-start grid, Ferdinand Piëch, at the time Supervisory Board Chairman of Volkswagen AG, expects to have the drivetrain changed also on car number 8. "There was no room for discussion about whether or not that was still possible, it was to be done! Resistance would not have accomplished anything but would have only cost time," Wolfgang Ullrich recalls. [23] Joest Team Principal Ralf Jüttner: "Of course, the thread of a screw got messed up on that occasion as well. The situation was awfully tight. With all due respect that I have always felt for Mr. Piëch, I said after the race that we won not because of but in spite of Mr. Piëch." [24]

Plenty of hard work

In the race, the refueling stops of the competitors already take place four laps earlier when, after 52 minutes, the two R10 TDI cars are heading for the pits for the first time. Their range is that long. [25] Two hours into the race, car number 7 with the yellow color coding is 19 seconds ahead of the sister car and the two Pescarolo. At 8.24 pm, the car of Capello and his colleagues requires the injectors on the right-hand cylinder bank to be changed. Looking back, Ulrich Baretzky says, "We checked the injectors at home but at cold temperatures the failure was no longer reproducible. Much later we noticed that the injectors were specified according to ISA (injector voltage adjustment) which is permanently programmed into the electronic control unit. During the development project, the injectors slightly changed and, due to temperature, migrated out of the ISA window. That resulted in misfiring because the nozzles no longer injected." [26] After a 20-minute time loss, Tom Kristensen, from 16th position, starts a comeback and is in fourth at midnight. About two hours later, a GT1 race car touches the Audi with Dindo Capello at the wheel. The repair of the damaged rear section takes eleven minutes. About an hour later, the underfloor separates and the car stops for another 18.50 minutes. At 3.47 am, Emanuele Pirro complains about problems with fifth gear. Thanks to a new design, the gearwheels can be changed in less than ten minutes but the car's advantage drops from four laps to one.

Long hours before victory

While car number 7 advances to third position again Marco Werner, at 7.51 am, has to have the front hood changed because of a defective headlight. Twelve minutes later, the mechanics change the left-hand turbocharger on Kristensen's car within just 15 minutes, and the Dane remains in third position. At 11.37 am, the radio system's microphone begins to fail so that the drivers can still hear the instructions but are no longer able to talk to the people in the pit lane. When the underfloor starts separating again, the car is told to reduce speed. After 380 laps, Emanuele Pirro crosses the finish line with a four-

Saturday after the warm-up: Not an ideal time for Thomas Bauch and his colleagues having to change the rear end once again

lap advantage over Hélary/Montagny/Loeb in the Pescarolo. For the current track, that sets a record. The sister car takes third place. It has led the race on 42 laps, the winners on 338, no one except Audi has run in front. The winners use only 40.34 liters of diesel fuel per 100 kilometers. A year earlier, Champion Racing's R8, with its output heavily reduced by the regulations, consumes 42.71 liters of gasoline while the FSI 2002 in its second year uses 45 liters. [27] In the final stage, Audi's drivers achieve a range of up to 16 laps on one tank filling. [28] Wolfgang Ullrich

Late wish by the chairman of the VW supervisory board: Stefan Grimm (steering) and the other mechanics have to push car number 8 from the pre-starting grid

[23] Transcript of interview with Dr. Wolfgang Ullrich on December 7, 2022
[24] Transcript of interview with Ralf Jüttner on November 17, 2022
[25] Audi Express 1, June 20, 2006, p. 2
[26] Transcript of interview with Ulrich Baretzky on December 19, 2022
[27] Consumption comparison. Contemporary information – internal document, undated
[28] Audi MediaInfo: Facts about Audi's historical Le Mans victory, June 20, 2006

summarizes: "This was already the sixth victory, but by far the most difficult and important one. [...] Le Mans always harbours some surprises that cannot be simulated on a test bed or a test track." [29]

To be continued

In the American Le Mans Series, the Audi R8 celebrates its last victory in July, at Lime Rock. Starting in mid-July, the R10 TDI continues Audi's string of success. In Utah, at Portland, Road America, Mosport, Road Atlanta and Laguna Seca, it remains unbeaten six times in a row. The title goes to Dindo Capello/ Allan McNish.

[29] Audi MediaInfo: Audi triumphs with TDI Power at Le Mans, June 18, 2006

Car number 8 secures the first diesel victory at Le Mans for Audi and the sixth in total (above).
On June 28, at the Donaukurier newspaper's initiative, Ingolstadt even blocks off the route from the Audi Piazza via Ettinger Straße to the city hall for Marco Werner's parade drive (below)

Diesel in motorsport

One of the reasons why the arrival of the Audi R10 TDI in 2006 attracts so much attention is that the diesel engine has so far been chanceless in motor racing's top categories – except for cross-country rallying, where Seat, BMW or VW in 2002 start scoring initial stage victories in the Dakar Rally. However, historically, the diesel engine has not always been the odd one out in circuit racing either. As early as in 1949, the Delettrez team is putting a 6-cylinder diesel powered car on the Le Mans grid, but it does not finish. [30] Freddy Agabashian claims pole position in the 1952 Indianapolis 500 – a Formula One round – in a Cummins Diesel Special powered by a 430-hp truck engine, but does not see the checkered flag either. [31] Somewhat off the classic motorsport scene, the diesel shows its skills in record-setting events in the nineteen-seventies. In Nardò, Mercedes-Benz and Volkswagen compete for new records with prototypes. In Wolfsburg, the ARVW with a frontal area of just 0.75 square meters is created for the Southern Italian high-speed track. A 2.4-liter six-cylinder swirl chamber diesel from the VW LT commercial vehicle with 175 horsepower accelerates it to a speed of up to 360 km/h while consuming 13.6 liters per 100 kilometers. [32]

While Audi in 1989 introduces the TDI engine and the market share of compression-ignition engines is growing in many markets, a diesel initiative starts emerging in motorsport only in the mid-nineteen-nineties. The Belgian automobile club RACB collaborates with former race driver, long-standing jour-

175 diesel-hp, consumption of 13.6 liters at 360 km/h, cd = 0.15: The record-setting ARVW in 1980 (left).
VW Golf TDI with 170 hp at the Nürburgring 24 Hours in 1997 (center).
Neil Simpson/Steve Martin in 1999 with the VW Golf TDI in the British Rally Championship (right)

nalist and Team Director Pierre Dieudonné. "I had a contact with Jean-François Chaumont, the promotor of the Spa 24 Hours. Just like Paul Frère in 1964 came up with the idea of establishing a 24-hour touring car race at Spa as a differentiation from Le Mans as a sports car race, I developed the idea for an experimental category as a technology laboratory for the future." [33] That leads to the Challenge EcoTech, which provides initial impetus to the utilization of modern diesel technology in a fast-growing number of motorsport classes. In 1995, Peugeot is the first manufacturer to become involved in the Challenge EcoTech; in 1996, Volkswagen follows suit with the Golf TDI. Organizers such as ADAC Nordrhein adopt the idea for the Nürburgring 24 Hours. BMW can take credit for having clinched the first overall diesel victory across 24 hours in this event in 1998.

Volkswagen subsequently transfers not only the idea but also the production-based technology to rallying – initially to sprint rallies and, starting in 2003, also to the Dakar Rally. In 2004, the Wolfsburg-based brand switches to five cylinders in the Race Touareg. Le Mans begins to open its field to diesel units in 2004. A privateer Lola-Caterpillar with a VW V10 TDI powerplant competes but does not finish. Later, the World Touring Car Championship (WTCC) permits diesel engines. In 2008, Seat immediately wins the title with a TDI powertrain – with Yvan Muller at the wheel who used to race for Audi.

[30] https://assets.lemans.org/explorer/pdf/courses/2020/24-heures-du-mans/press-kit/statistiques-historiques-fr.pdf, last retrieved on June 7, 2022
[31] Matthew Franey: Oil on the track, in Motor Sport, August 1998, p. 38–41
[32] Klaus-Rainer Deutenbach, Jürgen Nitz, Rolf Poltrock: ARVW – Konzept eines luftwiderstandsarmen Rekordfahrzeugs, in ATZ No. 5/1982, p. 211–219
[33] Transcript of interview with Pierre Dieudonné on July 29, 2022

Diesel stage wins at the Dakar Rally thanks to Seat Cordoba WRC 2002 (left), VW Tarek 2003 (center) and VW Race Touareg from 2004 on (right) that scores three overall victories between 2009 and 2011

Beginning of an era

2007 is the first year of a duel between Audi and Peugeot that would continue to fascinate fans for half a decade.

Marco Werner in the Audi R10 TDI in
front of Sébastien Bourdais/Pedro
Lamy/Stéphane Sarrazin's Peugeot

After his DTM crash, Tom Kristensen must fear for his Le Mans start until the last moment, announcing it only at a press conference during the race week

In 2007, Mattias Ekström comes into play as a stand-in for Tom Kristensen. The picture shows him sitting to the left of Lucas Luhr and Mike Rockenfeller (above). To be on the safe side, the fans have ten names printed on their T-shirts (right)

The parties have known each other for a while: Audi and Peugeot have been meeting with each other as early as in the World Rally Championship's Group B from 1984 to 1986, a year later at the Pikes Peak hillclimb in the U.S. and in Super Touring Car racing from 1996 on. Both brands are always among the best, the competitions are always a pleasure, but the manufacturers also repeatedly go separate ways in racing. Announced in June 2005, the French sports car program does not begin until November, after the end of the WRC Rally project. [1] Under Head of Sport Michel Barge and Technical Director Bruno Famin, the concept decision in favor of the closed cockpit is made in March 2006, the engine is up and running in September, and on December 31, the race car is doing its first laps. At Le Mans, Peugeot puts the 908 designated as car number 7 into the hands of Formula One test driver Marc Gené, sports car expert Nicolas Minassian and Jacques Villeneuve, the 1997 Formula One World Champion. Long-time GT driver Pedro Lamy, rally and circuit racer Stéphane Sarrazin

Visitors to the Audi garage include ACO President Jean-Claude Plassart, Health and Sports Minister Roselyne Bachelot-Narquin, Le Mans Mayor Jean-Claude Boulard and Prime Minister François Fillon

and Champ Car Champion Sébastien Bourdais share car number 8. At the 908 HDi FAP's debut, Nicolas Minassian and Marc Gené win the Monza 1,000 Kilometers in mid-April 2007 with a one-lap advantage in front of Pescarolo.

The LMP1 field has 16 entrants on the test day on June 3. Besides Audi and Peugeot, three Pescarolo Judd are on the grid – two fielded by Henri Pescarolo and one by the UK Rollcentre Racing team. Also racing with Judd power are a Dome, a Creation and a Lola. Two Courage and a Lola are powered by Aer. A Zytek and the Lola from Swiss Spirit with an Audi V8 TFSI engine complete the field. Pedro Lamy, Stéphane Sarrazin and Sébastien Bourdais at the front of the field are half a second faster than Biela/Pirro/Werner in the best Audi. The ACO endeavors to enhance the chances of gasoline engines: from 2007 on, diesel sports cars have nine liters less fuel per tank filling available than the year before.

Alternative planning at Audi

Before suspense sets in for Audi in the duel with Peugeot at Le Mans a state of suspense emerges in Ingolstadt for a far less pleasant reason. Audi Sport is continuing to plan with its two driver teams from the previous year and, for the first time since 2002, is fielding a third car, for three juniors this time. Mike Rockenfeller is 23, Alexandre Premat 25 and Lucas Luhr 27 years old when their first season for Audi in the LMP1 sports car as well as in the DTM begins. However, on April 22, all plans have gone awry. On the first lap of the DTM opener at Hockenheim, a serious accident occurs. Tom Kristensen's Audi spins after a collision, and the Dane's foot stays on the gas pedal. The spinning rear wheels produce an opaque cloud of smoke. At high speed, Mercedes driver Susie Stoddart, Alexandre Premat and Audi privateer Adam Carroll crash into the car of the Dane, who is exposed to extreme angular momentums. Externally unharmed, but unconscious for several minutes, Kristensen suffers severe whiplash. [2] The idea that he might be able to recover quickly soon evaporates.

[1] Peugeot press kit 24 Heures du Mans 2007, p. 2 et seq
[2] Tom Kristensen, Lars Krone: Tom Kristensen – The Book, no location, no publisher 2015, p. 182

Dindo Capello celebrates his 43rd birthday on race Sunday, June 17. He is leading with three laps to go when a wheel shears off. A year later, when the event ends on June 15, he is still 43 years old when he wins

Mike Rockenfeller and Lucas Luhr switch from Porsche to Audi.
Long-time Porsche engineer Roland Kussmaul stays in touch
with his former protegés after their departure

Wolfgang Ullrich changes plans and selects 2004
DTM Champion Mattias Ekström. If Kristensen is
unfit for racing, the Swede is supposed to drive
together with Lucas Luhr. Alexandre Premat, who
is able to recover from a vertebral injury at Hockenheim in time, is the third man. In this context, Mike
Rockenfeller is intended to be Dindo Capello and Allan McNish's teammate. On June 3, the ACO publishes a corresponding entry list, and that is the line-up
in which Audi starts the test day at La Sarthe as well.

As a race taxi driver during the DTM round at Brands
Hatch on June 9, Tom Kristensen, for the first time,
checks if he is fit again. 48 days after his accident,
his lap times are good immediately, he feels fine
after one hour of driving, and the doctors give him
the green light. Hence on June 13 – the Wednesday
of the Le Mans week and first practice day – Audi
announces that the Dane is going to race. [3] Even a
decade and a half later, Mattias Ekström, who will
go on to become 2016 World Rallycross Champion and contests the Dakar Rally with Audi from
2022 on, has no regrets about never having gotten
to race at La Sarthe: "I liked the LMP1 models but

Lucas Luhr together with Mike
Rockenfeller and Alexandre Premat
races in the LMP1 class for the first
time with Audi

Close fight in qualifying

Two red flags and rain showers on Wednesday mean that the Circuit des 24 Heures only dries off slowly. Driving on slicks does not make sense until the last minutes. When the checkered flag falls at midnight Allan McNish in the number 2 Audi is the front runner. However, at the very last moment, Stéphane Sarrazin beats him by 0.572 seconds. A day later, all hopes for better lap times dissolve in heavy rain. As a result, Sarrazin & company are in the top spot in front of McNish's car. Villeneuve and his partners are third in front of the two Audi cars of Biela and Luhr.

Early disappointment

Right in turn one, Dindo Capello takes the lead and pulls clear of his rivals. Frank Biela and Lucas Luhr overtake the Peugeot cars that started in front of them as well so that the three sports cars from Germany are running in front half an hour into the race. When rain showers set in in the second hour, track conditions are difficult. [5] The race is 23 laps old when Reinhold Joest and his team have to accept an experience they have never had with Audi at Le Mans before: a DNF. Mike Rockenfeller loses control of the 650-hp sports car, crashing with the rear end into the guard rails in the Tertre Rouge section. The on-board emergeny repair kit with tools and cable ties is truly of no help anymore in this case: when the TV cameras focus on the destroyed rear end it soon becomes obvious that the weekend is over for race engineer Brad Kettler and his crew. Rockenfeller, who is only driving his third lap, is inconsolable and apologizes to all team members with red eyes. What might be a reason for a pink slip somewhere else does not count for Audi's Head of Sport. 15 years

[3] Audi MediaInfo: Audi driver Tom Kristensen to start at Le Mans, June 13, 2007
[4] Information provided by Mattias Ekström on September 1, 2022
[5] Audi MediaInfo: Le Mans starts with mixed fortunes for Audi, June 16, 2007

driving in traffic with the four different classes never appealed to me." [4]

Audi DTM driver Vanina Ickx works for the TV channel Canal+ at Le Mans and talks to Alexandre Premat

Thorough preparation includes onboard tools with an emergency cell phone in case the driver needs to help himself on the track

Marco Werner and Frank Biela during a driver change

later, he explains, "Well, I never had any doubts about Rocky's abilities, not one second. Of course, I wasn't happy about it. But I immediately saw that he admitted his mistake himself. He said, I made a mistake and I'm terribly sorry about that. For me, it was clear that in a case like that, when you believe in the driver, you need to give him a chance again as soon as possible." [6] In fact, Rockenfeller goes on to win Le Mans for Audi three years later and the DTM another three years after that.

Number 2 delivers strong driving

After three hours, Capello, Kristensen and McNish are already one lap ahead of Bourdais' number 8 Peugeot and their own sister car driven by Biela/Pirro/Werner. Pescarolo with Jean-Christophe Boullion/Emmanuel Collard/Romain Dumas maintains fourth position in front of the number 7 Peugeot. This early trend continues throughout the night. When Marco Werner overtakes a GT1 sports car that car touches the body of the R10 TDI and destroys parts of it. At 6 in the morning, the team discovers a piece of concrete in a radiator shaft that must have come off a destroyed curb. [7] Consequently,

[6] Transcript of interview with Dr. Wolfgang Ullrich on December 7, 2022
[7] Gary Watkins: And then there was one, in Autosport, June 21, 2007, p. 62

Vaillante vs. Audi

How will a race car become unforgettable? Due to a string of success? An exceptional marketing campaign? A Hollywood movie? It, no doubt, will by appearing in Michel Vaillant's comics. After starting out as a locksmith, Jean Graton, who hails from France and emigrates to Belgium after the Second World War, evolves into a comic book illustrator. Franco-Belgian comics experience a heyday at the beginning of the second half of the century. Tintin and Snowy created by Hergé are still some of the most popular heroes today. [8] Another popular publication in Belgium at that time is Spirou, a comic book in which Graton applies his skills as a cartoonist for the first time. In 1957, he finds his calling on creating a character of his own, that of race driver Michel Vaillant. [9]

The comic book hero is unique because it is embedded in reality. Graton is not only a good scriptwriter but also an attentive observer. Vaillant's ambience

Young Jacky Ickx with Jean Graton, the inventor of the racing comic book series Michel Vaillant

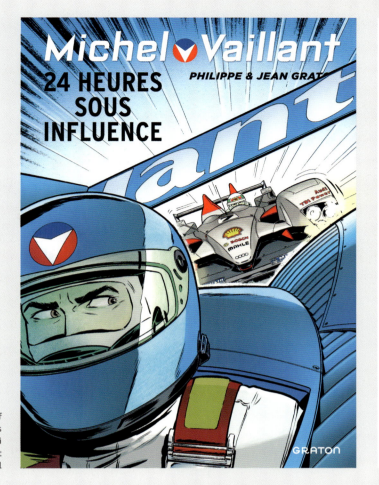

The 70th volume of the comic book series portrays the Audi R10 TDI with great attention to detail

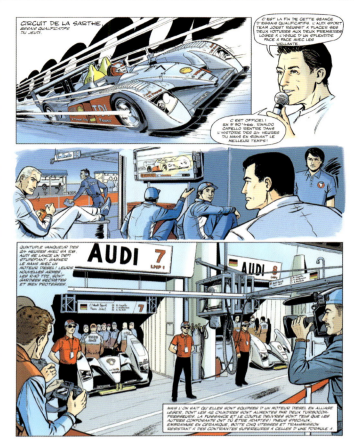

is by no means fictitious but takes cues from the motorsport landscape of the respective era for its characters, competitions, teams or race cars. Jean Graton attends car races, dedicates his attention to all details and delves into the world of the teams in their pit garages. He even befriends race drivers such as Belgian ace Jacky Ickx, who is at home initially in Formula One, then in sports cars and ultimately in desert rallying. His daughter, Vanina, is an Audi factory driver in the DTM in 2006 and 2007.

Jean Graton witnesses his comic book characters surviving even the turn to the 21st century. He is 97 years old when he dies in 2021. His youngest son, Philippe, continues his father's work for a long time. In 2007, a cooperation with Audi develops. Following 20 million albums sold, the comic book titled "24 Heures Sous Influence" is published in French, Dutch, English and German. Of course, the comic book car brand Vaillante is pitted against the Audi R10 TDI at Le Mans in that issue. The German diesel sports cars and Audi Sport Team Joest

are illustrated with great attention to detail. Jacky Ickx, a friend of the Graton family, presents Volume Number 70 at a press conference at Le Mans in 2007 together with Tom Kristensen. Philippe Graton even takes his three-member team of illustrators to the 24-hour race. To the guests' delight, Christian Papazoglakis, Robert Paquet and Nedzad Kamenica not only autograph the volumes but draw small individual scenes on the front endpapers of the 48-page book for anyone interested in such personalization.

Le Mans fans know that race cars sporting Vaillante wrap appear in real-world racing as well, for instance, whenever a new movie about the immortal comic book hero is in the making. The race at La Sarthe provides the backdrop for movies more than once. In 2002, for example, Luc Besson scripts the movie "Michel Vaillant." [10] The relevant race cars featuring a Vaillante livery are entrants of the 24-hour race. In 2017, the comic book hero returns to La Sarthe with the Vaillante Rebellion. [11]

Philippe Graton with Jacky Ickx and Tom Kristensen at Le Mans in 2007

[8] www.goethe.de/ins/be/de/kul/prj/com/20579059.html, last retrieved on January 22, 2023

[9] www.michel-vaillant.de/seiten/themen/werk_graton/_jean_graton.html, last retrieved on January 22, 2023

[10] www.lemans.org/fr/actualites/aco/fete-de-l-aco-michel-vaillant-une-exposition-et-un-film-video-21364, last retrieved on January 22, 2023

[11] www.speedweek.com/24hlemans/news/105150/Michel-Vaillant-und-sein-groc39fes-Comeback-in-Le-Mans.html, last retrieved on January 22, 2023

A last visit: The Belgian book author, journalist, race driver and former Le Mans winner Paul Frère, who died in 2008, is a regular guest at Audi's press conferences (in the center of the picture, sitting)

In pouring rain, Marco Werner, on scoring his third and final victory, crosses the finish line with a ten-lap advantage

the sister car's advantage keeps growing. Halfway through the race it is already two laps ahead and after 16 hours, its advantage has grown to more than three laps. The best Peugeot driven by Gené and his teammates has already lost seven laps. As sensational as the driving is that Tom Kristensen delivers together with his teammates following his comeback as spectacular and surprising is its ending on lap 263.

"I lost the rear left wheel at Indianapolis corner at approximately 260 km/h," Dindo Capello explains to his trackside team on his 43rd birthday. "It was a horrible feeling. I was just a passenger. I couldn't do anything to prevent a crash." [12] At 7.35 in the morning, at the exit of the fast right-hand turn, his R10 TDI spins toward the left, briefly lifts off but lands again on the remaining three wheels.

Capello is reminded of a test accident at Magny-Cours a long time ago in which his R8R lifts off and lands upside down: "I thought that I was flying again. This time it would have been more dangerous because the tire walls weren't far away. Fortunately, the car fell onto its wheels again and I crashed head-on into the tire wall. I was so shocked. Not about the accident, but about losing the race. Just like that. This retirement was painful. I only managed to get over that when Toyota stopped on the very last lap in 2016. That was even worse than our situation in 2007. How could I lose a wheel so long after a tire change? If it had happened after exiting the pit lane, I could have made it back to the pits on three wheels and we would still have won." [13]

The last tire change, in fact, took place 54 minutes earlier. With an improperly fastened wheel nut, Capello would have lost the wheel immediately. Former Head of Sport Ullrich comments on that today: "It took a long time for us to understand what happened there. We assume that during the mounting of the wheel an aluminum chip from the wheel nut got jammed while the wheel nut was being tightened. It then became compressed across many laps so that the preload of the nut degraded. [14] Once more, safety is the top priority for Audi. The motorsport squad together with Mega-Line develops a system that provides conclusions about the tightening torque of the wheel guns. Up until the end of the LMP era it indicates immediately after a pit stop if all four wheel nuts have been safely tightened.

Finale in the rain

Car number 1 is now the only remaining Audi. Before the last quarter of the race, the advantage of the car led by race engineer Ed Turner is four laps in front of the best Peugeot. Torrential rain in the last two hours mean a last final test for the driver trio. The safety car is leading the field almost during the entire last hour. Ten minutes before the race ends, Race Director Daniel Poissenot releases the competition once more. [15] Marco Werner crosses the finish line with a ten-lap advantage in front of Lamy/Sarrazin/Bourdais. For him, it is the third and last, and for the long-standing Audi factory drivers Biela and Pirro, it's their fifth and last Le Mans victory.

The normally calm and collected German Werner admits: "Of course, it's a great feeling to win but tomorrow for sure I will feel even better because there was gigantic pressure on our shoulders until the very end of the race. In the closing stages this Le Mans 24 Hours was more like a boat race. It was incredible that the race went green again under these conditions." [16] Emanuele Pirro finds kind words for the team and its rivals: "It was a tough race with some rain at the beginning which made tyre choice complicated and heavy rain at the end. I dedicate this victory to the mechanics of all three cars. There was a great battle with Peugeot. To beat such a competitor makes our victory even sweeter." [17]

Race engineer Ed Turner, shown here with Emanuele Pirro and Frank Biela, gets his car to cross the finish line as the only R10 TDI to do so (above). The collection of radios for a big team like Audi (right)

[12] Audi MediaInfo: Quotes after the retirement of the Audi R10 TDI Number 2, June 17, 2007
[13] Transcript of interview with Dindo Capello on November 24, 2022
[14] Transcript of interview with Dr. Wolfgang Ullrich on December 7, 2022
[15] Gary Watkins: And then there was one, in Autosport, June 21, 2007, p. 61
[16] Audi MediaInfo: Quotes after the race at Le Mans, June 17, 2007
[17] Ibid

Even the digital age still includes some manual work: Dieter Meissler records the pit stops and related jobs on a board

Limited dominance in America

For the eighth time Audi prevails also in the American Le Mans Series. Dindo Capello/Allan McNish win the title after nine LMP1 class victories with a 36-point advantage in front of Marco Werner. Class wins? The Italian and the Scot are overall winners only on three occasions. To add suspense to the competition, the LMP2 cars from Porsche are rated in a way enabling them to clinch overall victory in eight out of twelve races – an upside-down new world.

The second diesel victory at Le Mans again goes to Frank Biela, Emanuele Pirro and Marco Werner

Hosting
the world

Audi's marketing activities at Le Mans have modest beginnings: "The first two years, there was no marketing. The poshest thing we had was this small hospitality lounge for the team," former Chairman of the Management Board Franz-Josef Paefgen recalls. "Other than that, we were in the rooms above the team garages. Every now and then, a lady would show up asking us if we'd like a cup of coffee. One of the highlights was Mrs. Joest inviting us to her large motorhome for dinner." [18]

However, the company goes on to systematically develop its marketing activities. Le Mans evolves into an event that appeals to guests from all over the world. Never before nor after Le Mans does Audi succeed in making a motorsport event a worldwide attraction. As versatile and professional as the brand's appearances in the DTM or in Formula E may be in those and subsequent years, they do remain a stage for the local markets. With their factory-backed

Soul stars Beverley Knight and Seal are two of Audi's many VIP guests at Le Mans in 2007

The Audi Racing Arena along the straight in front of the Ford Chicane is one of various event locations, used here for a press conference

Christof Caspar and his team support the Le Mans 24 Hours on the part of the Marketing Department for many years

return to Le Mans in 2006, Audi establishes itself as an integral component around the track. From perimeter advertising to official cars, the public and the television cameras clearly notice the brand with the four rings at first glance. A wide variety of event locations with individual activities are created to accommodate a total of 600 or more guests from all over the world. Over the years, many names of typical locations imprint themselves on the visitors' memories: the Audi Racing Club across from the start and finish line, the Audi Sky Lounge at the same location, the Audi Racing Lounges directly above the team garages, the Audi Racing Garden and the Audi Racing Shop in the bustling Village pedestrian mall near the paddock or the Audi Racing Terrace located directly at the approach to the Dunlop Chicane behind the start and finish straight. Centrally located is the Audi Racing Arena in the Parc du Raccordement between the track sections of Maison Blanche and Ford Chicane.

The guests there experience far more than just the race on television screens and time monitors. Over the years, the displays also show race car data such as engine speed, centrifugal forces or vehicle speed from a virtual onboard perspective in real time. An Audi Sport studio is on the air under various names. In a corner of the studio, professional presenters welcome and host race drivers and officials providing first-hand reports from the race. Corner shuttles take interested guests to the particularly challenging sections such as Indianapolis or the Porsche Corners for a close-up experience of the fascination exuded by Le Mans. Those interested in the history of the race can obtain tickets to the Musée Automobile

de la Sarthe where some of the most beautiful race cars can be admired. Last but not least, international stars like to visit Audi as well: No Angels perform a concert, Seal, Beverley Knight, Vanessa Mae and many others are part of a long list of celebrities.

[18] Transcript of interview with Dr. Franz-Josef Paefgen on October 27, 2022

For years, Audi provides the official cars as official supplier (above). In later years, the Audi Sky Lounge offers guests a fascinating view of the start and finish straight (below)

Truth in 24

American director Keith Cossrow selects
Le Mans for filming the documentary "Truth in
24" about Audi. A good choice: The 76th edition
is a bigger thriller than any scripted production.

The ACO registers 22 race cars in the LMP1 class including the three Audi R10 TDI and, for the first time, three cars from Peugeot. While the driver line-up from Ingolstadt remains identical, the French change their squad: Pedro Lamy and Stéphane Sarrazin are teamed up with Alexander Wurz replacing Sébastien Bourdais. The trio of Marc Gené/Nicolas Minassian/Jacques Villeneuve remains unchanged. Christian Klien, Franck Montagny and Ricardo Zonta share a third 908. No fewer than four Pescarolo Judd cars, fielded by Pescarolo Sport, Rollcentre Racing and Saulnier Racing, are among the strongest gasoline-powered contenders. However, when it comes to the best lap times in the race, they fall short by ten seconds and more compared to their fastest diesel-powered rivals. The sports cars from Courage-Oreca, Lola Aston Martin, additional Lola prototypes, Dome, Creation and Epsilon Euskadi fill up the LMP1 class.

An Audi R10 TDI trio competes at Le Mans in 2008. The model remains unbeaten in its third race as well

Peugeot enlarges its team from two to three race cars (above). Lola Aston Martin is one of the pursuers from the group of gasoline engines within the LMP1 sports car category (left)

Biggest program ever

It is not without pride that Audi announces its biggest motorsport program in history to date. [1] Besides the three race cars in the Le Mans 24 Hours two Audi R10 TDI cars each compete in the American Le Mans Series and in the Le Mans Series in Europe, plus eight factory-fielded and two privateer Audi A4 DTM cars contest the DTM. In view of the fierce competition in all categories, winning all three championships and the crown jewel, Le Mans, would at best have been a dream at the beginning of the season. But exactly that

will come to pass. Never again will Audi run such a diverse factory-backed motorsport program with 28 factory-supported races, 15 of which the brand wins. [2]

Season starts well for Peugeot

Particularly in the sports prototype program Audi can clearly feel the strides that its competitor has made. Whereas the year before Peugeot could not keep its good qualifying pace in the race the French coupés are now stronger than ever in the battle with the R10 TDI that is already entering its third season. Although Audi wins at Sebring, the victorious Peugeot of Gené/Minassian in the LMS opener at Barcelona in early April laps the best R10 TDI of Premat/Rockenfeller once. Three weeks later, at Monza, Lamy/Sarrazin see the checkered flag 48 seconds before Audi's young duo does. Another 14 days later, at Spa, Audi finishes half a minute behind Peugeot. On the test day at Le Mans, on June 1, Lamy/Sarrazin/Wurz are 4.4 seconds faster than the sister car of Montagny/Klien/Zonta. They, in turn, are separated by six tenths of a second from their pursuers Biela/Pirro/Werner and Gené/Minassian/Villeneuve.

However, the conditions on that day are anything but balanced: bright sunshine, heavy rain and even hail whirl the work of the teams around. Yet that proves to be extremely valuable. "Michelin had two

Peugeot also loses its second Le Mans race against Audi, here with Capello/Kristensen/McNish

Allan McNish, Ralf Jüttner, Dindo Capello, Wolfgang Ullrich and Tom Kristensen are obviously overjoyed at their hard-fought victory

different rain tires that year," Joest's Team Principal Ralf Jüttner recalls. "As early as on the test day we realized that one of the versions did not work and the other one was massively faster. Plus, before the race weekend, we knew that there was a very high probability of rain."[3]

Until then, Audi sticks to its virtues and remains modest: "Audi relies on efficiency and reliability for its tenth appearance in Le Mans. The Audi R10 TDI, now in its third year of service, is no longer the fastest prototype on the grid – at least over a single lap. However, over the distance Audi Sport Team Joest has a good chance of winning because in Le Mans it's all about losing as little time as possible in the pits," the brand announces before the start. [4] Auto-

sport magazine expresses this opinion before the race weekend: "The Peugeot is the faster car, it's newer, more aerodynamically efficient and has better weight distribution."[5]

Despite major differences in age and experience, the magazine sees Audi and Peugeot on a par in terms of their driver squads as well as in terms of fuel efficiency. Concerning reliability, pit stops and ease of maintenance, the editors concede that the Germans, in part, have clear advantages. The author concludes that, "Peugeot has the pace to win the 2008 Le Mans 24 Hours, so long as at least one of the 908s makes it through without spending too long in the pits. The inexperience of some of the drivers and the time it takes to repair the French car could hinder that. But

[1] Audi MediaInfo: Audi with clear commitment to motorsport, November 30, 2007
[2] Audi Motorsport Communications: Press kit Audi in Motorsport 2008/2009
[3] Transcript of interview with Ralf Jüttner on November 17, 2022
[4] Audi MediaInfo: Audi relies on efficiency for Le Mans anniversary, June 6, 2008
[5] Autosport Le Mans Guide 2008, p. 8

Following their own mishap, last year's winners Pirro/Werner/Biela put themselves at the service of the team

McNish has probably got it right when he says: 'It is Peugeot's race to lose.'" [6]

In the first qualifying session, the three Audi trail three Peugeot cars, with a time gap of roughly five and a half seconds in between. After the second qualifying day, positions four for Dindo Capello/ Tom Kristensen/Allan McNish, five for Lucas Luhr/ Alexandre Premat/Mike Rockenfeller and seven for Frank Biela/Emanuele Pirro/Marco Werner behind a Lola Aston Martin have been determined. The best Audi is lacking five seconds per lap compared to the fastest Peugeot driven by Lamy/Sarrazin/Wurz. The commentaries afterwards seem almost prophetic: "This will for sure be a very exciting race," predicts Head of Sport Wolfgang Ullrich. "The lap times were very close together on Thursday and on a very high level. We consistently ran through our programme and worked out a good dry set-up for all three cars with which all drivers coped with well. It can also be changed quickly into a good rain set-up in case this will be necessary." [7] Dindo Capello adds, "We improved the car compared with the previous day. Now the car is easier to drive. It is faster even with a lot of fuel and used tyres. That's what we need – a race car that handles easily and allows you to push where you need it without taking big risks." [8]

One of Audi Sport Team Joest's secrets of success can be seen here: The wide-angle shot shows a perfectly prepared garage tent. Since the test day the team has known which tires are best

Efficiently forward

At the beginning of its racing section, the film "Truth in 24" is focused on Howden Haynes. On the time monitors, Dindo Capello, Tom Kristensen and Allan McNish's race engineer has to helplessly watch how Peugeot hurries away after the start, gaining three seconds per lap. No one in the camp of the Ingolstadt and Neckarsulm squad is surprised. After the end of the race, the fastest lap set by the winners that Haynes supports proves to be 4.758 seconds slower than the one of the best Peugeot driven by Lamy/Sarrazin/Wurz. Even so, it is a statistic that could hardly be less relevant because at Le Mans in 2008 it is something else that matters. "Everyone in the team is focused on this: we make no mistakes," Wolfgang Ullrich analyzes a decade and a half later. "We consistently extract the maximum from the package for 24 hours straight. And if the others make a small mistake, then that may be enough for us to be in contention again at the front. The experience of our squad has shown that mistakes happen again and again. You don't have to be a poor performer for that to be the case because it just happens. Seeing that we were slower on the race track, we tried to save time with the pit stops." [9]

The organizers' analysis subsequently confirms that the victorious Audi with chassis number 204 spends 31m56s at 32 service stops. The second-placed Peugeot of Gené, Minassian and Villeneuve requires 41m40s for 36 stops – almost exactly ten minutes longer. Nearly more impressive is the time that the mechanics really need. The internal calculation reveals that the number 2 Audi really stopped only 19m51s in total. [10] The remainder between the measuring loops in the pit lane is attributable to approach and departure times.

Aside from the excellent job done by Audi Sport Team Joest there are other factors that come into play. The Audi R10 TDI has a range of twelve laps per tank filling whereas Peugeot needs to refuel one lap earlier. As a result, Capello/Kristensen/McNish initially take the lead lap per lap and from lap 41 forward, they are running in front by seven laps straight. The leading intervals subsequently grow. In his internal race report, race engineer Howden Haynes notes, "The strategy was simple: drive as fast as possible for as

To Emanuele Pirro's great regret, he misses a tenth podium finish in a row

Carl Erik Kristensen brought his son, Tom, into motorsport and occasionally accompanies him to his races

[6] Autosport Le Mans Guide 2008, p. 11
[7] Audi MediaInfo: Audi starts from the second row at Le Mans, June 13, 2008
[8] Ibid
[9] Transcript of interview with Dr. Wolfgang Ullrich on December 7, 2022
[10] Internal report by Howden Haynes: Le Mans 2008 Race Week Chassis R10T–204

In the years of the R10 TDI, Audi enters into an agreement with its partner Red Bull about using the F1 Energy Station. Guests love the open team hospitality lounge with a terrace (both images)

In fourth position, Alexandre Premat and his teammates see the finish line at Le Mans for the first time

Reinhold Joest and Ralf Jüttner experience a perfect season at Le Mans and in the LMS with Audi Sport

long as possible, stay out of the pits, quadruple stint each driver, double stint every set of tyres and when experiencing adverse weather, take the safe option for tyre choice and stick with it regardless of short term performance loss." [11]

Night owls

There is no shortage of bad weather, quite to the contrary. Blessed are those who have a precise weather forecast. Audi has its own on-site weather service, the UK specialists from Racemet. Peugeot books the national French weather service Météo France, whose employees are less interested in motorsport than in a concurrent call for a strike issued by three unions. [12] "We had nothing to do with that. We didn't incite them," Ralf Jüttner says, still amused about events back then. [13]

The race begins to slip through the French squad's fingers. After car number 8 that is leading with a 40-second advantage encounters a shifting problem three hours into the race, car number 9 has to serve a penalty and have a new hood installed due to a failed headlamp. In the 13th hour of racing, at night, overheating issues torment all three coupés of the

brand sporting the lion. Track dirt and tire wear combine with rain into a mix that clogs the radiators. [14]

From the 14th hour of racing on, F1 World Champion Jacques Villeneuve in car number 7 cannot enjoy his lead very long: the fastest Audi overtakes the Canadian at 5.17 in the morning. Tom Kristensen together with Allan McNish achieves an advantage of nearly one lap before Dindo Capello, at 9.30 am, even laps the Peugeot. "The car was a nightmare to drive," admits former Grand Prix driver Villeneuve, whose coupé, just like its sister cars, are racing with a setup purely for dry conditions. Team Manager Serge Saulnier openly admits the mistake: "You have to make a decision: do you go for a compromise set-up that means you are less competitive in the dry? That was not our choice, but I think we learnt a lesson today: a good 24-hour car must be a good car in all conditions." [15]

Successful strategy

Starting on lap 235, Audi's car number 2 is at the front of the field and running impeccably. However, for Audi Sport Team Joest, the weekend is not

completely trouble-free either. Luhr, Premat and Rockenfeller are deprived of a chance for a podium when the mechanics have to change an oil filter in the penultimate hour and number 3 drops down to fourth position. The winners of the two previous years – Frank Biela, Emanuele Pirro and Marco Werner – drop down to sixth position due to a clutch change. Starting in second gear following a spin has overtaxed the module. [16]

The seasoned squad of Audi Sport Team Joest can even turn this disadvantage into an advantage: Following the 33-minute repair, the chanceless last

[11] Internal report by Howden Haynes: Le Mans 2008 Race Week Chassis R10T–204
[12] www.ladepeche.fr/article/2008/06/11/459115-meteo-france-preavis-de-greve-jusqu-au-24-juin.html, last retrieved on January 24, 2023
[13] Transcript of interview with Ralf Jüttner on November 17, 2022
[14] Gary Watkins: Audi takes the rains, in Autosport, June 19, 2008, p. 42 et seq
[15] Ibid
[16] Audi MediaInfo: Audi achieves second Le Mans hat-trick, June 15, 2008

Ten years after his first Le Mans victory with Porsche, Scotsman Allan McNish achieves this success with Audi

143

Race engineer Howden Haynes, in front of the car, wearing red overalls and a headset, leads Tom Kristensen and his teammates to victory (above). A clear tally (below)

year's winners, in changeable weather, test which of the many tire versions best match the current track conditions. Racemet predicts with high precision where and how long it is going to rain on the more than 13-kilometer track. Hence Biela/Pirro/Werner are running tire tests in the race. Their teammates in car number 2 that is in contention for victory use the resulting advice to their advantage. The wide variety of compounds and unstable weather cause a certain level of stress. "Michelin had only a limited number of specific rain tires that we couldn't store in our garage," reveals Ralf Jüttner. "We were able to remove only one set and install the next one. And then it took a while for the newly mounted set from Michelin to arrive again. We consistently did that, even at the risk of a car coming in with tire failure

Think big

In America, everything is a bit bigger. This VW Touareg is 110.5 percent the size of its production counterpart. [17] And its engine comes from Le Mans: It is the V12 from the Audi R10 TDI. VW contests the famous offroad event Baja 1000 with it on November 21 and 22, 2008. Arciero Miller Racing designs the "Trophy Truck" around a tubular frame.

Contact with Audi Sport is established through VW's engine man Donatus Wichelhaus. Trophy Truck designer Don Tebbe travels from Foothill Ranch near Los Angeles to Neckarsulm to sort out how the V12 TDI

Designer Don Tebbe in conversation with engine engineer Timo Witt

Rear-wheel drive, no windows, 63 centimeters of front suspension travel and 76 at the rear: That is the 2008 Volkswagen Red Bull Baja Race Touareg TDI

can be integrated as a mid-engine. "We implemented the entire packaging with the upward relocation of the turbocharger in the space of three hours," engine engineer Timo Witt recalls. [18] The driver pairings Mark Miller/Willie Valdez jr. and Ryan Arciero/Benny Metcalf jr. are surprised by the power. "In tests in the Mojave Desert, an uphill section in deep sand had to be mastered," says Witt. "The other Trophy Trucks with Nascar engines drove 80 miles there, we drove over 110 miles, and the car continued accelerating. You could hear the laughter over the radio. At more than 200 km/h, the wheels kept spinning, so we reduced the power to 75 percent."

In the race, the team encounters a problem with a seal and has to change the rear differential. Miller achieves 13th place. After the first race, the financial crisis puts an end to the project that was designed to be run for several years.

[17] Volkswagen Motorsport Information: First time with Clean Diesel Technology: Volkswagen masters Baja 1000, November 22, 2008
[18] Transcript of interview with Timo Witt on October 28, 2022

and exactly that type of tire then missing. It was great that Dr. Ullrich just let us do our thing the whole time without telling us what to do. I thought that was sensational." [19]

The mechanics handle not only this intensive task with aplomb but also play a completely legal tactical game with their rivals on the sidelines. "Before a pit stop, we set out other tires than those we were planning to use," recalls Thomas Bauch, who was working on the car of Premat and company at the time. "Peugeot were watching our tire choices with their spies. We'd set out slicks, for instance. You could recognize the spies, and when they left and our car was coming in, we put the slicks away and mounted rain tires." [20]

Despite a spin by Tom Kristensen following a collision with a lapped car in the final stage, the trio that had been formed two years earlier achieves its first joint Le Mans victory. For the Dane, it is the eighth, for Dindo Capello, the third and last, and for Allan McNish, the second in total and the first one with Audi – exactly ten years after his first success. Audi completes a hat-trick with Audi Sport Team

Alexandre Premat and Mike Rockenfeller win the 2008 LMS together without a single race victory

Audi prevails in the American Le Mans Series for the last time, here with Lucas Luhr in front of Emanuele Pirro

Joest for the second time, as it did before between 2000 and 2002. Engines from Neckarsulm, including the Bentley victory, remain unbeaten for the ninth consecutive time. "Peugeot was in a different league," says Capello. "The team spirit made the difference. The strategy was perfect. Peugeot came under pressure and made mistakes. At Le Mans, it's not necessarily the fastest car that wins. In 2008, the best team won." [21] Allan McNish feels like a weight has been lifted off his shoulders: "I'm overjoyed to have finally won the Le Mans 24 Hours with Audi. I've come very close on numerous occasions in the past but despite fierce opposition [...] and unpredictable weather, I've finally done it. [...] Thankfully, the car was very sure-footed." [22]

The dream continues

The American television crew has a topic that even Hollywood could hardly have invented more impressively. "Truth in 24" evolves into a cult film for motorsport enthusiasts. Three years later, after the thrilling 2011 race, the next episode, "Truth in 24 II," follows. For Audi, as well, the season continues like a dream after the 2008 Le Mans success. Alexandre

Premat/Mike Rockenfeller win the LMS title. In the American Le Mans Series, Lucas Luhr/Marco Werner in front of Emanuele Pirro decide the title in their favor in the year of Audi's last participation.

This marks the end of the R10 TDI's factory career. But Colin Kolles' privateer team races with the proven sports car at Le Mans the two following years and launches two programs for the Le Mans Series and the Asian Le Mans Series. The 2009 Le Mans 24 Hours will become an unforgettable event. On returning from the grid, Narain Karthikeyan leaps across the pit wall, dislocates a shoulder and is no longer able to contest the race. With only two drivers left, the R10 TDI loses its right to race but the ACO allows the team to participate with the Dutch-German driver duo of Charles Zwolsman/André Lotterer.

The German, who has disappeared in Europe but long become a successful pro in Japan, even has to provide a budget for his first start at Le Mans. [23] It is money well invested: Thanks to strong lap times, Lotterer and his teammate achieve a remarkable seventh place overall. With that, he attracts Audi's interest, is signed under a factory agreement a year later and goes on to win Le Mans three times.

[19] Transcript of interview with Ralf Jüttner on November 17, 2022
[20] Transcript of interview with Thomas Bauch on October 28, 2022
[21] Transcript of interview with Dindo Capello on November 24, 2022
[22] Audi MediaInfo: Quotes after the Le Mans 24 Hours, June 15, 2008
[23] www.dailysportscar.com/2013/10/12/andre-lotterer-the-big-break.html, last retrieved on January 24, 2023

André Lotterer and Charles Zwolsman drive as a pairing at Le Mans in 2009 after Narain Karthikeyan has sustained an injury

After the factory program has ended in 2008, the R10 TDI's career continues for two more years. The team of Colin Kolles competes at Le Mans in 2009 and at other events, here with André Lotterer, Charles Zwolsman, Narain Karthikeyan, Christijan Albers, Giorgio Mondini and Christian Bakkerud

In push mode

All too often during its Le Mans
debut the mechanics must push the
Audi R15 TDI into the garages. Combined
with other problems Audi is chanceless.

In the 2009 race, Audi has to make unscheduled pit stops more than once

Second diesel generation

Audi Sport has been working on the R15 TDI since 2007. The sophisticated aerodynamics design is focused on airflow around and through the car. The rear wing suspended from the top compensates for the losses caused by a drastic cut. [1] The regulations reduce its width from two meters to 1.60 meters and its length from 30 centimeters to 25. Unusual are the curved contours, surfaces and openings of the side pods. For the first time, Audi uses a lithium-ion

The bodywork of the R15 TDI features many radically styled segments and revolutionary aerodynamics enabling airflow through the car

battery. It weighs less than a conventional battery and supplies higher onboard voltage.

To downsize the powerplant – while retaining its displacement of 5.5 liters – the engineers compare the advantages and disadvantages of eight, ten and twelve cylinders. [2] Concept studies begin in summer of 2007 and the V10 is chosen in September. A V12 would have had a lower installed height but disadvantages in terms of length. An eight-cylinder unit would have had to cope with a 50-percent increase per cylinder volume and correspondingly high loads. At the end of 2007, initial single-cylinder trials are successful. In July 2008, the V10 fires for the first time, and in December the first test on a track follows.

The 20-percent increase of single-cylinder volume also entails an increase in the required quantity of injected fuel. The new hydraulic system raises rail pressure from 2,000 to 2,400 bar. [3] The piston area load increases by 12 percent while ignition pressure remains unchanged. That is why Mahle replaces the aluminum pistons that have a fiber-reinforced bowl edge by steel pistons. [4] The high temperature strength of steel enables a lower top land height resulting in a lower cylinder block. The pin bore absorbs higher forces so that the piston pin is shorter. As a result, a steel piston can even be lighter than an aluminum piston. [5]

The turbocharger is the first to feature a variable turbine geometry (VTG). Whereas this technology has been available in production vehicles since 1991 [6], it is deemed to be hard to manage in racing. The exhaust temperatures make maximum demands on the compartmentalized system that depends on exact clearances and accurate free travel – at up to 1,050 degrees centigrade. A passenger car reaches a maximum of 800 degrees.

The VTG control unit loads the turbine wheel with a larger or smaller amount of exhaust gas, thus replacing the wastegate. Shift times in the transmission of

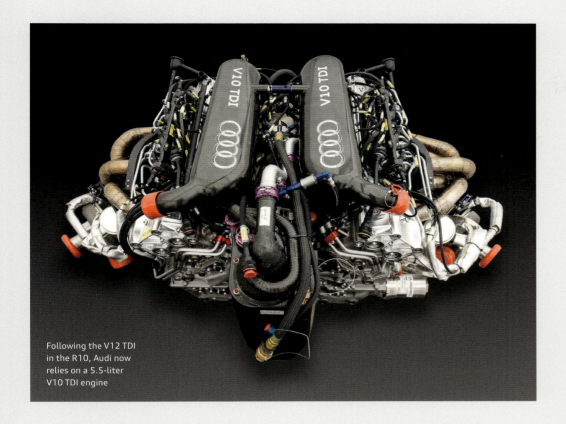

Following the V12 TDI in the R10, Audi now relies on a 5.5-liter V10 TDI engine

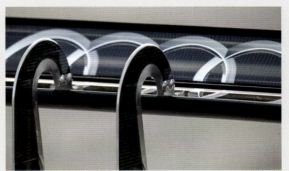

Covered wishbones on the front suspension, a rear wing suspended from the top, louvres for venting of radiator sections and turbochargers with variable turbine geometry define the R15 TDI (from top to bottom)

merely around 30 milliseconds are hard on the boost controller because pressure is not supposed to drop when the engine control unit (ECU) cuts injection during shifting events. The VTG system closes the blades, thus accelerating the exhaust gas flow and increasing turbocharger speed.

The changes enable an 8-percent increase in turbocharger speed combined with a roughly 15-percent reduction of exhaust gas back pressure. The rotational speed range of the maximum boost pressure extends downward by 250 revolutions. The charge air temperature drops by as much as 12 percent. The intercooler can be downsized and aerodynamic drag drops. Responsiveness and power delivery are clearly enhanced. The boost pressure level is higher during overrun as well. In the transient range – during the transition from overrun to full throttle – boost pressure builds up faster. [7] With that, Audi achieves valuable improvements in times of more stringent restrictions: In 2009, the restrictor cross section drops by 9.8 percent to 37.9 millimeters per bank and boost pressure by 6.5 percent to 2,760 millibar. A year later, the cross section decreases to 37.5 millimeters and pressure to 2,590 millibar.

[1] Gary Watkins: That petrol emotion, in Autosport, March 12, 2009, p. 46

[2] The architecture of a diesel, in Racecar Engineering Le Mans 2012 Special Edition, p. 79 et seq

[3] Michael Hackethal: Markenbotschafter, in Motorsport Guide 14, 11/2011–1/2012, p. 58

[4] Michael Hackethal: Markenbotschafter, in Motorsport Guide 13, May/June/July 2011, p. 46 et seq

[5] The architecture of a diesel, in Racecar Engineering Le Mans 2012 Special Edition, p. 83

[6] www.audi-mediacenter.com/en/the-audi-tdi-tech-workshop-2014-3039/technology-milestones-3129, last retrieved on October 12, 2022

[7] Michael Hackethal: Markenbotschafter, in Motorsport Guide 14, 11/2011–1/2012, p. 60

Daniel Perdrix from the ACO ascertains the legality of the R15 TDI

Peugeot makes its third attempt in 2009 (above).
Aston Martin enters the race with three prototypes (below)

Dindo Capello, Tom Kristensen and Allan McNish return in car number 1 as last year's winners. Frank Biela and Emanuele Pirro – the 2006 and 2007 overall winners – have retired from their sports car careers as Audi factory drivers. Marco Werner in the number 2 Audi takes turns at the wheel for the first time with Mike Rockenfeller and Lucas Luhr. Alexandre Premat shares number 3 with Romain Dumas and Timo Bernhard. Porsche makes both drivers available for four years. They know Le Mans from the GT cockpit and have achieved victories and titles in the LMP2 class.

Strong rivals

Peugeot analyzes the deficits from 2008. "The main problems which needed to be sorted out were the coggling of the radiators, skid resistance and traction control and the time taken for wheel changes in the pits. At the same time as working on these areas, we had to incorporate into our 908 HDi FAP vehicles certain technical modifications which had been imposed by the new ACO regulations," explains Technical Director Bruno Famin. [8] Unlike Audi, Peugeot does not build a new model. The names of the drivers are largely known, but have been regrouped. Pedro Lamy, Christian Klien and Nicolas Minassian compete in car number 7. In number 8, returnee Sébastien Bourdais races together with Franck Montagny and Stéphane Sarrazin. Marc Gené and Alexander Wurz in number 9 work together with David Brabham, the only new signing. Peugeot provides Henri Pescarolo with a fourth 908 HDi FAP.

The other competitors contest the race with gasoline engines. In addition to the Peugeot, Henri Pescarolo enters a Pescarolo Judd 01. [9] Aston Martin with Prodrive moves up into the LMP1 category. For cost reasons, the model is based on a Lola chassis with a nearly new body. Prodrive initially tries to homologate the LMP1 coupé as an Aston Martin. Lola insists that the car continues to be a model from its proprietary production. Ultimately, the coupé is put on the grid as Lola Aston Martin B09/60. [10] As the best gasoline-powered model, one of the cars clinches fourth position. The Swiss Speedy Racing team relies on a Lola chassis and Aston Martin power as well. Oreca competes for the first time with the self-constructed "01" based on the monocoque of a Courage LC70. A Courage LC70 from Signature Plus, Creation Autosportif with its own CA07, and Teams LNT and Strakka Racing with a Zytek 09S complete the LMP1 field.

Honda's US subsidiary Acura joins the LMP1 class in 2009. The car's striking features are a high nose, a rear wing suspended from the top and wider front tires for more grip that will soon be setting the trend. [11] Acura races exclusively in the ALMS and dominates there.

Deceptive success?

At Sebring, Acura impresses with pole position. For the Audi R15 TDI, it is its premiere. Allan McNish says, "I had a smile on my face after my first lap in the car. The R15 did everything I wanted it to do, all the things that the R10 didn't do." [12] Capello/Kristensen/McNish win the race in front of Peugeot after the lead between the two brands has changed 22 times. The second R15 TDI achieves position three. "We had too many small problems," says Peugeot's Team Principal Serge Saulnier. "Look at Audi: it has a new car but didn't have too many problems over the week." [13]

Tom Kristensen, Romain Dumas, Alexandre Premat, Dindo Capello and Timo Bernhard at the beginning of the race week

[8] Jean-Marc Teissedre: The Quest for Le Mans, Paris: EPA Publishing, 2009, p. 16
[9] Gary Watkins: The Petrol-Powered Push for the Le Mans podium, in Autosport June 11, 2009, p. 68 et seq
[10] Gary Watkins: Gulf Scream, in Autosport, April 2, 2009, p. 64 et seq
[11] www.racecar-engineering.com/articles/lmp1-acura-arx-02/, last retrieved on January 28, 2023
[12] Gary Watkins: Silence is silver, in Autosport, March 19, 2009, p. 96
[13] Gary Watkins: New car means old tricks for Audi, in Autosport, March 26, 2009, p. 65

On making its racing debut at Sebring in March, the R15 TDI achieves a victory against Peugeot and Acura

Marco Werner and Mike Rockenfeller at the wheel of a Horch 830 during the parade on Friday are still in an upbeat mood

At Arnage, an autograph session has been set up for German drivers, here with Lucas Luhr (right) and Mike Rockenfeller

Yet in retrospect, the question arises whether that success belies potential deficits? Wolfgang Ullrich is slightly surprised: "This is a great result for a brand new car which came to Sebring with less mileage under its wheels than we had planned." Dindo Capello adds, "I honestly did not expect to win with the R15 TDI at Sebring because the car is so new and had little testing in Europe." [14]

Following initial trials in December, the test program falls behind schedule due to bad weather. Temperatures in Europe are never warmer than 15 degrees centigrade while in part they are more than twice as high at Sebring. [15] After Dindo Capello crashes at Sebring in March following a suspension failure and the team stops the trials, Alexandre Premat during the 30-hour test in April at Le Castellet hits the barrier at high speed. At the same time, the ACO reduc-

es the diameter of the refueling system for diesel sports cars from 38 to 33 millimeters and imposes a 30 kilograms higher minimum weight on them on short notice. Due to the worldwide financial crisis, the prequalifying is cancelled. [16] Consequently, Audi has no database whatsoever with the new R15 TDI at La Sarthe.

Rivals have legal doubts

Peugeot and other rivals have been doubting the legality of the R15 TDI since March: A small profile above the front splitter allegedly represents a prohibited aerodynamic element. Openings in the engine cover and the side pods arouse suspicion as well. [17] Wolfgang Ullrich counters, "The Audi R15 TDI has been created according to 2009

After setbacks, Allan McNish and Dindo Capello with their teammate Tom Kristensen still finish in third position

During Technical Scrutineering at Le Mans, Peugeot warily watches Audi and files a protest on Wednesday, June 10. The French complain about flaps and other components on the front fenders. Peugeot's Sport Director Olivier Quesnel desires a clarification of the rules. [20] Today, Andreas Köppen, then Audi's regulatory expert, is still surprised: "In my view, the protest, if for no other reason, could not be successful because it was filed against a homologated car. In any event, a protest can only mean that the car does not correspond to the homologation sheet or that there have been further modifications made compared to the homologation sheet that are not permissible. Neither was the case. The car corresponded exactly to the homologation sheet." [21]

ACO regulations. The ACO was involved in this development and approved that car in the condition in which it raced at Sebring. The R15 TDI is homologated and passed Technical Scrutineering at Sebring. That clearly shows that our car is legal." [18] When Audi modifies the aerodynamics for Le Mans, the waters have by no means been smoothed. The Head of Audi Sport comments: "We had planned two aerodynamic configurations from the very beginning. A version for Sebring with maximum downforce, and one for Le Mans with greater emphasis on the aerodynamic efficiency. The basic concept is, however, exactly the same." [19]

[14] Audi MediaInfo: Perfect debut for the Audi R15 TDI, March 22, 2009
[15] Ibid
[16] www.24h-lemans.com/en/news/test-day-an-intermittent-history-7093, last retrieved on October 12, 2022
[17] Rivals query R15 legality, in Autosport, April 9, 2009, p. 20
[18] Manuscript of interview with Dr. Wolfgang Ullrich on March 31, 2009
[19] Audi hits out at LMP1 rivals, in Autosport, June 4, 2009, p. 31, and Audi MediaInfo: Audi R15 TDI in the limelight at Le Mans, June 9, 2009
[20] Press release Team Peugeot Total, June 10, 2009
[21] Transcript of interview with Andreas Köppen on October 27, 2022

In his last Le Mans participation for Audi, Marco Werner, following a teammate's accident, does not see the checkered flag

Audi contests the race with the car in its homologated condition. The stewards reject the protest and Peugeot appeals their decision. Despite contrary intentions, the French ultimately drop their request for an appeal and there is no hearing. [22]

Need to catch up at La Sarthe

Following this tug of war, Audi focuses on the setup and tires in qualifying. Tire changes should be avoided because the new regulations only allow two mechanics to use one wheelgun anymore. Pitting time doubles. Capello/Kristensen/McNish simulate four driving stints straight on one set of Michelin tires. The Scot starts the time chase only at the end and has to admit defeat to Peugeot's Stéphane Sarrazin

by 0.762 seconds. Bernhard/Dumas/Premat completely do without a qualifying attempt, drive tire tests, and achieve seventh position on the grid. [23] Luhr/Rockenfeller/Werner secure sixth.

A rude awakening

The beginning of the Race Saturday is hectic. In the warm-up session, Tom Kristensen drives through the gravel trap because a cable that has separated in the footwell after a pit stop jams the gas pedal. Marco Werner spins before the start and finish straight due to avoiding a GT2 rival. [24] Yet those are rather minor concerns. "Our three cars are suffering from inexplicable understeer for which we find no solution," Dindo Capello tells the French sports paper L'Équipe. [25]

Timo Bernhard and his teammates lose a lot of time due to an early defect

Peugeot vs. Audi – in the third year of the duel, the lion brand wins for the first time (above).
Presenter Bruno Vandestick, here with Romain Dumas, is the voice of the Le Mans 24 Hours.
The drivers call him Bruno "Fantastique" (right)

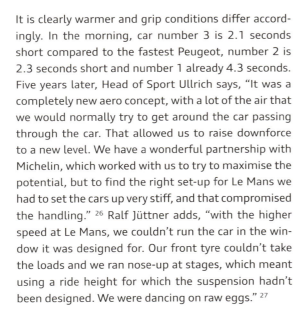

It is clearly warmer and grip conditions differ accordingly. In the morning, car number 3 is 2.1 seconds short compared to the fastest Peugeot, number 2 is 2.3 seconds short and number 1 already 4.3 seconds. Five years later, Head of Sport Ullrich says, "It was a completely new aero concept, with a lot of the air that we would normally try to get around the car passing through the car. That allowed us to raise downforce to a new level. We have a wonderful partnership with Michelin, which worked with us to try to maximise the potential, but to find the right set-up for Le Mans we had to set the cars up very stiff, and that compromised the handling." [26] Ralf Jüttner adds, "with the higher speed at Le Mans, we couldn't run the car in the window it was designed for. Our front tyre couldn't take the loads and we ran nose-up at stages, which meant using a ride height for which the suspension hadn't been designed. We were dancing on raw eggs." [27]

Today, Wolfgang Ullrich judges the fact that Michelin, as Audi's continually capable partner, struggles with the aero values, like this: "The car had very high aerodynamic efficiency which overtaxed the tires. That is why we had to adjust ground clearance in such a way that we were no longer driving with optimal efficiency. But unfortunately, the car did not work in that window at all. There were communication problems between our people and the ones at Michelin. In our operation at that time, a new man was responsible for this liaison between the aerodynamics depart-

ment and Michelin. And they didn't communicate well with each other. They did the development with values that were different from those that our car was capable of. That wasn't so noticeable at Sebring, because you need to drive differently there anyway." [28]

By the second hour of racing Audi cars number 1 and 2 are already 1.56 and 2.03 minutes behind the leading Peugeot. Four hours into the race, two French coupés have even gained more than one lap. On Saturday night, shortly before 7 pm, Audi installs hoods with higher downforce for rainy weather despite dry conditions. "Our car was very good after the changes," says Tom Kristensen. [29] Then Audi experiences what happened to Peugeot the year before:

[22] Gary Watkins: Peugeot: no plan to drop protest, in Autosport June 18, 2009, p. 26, and Christian Borel, Mario Luini, Gérard Vallat, Benoît Wyder, Jean-Marie Wyder: Les Suisses au Mans 2009, Couvet: turbo éditions, 2009, p. 24, and transcript of interview with Andreas Köppen on October 27, 2022
[23] Audi MediaInfo: Audi R15 TDI on front row for Le Mans début, June 11, 2009
[24] Audi MediaInfo: Audi names start drivers for Le Mans, June 13, 2009
[25] Carole Capitaine: Audi découvre l'échec, in L'Équipe, June 15, 2009, p. 23
[26] Simon Taylor: Lunch with Dr. Wolfgang Ullrich, in Motor Sport, June 2014, p. 91
[27] Motor Sport, July 2013, p. 86
[28] Transcript of interview with Dr. Wolfgang Ullrich on December 7, 2022
[29] Audi MediaInfo: Audi on the podium again at Le Mans, June 14, 2009

dirt clogs the intercoolers. [30] Audi Sport Team Joest has to repeatedly clear them using a high-pressure cleaner, and the engine engineers must reduce power due to rising charge air temperatures. [31] Audi learns from that, redesigns the car for 2010 and tests also on deliberately dirtied tracks.

When six and a half hours into the race Lucas Luhr loses his car on a bump in the fast Porsche Corners and crashes backwards into the barrier, his race is over. His teammate Marco Werner comes to his defense: "I can't blame Lucas because the car was really difficult to drive." [32]

On car number 3, the power steering system fails after nine minutes, and Alexandre Premat has an off-track excursion. Changing the unit takes only three minutes. Five hours into the race a high-pressure diesel pump disables the left cylinder bank. "That was a failure that has never occurred before," says a surprised engine engineer Timo Witt. "The CP4 injection pumps sat on the front side of the engine and the shaft had sheared off on one of them." [33] After a loss of 2:17 hours, the car eventually finishes in 17th position.

Erwin Gassner from Mega-Line has supported Audi's Le Mans project from the beginning and supplies the pneumatic gearshift, among other things (above).
Tom Kristensen's fan community grows once more following last year's victory (below)

With fast lap times, Capello, Kristensen and McNish exert pressure again up until Sunday noon even though they are one lap behind. However, during the 21st hour of racing the replacement of an electrical component and changing the right rear suspension costs them four laps. [34] As a result, they clinch third position behind the Peugeot cars of David Brabham/Marc Gené/Alexander Wurz and Sébastien Bourdais/Franck Montagny/Stéphane Sarrazin. For Brabham, it is a nice chapter of family history: Jack, his father, and a three-time Formula One World Champion, in 1967 wins the only French GP ever held on Circuit Bugatti and Geoff, his older brother, wins the 24-hour race in 1993 – with Peugeot. [35]

Bitten by the lion

The lion brand wins thanks to better preparation. As early as in March at Sebring, attentive observers discover that "The Peugeot Sport looked a more coherent, well-drilled team than ever before. Most important – or of most concern for its German

Misleading impression: Audi's weekend is shaped by stress and hard work rather than by rural idyll and relaxation

rival – was a new air of serenity in the Peugeot camp." [36] In addition, the leadership of the racing department issues a team order on which Bruno Famin comments: "At 4:00 AM, we asked the n° 8 908 to slow down [...]. We were well aware of the kind of problems that the Audi R15s were encountering, as we have experienced them ourselves in 2008. From then on, it would have been suicidal to let two of our cars compete against each other at the front even if all our indicators clearly showed that the n° 8 was faster than the n° 9 car." [37] The brand advertises its victory with a tongue-in-cheek statement: "The Peugeot 908 HDi FAP has won the 24hrs of Le Mans thanks to PTW* technology." PTW stands for: * Peugeot Team Work. [38]

Following its departure from the American Le Mans Series, only the Petit Le Mans race remains on Audi's calendar. The R15 TDI leads the event at Road Atlanta for 167 laps but heavy rain forces the race to be stopped. The prototypes – including the two Audi

cars – spin off track even behind the safety car. In the end, Dindo Capello/Allan McNish finish in third position in front of Lucas Luhr/Marco Werner. Winning the Michelin GreenX Challenge efficiency classification remains cold comfort. [39]

Team Principal Ralf Jüttner in conversation with Allan McNish

[30] Gary Watkins: Audi takes the rains, in Autosport, June 18, 2008, p. 44
[31] Audi MediaInfo: Audi on the podium again at Le Mans, June 14, 2009
[32] Gary Watkins: Third-time plucky for Peugeot, in Autosport, June 18, 2009, p. 38
[33] Transcript of interview with Timo Witt on October 27, 2022
[34] Audi MediaInfo: Audi on the podium again at Le Mans, June 14, 2009
[35] Stéphane Barbé: Peugeot a dompté Le Mans, in L'Équipe, June 15, 2009, p. 20
[36] Gary Watkins: New car means old tricks for Audi, in Autosport, March 26, 2009, p. 65
[37] Jean-Marc Teissedre: The Quest for Le Mans, Paris EPA Publishing, 2009, p. 137
[38] Autosport June 18, 2009, p. 42
[39] Audi MediaInfo: Audi R15 TDI wins efficiency trophy in the U.S., September 27, 2009

The scores are tallied at the end

Much of 2010 looks like it is going to see another Peugeot victory, but then Audi drivers Timo Bernhard, Romain Dumas and Mike Rockenfeller end up winning – setting a distance and speed record in the process.

Record run: Mike Rockenfeller
in the victorious Audi R15 plus

Dindo Capello and Allan McNish clinch victory when the Audi R15 plus debuts at Paul Ricard in mid-April (above).
Marcel Fässler, Benoît Tréluyer and André Lotterer form a driver team for the first time in 2010 (above, right)

In 1971, Helmut Marko and Gijs van Lennep in a Porsche 917 set a distance record deemed to be unbeatable

Flashback to 1971. Porsche competes for the third time at Le Mans with the 917, the car with which the brand scored its first overall victory at La Sarthe the year before. Now, Gijs van Lennep and Helmut Marko in the 630-hp 917 clinch the second win across a distance of 5,335.313 kilometers – more than any other winners ever have. The average speed during their triumphant drive: 222.304 km/h, which sets another record. When these records are still valid in 1990, and two chicanes defuse the 5.8-kilometer Hunaudières straight [1] – on which 400 km/h are still possible in 1989 – only few people believe that Porsche's record will ever be broken. In line with that belief, the authors of a book about the Porsche 917, in 2006, write that those were "records for eternity, which – due to the subsequent modification of the track – are still valid today and likely to remain so forever." [2] However, being broken is in the nature of records, and that is what Audi does 39 years after Porsche's victory.

Audi signs new driver trio

The driver lineup in 2010 clearly differs from the one in the previous year. While Dindo Capello, Tom Kristensen and Allan McNish celebrate their fifth joint race at La Sarthe, Marcel Fässler, André Lotterer and Benoît Tréluyer are new to the squad. In 2008, Fässler contested initial Audi LMP1 races in the ALMS and is now signed as a regular driver. Lotterer, a former F1 test driver and two-time champion in the Japanese Super GT series, joins the four rings based on a recommendation by Jo Hausner following his strong debut in the Kolles Audi R10 TDI. [3] Tréluyer, as well, has been most recently active in Japan, having won several titles there. Of all cars, the five-time Le Mans contender in 2009 drove a Peugeot, but had a serious accident in the race. "In view of our strong competitors, we want to – and have to – be perfectly positioned in terms of drivers too," says Wolfgang Ullrich. "Therefore, we decided to extend our driver line-up." [4] In the third R15, entered by Audi Sport North America, Mike Rockenfeller complements Porsche factory drivers Timo Bernhard and Romain Dumas. Audi Sport employees such as race engineer Dominic Zeidtler and chief mechanic Michael Strehler are predominantly assigned to that car.

Once again, Audi reels off an extensive test program. In January, at Sebring, the brand based in Ingolstadt tests an interim version of the R15, and the Audi R15 plus does initial laps on March 3, in Neustadt, followed by aerodynamics testing in Homestead, before a five-day endurance run is coming up at Sebring. [5] A participation in the 12-hour race there is not on the agenda: because the ACO adopts the regulations for 2010 at a late stage and the development of the R15 plus has not been completed, there is no time for a racing commitment. A request for competing with the 2009 R15 is vetoed by Peugeot. [6]

Lions, F1 champions and underdogs

In 2010, the brand with the lion logo competes again with the 908 HDi FAP, which Peugeot updates once more in many areas. They include a modified front diffusor, updated wheel well vents and a new engine cover, among other things. The power plant is modified as well. Like the Audi engine, the turbo-

[1] https://assets.lemans.org/explorer/pdf/courses/2018/24-heures-du-mans/press-kit/uk/statistiques-historiques-en.pdf, last retrieved on February 8, 2023
[2] Jörg Thomas Födisch, Jost Nesshöver, Rainer Rossbach, Harold Schwarz: Porsche 917: Die Helden, die Sieger, der Mythos, Cologne: Verlag Reinhard Klein, 2006, p. 129
[3] Transcript of interview with Dr. Wolfgang Ullrich on December 8, 2022
[4] Audi MediaInfo: New driver trio for the Audi R15 TDI, January 28, 2010
[5] Audi MediaInfo: Audi R15 plus on front row on its début, April 10, 2010
[6] Audi Motorsport Communications Q&A, March 11, 2010

Clearly an evolution

For the 2010 season, the Audi R15 TDI has "plus" added to its name, a suffix which has previously been used only with DTM race cars. The original two-year plan does not provide for a major evolution because a new race car with a roof – the R18 – is in the making for the 2011 season. "However, the changes to the regulations from 2009 to 2010 no longer permitted our aerodynamics," legal counsel Andreas Köppen recalls. [7] The late change in regulations effective November 2009 forces Audi Sport to completely modify the front section, resulting in the distinctive split nose. In addition, the aerodynamicists improve many of the R15's body sections. All the work is focused on efficiency. The diameter of the engine's air restrictors must be reduced by two percent from 37.9 to 37.5 millimeters and boost pressure even by 5.8 percent from 2.75 to 2.59 bar. Even so, following a lot of detailed work, the engine developers continue to report power output of more than 440 kW (598 hp). The cooling and fuel tank systems are subjected to an optimization process as well. "There were about 20 important points on our specification sheet," says Technical Director Martin Mühlmeier. [8]

[7] Transcript of interview with Andreas Köppen, October 27, 2022
[8] Audi Motorsport Communications: Booklet Audi R15 TDI 2010, p. 12

The "plus" version on the right is readily recognizable as an R15 but differs in many details

Every year, thousands of Danish fans set up their tents in the so-called Danish camp

diesel unit must now make do with 2.59 bar of boost pressure. The restrictor size decreases to a diameter of 37.8 millimeters but is still 0.3 millimeters larger than that of the R15 – an advantage that the regulations grant to closed prototypes. In collaboration with lubricant manufacturer Total, the French reduce the internal friction of their engine and optimize the volumetric efficiency in the intake and exhaust system. [9] As an additional measure, the engines receive lighter-weight titanium instead of steel con rods. Peugeot reports 700 horsepower and torque of 1,200 newton meters. [10] The drivers are impressed by the update as Nicolas Minassian relates: "We were doing an endurance test at Paul Ricard, and it gained us 10 kph on the straight. A huge amount. At Ricard we did more than 30 hours with the engine – no problem." [11] Even so, Peugeot wants to play it safe and fit only two cars with new components, but that option ceases to exist following problems with a supplier and on the engine dyno. [12] This time, a 908 of the Oreca team complements the three race cars entered by Peugeot Sport. The driver squad sees changes as well. Since rallying ace Sébastien

Loeb declines, Peugeot signs ex-F1 driver Anthony Davidson, who shares a car with last year's winners Marc Gené and Alexander Wurz. [13] Nicolas Minassian supports Franck Montagny and Stéphane Sarrazin, and Pedro Lamy, Sébastien Bourdais and Simon Pagenaud share the third 908. Loïc Duval, Olivier Panis and Nicolas Lapierre sit in the Oreca 908. The team's second car is the 01 it has constructed itself. In the end, in fourth overall, it is the best gasoline-powered car at Le Mans.

Lola provides the largest lineup in the LMP1 field, with two Lola-Aston Martin cars spearheading the septet. The Prodrive factory team clinches sixth position. The privateer car from Signature Plus does not figure prominently in the race. Rebellion Racing debuts with two Lola Judd cars. Former UK Minister Lord Paul Drayson relies on former Audi factory driver Emanuele Pirro in his Lola Judd. An obsolete Spider from Team Autocon completes the Lola lineup.

Nigel Mansell's Le Mans debut causes a sensation. The 1992 F1 World Champion shares a Ginetta-Zytek with his sons Leo and Greg. But the Brit's appearance is brief: on lap five, he slips off the track due to a puncture. The Kolles team completes the LMP1 field with two Audi R10 TDI cars.

Tom Kristensen, pictured with Allan McNish, and his teammates regularly stop by to see them at the marquee

Season opener on the Mediterranean coast

Unlike Audi, Peugeot competes in the 12-hour race at Sebring and scores a one-two win. The updated Audi celebrates its first outing in a race on April 11, at Paul Ricard. Capello and McNish drive the R15. The outing is victorious. Following a 30-hour test at the same venue, Audi meets with Peugeot for the first time at the beginning of May, at Spa. The "dress rehearsal," though, does not take place under identical prerequisites. While Peugeot contests the event using sprint aerodynamics and has an advantage due to higher downforce, Audi already uses the aeropack for Le Mans. Even so, the two manufacturers are on an equal footing for a long time. However, when rain sets in and Audi makes a wrong tire choice, Peugeot goes on to claim a one-two victory. Capello/Kristensen/McNish have to settle for third position, followed by Bernhard/

Dumas/Rockenfeller in fourth. Following a slip, twelfth place is the best result that the third R15 of Fässler/Lotterer/Tréluyer can achieve.

Peugeot fast, Audi reliable

Initially, the race weekend at Le Mans is dominated by Peugeot. Following the three qualifying sessions of more than six hours in total, Sébastien Bourdais is the front runner. His best time of 3m19.711s shows what strides Peugeot has made: He beats last year's pole by 3.1 seconds. The other 908 cars take the subsequent positions. Due to the dominance of the

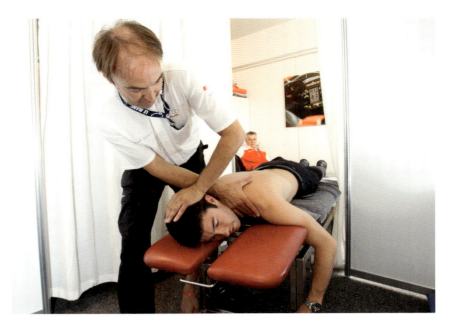

From 1983 to 2014 the well-being of Audi's drivers, not only at Le Mans, is in the hands of team physician Christian John

[9] Peugeot press kit: Peugeot 908 HDi FAP, February 22, 2010
[10] Ibid
[11] Damien Smith: Audi vs. Peugeot: Inside the duel, in Motor Sport 10/2012, p. 106 et seq
[12] Gary Watkins: Close, but one cigar, in Racer, October/November 2022, p. 55
[13] Peugeot press kit: Peugeot 908 HDi FAP, February 22, 2010

Following an evasive maneuver while lapping a GT2 BMW, Dindo Capello, Tom Kristensen and Allan McNish lose their chances of victory

Runners-up: Marcel Fässler, André Lotterer and Benoît Tréluyer (pictured) clinch a spot on the podium in their first Le Mans race with Audi

Over the years, Stefan Grimm, chief mechanic of car number 7, together with his crew, develops many practical ideas for improving the pit stops

opposition, Audi chooses not to battle for the fastest time. Mike Rockenfeller, clocked with a best time of 3m21.981s as Audi's quickest driver, takes fifth, beating Audi's best lap time in 2009 by 1.7 seconds. Allan McNish and Marcel Fässler follow in positions six and seven.

When the 24-hour chase begins on Saturday, no one suspects that it will end in an Audi one-two-three triumph. The four Peugeot are up to two seconds faster per lap than Audi and defend their positions at the front of the field. "The name of the duel at Le Mans in 2010 was absolute reliability vs. absolute performance. Peugeot – that is the learning from the race – went to the limits and beyond to produce their awesome speed. That was possible only because the engineers squeezed a car with a five-year-old basic concept like a lemon. Audi made a leap forward in terms of performance compared to 2009 with the new R15 TDI plus, but without compromising reliability." [14]

Reliability soon becomes an issue for Peugeot: Two-and-a-half hours into the race Pedro Lamy has to park the car that started from pole position when a front wishbone breaks and damages the monocoque. After the first quarter of the race, the remaining 908 cars defend the top three spots, followed by the Audi cars of Bernhard/Dumas/Rockenfeller and Fässler/Lotterer/Tréluyer. At that time, the R15 of Capello/Kristensen/McNish has already lost several minutes because the Dane has to avoid a GT2 BMW and damages his car in the process. After six hours, car number 7 is running in seventh position. Shortly before 11 pm, Peugeot suffers the next setback. The leading 908 of Davidson/Gené/Wurz loses three laps due to a defective alternator. The Audi cars advance to positions three, four and six. At the race's midpoint, Minassian/Montagny/Sarrazin are clearly leading but the R15 are alreading following in two, three and four because misfortune strikes another "lion," the Oreca 908 that has to pit for a repair of the drive shaft.

To finish first,
you first have to finish

During the night the Peugeot cars continue to reel off clearly faster lap times. "We can do 3m33s, but a 22 is not a 20. They are playing with us" says a frustrated Romain Dumas. [15] But then the tide turns: shortly after seven on Sunday morning, the dream of victory ends for the next Peugeot. With an advan-

tage of nearly two laps, Minassian coasts to a stop with engine failure. It will not be the last because in an unparalleled series of mishaps, the powerplants of the two remaining 908 fail as well.

A record run

That clears the way for Audi to claim a sensational triumph. Bernhard/Dumas/Rockenfeller take the top spot and will maintain it up to the finish. Except for a slow puncture and loss of a right-hand outside mirror – a member of the media had stood in the car's way in the pit lane – the trio has a trouble-free race, skillfully leveraging its own fortes: "Our strength was that, unlike the year before, we no longer had any teething problems. The R15 plus was technically sorted and running like clockwork. We were able to push full force with all three cars in the race right from the beginning – and so drove the Peugeot cars to their doom," says Mike Rockenfeller in summing up the event after his first victory. [16] It is a very special

[14] Andrew Cotton and Marcus Schurig: Hätte, wäre, wenn, in sport auto, July 2010, p. 127
[15] Gary Watkins: Audis waltz as Peugeot wilt, in Autosport, June 17, 2010, p. 42
[16] Thomas Voigt: Rocky der Rennfahrer, Hamburg: Adrenalin Verlag 2014, p. 124

The Peugeot cars drop out of the race with engine failure one by one – pictured here is Franck Montagny (left).
Audi's pit crew is watching the three R15 with bated breath (above)

The Audi R15 cars score a surprise one-two-three win (left).
The nine Audi drivers celebrate their sensational triumph on the podium together with Wolfgang Ullrich (red suit, below left)

win because those who clinch it succeed in achieving what has been thought to be impossible. They set a new distance record of 5,405.472 kilometers. A winners' average of 225.228 km/h makes the 78th edition the fastest one in history. The Audi cars of Fässler/Lotterer/Tréluyer and Capello/Kristensen/McNish in second and third positions break Porsche's 1971 record as well. The new record has remained unbeaten up until the publication of this book in spring of 2023. With its fourth one-two-three win after 2000, 2002 and 2004, Audi, with nine Le Mans victories, closes the gap to Ferrari. Ullrich explains the result like this: "From the outset we planned our strategy to do as long stints as possible and we used every opportunity that was offered with efficiency and reliability to achieve our goal." [17]

Peugeot on the other hand is devastated. Bruno Famin puts it in a nutshell: "That is not acceptable," [18] and immediately starts an analysis of the defective engines. At the beginning of July, Peugeot announces the results. "The track benefited from high levels of grip this year, so the engines spent longer at full throttle than we expected", explains the technician. "At the same time, the weather stayed cool and, unlike previous years, the air/air intercoolers did not become clogged up. The filling of the combustion chambers remained extremely efficient throughout, which in turn meant that the performance delivered by the engines was particularly high. Okay, the conditions were the same for all competitors, but we were running new conrods this year. That said, they

[17] Audi MediaInfo: Quotes after the race at Le Mans, June 13, 2010
[18] Carole Capitaine: Ce n'est pas acceptable, in L'Equipe, June 14, 2010, p. 3

Get-together at the Audi team hospitality: Allan and Kelly McNish with Julia and Alexander Wurz (left), Ralf and Sigrun Jüttner with Bruno Famin and Pedro Lamy (center). This tradition continues later, here in 2014 with Wolfgang Ullrich, Filipe Albuquerque, Timo Bernhard, Kyle Wilson-Clarke, Oliver Jarvis and Mark Webber (right)

Competition in style

A friendly handshake in the pit lane or on the podium is customary among racers. The way Audi and Peugeot have been meeting since 2007 is altogether different. "I spontaneously told Peugeot's Technical Director Bruno Famin at the podium ceremony that we'd be incredibly happy if he and his team subsequently joined us for our party," Wolfgang Ullrich recalls. "I'll never forget that while I was delivering my thank you speech I saw the door opening and some Peugeot mechanics walking in. I spontaneously said, "I think it's great that you're actually coming to our party now, and you've done a superb job. And all the 'Audians' got up and gave the Peugeot guys a round of applause. And they were so taken with that atmosphere that after half an hour the whole team joined us. It turned into an incredibly great joint celebration." [19] Bruno Famin adds, "The principle was for the winning team to receive their rivals at its facilities on Sunday night. Even though it, no doubt, takes an effort to go see the opponent that has just defeated you, it's an effort you don't regret because the reception you receive is so warm and appreciative. And seeing how the Audi team moved into the Peugeot hospitality in 2009 [...], leaves me with a memory that's almost as strong as the one of having stood on the podium with the big trophy." [20] That

tradition is retained even after Peugeot's withdrawal as the picture showing the Porsche visitors at Audi in 2014 illustrates.

[19] Transcript of Interview with Dr. Wolfgang Ullrich on December 7, 2022
[20] Bruno Famin: Sportivité, in L'Équipe, June 18, 2012, p. 3

The Head of Audi Sport during the traditional thank you speech in front of his team and in the presence of Peugeot employees Pascal Dimitri and Bruno Famin

LMP1 meets GT3: Tom Kristensen and Allan McNish also meet with the Audi R8 LMS at the ILMC finale at Zhuhai

had undergone thorough testing [...]. We didn't observe the slightest problem with them during any of these test sessions, so there was nothing to suggest that we were closer to the limit than we had imagined." [21] Nicolas Minassian later admits that this operation at the limit is often a high-wire act at Peugeot: "I wouldn't criticize the Peugeot programme. For a driver, it was great. To work with the engineers and the way they pushed for performance, it was like Formula 1. But I would say that for Le Mans it wasn't the right way to do it, because the team won only once in five years. Still, the car was always the fastest." [22]

The people at Audi have yet another theory: "At Le Mans, the ambient air pressure was always a few hundred millibar higher than on the engine dyno in Germany," relates engines engineer Timo Witt. "In 2010, the ambient air pressure was even particularly high, which resulted in significant additional output of definitely more than 100 horsepower. With skill and after many discussions, we adjusted the engine's track application to that. Our assumption was that Peugeot may not have pursued that issue to quite the same extent and so presented a poorer

picture." [23] Legal counsel Andreas Köppen adds that the track is partly given new asphalt shortly before the race. This increases the proportion of full load and the stresses compared to test bench runs. [24]

Three ILMC events

After Le Mans, three other events with the R15 plus are on Audi's agenda. The races at Silverstone, Road Atlanta and Zhuhai are all part of the new Intercontinental Le Mans Cup (ILMC), a racing series that the ACO introduces in December 2009. [25] It adopts the technical regulations of the world's most important sports car race and is intended to serve as the starting base of an Endurance World Cup. [26] In addition to Audi, Peugeot enters the series as well. To be better prepared for the slower ILMC tracks, the R15 cars receive an aeropack with more downforce. However, victories and titles go to Peugeot. There is one more – final – appearance in store for the R15: In the ILMC opener at Sebring in 2011, Audi does not yet field the new R18 TDI but relies on the fully developed predecessor. However, the R15 cars have to settle for positions four and five in their farewell race.

Men in the background: Siegfried Krause (Partnerships), Klaus Wendel (Test and race organization), Andreas Köppen (Legal Affairs) and Elmar Adler (Partnerships)

[21] Peugeot press release: Technical report, and looking forward to the future after the 2010 Le Mans 24 Hours, July 5, 2010
[22] Damien Smith: Audi vs. Peugeot: Inside the duel, in Motor Sport 10/2012, p. 107
[23] Transcript of interview with Timo Witt on October 27, 2022
[24] Transcript of interview with Andreas Köppen on October 27, 2022
[25] ACO press release: The ACO launches the 2010 Le Mans Intercontinental Cup, December 8, 2009
[26] www.24h-lemans.com/en/news/aco-press-conference-ilmc-2010-626, last retrieved on September 27, 2022

For eternity

Alain Loqx (left) and Bernard Warain (right) take winner Timo Bernhard's handprint directly after the race

A special tradition was started at Le Mans in 1991: Since then, the handprints of the winners cast into bronze plaques have been placed in the pavement in the center of the French city – including those of the 15 Audi drivers that won the race between 2000 and 2014. Bernard Warain and Alain Loxq, the owners of a small metalworking factory, had the idea of establishing this unique Walk of Fame. "We wanted to create something that would last, for the people in Le Mans, who identify so much with this race. But of course also to offer an attraction to the many tourists and motorsport fans visiting Le Mans," explains Warain. [27] Immediately following the podium ceremony, amidst all the excitement of celebrating the race winners, they take the winners' handprints in plaster from which a metal mold is created as the basis for casting the 72 by 72 centimeter bronze plaques weighing around 90 kilograms that can be admired on and around Place Saint-Nicolas. The completely handmade plaques are officially unveiled the following year in the presence of the protagonists. "Being honored as the winner of this great race in this way is truly special. A really nice tradition," says five-time Le Mans winner Frank Biela. [28]

[27] Thomas Arndt: Für immer Sieger, in revvv 01. Mythos Le Mans, 2014, p. 235 f.
[28] Ibid

A memorial in the city center of Le Mans explains the idea of the handprints (left). Timo Bernhard, Romain Dumas and Mike Rockenfeller at the unveiling of their bronze plaque before the 2011 edition of the 24-hour race (center, from left). Wolfgang Ullrich also receives such recognition for his successes (right)

Against all odds

While 2011 sees two of the new Audi R18 TDI not finishing the race at Le Mans due to spectacular accidents Marcel Fässler, André Lotterer and Benoît Tréluyer in the number 2 Audi prevail against four Peugeot cars.

The last hours of racing reflect a magnified image of all the stress. Four Peugeot are chasing the only remaining Audi. A misunderstanding makes the situation even more precarious. When race engineer Leena Gade radioes the pure gap in ascending numbers her driver interprets it as a deficit and ups the ante, realizing that he is leading the race only a while later. [1] However, an advantage of 1m21s over Simon Pagenaud does not amount to much when the left rear tire starts losing air shortly after the pit stop at 2.05 pm, causing Wolfgang Ullrich, Ralf Jüttner and Jo Hausner to rack their brains: if the car pits immediately there won't be enough fuel to finish. If you wait the threat of a tire blowout with a crash and damage looms. Tom Kristensen recommends changing all four tires. [2] Lotterer does two more laps with decreasing inflation pressure. Almost at the same time, Pagenaud pits for refueling without changing tires. Audi's stop takes 68.5 seconds, its rival's 54.6 seconds. Lotterer remains in front with 6.4 seconds. [3] In the end, Audi wins with an advantage of 13.854 seconds. The race at Le Mans has seen a closer finish only on three other occasions.

[1] Transcript of interview with Leena Gade on December 13, 2022
[2] Transcript of interview with Tom Kristensen on December 6, 2022. Changing four tires takes longer than changing the defective tire, but Kristensen is convinced that this disadvantage can be more than just compensated for. Events will prove him right.
[3] http://fiawec.alkamelsystems.com/Results/01_2011/02_LE%20MANS/27_24%20HEURES%20DU%20MANS/201106111500_Race/27_Hour%2024/19_AnalysisByLap_Race.PDF, last retrieved on September 29, 2022

For the victory celebration, the ACO traditionally opens the gates for the crowd, creating a unique atmosphere

All-new technology

The name R18 replaces the previously used consecutive numbering by a dedicated model name across vehicle generations – just like in the case of production cars. A V6 TDI engine with merely 3.7 liters of displacement powers the R18 TDI, which is a coupé. There is a correlation between the engine and the bodystyle: due to the forced displacement reduction by one third, power output significantly decreases, and other factors, such as the coupé's better aerodynamics, gain importance in terms of overall performance. As an additional aspect, the advantage of faster driver changes with open-top cars has been lost ever since the regulations started limiting the number of mechanics to two in 2009, resulting in longer tire changes. [4]

Audi relies on a single-piece monocoque instead of the usual multi-sectional manufacturing and joining methods, enabling better stiffness and strength. [5] The CFRP content in the transmission housing increases and an electric gearshift replaces the pneumatic system. Plus, thanks to effective venting, Audi complies with the permissible cockpit temperatures even without an air conditioning system. The coupé uses AUDI AG's new climatic wind tunnel with wind speeds of up to 300 kilometers per hour in the range of minus 25 to plus 55 degrees centigrade. The tests are focused on the interior venting, the windshield and the windshield wiper of the R18. [6]

Audi ultra lightweight technology is a new feature. The term initially pools the brand's lightweight engineering expertise. [7] Subsequently, it will stand for "consistent sustainability in manufacturing and with the cars." [8] While motorsport pioneers the promotion of this theme Audi does not launch the same idea for its products until the International Motor Show (IAA). [9] The outside world has not yet fully understood why of all cars an LMP1 model with its small V6 engine has been trimmed for lightweight design, even though the objective is by no means a secret. Concerning the introduction of hybrid powertrains in 2012 then Chief Technology Officer Michael Dick officially comments as early as in 2011, "We are working on it, but as is the case everywhere in racing we'll only compete with hybrid power when it proves to be a more efficient concept than a conventional powertrain." [10]

From the first to the second evolution the delicately crafted bodywork loses 40 kilograms in weight, which calls for cautious handling. [11] The engine weighs about 25 percent less than the 440-kW (598-hp) V10 TDI. [12] Its power output drops by 9.7 percent to 397 kW (540 hp). To lower the center of gravity and to enhance airflow through the car, the exhaust manifolds are located between the cylinder banks. Audi combines this arrangement ("hot side inside") known from Formula One with a single turbocharger fed by a dual mass flow. On the turbine

[4] The authors owe the reference to this factor in the concept decision, which the contemporary MediaInfo releases do not emphasize, to two contemporary witnesses: Transcripts of interviews with Andreas Köppen on October 27, 2022 and Dr. Wolfgang Ullrich on December 7, 2022

[5] Trackstar – Das Audi-Motorsportmagazin: Saison 2015 Highlights, p. 39

[6] Audi MediaInfo Magazin: Motorsport and Production, 2011, p. 36

[7] Ibid, p. 20, and Audi MediaInfo: Audi relying on ultra lightweight technology for Le Mans, April 21, 2011

[8] www.audi-mediacenter.com/de/audi-im-ueberblick-3682/ausblicke-auf-die-zukunft-die-neuen-audi-modelle-2015-3685, last retrieved on September 28, 2022

[9] Leichtbau – Die Audi Kernkompetenz, internal paper, department I/VS-21, 2011, p. 30

[10] Audi MediaInfo Magazin: Motorsport and Production, 2011, p. 9

[11] Audi MediaInfo: Audi relying on ultra lightweight technology for Le Mans, April 21, 2011

[12] Ibid

For the first time since the 1999 R8C Audi uses a closed monocoque again

Aerodynamicist Martin
Gerspacher with
the Audi R18 TDI in
AUDI AG's wind tunnel

The step from the open R15 TDI
to the closed R18 TDI marks a
major move (above, right).
The daytime running light of
the headlights symbolizes a "1"
(above, left).
In the climatic wind tunnel, Audi
investigates weather phenomena
affecting cockpit venting, the
windshield and windshield
wiper (left)

side the exhaust gas flows through both manifolds onto a single turbine wheel. The housing around the compressor wheel has been designed accordingly. Only the variable turbine geometry (VTG) enables good responsiveness.

Preliminary work starts in spring of 2009. The basic concept of the V6 is even retained up until the end of the LMP program in 2016. Initially, Audi does not exclude the possibility of using a gasoline engine. [13] About 20 months pass from the beginning of the design stage in August 2009 to the first dyno test in July of 2010 and the first on-track test in October to the unit's racing debut. Audi also investigates

a V8 as used by Peugeot. However, the engine developers led by Ulrich Baretzky prefer the V6 due to advantages in the areas of weight, dimensions and friction losses. The strides that have been made since the beginning of the diesel era in 2006 are impressive: by 2011, due to the regulations, the air mass intake through the restrictors is reduced by 29.5 and displacement by 32.7 percent. However, power output in relation to displacement increases by 23.8 percent. The specific progress achieved is even more significant. The volume of each cylinder increases by 34.5 percent. Using the air mass from 2006 as the base value, it has increased by 41 percent per combustion chamber by 2011. Thanks to

Proud of the new engine generation: Karl Hasenbichler, Michael Grübsch, Thibaut Meunier, Stefan Dreyer, Gerhard Ziegler, Wolfgang Kotauschek, Matthias Condiescu, Friedrich Gabel, Timo Hartmann, Hartmut Diel, Daniel Mack, Manfred Schwarz, Timo Witt, Erwin Fischer, Frank Axthelm, Bernhard Strassburger and Ulrich Baretzky, Head of Engine Development (from left)

the progress made with the combustion technology, with the components and in tribology, output per cylinder has seen a disproportionate growth by 67.5 percent. [14] The 120-degree cylinder bank angle results from the "hot side inside" concept, the lower center of gravity, the location of the ancillaries and the firing order. The cylinder bores are larger than those of the V10 TDI so that the power per unit piston area (or specific power) with the same ignition pressure is about five percent higher. [15]

In terms of light and sight, Audi introduces 16 high-performance light diodes with passive air cooling distributed to both headlights. Tom Kristensen is thrilled: "The light is stronger and vibrates less than a normal headlight. This is a clear advantage and specifically at Le Mans, a track with many dark braking points in the night." [16] The design of the daytime running light in the left headlight features the shape of a "1" like the former Audi logo. For reasons of symmetry, the number is mirrored on the right. [17]

The lightweight bodywork calls for caution – the drivers may support themselves only in the area delimited in yellow (above, left).
The dyno makes the "hot side inside" visible (below).
The V6 is extremely compact and short (above, right).
Dual mass flow on the encapsulated turbine side and respective outlets on the compressor side characterizes the innovative mono-turbocharger with VTG control (below)

[13] Race Tech Magazine Vol 20 Issue 8: Secrets of Le Mans success, June 2013, p. 42
[14] Ibid, p. 44
[15] Ibid, p. 46 et seq
[16] Audi MediaInfo Magazin: Motorsport and Production, 2011, p. 58
[17] Audi MediaInfo: Audi extends motorsport commitment, December 10, 2010.
   Audi used this logo between 1923 and 1940

Same drivers, same main rival

The driver squad with Timo Bernhard, Romain Dumas and Mike Rockenfeller, the trio of Dindo Capello, Tom Kristensen and Allan McNish as well as Marcel Fässler, André Lotterer and Benoît Tréluyer remains unchanged. Marco Bonanomi is the new test and reserve driver.

In the group of 17 LMP1 race cars Peugeot with a new 908 and 3.7-liter V8 turbo diesel engine remains the main rival. Head of Sport Olivier Quesnel continues to rely on Anthony Davidson/Marc Gené/Alex Wurz, Nicolas Minassian/Franck Montagny/Stéphane Sarrazin and Sébastien Bourdais/Pedro Lamy/Simon Pagenaud. In addition, Oreca is fielding an older 5.5-liter model, albeit with smaller restrictors and lower boost pressure as required by the regulations. Aston Martin, together with Pro-

In the lull before the storm Benoît Tréluyer shows daddy's fast company car to his son Jules

In the R18's debut at Spa, Capello/Kristensen/McNish clinch third position after spinning, accidentally activating the pit limiter on track with a 20-second time loss, and a puncture

drive, has put a new car with a straight-six engine on wheels. [18] But the AMR-One proves to be slow and unreliable. At Le Mans, both cars combined manage merely six laps in the race and are more than 20 seconds slower than the front runner. Arguably the fastest new LMP1 model with a gasoline engine is provided by Honda's American subsidiary Acura. In the Sebring 12 Hours, the ARX01-e as the overall runner-up celebrates a strong debut, but Highcroft Racing withdraws its entry 23 days before qualifying starts at Le Mans: the consequences of the earthquake and the tsunami in Japan have led to budget cuts at Honda. [19] The Oreca-SwissHyTech is a novelty. The Swiss Hope Racing team ventures fielding a hybrid powertrain with a flywheel but the car suffers a setback due to teething troubles.

Audi enters the Intercontinental Le Mans Cup (ILMC) that has been expanded from three to seven rounds. At Sebring, the old Peugeot from Oreca, beating the two new Peugeot and the once-again reactivated Audi R15 cars, scores a surprise victory.

Initial strength test

Following a two-year break, Le Mans has reinstated a test day. On April 24, the three new Audi and two of three new Peugeot cars are running within just 0.617 seconds of each other. Tom Kristensen clocks the best time ahead of Mike Rockenfeller. In May, at Spa, the new diesel sports cars meet in the race as well. Peugeot scores a one-two win. The three Audi cars are promising but suffer setbacks due to some minor issues. Capello, Kristensen and McNish achieve third position.

Dramatic 24 hours

249,500 spectators [20] witness a competition that sport auto calls a "Höllen-Rennen" ("race from hell"). [21] In the third qualifying session, Benoît Tréluyer in a race simulation on his 21st lap clinches the top spot on used tires. After the start, Tréluyer and Timo Bernhard slightly break away toward the front. Allan McNish overtakes two Peugeot cars. At 3.51 pm, the Scotsman passes Bernhard on the inside after the Dunlop Bridge and intends to pass the

Aston Martin, Audi and Peugeot on the front row during the photo shoot on test day

lapped Ferrari of Anthony Beltoise as well. Both cars touch. McNish's Audi crashes into the tire walls, rises and drops. There are also many parts that have come off the car but luckily do not hit any photographers or track marshals. The safety cell of the R18 is intact and McNish unharmed. "It was a racing accident," he says later. "No one is to blame. Anthony Beltoise is a very experienced opponent. I understood that he didn't see me coming and that he thought there was only one Audi behind him. [...] I don't think I took a rash risk when I took the inside of the corner. I left enough distance so that the driver [...] had the greatest possible view. It was even safer for me. Timo was ahead of me and ran wide on the outside of the astroturf in the Dunlop chicane. I overtook him on the inside when he came back onto the track under the Dunlop bend. That's when we ran into the Ferrari. Not overtaking him would even have meant

Marco Bonanomi from Italy complements the driver squad as the new test and reserve driver

[18] www.motorsportmagazine.com/archive/article/june-2011/50/le-mans-2011-preview, last retrieved on September 27, 2022

[19] www.autosport.com/wec/news/highcroft-withdraws-from-le-mans-4444931/4444931/, last retrieved on September 27, 2022

[20] Alain Bienvenu, Christian Moity and Jean-Marc Teissedre: Le Mans 24 Hours 2011, Waterloo: Apach, p. 244

[21] Andrew Cotton and Marcus Schurig: Nummer 2 überlebt, in sport auto, 07/2011, p. 118

André Lotterer, Leena Gade, Benoît Tréluyer and Marcel Fässler beaming with pride after pole position on Thursday night

having an accident with Timo [...]" [22] After the clean-up operation, the Audi of Fässler/Tréluyer/Lotterer and the Peugeot of Davidson/Gené/Wurz take turns at the front of the field.

Drama around "Rocky"

Mike Rockenfeller is the fastest driver at night, advancing from fifth to second position. At 10.41 pm, he has an accident. Race engineer Kyle Wilson-Clarke radioes him but receives no response. On the way toward the Indianapolis Corner, the Audi driver is in the process of overtaking the Ferrari of American Le Mans rookie Rob Kauffman on the right. Suddenly, the privateer turns the wheel toward the right, hitting the R18. In his biography, the German recalls: "When you make a ninety-degree turn at more than 300 km/h, there's only the width of the road, the field and the guard rail. It all happened incredibly fast but seemed extremely long to me. The impact was mega hard. I hung on inside the car and screamed in pain when my car hit the guard rail. I kept feeling this awesome force that was acting on me for a very long time. [...] I then got out of the car myself, jumped across the guard rail and lost consciousness. I woke up again when someone was shining a flashlight at my eyes and reported in French that my pupils were reacting. I had pretty strong pains on the back of my neck that was also slightly swollen [...]. The helmet was partially broken at the top." [23] Subsequently, race control excludes crash opponent Kauffman from the remainder of the race. To better prepare inexperienced rookies, the ACO introduces a mandatory session in a race simulator from 2014 on. [24] Looking back, Wolfgang Ullrich reveals that he considered a withdrawal as well: "We massively thought about whether we could have justified continuing the race if something had happened to Mike after all." [25]

The duel intensifies

Fässler/Lotterer/Tréluyer are leading the race with a two-minute advantage over four Peugeot cars. "The complexion of the race changed, paradoxically, as a result of a drop in temperatures. Peugeot hit a pur-

Allan McNish explains his accident in the presence of Audi's PR people Martyn Pass (red jacket) and Jürgen Pippig (white shirt). The audience includes Guido Quirmbach, Andrew Cotton, Gregor Messer, Simon Taylor, Stéphane Barbé and others

ple patch during the night when it swapped to the soft-compound Michelin as planned. On the new tyre and a rubbered-in track surface, the 908 came alive. Audi, on the other hand, struggled with this tyre and quickly went back to the medium." [26] 14 hours into the race, Sébastien Bourdais and Simon Pagenaud are at the front of the field while Fässler drops back to third position. In addition, a rival's oil dirties the windshield. [27] Lotterer takes over and at 7.08 am sets the fastest lap of the race at 3m25.289s, beating pole time by half a second. [28] During another safety car period Audi changes drivers earlier than planned. Shortly before 8 am, Tréluyer has to get into the car directly out of bed: "I had two minutes to get ready. I hadn't eaten anything at night when I went to bed and had no time for breakfast. [...] I knew that I'd be driving a quintuple stint. We had saved that if worst came to worst." [29]

When temperatures rise he fights his way toward the front of the field – in five stints across 54 laps – marking a first for the Michelin tires. The lead

Tom Kristensen and Jerôme Mondain help out with valuable advice during the crucial last pit stop

[22] Stéphane Barbé: On a eu de la chance, in L'Équipe, June 13, 2011, p. 2

[23] Thomas Voigt: Rocky. Der Rennfahrer, Hamburg: Adrenalin Verlag 2014, p. 140 et seq

[24] www.fiawec.com/en/news/le-mans-simulator-training-an-insiders-view/4054, last retrieved on September 27, 2022

[25] Transcript of interview with Dr. Wolfgang Ullrich on December 7, 2022

[26] Gary Watkins: Anguish and Joy for Audi, in Autosport, June 16, 2011, p. 47. Factually, Audi ran on the "Soft-Medium" (W/Q) compound between 3.30 am and 6.37 am during Marcel Fässler's quadruple stint, in Le Mans 2011 Race Statistics (internal Audi Sport source)

[27] Transcript of interview with Marcel Fässler on November 15, 2022

[28] http://fiawec.alkamelsystems.com/Results/01_2011/02_LE%20MANS/27_24%20HEURES%20 DU%20MANS/201106111500_Race/27_Hour%2024/17_FastestLapSequence_Race.PDF, last retrieved on September 29, 2022

[29] Carole Capitaine: Gravé dans ma mémoire, in L'Équipe, June 13, 2011, p. 4. Leena Gade recalls that the team had no prior experience with five stints but trusted Michelin's advice in order to reduce the number of pit stops in the battle with Peugeot. Transcript of interview with Leena Gade on December 13, 2022

Number 1 does not bring good luck to last year's winners Timo Bernhard, Romain Dumas and Mike Rockenfeller

between Audi and Peugeot alternates several times. Sarrazin is handed a one-minute stop-and-go penalty, and runner-up Alexander Wurz subsequently slips into the gravel trap. The four-way battle turns into a duel: the number 2 Audi versus the number 9 Peugeot. But the other Peugeot cars cause plenty of trouble for Audi. Marc Gené even touches the only R18. Wolfgang Ullrich makes it clear to the opponents in their pit perch that he prefers a fair competition. [30] The drivers go to the limits – and beyond. Joest's Team Principal Ralf Jüttner recalls: "In 2011 I also take some credit for victory. Of the 24 hours I subjectively spent 14 with the stewards because there so many violations. In the end, lawyer Andreas Köppen joined me too. While overtaking a Peugeot and a Corvette, Ben Tréluyer went beyond the track limits on the right. We got rid of that allegation because we said that it was the only way to avoid an accident …" [31] Even today, not all three winners

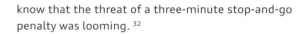

Faces that speak volumes: Olivier Quesnel, Pedro Lamy, Simon Pagenaud, Sébastien Bourdais, Benoît Tréluyer, André Lotterer, Ralf Jüttner, Marcel Fässler, Wolfgang Ullrich, Stéphane Sarrazin, Nicolas Minassian, Jean-Marc Gales, Franck Montagny (from left)

Gold for the winner (above).
A moment of peace and quiet for Timo Bernhard with his wife, Katharina, and his parents (below)

know that the threat of a three-minute stop-and-go penalty was looming. [32]

Chase up until the finish

In the morning, the R18 achieves an advantage of more than one minute even though the fuel tank cannot always be filled fully. At noon, in the rain, Simon Pagenaud narrows the gap to 24 seconds within just three laps. When the track dries off Lotterer breaks away again. The last hour then sees the slow puncture drama. Leena Gade emphasizes that advice from Jérôme Mondain tips the scales. Michelin's endurance racing manager recommends to continue racing and keeping the pace. [33] Looking back, Wolfgang Ullrich points out that "Every stop poses a risk such as engine stall. By changing all four tires we could have also dropped behind Peugeot. That makes overtaking difficult." [34] But in the end, Audi clinches its tenth victory. [35] Autosport comments on it: "There

[30] Transcript of interview with Dr. Wolfgang Ullrich on December 7, 2022

[31] Transcripts of interviews with Ralf Jüttner on November 17, 2022 and Andreas Köppen on October 27, 2022. The scene in detail: www.facebook.com/AudiSport/videos/le-mans-highlight-film-2011/1159178444166796 (10m28s), last retrieved on December 8, 2022

[32] Transcripts of interviews with Andreas Köppen on October 27, 2022 and Marcel Fässler on November 15, 2022

[33] Transcript of interview with Leena Gade on December 13, 2022

[34] Transcript of interview with Dr. Wolfgang Ullrich on December 7, 2022

[35] Despite the close duel, Audi and Peugeot are both around six seconds slower on the last lap than before. After talking to a colleague from Peugeot, Ulrich Baretzky said that both were running on their last drops of fuel. Transcript of interview with Ulrich Baretzky on January 23, 2023

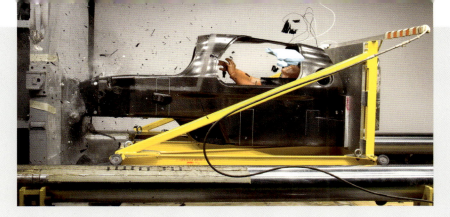

The crash test for the monocoque including the crash nose is one of many tests for the safety cell

Safety

Allan McNish's crash occurs at 180 km/h. [36] The airborne R18 flips around several axes, and the energy dissipates favorably. "Not even a piece of gravel entered the cockpit and both doors could be opened and closed neatly," says designer Axel Löffler. [37] "McNish thanked me for the sturdy cockpit. That was very moving." [38] The safety cell has to absorb clearly more energy in Mike Rockenfeller's accident. That impact occurs at 255 km/h. [39] The monocoque must withstand static test loads designed, for instance, for the rear rollover structure (119 kN) or the sidewalls (30 kN), plus a dynamic frontal impact at 14 meters per second (50 km/h), resulting in a maximum average deceleration of 25 g. The monocoque has to remain intact. Rockenfeller's impact occurs at fivefold speed and deceleration of 20 to 25 g. The front CFRP crash structure degrades the speed by about 40 km/h, and the guard rail by another 40 km/h. [40] The HANS system reduces the strain on the cervical vertebrae.

Three years later, Loïc Duval has an accident in the Porsche Corners. At the time of crashing into the edge of a concrete wall the cockpit absorbs a huge load within a very small area, and parts of the CFRP structure collapse. "A modern monocoque must be able to easily withstand an accident like McNish's," says Löffler. For Rockenfeller and Duval he provides this caveat: "Those are speeds at which enormously high energies must be dissipated [...]. It is the interaction between the safety measures in the race car and the trackside safety measures that save the drivers' lives in high-speed accidents." [41]

Those measures include run-off areas, safety fences, plastic tarps in front of tire walls and the interconnected Tecpro barriers, as well as guard rails, provided they have room to yield. That is not the case in 2013 when Allan Simonsen laterally crashes into the track barriers and dies because there are trees directly behind the steel rails. The ACO responds by moving these guard rails forward, enlarging run-off areas, introducing LED lamps for track lighting, creating new display systems for track marshals, and equipping the Porsche Corners with Tecpro elements. [42]

The limited visibility motivates the ACO to issue new cockpit rules. [43] From 2014 on, the driver's seating position is raised and moved forward. Audi experiments with transparent bodywork and in 2012 introduces a digital rear-view mirror with a camera. Higher test loads require a stiffer cockpit from 2014 on. A zylon layer improves side impact protection against objects, and for the first time a crash box is provided at the rear.

From 2011 on, the tail fin is intended to increase aerodynamic stability to prevent accidents. In 2012, this feature is complemented by openings on the surface of the four fenders. They prevent air from accumulating in the wheel wells at larger yaw angles, reducing lift that is conducive to the car becoming airborne. A skid block installed underneath the underfloor is supposed to reduce aerodynamic sensitivity as well. From 2014 on, wheel tethers that must withstand 80 kilonewtons, are mandatory as well. [44]

Axel Löffler is responsible for the safety concept (above). The HANS system reduces the strain on Mike Rockenfeller's cervical vertebrae by absorbing the centrifugal force from the helmet and head and shifting it toward the shoulder girdle (below)

[36] Trackstar – Das Audi-Motorsportmagazin: Saison 2015 Highlights, p. 38
[37] Ibid
[38] Alexander von Wegner: Fueling success, in Audi's Annual Report 2011, p. 75
[39] Claus Mühlberger: Happy End, in auto motor und sport 17/2011, p. 150
[40] Ibid, p. 149
[41] Trackstar – Das Audi-Motorsportmagazin: Saison 2015 Highlights, p. 38
[42] www.fiawec.com/en/news/24h-du-mans-safety-changes-to-the-track-for-2014/2077, last retrieved on September 29, 2022, and www.lemans.org/fr/news/circuit-des-24-heures-du-mans-le-virage-porsche-securise/48433, last retrieved on September 29, 2022
[43] Head of Audi Sport Wolfgang Ullrich takes the deficit very seriously too and personally sits in the cockpit during a test of the R18 to do a few laps and to assess visibility. Transcript of interview with Dr. Wolfgang Ullrich on December 7, 2022
[44] ACO Press Information: 2014 LM P1 prototype regulations, June 14, 2012

The gaps between Audi and Peugeot resemble those in a sprint race

In high spirits: Following the official celebrations, the team gathers around the trophies and winners at the garage tent on Sunday afternoon

have been closer finishes at the Le Mans 24 Hours, but never has an edition of the French endurance classic been so close for so long." [45] The fact that the lead between Audi and Peugeot changes 46 times underscores that as well. Six-time winner Jacky Ickx even compares this success with 1977 when clinching victory together with Jürgen Barth and Hurley Haywood despite a 15-lap deficit. [46]

Peugeot dominates rest of season

Peugeot celebrates a one-two win in the ILMC at Imola and clinches a dominant win at Silverstone as well where Audi finishes runner-up. At Road Atlanta, Audi suffers a double DNF. In the finale at Zhuhai, Peugeot bids farewell with a one-two win and tests an electrified version of the 908 for 2012. [47] At the beginning of 2012, the R18 TDI races for the last time in the new FIA World Endurance Championship (WEC): at Sebring, Dindo Capello/Tom Kristensen/Allan McNish win in front of Timo Bernhard/Romain Dumas/Loïc Duval. [48]

After podium and press conference, the three winners proudly carry their trophies to the team's garage tent behind the pits (above).
In its last race the Audi R18 TDI clinches a one-two win at Sebring in 2012 (below)

[45] Gary Watkins: Anguish and Joy for Audi, in Autosport, June 16, 2011, p. 46
[46] Michael Schmidt: Jacky Ickx: Es gab nur eine Devise und die hieß Vollgas, in auto motor und sport 20/2011, p. 158 et seq.
[47] Peugeot Sport press release: The 908 HYbrid 4 Takes to the track, October 17, 2011
[48] Audi MediaInfo: Audi one-two victory at FIA World Endurance Championship opener, March 17, 2012

  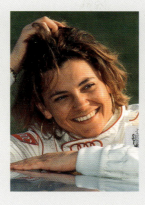   

Michèle Mouton and Fabrizia Pons put the fear of God into their opponents in the World Rally Championship, Tamara Vidali achieves good results in STW racing. Vanina Ickx as well as Katherine Legge and Rahel Frey are Audi's female faces in the DTM (from left)

Women power

In 2011, Leena Gade makes for a premiere. She is the first woman to win Le Mans as a race engineer – a feat she achieves in spite of having been on the verge of giving up her role in the team after two disastrous races at Sebring and at Spa. Instead, she confides in engine engineer Timo Witt, who advises her not to give up. She works with chief mechanic Ronny Reinhardt on communications, practices exchanging parts more frequently and engages in an open dialog with the team. [49] The Briton plays down her own achievements: "Such success for Audi is of course a team effort." [50] The human aspect is important to her: "I am 50 percent engineer and 50 percent psychologist. The drivers trust my decisions and want to be guided. [...]. You have to be very sensitive when dealing with people." [51] After graduating from university, Gade, at age 22, starts working in the automotive industry and switches to motorsport in 2003. In 2007, she assumes her first role at Audi as a data engineer and becomes a race engineer in 2010. "There needs to be more of us," she says. [52] In schools, she inspires girls' enthusiasm for so-called STEM subjects, and in 2013 starts serving as an ambassador of the FIA Women in Motorsport Commission. [53]

Gade is not the first woman to have carved out a career at Audi Sport. In 1982, Michèle Mouton in an Audi quattro with co-driver Fabrizia Pons finishes runner-up and clinches four victories in the World Rally Championship. Subsequently, women race in touring cars with Audi. They include Tamara Vidali in an A4 quattro and, from 2006 on, Vanina Ickx, followed by Katherine Legge and Rahel Frey in the DTM. The latter spends a total of eleven years with Audi, celebrating six GT3 victories worldwide.

[49] www.fia.com/multimedia/publication/auto-women-motor-sport-3, last retrieved on September 29, 2022 and transcript of interview with Leena Gade on December 13, 2022
[50] Transcript of interview with Leena Gade on June 9, 2013
[51] Alexander von Wegner: A woman sets the pace, in Audi Annual Report 2012, p. 46
[52] www.fia.com/news/winning-equal-terms-leena-gade-success-story, last retrieved on September 27, 2022
[53] www.fia.com/news/women-motorsport-ambassador-engineers-victory-le-mans, last retrieved on September 27, 2022

Leena Gade with chief mechanic Ronny Reinhardt after the first victory

Electrified
Vorsprung durch Technik

On June 9, 2011, the FIA announces that, starting in 2012, it will sanction a world championship for sports prototypes again for the first time since the era from 1953 to 1992: the WEC (World Endurance Championship). Audi relies on a hybrid powertrain.

Marcel Fässler, André Lotterer
and Benoît Tréluyer repeat
last year's victory

The WEC makes a long-held dream come true for Wolfgang Ullrich. [1] The FIA and the ACO team up, establishing an endurance racing commission in which members of the ACO hold the majority and whose resolutions the FIA World Council subsequently verifies – a constellation that sport auto views skeptically: A loss in autonomy of the ACO was one aspect, the assumption that FIA President Jean Todt only intended to weaken Bernie Ecclestone's Formula One by means of the WEC before the ACO and FIA went separate ways again, another one. [2] A view, however, that will not prove to be true.

An abyss opens when on January 19, 2012 Peugeot surprisingly announces the end of its LMP program. [3] The ACO issues the following announcement: "It is a big disappointment for the 24 Hours of Le Mans

In FIA President Jean Todt Wolfgang Ullrich finds an official to talk to who promotes a world championship for sports cars

André Lotterer, Benoît Tréluyer, Marcel Fässler, Mike Rockenfeller, Romain Dumas, Tom Kristensen, race engineer Howden Haynes, Marco Bonanomi, race engineer Kyle Wilson-Clarke and Dindo Capello receive emergency instructions from Joest's Team Principal Ralf Jüttner. A kit on board of each R18 contains tools and a cell phone

and the FIA World Endurance Championship, which begins in the year 2012. A competition created at the request of manufacturers in general and in particular Peugeot." [4] Audi's Head of Sport is surprised as well when he learns the news during the traditional teambuilding event with his drivers and Team Principals in Ofterschwang. [5] Behind the scenes, the officials succeed in motivating Toyota to launch a full-fledged program early. [6] At the beginning of February, the Japanese announce that, instead of sporadic entries in preparation for 2013, they are going to contest the full WEC season starting with round two at Spa. [7]

The new rival: Toyota

At that time, Toyota has been the world's largest automobile manufacturer since 2007. [8] That makes the Japanese carmaker the main rival of Martin Winterkorn, the Chairman of the Management Board of Volkswagen AG, who, on January 1, 2007, had announced the goal of bumping Toyota from the top spot. [9] Toyota is deemed to be the pioneer in hybrid technology and since 1997 has sold more than 4 million cars worldwide using this type of drivetrain. [10] In motorsport, the Japanese have experience in a wide variety of disciplines, be it in the World Rally Championship, sports car racing or Formula One. Toyota Motorsport GmbH (TMG) signs Oreca as a team.

The Toyota TS030 uses a 3.4-liter V8 naturally aspirated engine and an electric motor delivering its output to the rear axle as well. While the original plan called for electrically powering the front wheels, Toyota abandons this option when the FIA and the ACO announce the 120-km/h minimum limit. [11]

[1] He had been espousing the idea of a world championship for a long time and, looking back, assesses Jean Todt's stint as FIA President as conducive to realizing it. Transcript of interview with Dr. Wolfgang Ullrich on December 7, 2022

[2] Background information on the new World Endurance Championship in sport auto, July 2011, p. 116

[3] The manufacturer states economic reasons, Peugeot press release: Peugeot 908, January 19, 2012

[4] www.24h-lemans.com/en/news/response-by-the-aco-to-the-news-of-the-cancellation-of-peugeots-endurance-racing-programme-6009, last retrieved on July 15, 2022

[5] Transcript of interview with Dr. Wolfgang Ullrich on December 7, 2022

[6] www.auto-motor-und-sport.de/motorsport/toyota-hybrid-lmp1-toyota-feiert-2012-le-mans-comeback/, last retrieved on July 15, 2022

[7] www.toyota-media.de/blog/unternehmen/artikel/toyota-bestatigt-teilnahme-an-der-fia-langstrecken-wm/text, last retrieved on July 15, 2022

[8] www.welt.de/motor/article830457/Toyota-erstmals-groesster-Autobauer-der-Welt.html, last retrieved on July 15, 2022

[9] Volkswagen Annual Report 2007, p. 14

[10] www.toyota-media.de/blog/technik/artikel/elektrisch-durch-die-boxengasse/text, last retrieved on July 15, 2022

[11] www.24h-lemans.com/en/news/2012-technical-and-sporting-regulations-5410, last retrieved on July 15, 2022

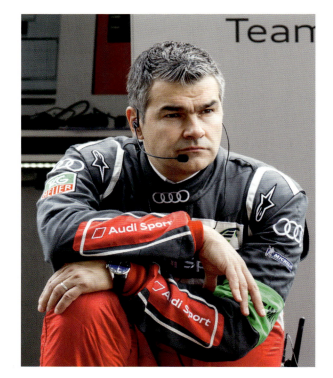

Supercapacitors serve as energy storage systems. With that, Toyota relies on a completely different concept than Audi within the broad scope offered by the LMP1 regulations. A lot of Formula One know-how, including two wind tunnels, is fed into the sports car project. Former Formula One drivers Anthony Davidson, Sébastien Buemi, Stéphane Sarrazin, Alex Wurz and Kazuki Nakajima as well as sports car specialist Nicolas Lapierre are on board as the driver squad.

Privateers in the LMP1 class include the Swiss Rebellion team with two Lola-Toyota cars and the British JRM and Strakka outfits putting the LMP1 prototypes from Honda's subsidiary HPD on the grid. The squad of four-time Le Mans winner Henri Pescarolo competes with proprietary designs and a Japanese Dome chassis but is forced to quit after Le Mans for financial reasons.

Audi with four cars and two concepts

For the first time since 1999 Audi enters four factory-fielded cars at Le Mans. Marcel Fässler/André Lotterer/Benoît Tréluyer and Dindo Capello/Tom Kristensen/Allan McNish drive the hybrid sports cars. For the two ultra models, Timo Bernhard and Romain Dumas receive Frenchman Loïc Duval as a new teammate. When an injury prevents Bernhard from racing after March, Spanish reserve driver Marc Gené, winner of 2009, who switched from Peugeot to Audi, takes his place. Mike Rockenfeller shares a cockpit with Italian Marco Bonanomi, who is promoted from test to race driver. Briton Oliver Jarvis switching from the DTM to the sports car squad completes the trio. The management team changes as well. Dieter Gass, who used to work as an engineer for Audi Sport until 2001, has joined the four rings again following his Formula One stint. He is the new Head of Racing and, from 2012 on, also Head of WEC at Audi Sport. [12]

Dieter Gass returns to Audi (above).
The Audi squad learns about Peugeot's surprise withdrawal at the teambuilding event in Ofterschwang (below)

[12] Audi MediaInfo: Dieter Gass to reinforce Audi
   Sport, December 19, 2011

A twin pack of sophisticated tech

2012 sees the introduction of an electrified powertrain at Audi – a move that the brand has been openly talking about beforehand. "If, in our opinion, this technology is the most efficient we will use it at Le Mans," says Wolfgang Ullrich as early as in 2011 when he presents the R18 TDI.[13] The new project is initially run under the code name R18-X.[14] It starts in February 2010.[15] From 2011 on, the compact V6 TDI engine and ultra-lightweight design create the essential prerequisites for integrating a hybrid system. The tight space and minimum weight of 900 kilograms pose the greatest challenges. The volume of the drinking system for the driver decreasing from 1.2 to 0.5 liters and the gas pedal now being made of CFRP instead of metal are two extreme examples of saving kilos.

Visually akin to its predecessor, the 2012 "RP2" with a modified monocoque is largely new.[16] The cell is longer at the front due to the hybrid system, whereas the front crasher is shorter, which raises the crash testing requirements.[17] Plus, not just one but two models are created: an ultra base model without a hybrid powertrain and the subsequent e-tron quattro version using an electric system. Audi's Head of Sport assesses the project: "To develop the hybrid technology for Le Mans is at least as ambitious and challenging as our diesel project was in its early stages."[18] The differences also include compensation for the changed distribution of weight and the fuel tank that has been reduced by 2 to 58 liters on the hybrid model.

In classic style, a conventional internal combustion engine accelerates the car, converting chemically bound energy into kinetic energy in the process. While braking, this kinetic energy escapes unused as heat. It can be partially recovered and reused only with a hybrid powertrain. Acting in parallel with the hydraulic brake, the motor-generator unit (MGU) produces an additional braking effect by converting the rotational motion of the front wheels into electrical energy like a dynamo. Audi feeds this energy into a flywheel energy storage system with a capacity of up to 500 kilojoules. The current accelerates a carbon ring in the storage system's housing to more than 45,000 revolutions. After cornering, not only

[13] Audi Motorsport Communications: Booklet Audi Sports Prototypes 2011, p. 10
[14] Audi MediaInfo Magazine: Motorsport and Production, 2011, p. 35
[15] Audi MediaInfo: Audi brings the quattro back to the race track, February 29, 2012
[16] Audi Motorsport Communications: Booklet Audi Sports Prototypes 2012, p. 11
[17] Authors' research manuscript dated May 10, 2012
[18] Audi MediaInfo: Audi with hybrid drive at Le Mans for the first time, February 2, 2012. Ten years later, he adds the detail that the ultra marked the first stage in which hybrid drive could be integrated following the decision to adopt electrification. Transcript of interview with Dr. Wolfgang Ullrich on December 7, 2022

On the occasion of quattro all-wheel drive's return to racing, Audi Tradition contributes a rally quattro for a photo shoot

Boost mode

Audi R18 e-tron quattro

Brake recuperation

Audi R18 e-tron quattro

This is how hybrid works: In boost mode, the flywheel energy storage system delivers energy to the front axle (above) and during recuperation in braking phases, it flows back into the storage system in the cockpit (below)

That results in a proposal from Ingolstadt for powering the second axle that the ACO and the FIA welcome. However, following successively are a range of restrictions because Peugeot vehemently opposes this all-wheel drive system. [21] The French continue to exert influence on the regulations up until 2011. Although the brand with the lion logo leaves the LMP stage before electrification commences the negotiated restrictions remain in effect. The recuperated energy is allowed to assist in acceleration again only above 120 km/h. By the same token, a ban is issued on selective distribution of torque to each front wheel using torque vectoring to affect turn-in behavior. At that time, Audi has already integrated two separate electric motors in one housing. In a post-test comment on turn-in agility, Marcel Fässler says, "Well, it handles like a forklift truck." However, in the FIA WEC, the input power of both electric motors must always be identical. The 120 km/h speed limit is not rescinded until 2014.

At that time, the Technical Development division at AUDI AG has already made the parallel hybrid idea with traction force addition a reality – albeit in inverse topology – in a mule based on the Audi A5. An internal combustion engine drives the front axle and a plug-in hybrid system the rear axle. [22] In preparation for its use in the LMP sports car, Audi Sport initially experiments with an Audi R8 GT. [23]

the V6 TDI engine propels the car but the electrical energy flows back from the storage system to the front axle. At that time, the MGU operates as an electric motor with up to 150 kW (204 hp). Both systems complement each other to create the e-tron quattro all-wheel drive system without any mechanical connection, using strictly electronic control strategies. [19]

Le Mans organizer ACO initially proposes a serial configuration of the electric motor and the internal combustion engine. Audi does not consider this serial arrangement to be effective for the intended purpose and analyzes four parallel hybrid system topologies, offering the choice between rotational speed addition, torque addition in a single-shaft or a dual-shaft system plus traction force addition. Narrowed down to the choice between single-shaft torque addition and traction force addition, the engineers ultimately opt for the latter. Audi sees advantages in terms of traction, tire wear and weight distribution. [20]

The Technical Development division at AUDI AG is already working on a parallel hybrid concept using an A5 as a mule

The space for the MGU in the silver-colored metal housing between the footbox and the crash nose is minimal

For safety reasons, the high-voltage system sits inside the LMP monocoque, which concerns three of the five main components: the motor-generator unit, the flywheel energy storage system and the electronic control unit. Only the drive shafts and the part of the cooling system sitting in the left-hand sidepod are located on the outside. All components combined tip the scales at around 70 kilograms. The monocoque is tightly packed: the regulations prohibit locating the MGU between the footbox and the steering wheel. Toward the front, the removable crash box is the limiting factor. Due to the wheel suspensions, springs, dampers and steering components, the space remaining in the place where the MGU has to sit is scarce.

Together with Bosch Audi achieves a highly integrative, extremely compact MGU. A 400-volt system is the prerequisite for the small design size. The MGU has to deliver clearly more output than its contemporary counterparts in Formula One, which uses only one boost per lap. Two permanently excited synchronous motors, each with output of 75 kW and torque of 300 Nm, are highly efficient units operating at low rotational speeds. They can be integrated into the powertrain with a fixed gear not requiring an additional manually shifted transmission. [24]

The MGU operates torque-based whereas the flywheel does so in a voltage range remaining as constant as possible. The regulations provide for seven on-track braking zones, each permitting the use of 500 kilojoules of recuperated energy. Even decelerating from more than 300 to around 120 km/h in front of the Hunaudières Chicanes takes modern

The MGU combines high component density in a small design space (above). To reduce weight, the transmission housing is made of CFRP (below)

[19] Audi MediaInfo: Audi brings the quattro back to the race track, February 29, 2012

[20] Authors' research manuscript dated November 9, 2012. For the classification of these drive systems, see Peter Hofmann: Hybridfahrzeuge. Vienna: Springer-Verlag, 2014, p. 23 et seq

[21] www.racecar-engineering.com/articles/peugeot-hybrid4/, last retrieved on August 15, 2022

[22] Audi Motorsport Communications: Booklet Audi Sports Prototypes 2012, p. 7

[23] Transcript of interview with Dr. Wolfgang Ullrich on April 30, 2012

[24] Authors' research manuscript dated May 10, 2012

Recuperation at Le Mans

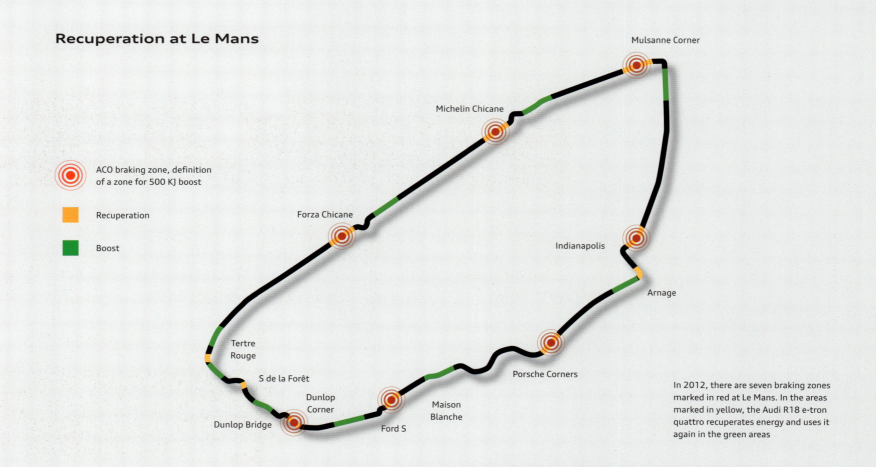

Mulsanne Corner

Michelin Chicane

⊙ ACO braking zone, definition
of a zone for 500 KJ boost

🟧 Recuperation

🟩 Boost

Forza Chicane

Indianapolis

Arnage

Tertre Rouge

S de la Forêt

Porsche Corners

Dunlop Corner

Maison Blanche

Dunlop Bridge

Ford S

In 2012, there are seven braking zones marked in red at Le Mans. In the areas marked in yellow, the Audi R18 e-tron quattro recuperates energy and uses it again in the green areas

Development timeline

02/2010: Management board decision adopting the Hybrid in 2012
05/2010: 400-volt hybrid e-quattro
06/2011: Initial operation of the MGU on the test bench
08/2011: R8 GT H rollout
11/2011: R18H rollout at Le Castellet
04/2012: Endurance testing
05/2012: First race at Spa
06/2012: Victory at Le Mans

LMP sports cars only about three seconds. That calls for a high-performance storage medium with high cycle stability whereas the storage period is very limited. Consequently, due to the system's weight and the cooling concept, the engineers choose flywheel energy storage instead of battery storage or electrostatic storage in capacitors. The flywheel energy storage system is created in collaboration with WHP, Williams Hybrid Power. [25]

The hybrid system is designed according to the isolated-terra (IT) principle providing electrical insulation against the car. A high-voltage insulation monitoring device measures the insulation and deactivates the system when a threshold has been reached. The DC cables are high-temperature-resistant, double-insulated and covered. All high-voltage contacts are secured by a pilot line integrated as a loop into all plug-in connectors. The system shuts down in the event of a loose connector. On the lap back to the pits, the system already discharges the flywheel energy storage unit, and two relays on both terminals disconnect it from the high-voltage system. When the system switches from the high-voltage to the low-voltage range, a light-emitting diode on the outside of the cockpit switches from green to flashing green. The rotor in the storage system is made of CFRP to ensure that the centrifugal forces remain manageable at 45,000 revolutions and circumferential speeds beyond the speed of sound. To prevent air friction and thus heating, the rotor spins in a high-vacuum environment. Due to outgassing of the CFRP material, a twin-stage pump permanently evacuates the housing. The rotor is mounted in a way that causes it to wobble instead of entering into a rotary motion in case of an unplanned event. The CFRP abrades on the inside wall of the aluminum housing in the process while the resulting gas development

decelerates the flywheel and generates overpressure. In the event of excessive pressure, rupture discs open the path to the channels that dissipate the carbon fiber dust toward the outside to prevent contamination of the driver. A low-temperature circuit for power electronics, the flywheel energy storage system and the MGU ensures thermal safety.

Application and control strategies are conclusive. Brake pressure, gas pedal position and program pre-selection are parameters the drivers can influence. On the steering wheel, they can determine the ratio between braking pressure and recuperation torque during deceleration. During acceleration, the program defines the relation between load and boost torque. The maps must correspond to defined algorithms; the drivers are not allowed to vary them freely. In the event of a hybrid malfunction, brake balance automatically shifts toward the front axle. In that way, the car compensates for the abrupt absence of the hybrid system's superimposed braking torque, and handling remains predictable. What Audi is keeping under wraps at the time is the corner point of the design. It puts the maximum power output of the electric motor in relation to pace and is located on the level of top speed. The torque level during deceleration then remains constant until the car stops. That is the only way in which the system can guarantee stable support during braking events because the distribution of braking force must not be varied during deceleration. A lower level of the corner point would result in different torque curves and instability of the car. In testing, Audi simulated system failure during braking. Proficient people like race drivers can safely decelerate the car even under such circumstances. [26]

Rain makes for an intriguing scenario because the driver brakes earlier. That extends the recuperation phase, and the amount of recuperated energy in-

creases. To prevent a complete filling of the storage system before the end of the braking event, the development engineers reduce its state-of-charge profile. Otherwise the electronics would have to abort recuperation during braking, resulting in a sudden change of braking behavior. [27]

The distinct color difference between the R18 ultra and the e-tron quattro belies the fact that both race cars are visually identical except for the hybrid warning lamps in the B-pillar. Only the hybrid system separates the two models from each other. The ultra version even uses the same sidepods to reduce complexity. The cooling circuit for the hybrid system located there is retained but not connected. In total, the difference between the models amounts to only about 200 parts.

The V6 TDI engine in the R18 e-tron quattro drives the rear axle; there is no mechanical connection with the electric front-wheel drive (above).
The driver sits on the right-hand side in the cockpit and the flywheel next to him on the left (below)

[25] Authors' research manuscript dated November 9, 2012.
    WHP is a subsidiary of Formula One Team Williams
[26] Authors' research manuscript dated May 10, 2012
[27] Authors' research manuscript dated November 9, 2012

The R18 e-tron quattro (number 1) and ultra (number 3) cars debut at Spa in May 2012 and can be distinguished from each other only by their liveries

WEC begins at Sebring

Following the race at Sebring with last year's model, Audi tests the new R18 generation in Florida. Timo Bernhard has a test accident when the front suspension breaks, sustaining a hairline fracture of the fourth cervical vertebra. [28] Hence he cannot race at Le Mans.

Hybrid premiere and initial meetings

In the second WEC round at Spa, the R18 ultra and the R18 e-tron quattro make their debuts. Toyota is absent following a test accident. [29] In the race, André Lotterer in the hybrid model builds an advantage of nearly one minute, but in the end, the R18 ultra of Romain Dumas, Loïc Duval and Marc Gené is the front runner. Substitute driver Gené lays the foundation for victory on a drying track. At times, he is four seconds faster because he is the first to switch to "D soft slick" tires. Audi keeps these intermediates without grooves under wraps, not only publicly but even in radio communications.

Fässler/Tréluyer/Lotterer in the fastest R18 e-tron quattro take the runner-up's spot, followed by Oliver Jarvis and Marco Bonanomi in the R18 ultra, whose regular partner, Mike Rockenfeller, is racing in a concurrent DTM event. Completing the Audi quar-

tet at the front are Capello/Kristensen/McNish in the second R18 e-tron quattro. Capello tests a set of tires across three stints but the tires degrade too heavily. [30] Another factor deciding the ultra's victory: both e-tron quattro race cars with 58 liters of fuel tank capacity make their first refueling stops after 23 laps, the ultra cars, however, only after 24 and 25 laps, respectively. Audi also admits to not yet fully exploiting the potential of the hybrid system. [31]

André Lotterer celebrates his first pole position in the presence of ACO President Pierre Fillon and Dominique Le Mèner from Conseil Général de la Sarthe

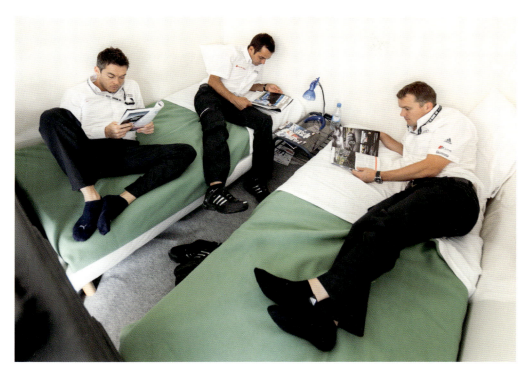

Audi and Toyota meet for the first time on the Le Mans test day that sees the R18 shining with first, second, third and sixth positions. The race week at Le Mans kicks off with Scrutineering at Place de la République. [32] Audi is regarded as the favorite. Autosport refers to Toyota's lack of Le Mans experience: "The conclusion has to be that Toyota can't challenge Audi over the full distance, it's just too early." [33] sport auto writes, "There can only be one winner at Le Mans, and those who bet on Audi at the bookies in 2012 should expect low odds. An exceedingly exciting question is which Audi is faster and allowed to win: hybrid or ultra." [34]

Record in qualifying

At 3m25.453s, André Lotterer beats last year's best time in the first qualifying session by 0.285 seconds. On Thursday, the German, improving to 3m23.787s, clinches his first pole position.

André Lotterer, Benoît Tréluyer and Marcel Fässler enjoy the calm before the storm in their container behind the team garage (above). Dominik Zeidtler as race engineer takes care of the R18 driven by Allan McNish and his teammates Dindo Capello and Tom Kristensen (center). Yoshiyaki Kinoshita as Team President of Toyota is an excellent challenger for Audi (below)

[28] Peter Schäffner: The Story of a Champion. Timo Bernhard, Duisburg: Gruppe C Motorsport Verlag 2015, p. 100 et seq. The cause is a broken bolt, transcript of interview with Dr. Wolfgang Ullrich on December 7, 2022
[29] www.toyota-media.de/blog/unternehmen/artikel/toyota-racing-verschiebt-saison-debut/text, last retrieved on July 15, 2022
[30] Audi MediaInfo: Audi 1-2-3-4 victory at Spa on Premiere, May 5, 2012
[31] Transcript of Dr. Wolfgang Ullrich's interview with Yumiko Kaijima, May 20, 2012
[32] The previously used area in front of the cathedral is blocked due to the conversion of Espace Culturel des Jacobins and construction of the second streetcar line: www.autonewsinfo.com/2012/05/14/24-heures-du-mans-la-place-de-la-republique-accueillera-le-traditionnel-pesage-47589.html, last retrieved on July 15, 2022
[33] Gary Watkins: Can a Hybrid win Le Mans? in Autosport, Le Mans Special 2012, p. 7
[34] Marcus Schurig: Der Favorit, in sport auto, June 2012, p. 114

Hybrid in motorsport

In 2012, Audi and Toyota are ringing in the hybrid era at Le Mans. Even so, it is not a premiere because Chrysler presents the Patriot sports car as far back as in 1994. It uses a liquid gas turbine driving an alternator, a flywheel energy storage system and an electric final drive system. However, the car to the development of which the Clinton administration has contributed, never runs. [35] Four years later, Don Panoz ventures racing at Le Mans with his gasoline-electric model Q9 but fails to pass the pre-qualifying. This vehicle competes in the Petit Le Mans race at Road Atlanta, also in 1998. [36] In Japan, Toyota makes history in 2007 when the Supra HV-R hybrid GT sports car clinches victory in the Tokachi 24 Hours. BMW in 2008 is the first manufacturer to test hybrid drive for Formula One while Peugeot showcases the 908 HY, an LMP concept car with an electrified powertrain. In 2009, several Formula One teams rely on hybrid systems in racing, and a

Heinz-Harald Frentzen HHF Hybrid Concept based on a Gumpert Apollo contests the Nürburgring 24 Hours. [37] In 2010, Porsche unveils the 911 GT3 R Hybrid for the Nordschleife, and in May 2011 wins a VLN race. [38] The Swiss privateer Hope Polevision team in 2011 – 13 years after Panoz – actually puts a hybrid powertrain on the Le Mans grid for the first time. [39] However, the technology achieves its breakthrough in endurance racing only through the Volkswagen Group's effort. Three victories scored by Audi starting in 2012 are followed by three Porsche wins. Following the withdrawal of both manufacturers, Toyota has remained unbeaten at Le Mans with hybrid drive from 2018 to 2022.

[35] Ian Sharp: 20 Years on, Patriot dream is re-ignited, in: Race Tech International No. 152, June 2013, p. 24–31
[36] www.roadandtrack.com/motorsports/a23119322/don-panoz-hybrid-race-car/, last retrieved on August 22, 2022 and https://panoz.com/past-projects/, last retrieved on August 22, 2022
[37] Gary Watkins: Are Frentz electric? in Autosport March 5, 2009, p. 56–59
[38] Porsche press release: 25 Jahre Manthey Racing, June 4, 2021
[39] Christian Borel, Mario Luini, Gérard Vallat, Benoît Wyder, Jean-Marie Wyder: Die Schweizer in Le Mans 2011, Saint-Sulpice: turbo éditions, 2011, p. 48

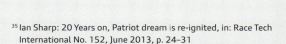

Porsche uses a parallel hybrid with a flywheel energy storage system in the 911 GT3 R Hybrid. Shortly afterwards Audi integrates such a system in the much tighter dimensions of an LMP1 cockpit

The Chrysler Patriot with a turbine and electric drive is a technology trailblazer but never runs. Panoz fails to pass the pre-qualification at Le Mans. Toyota scores an endurance racing victory in Japan with a hybrid powertrain. Before quitting its LMP program Peugeot experiments with hybrid drive in the 908. The HHF Hybrid Concept is created on the basis of a Gumpert Apollo (from top to bottom)

Christian Weck fulfills the double function of Project Manager LMP and organization LMP for many years

Loïc Duval qualifies for the front row as well. The other two Audi cars secure grid positions four and six, with Toyota in between.

Changing lead

André Lotterer defends his position at the start against Allan McNish. Three hours into the race Tom Kristensen, who takes over from McNish, makes an unscheduled pit stop to have rubber removed that he has picked up from the track, causing him to lose one lap. The Dane is in fourth position behind the two Toyota. The Japanese cars clearly increase their pace as auto, motor und sport analyzes: "On a clear track one hour into the race, Toyota, on average, was two and a half seconds per lap slower than the Audi R18 cars. Although three, four and five hours into the race Toyota managed to close the gap to some extent again [...]. After they saw at Audi that Toyota did not pose a real threat they switched from 11- to 12-hour stints [...]. Second, the TS030-Hybrid stayed on one set of tires longer. The Toyota drivers reeled off up to four consecutive stints at a stretch. That saved time in the pit lane. And third, the Toyota seemingly tended to benefit from the rubber on the track more than Audi [...]." [40] Racecar Engineering

[40] www.auto-motor-und-sport.de/motorsport/24h-le-mans-analyse-2012-audi-vs-toyota/, last retrieved on July 15, 2022

After Toyota's DNF, Audi can only defeat itself

adds that for the setup Audi focuses on the later stages of the race. [41] After almost exactly five hours, Toyota driver Nicolas Lapierre manages to overtake the leading number 1 Audi and continues to lead the race for three laps. Anthony Davidson collides with a GT car nearly at the same time. His Toyota is lifted up and the Briton sustains a vertebral injury. During a safety car period Audi takes the lead from Toyota again thanks to a faster pit stop. After the race is restarted, Kazuki Nakajima attacks the leading Fässler but collides with a rival and has to pit twice for repairs. The Toyota show is over.

Audi's duel for victory

In the next hours of racing Fässler, Lotterer and Tréluyer are in front of Capello/Kristensen/McNish. That will only change 14 hours into the race. Fässler spins in the Porsche Corners, touches the barrier and pits early. However, there is nothing to repair for Crew Chief Stefan Grimm, Chief Mechanic Ronny Reinhardt and their colleagues. Due to an incomplete radio message, the team changes drivers but not the tires. [42] McNish takes over at the front of the field.

Because the sequences vary at which the two R18 cars pit the lead keeps changing. On Sunday morn-

Audi's new signing Loïc Duval celebrates his 30th birthday on June 12

Number 2 has chances for victory up until Allan McNish's accident

ing, Fässler has to get out of a GT car's way in the Mulsanne Corner. He drives through the gravel trap and touches the track barrier. He finishes his stint but the pit stop reveals the need for a new rear and engine hood. Then, shortly after noon on Sunday, misfortune strikes McNish while leading the race with a 50-second advantage. McNish is devastated: "I caught a slower GT vehicle in the Porsche corners and expected the driver to stay on the right-hand side. But he didn't. I haven't got a clue why. I spun and crashed into the guard rail with the right front." [43] The repair during which Chief Mechanic Michael Strehler and his crew change the front bodywork and the rear hood costs one lap.

378 laps into the race Marcel Fässler, André Lotterer and Benoit Tréluyer clinch the first Le Mans victory of a hybrid sports car with "Electra," the name the mechanics have given to Chassis 208H. Yet before that happens the trio has a few moments of trepidation when the hybrid system fails to develop its

full potential. During the subsequent stops the engineers keep trying to restore the system's functionality. A decade later, Leena Gade reveals: "When the new flywheel came in during practice it made this horrendous noise. We couldn't switch back to the old flywheel. It would have meant that we would have gone over the mileage with regard to the race distance. Despite the malfunctioning, our lap times were good. It did help us further down the line to understand that with the hybrid system, we had to push it much more to its limit and make it much more powerful so that it actually gave us a distinct advantage." [44] Capello, Kristensen and McNish finish runners-up but can defend their top spot in the WEC drivers' standings with a narrow margin in front of the Le Mans winners. For Capello, who already wanted to quit in 2011 but did not get to drive that year due to the accident of his teammate McNish, it is the last sports car race. [45]

Head of Sport Wolfgang Ullrich remains committed to his choice of not issuing a team order: "Of course, that could have gone wrong but I have full confidence in our drivers and am proud of us having permitted an open race and securing a podium lockout nonetheless. I think that for the fans and Le Mans it was the right choice." [46] The sports media respond benevolently. sport auto writes: "In that way, Audi gave us eight highly entertaining hours [...]. Audi did not take the easy way out at Le Mans but the hard way. [...] The media were no less impressed than the trackside fans. [...] Yes, at Le Mans, Audi was the cherished winner." [47] Christian Borel headlines his

[41] Paul Truswell: First among equals, in Racecar Engineering, August 2012, p. 19

[42] Looking back, Leena Gade says that her announcement was wrong. That is why, 33 minutes later, car number 1 pits again for the required tire change during a safety car period. Transcript of interview with Leena Gade on December 13, 2022

[43] www.audi-mediacenter.com/en/press-releases/quotes-after-the-audi-triumph-at-le-mans-1645, last retrieved on July 15, 2022

[44] Transcript of interview with Leena Gade on December 13, 2022

[45] Transcript of interview with Dindo Capello on November 24, 2022

[46] Transcript of interview with Dr. Wolfgang Ullrich on June 20, 2012

[47] Marcus Schurig: Der geliebte Sieger, in sport auto, August 2012, p. 93

André Lotterer, Ralf Jüttner, Benoît Tréluyer, Wolfgang Ullrich and Marcel Fässler in the first flush of victory (above). Dindo Capello races at Le Mans for the last time in 2012 (below)

Following their Le Mans victory, Tréluyer, Lotterer and Fässler are also the first WEC champions (right). A large Danish fan community visits Tom Kristensen at the 24-hour race year after year (below). Audi employs its own weather service: Dave Morton's Racemet (bottom)

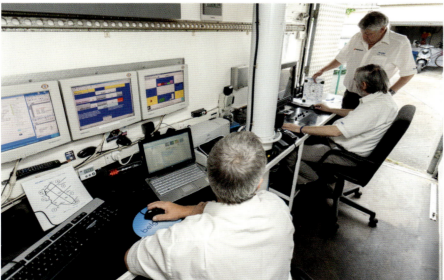

article approvingly "Merci Docteur" but expresses near-disbelief about the open outcome. [48]

During a pit stop to check the rear suspension, the third-placed Audi R18 ultra loses a lap in the early stage of the race. Following problems with a transmission sensor on Sunday morning, a gear gets stuck twice. Marco Bonanomi and Oliver Jarvis mount the podium for the first time, and Mike Rockenfeller returns to the podium together with them one year after his serious accident.

Due to two near-identical slips, the number 3 Audi R18 ultra loses its chances. On Sunday night, Romain Dumas hits the dirty part of the track in the first chicane and slides into the track barrier. A similar thing happens to Marc Gené at noon on Sunday. However, the post-incident repairs cost the car twelve laps. Loïc Duval improves the fastest race lap an amazing five times on Sunday morning and is hardly slower than in qualifying.

Two WEC titles for Audi

Capello's previous teammates continue racing as a twosome in the next rounds. At Silverstone, Fässler, Lotterer and Tréluyer in the R18 e-tron quattro score another victory, taking the top spot in the standings for the first time. Kristensen and

McNish finish third in the ultra. As a result, Audi wins the manufacturers' championship in the fourth of eight races. It is the first FIA World Championship title for Audi since the 1984 World Rally Championship.

Toyota continues developing the TS030 at a fast pace. As early as in round five at São Paulo, marking the brand's third event, it scores its first victory. Fässler, Lotterer and Tréluyer finish runners-up. Third position goes to Kristensen, McNish and local hero Lucas di Grassi, who is deployed as the third driver. In Bahrain, Audi clinches a one-two win with two hybrid models by Fässler/Lotterer/Tréluyer in front of Kristensen/McNish. The last two races at Fuji and Shanghai go to Toyota again while Audi claims second and third place, respectively. Following three victories, Marcel Fässler, André Lotterer and Benoît Tréluyer are the first WEC driver champions. But Toyota has emerged as a new rival pulling off a strong debut with three victories of the season and as a short-handed squad.

48 Christian Borel, Mario Luini, Gérard Vallat, Benoît Wyder, Jean-Marie Wyder: Les Suisses au Mans 2012, Saint-Sulpice: turbo éditions, 2012, p. 57 et seq. Borel surprises with an opposing rationale according to which a team order in favor of car number 2 on the occasion of Dindo Capello's 48th birthday and retirement from racing as well as a ninth victory by Tom Kristensen would probably have produced huge media response

Compared to their hybrid sister models the two R18 ultra are amazingly fast, number 3 even sets the fastest race lap

Victory without joy

In 2013, Audi wins at Le Mans for the twelfth time.
However, a fatal accident casts a shadow over that success.

Extremely changeable weather
shapes Le Mans in 2013 when
car number 2 scores victory

Systematic steps

After the R18 from 2012 is an extensively updated version compared to its predecessor named RP1 the car for 2013 is a development of the RP2. With that, Audi Sport switches to a two-year cycle up until the end of the LMP program. The basic structure consisting of the monocoque and powertrain is retained. Visually, though, the prototypes change significantly due to the rapid progress in aerodynamics. Despite this two-year lifecycle the sports cars are provided sequentially with new internal abbreviations, now it is the RP3.

Audi prefers an "evolution to a revolution." The minimum weight of the race cars must increase from

The RP3 is based on the 2012 RP2 but represents a further development in terms of aerodynamics

900 to 915 kilograms. Consequently, there is greater scope for ballast weight with which the center of gravity can be influenced.

The flywheel energy storage system is more powerful in the second season, while the basic system topology remains the same. Each of the two electric motors for each front wheel now deliver 80 instead of 75 kilowatts equating to 218 horsepower in total. Optimized components and enhanced thermal management help increase output. The ratios of the two planetary gearsets in the motor-generator unit that for the first time can be adjusted to the characteristics of the individual circuits result in track-specific efficiency increases. As before, the R18 may not use more than 500 kilojoules of energy for acceleration between two braking zones at Le Mans. Modified algorithms enhance its efficiency.

The engineers invest a lot work in aerodynamics. The entire airflow from the front to the rear has been designed for greater efficiency. Winglets above the rear fenders complement the contour of the rear wing. The air behind the front wheels now flows differently as well. New openings and turning vanes in the side pod improve venting of the front wheel arches. [1]

Audi continues relying on the 3.7-liter V6 TDI. The regulations reduce the size of the air restrictor by 0.7 to 45.1 millimeters, and output drops by 20 to around 490 horsepower. Not actively published is information about the modified exhaust system. After combustion, the gases drive the mono turbocharger as usual but, for the first time, subsequently flow to the rear diffusor through a split system. As a result, they accelerate airflow and enhance downforce. That is one of the elements for achieving better lap times.

There is another system that Audi tests in 2013 but rejects afterwards. In preparation for the deployment of several hybrid systems per car in the future, the engineers design a compressed air hybrid. In braking phases without fuel injection, the fresh air that is compressed by the engine flows through a valve in the exhaust pipe into a pressure accumulator. During acceleration the vessel in front of the right rear wheel releases the compressed air into the intake system

The maximum wing width of 1.60 meters has been adhered to but the remaining area can be used creatively

again, so enabling excellent responsiveness. The idea proves its potential in tests. However, in response to potential queries, Audi has prepared an answer even before Le Mans 2013: "Currently, Audi is not using the system on race weekends. The interpretation of the regulations that will be valid in 2014 suggests that its utilization will be improbable." [2]

[1] Audi Motorsport Communications: Booklet Audi Sports Prototypes 2013, p. 15 et seq
[2] Internal position paper of Audi Motorsport Communications: Topics of the Weekend, WEC Test Day Le Mans, June 4, 2013

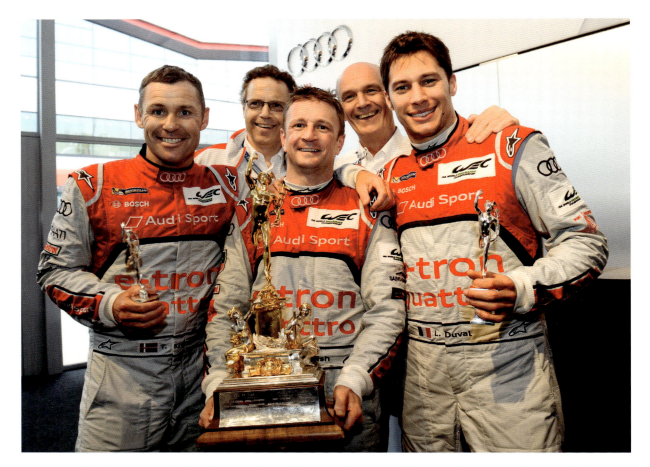

With the victory scored by Tom Kristensen, Allan McNish and Loïc Duval in the WEC opener at Silverstone, Audi also wins the Tourist Trophy that the Royal Automobile Club RAC presented for the first time in 1905. The figure of Hermes consists of 18 carat gold

Goodbye to Sebring

The Sebring 12 Hours are no longer part of the WEC in 2013. Due to the merger of the ALMS and Grand-Am series, LMP1 models are not admitted anymore from 2014 on. Consequently, Audi bids farewell to the race with which the LMP program began in 1999. Marcel Fässler shares a previous-generation car with Oliver Jarvis and Benoît Tréluyer. Lucas di Grassi, Tom Kristensen and Allan McNish drive an R18 Type RP3. In the race, the lead between them changes 20 times; ultimately, the old car leads with a 7.679-second advantage. In the WEC opener at Silverstone, Duval/McNish/Kristensen clinch victory although, due to 20 percent less fuel tank capacity (58 vs. 73 liters), they have to make one more refueling stop than the last-generation cars from Toyota. Fässler/Lotterer/Tréluyer are separated from them by 3.4 seconds.

New handicaps for Audi

From Spa onward, the refueling orifice for Toyota may be 26 instead of the previous 25 millimeters (as for Audi). That shortens the stops. Audi fields two body-shells with high downforce and a third one for Gené and his colleagues featuring the Le Mans configura-

Marcel Fässler, André Lotterer and Benoît Tréluyer are again forming a driver trio; in the second car, Loïc Duval supports Tom Kristensen and Allan McNish. After Le Mans 2012, Kristensen asked Duval if he would like to switch to his cockpit in the upcoming year. [3] At Spa and at Le Mans, Marc Gené, Lucas di Grassi and Oliver Jarvis are additional drivers. New Project Leader LMP at Audi Sport is Chris Reinke, the previous Technical Project Leader. [4] He succeeds Dieter Gass, the new Head of DTM at Audi Sport. [5]

Toyota introduces innovations for the monocoque, aerodynamics and powertrain on the TS030. [6] The driver lineup remains the same. Besides the factory teams only the privateer race teams Rebellion Racing with two Lola Toyota cars and Strakka Racing with one HPD 03c compete in the LMP1 class. A third place clinched by Rebellion at São Paulo remains their best result.

The fans at Le Mans look forward to another duel between Audi and Toyota

At Sebring, the LMP1 prototypes are allowed to contest a final race. Audi says goodbye to the fans with the eleventh victory. Tom Kristensen, Dindo Capello, Emanuele Pirro, Frank Biela, Marco Werner, Marcel Fässler, Lucas di Grassi, Dieter Gass (back row, from left) and Oliver Jarvis, Allan McNish, Wolfgang Ullrich and Benoît Tréluyer (kneeling) in a group photo

tion. Despite an early puncture – causing Lotterer/ Fässler/Tréluyer to drop to seventh position – the trio wins in front of Duval as well as di Grassi and their respective teammates. The new Toyota leads the race until suffering a defect of the hybrid system. The Japanese admit, "We are very disappointed by the final result because we were fighting for the win. Even if we are a little bit slower than them, I think it would have been close. [...] Considering we were using the Le Mans package, we are back in the game." [7] An about-face follows a few days later: Technical Director Pascal Vasselon demands a new rating because Audi has allegedly increased engine power so much that the good lap times overcompensated for the fuel consumption disadvantage: "The rulemakers' mistake [...] was to ignore this possibility. It was wrong to concentrate only on the power side and leave the fuel [capacity]. If we leave one of the two open, then diesel technology can exploit this." [8]

Chris Reinke is new Project Leader LMP at Audi Sport from 2013 on while his predecessor, Dieter Gass, switches to the DTM (right). Toyota remains Audi's rival in the hybrid class (below)

[3] Carole Capitaine: Y a rien de comparable, in L'Équipe, June 24, 2013, p. 18
[4] www.audi-mediacenter.com/en/press-releases/chris-reinke-achieving-aims-with-positive-energy-3569, last retrieved on October 18, 2022
[5] Audi MediaInfo: Dieter Gass Head of DTM at Audi, April 18, 2013
[6] https://newsroom.toyota.eu/2019-toyota-racing-reveals-updated-ts030-hybrid-for-2013, last retrieved on October 18, 2022
[7] https://newsroom.toyota.eu/2019-eventful-race-for-toyota-racing-at-spa/, last retrieved on October 18, 2022
[8] Gary Watkins: As it is, our chances are very small, in Motor Sport 07/2013, p. 123

After Allan Simonsen's accident, the field follows the safety car during the first hour (above).
His teammates already know what it feels like to win but for Loïc Duval – shown here with race engineer
Kyle Wilson-Clarke – it is a new experience (below)

Wolfgang Ullrich decisively rejects that kind of criticism: "How can someone come to the first race without their new car and then bring one to the second race and complete only half the race and ask for a change in the BoP? The new Toyota [...] was at least comparable to our Le Mans car." [9] Even so, the FIA Endurance Committee, on May 24, increases the fuel tank capacity of the LMP1 gasoline engines by three to 76 liters. [10] As a result, Audi manages ten laps straight at Le Mans and Toyota twelve. Across the distance, that amounts to six stops, i.e., around a 6-minute difference in stopping time. [11] That is already the third move at Audi's expense following the smaller air restrictor on January 16 and the change of the refueling orifice on May 2. "Factually, they led to the reversal of an experience everyday drivers are

familiar with," Chris Reinke recalls. "As the range of our TDI race cars was suddenly lower than those of our opponents using gasoline engines." [12]

In qualifying at Le Mans, Loïc Duval secures his first pole position, Audi its eighth. Second place goes to André Lotterer. Oliver Jarvis and his teammates are third in front of both Toyota cars.

Le Mans in mourning

After the start in front of 245,000 fans, André Lotterer is in front, followed by Nicolas Lapierre in a Toyota. As early as on lap three, Allan Simonsen in an Aston Martin crashes sideways into the guard rail in the Tertre Rouge section. Rescue squads retrieve the Dane who succumbs to his injuries shortly afterwards. The congenial driver is known and popular around the world – also at Audi. Based on Tom Kristensen's good offices, he contests the Nürburgring 24 Hours in an Audi R8 LMS in 2012. One of his teammates back then was Oliver Jarvis, who happens to be at the wheel of car number 3 at Le Mans when the news of Simonson's death arrives at 6.21 pm. [13]

Following a 50-minute neutralization period, the safety cars release the race again. Audi pulls clear of its rivals by more than 50 seconds. Fässler/Lotterer/Tréluyer lead 96 of the first 100 laps before the generator fails. "It is not rated as a quick-change component in our operation because it normally does not fail and should never fail either," says engine developer Ulrich Baretzky. [14] 43 minutes are lost, equating to twelve laps. Then, while running in third position, Oliver Jarvis spins following a collision due to a puncture. He has to limp back to the pits on a defective tire for nearly one lap. After the wheel change and subsequent repair, his car, with a two-lap deficit, is in fourth position. For Audi, having three strong driver squads now pays off because car number 2 continues battling with Toyota.

About halfway through the race Duval/Kristensen/McNish have a one-lap advantage. Rain repeatedly calls for maximum concentration – by the drivers as well as by race engineer Kyle Wilson-Clarke. McNish experiences "one of the most mentally difficult races

Just one year before his death Allan Simonsen (above, left) was part of an Audi driver quartet with Edward Sandström, Andrea Piccini and Oliver Jarvis in an Audi R8 LMS at the Nürburgring 24 Hours

9   www.autosport.com/wec/news/toyota-calls-for-le-mans-rules-
    redress-after-audi-spa-performance-4465925, last retrieved on
    October 18, 2022
10 www.fiawec.com/en/news/24h-le-mans-balance-of-performance-
    lmp1/1142, last retrieved on October 18, 2022
11 www.auto-motor-und-sport.de/news/analyse-vom-24h-rennen-
    in-le-mans-2013-das-langstreckenrennen-des-jahres, last
    retrieved on October 18, 2022
12 www.audi-mediacenter.com/en/press-releases/flashback-le-
    mans-2013-and-the-audi-win-under-unequal-prerequisites-4210
    last retrieved on October 18, 2022
13 www.fiawec.com/en/news/24h-le-mans-aco-statement-on-the-
    death-of-allan-simonsen/1221, last retrieved on October 18,
    2022
14 www.auto-motor-und-sport.de/news/analyse-vom-24h-rennen-
    in-le-mans-2013-das-langstreckenrennen-des-jahres, last
    retrieved on October 18, 2022

Wolfgang Ullrich traditionally invokes the team spirit with his drivers before the start of the race with a battle cry

Marc Gené, Lucas di Grassi and Oliver Jarvis manage the leap onto the podium

After the fatal accident, Allan McNish, Wolfgang Ullrich, Tom Kristensen, Loïc Duval, Ralf Jüttner, Oliver Jarvis, Marc Gené and Lucas di Grassi feel no joy on the podium (right). The victorious Audi also receives a round of applause from a row of Toyota team members (below)

A momentous mistake in handling a rain protection cover costs valuable points in Japan

of my career. There was no stint that was completely wet or dry. Every lap, every corner was an adventure – an adventure at 300 km/h." [15] The media praise the drivers: "They make no mistake despite the pressure exerted by Toyota." [16] Shortly before the end of the penultimate hour, Lapierre, in third position in a Toyota, slips into the tire wall in the Porsche Corners during a rain shower, loses one position and paves the way to the podium for Audi's car number 3.

Factors of the victory

Tom Kristensen achieves his ninth victory and Audi its twelfth. Allan McNish is on the top step of the podium for the third and Loïc Duval for the first time. With a one-lap deficit, Sébastien Buemi, Anthony Davidson and Stéphane Sarrazin are the runners-up for Toyota. Notably, the winners theoretically had a maximum of 1,972 liters of diesel fuel available to them whereas Toyota was allowed to fill up on 2,280 liters of gasoline. [17] Gené's car finishes in third, Tréluyer's in fifth place.

An exuberant mood does not develop. Tom Kristensen is particularly distraught: "Unfortunately, we lost someone yesterday who had the same dream. He was a very modest and nice person. [...] I'm driving with determination and the ambition my father inspired in me. He died in March. Before his death, he told me that I'd win Le Mans this year [...]. I'm hoping that one day I'll be able to celebrate another victory with Loïc and Allan that I can dedicate to my father. Because this Le Mans success I'm dedicating to Allan Simonsen." [18] The race remains neutralized twelve times for a total of 5.27 hours – setting a new negative record. [19] As a result, Toyota cannot take advantage of its large fuel supply [20] even though car number 8 stopping for 43m20.1s spends four minutes less standing in the pit lane than the winning Audi. [21] There are two additional factors: car number 8, the ultimate runner-up, has a temporary fuel pump problem. [22] Plus, Audi, say the media, benefited from a massive performance increase. [23] auto motor und sport writes, "Toyota driver Alexander Wurz noted that 'Audi just invested the additional performance in downforce.' Consequently, the performance advantage remained invisible in terms of top speed and downforce, as is commonly known, is also beneficial for tire wear." [24] The heavier wear of the rubber has two disadvantages: on the one hand, Toyota achieves only four stints while Audi does five. [25] On the other hand, lap times suffer: "Toyota should not have lost more than one second per lap but they regularly lost two or even three seconds." [26] Following this emotional weekend, Audi's workforce once again welcome their winners to the plant for a traditional event featuring an honorary lap and autograph session.

Both WEC titles again go to Audi

In the following race at Brazil, Audi scores a one-two win with number 1 in front of number 2. The only Toyota collides with a rival. In the WEC premiere at Austin, Duval and company clinch the 100th LMP victory for Audi. At Fuji, the field starts behind the safety car in heavy rain. This first starting attempt up until the red flag is waved is equally futile as all the following ones, but the clock keeps running. That results in a classification in which Toyota traipses toward its first victory of the season. Audi makes a momentous mistake: during the pre-start warm-up of car number 1 on pole position the engine sucks in the rain protection cover through the air scoop on the roof. The vacuum causes pieces of the delicate CFRP intake pipe to break, partially blocking the air supply. During the formation lap Lotterer reports a loss of power. While Fuji specialists Lotterer and Tréluyer do not expect the

[15] Transcript of interview with Allan McNish on April 11, 2015
[16] Stéphane Barbé: Du neuf avec du vieux, in L'Equipe, June 24, 2013, p. 18
[17] www.audi-mediacenter.com/en/press-releases/audi-most-efficient-in-the-field-facts-on-the-twelfth-victory-at-le-mans-1279, last retrieved on October 18, 2022
[18] www.audi-mediacenter.com/en/press-releases/quotes-after-the-audi-victory-at-le-mans-765, last retrieved on October 18, 2022
[19] Alain Bienvenu, Christian Moity, Jean-Marc Teissedre: Le Mans 24 Hours 2013, Antony: E-T-A-I 2013, p. 252
[20] www.auto-motor-und-sport.de/news/analyse-vom-24h-rennen-in-le-mans-2013-das-langstreckenrennen-des-jahres, last retrieved on October 18, 2022
[21] Paul Truswell: Strategic Calls, in Racecar Engineering, August 2013, p. 48
[22] Didier Braillon: Toyota, encore derrière, in L'Equipe, June 24, 2013, p. 17
[23] Ibid
[24] www.auto-motor-und-sport.de/news/analyse-vom-24h-rennen-in-le-mans-2013-das-langstreckenrennen-des-jahres, last retrieved October 18, 2022
[25] Ibid
[26] Christian Borel, Mario Luini, Gérard Vallat, Benoît Wyder, Jean-Marie Wyder: Les Suisses au Mans 2013, Saint-Sulpice: turbo éditions, 2013, p. 64

Following the Le Mans victory, Audi Sport proudly presents itself at the Neckarsulm location. Works Council Chairman Norbert Rank (yellow polo shirt) together with the workforce he represents is a backbone of the brand's success in racing

start to be released in the rain and want to stay behind the safety car, the team expects a later release of the race and summons Lotterer to the pit lane. Following the change of the intake pipe, he is in the last position which, in retrospect, proves to be the wrong decision: the car could have followed the safety car even without the repair and have even won due to an overtaking ban under yellow flags. Instead, it finishes in 26th place overall and fourth in the LMP1 class. Otherwise, the driver trio with a 1.5-point advantage could have become world champions for the second time – if strategies and driving styles had remained the same until the end of the season.

Due to the short distance, only half the points are awarded in Japan; Audi wins the manufacturers' title early. At Shanghai, car number 1 scores the third victory of the season. For the sister car, third position suffices to claim the drivers' title. After nine Le Mans victories, Kristensen is finally world champion: "We beat the increasingly competitive Toyota and defending champions Marcel Fässler, André Lotterer and Benoît Tréluyer. It was an incredible feeling to win the World Championship. [27] At the finale in Bahrain, Fässler/Lotterer/Tréluyer take the runner-up's spot. Allan McNish ends his career in the middle of December with the conclusion: "I can't wish for more than what we've achieved this year." [28]

[27] Tom Kristensen, Lars Krone: Tom Kristensen – The Book, no location, no publisher, 2015, p. 200
[28] Audi MediaInfo: Parting at the pinnacle: Audi driver Allan McNish ends LMP career, December 17, 2013

For the second time in a row, the WEC title goes to Audi

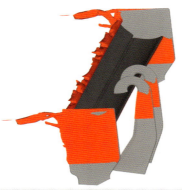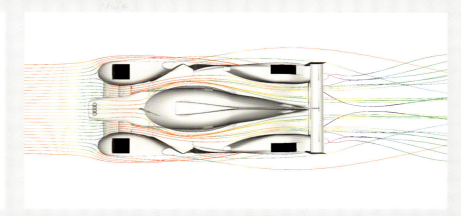

The rear wing that in the picture is shown with air flowing toward it from the right works clearly more efficiently when it is no longer supported from the bottom but, since 2009, suspended from the top (left and center). The colors of the lines provide information to the engineers about the individual pressure conditions in decisive body sections of the LMP sports car (right)

Shaped by the wind

Jan Monchaux and his team cause Audi to move forward in the area of aerodynamics

Audi initially uses three wind tunnels for the individual development steps: In Stuttgart, the bodywork of the R8 is created on a 1:4 model; the main development on a 1:2.5 model takes place at Fondmetal. Audi verifies the calculations on the race cars in its own aeroacoustics wind tunnel. [29] Subsequently, Audi cooperates with Sauber in Switzerland. "Today we've reached a model size of 60 percent. Thanks to rubber tires and a moving floor we can create the airflow with a lot more realism. The suspensions of the models have also been fully emulated," says Axel Löffler, Head of Design Chassis/Bodywork. He is responsible for aerodynamics until 2013, before Jan Monchaux arrives from the Ferrari F1 team. [30]

In 1999, the rear wing is allowed to be 2 meters wide, 40 centimeters long and 15 centimeters high. In 2009, the dimensions drop to 1.60 meters and 25 centimeters while the height remains unchanged. The rear wing suspended from the top however compensates for a major portion of the loss in downforce. On the underbody, the profile cross section must increase by seven degrees from the center toward the outer edges ever since the R10 TDI. While on the R8 the desired downforce versions could still be implemented with one bodyshell, a long-tail version is cre-

ated for 2013. The maximum length of 4.65 meters is retained but the body now extends all the way below the rear wing. Despite all the restrictions aerodynamic efficiency (downforce in relation to drag) from 1999 to 2013 increases by 65 percent. [31]

[29] Michael Pfadenhauer: Aerodynamikentwicklung im Rennsport am Beispiel Audi R8, in Michael Bargende, Jochen Wiedemann (Publishers): Kraftfahrwesen und Verbrennungsmotoren, Renningen: expert verlag 2001, p. 357
[30] Audi MediaInfo Magazine: Motorsport and Production. Audi Le Mans Prototypes 1999–2013, 2013, p. 43 et seq, and https://ch.linkedin.com/in/jan-monchaux-2a8b563, last retrieved on October 19, 2022
[31] Audi MediaInfo Magazine: Motorsport and Production. Audi Le Mans Prototypes 1999–2013, 2013, p. 44 et seq

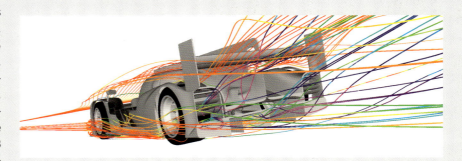

The virtual analysis of the airflow enables Audi to draw initial conclusions on the computer

Intensified conditions

The FIA WEC and Le Mans along with it are clearly evolving: new energy regulations entail major change and Porsche's entry fuels the competition.

Porsche's return marks something that sports car enthusiasts around the world have been waiting for: 16 years after its last race at Le Mans with a car that was in contention for overall victory, the Stuttgart-based brand, after years in the smaller GT and LMP2 categories, is finally competing in the top category again. A record winner with 16 successes at La Sarthe, the marque attracts strong interest by both media and fans. The Porsche 919 with a V4 turbo engine and a kinetic as well as a thermal hybrid system uses a totally different powertrain concept than its rivals at Audi and Toyota. Just one thing unites the Swabians and the Japanese: they compete with their gasoline engines in the 6-megajoule class. [1]

For its driver squads, Porsche relies on Romain Dumas and Marc Lieb who have been with the brand for years and are competing together with former F1 test driver and endurance racer Neel Jani. Timo Bernhard, an old hand like Dumas, who is returning

[1] Peter Wright: The question of equivalence, in Racecar Engineering July 2014, p. 12

Last chance for a ride: André Lotterer, Ralf Jüttner, Marcel Fässler and Wolfgang Ullrich heading for the podium with Benoît Tréluyer, the driver of the final stint

Porsche with a track record of 16 victories is a formidable rival for Audi at Le Mans. The Stuttgart-based brand is now part of the same corporation

Lucas di Grassi, Loïc Duval, Tom Kristensen, Marcel Fässler, André Lotterer, Benoît Tréluyer, Filipe Albuquerque, Marco Bonanomi and Oliver Jarvis (above, from left). Toyota is developing a new car for 2014 as well (below)

to Porsche with Audi LMP1 experience, is entering the race together with two pros from the southern hemisphere. New Zealander Brendon Hartley brings Formula One testing experience to the squad, and Australian Mark Webber, after twelve years in Formula One, is returning to the venue of which he does not have the fondest memories ever since his "flight" in a Mercedes in 1999.

Toyota is building the TS040 Hybrid whose naturally aspirated V8 engine now has 3.7 instead of 3.4 liters of displacement. In addition to kinetic energy recovery at the rear axle, such a system is now also being used at the front. Furthermore, the Japanese are the only squad to rely on supercapacitors as energy storage systems. Kazuki Nakajima, Stéphane Sarrazin and Alexander Wurz form one driver lineup and Sébastien Buemi, Anthony Davidson and Nicolas Lapierre the other one. Sarrazin and Lapierre have

swapped their places in the six-member driver squad compared to 2013.

At Audi, Lucas di Grassi succeeds Allan McNish in the lineup of last year's winners after McNish's retirement, forming the new trio with Loïc Duval and Tom Kristensen. Marcel Fässler, André Lotterer and Benoît Tréluyer remain together as before. Filipe Albuquerque from the DTM and Marco Bonanomi move up as Oliver Jarvis' teammates. These two slots are vacant after di Grassi has switched to the sister car and Marc Gené to the status of a reserve driver.

Winds of change

Audi welcomes Porsche, its sister brand in the VW Group, with a creative "welcome back" video that three years later prompts Porsche to issue an equally

Porsche Chairman Matthias Müller, Head of Motorsport
Fritz Enzinger and Wolfgang Ullrich

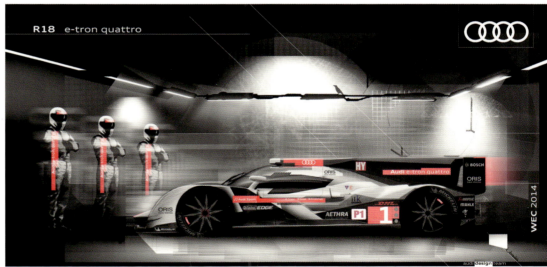

While the Audi Sport engineers are forming the body shell according to the regulations and technical requirements Audi Design is styling the surface. Tobias Drews' design shows the highly geometric styling created for the 2014 season with distinctly angled red areas

humorous farewell message following Audi's departure. [2] None other than Ferdinand Piëch personally had brought the sports car brand's entry into play as far back as in fall of 2010. [3]

"Honestly, we didn't know that something was coming," says Wolfgang Ullrich, looking back on the program of the Stuttgart-based brand after having included two Porsche drivers, Timo Bernhard and Romain Dumas, on loan into his squad from 2009 on. Politically, he does not see any risk for his program in Piëch's 2010 announcement. "That didn't surprise me. It was clear to me that that could easily happen when two different technologies are on the race track. And I didn't worry a lot about us at that juncture because I was convinced that it wasn't the time at which Porsche would introduce a diesel." [4]

Presentation in urban traffic

To present the 2014 LMP program, Audi's PR department comes up with an unusual campaign: a series of 20 papers called "Countdown" provides detailed introductions of the race car, project and drivers. One of the episodes consists of the presentation of the new R18 e-tron quattro in urban traffic in Le Mans on March 25. The ACO and the city of Le Mans support the activity that begins on Place des Jacobins

[2] www.youtube.com/watch?v=Wg8TtuXvkug, last retrieved on January 31, 2023
[3] www.24h-lemans.com/en/news/porsche-considering-an-lm-p1-1947, last retrieved on January 31, 2023
[4] Transcript of interview with Dr. Wolfgang Ullrich on December 7, 2022

New in every detail

It only seems like the 2014 R18 e-tron quattro continues the line of its predecessors: LMP1 class, parallel hybrid, V6 TDI engine, kinetic energy recovery at the front axle and flywheel energy storage. In reality, the evolution called RP4 is new in every detail. For the first time, the car's absolute energy consumption is subject to lap-specific limitation.

The amount of energy in Group C is limited as early as in the nineteen-eighties. In 1982, the race cars at Le Mans may fill their tanks with a maximum capacity of 100 liter no more than 24 times. [5] That limits the absolute amount of energy but not its distribution across the distance. Therefore, the media fear so-called "economy runs:" excessive consumption at the beginning is compensated for by slower driving at the end. That happens more than once in 1,000-kilometer sports car races. Even when in 1985 the allocated amount of fuel drops by 15 percent the winners clocking 5,088 kilometers break all racing distances ever driven since 1972. [6]

A different idea is adopted in the FIA WEC starting in 2014: The energy consumption is limited per lap, resulting in balanced competition. A fuel flow meter measures fuel consumption and radios it to the ACO and FIA in real time. In qualifying, the race cars must strictly comply with the quantity. In the race, if they use more than the permitted quantity, they must compensate for the additional consumption on the following two laps by a corresponding reduction, or else may be penalized. If a car does not use the allocated energy per lap, that energy is forfeited. What sounds so simple encompasses the permanent analysis of no less than 240 channels. [7] The ACO devotes five years of work to that idea. [8]

Energy restriction is by no means just limited to the engine. Any reduction of tractive resistances such

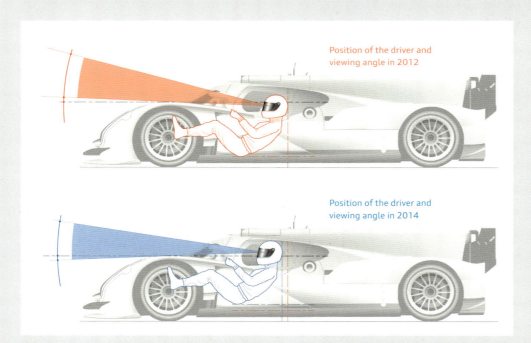

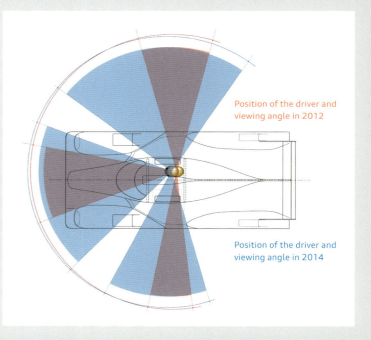

The poor vision from the closed-cockpit prototypes motivates the ACO to issue different requirements. From 2014 on, the driver's seating position in the cockpit is elevated, providing a more favorable line of sight (left). Likewise, new requirements dramatically reduce the blind spots in the 360-degree view (right)

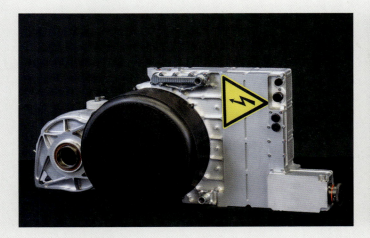

A completely new MGU in the black housing including power electronics and inverter in the metal housing drives the front wheels via a differential (left).
The displacement of the V6 engine increases to 4 liters (right)

as aerodynamic drag, rolling resistance, as well as more efficient electrical energy consumers, enhance the energy budget. This holistic approach is fully in line with the objectives of the automotive manufacturers, who must comply with statutory CO_2 emission limits for road-going vehicles. "A fundamental approach so typical in motorsport is abandoned," says Chris Reinke, Head of LMP at Audi Sport. "Instead of power, the energy use is restricted – this reflects the Zeitgeist and gives engineers enormous technical freedom." [9]

The width of the body that has been reduced by ten centimeters and slimmer tires also help save energy. This helps reducing the dimensions of the frontal area. Further energy can be conserved with a minimum weight of 870 instead of 915 kilos. In addition to lightweight design, the car must comply with new safety regulations as well: The test loads for the monocoque increase, Zylon panels reinforce the lateral area, wheel tethers and a rear crasher are required for the first time. [10]

The new Audi Laser Light now illuminates the track even more effectively. [11] Thanks to a redefined seating position and cockpit dimensions, the driver has a better all-round visibility. In the cockpit, ergonomics and controls have been updated. The clutch is now operated by means of paddle shifters instead of a pedal. [12]

[5] https://assets.lemans.org/explorer/pdf/courses/2018/24-heures-du-mans/press-kit/fr/statistiques-historiques-fr.pdf, last retrieved on May 12, 2022
[6] Ibid
[7] Romain Bernard: Energy control, in Programme Officiel 24h Le Mans 2015, p. 74 et seq
[8] Philippe Séclier: Pierre Fillon: We needed to go further, in Programme Officiel 24h Le Mans 2014, p. 8
[9] Audi Motorsport Communications: Booklet Audi Sports Prototypes 2014, p. 15
[10] Ibid, p. 17 et seq
[11] Audi MediaInfo: Laser light assists the Audi drivers at Le Mans, January 20, 2014
[12] Audi MediaInfo: Improved ergonomics for Audi's WEC drivers, April 1, 2014

View from behind of the rear axle and the new CFRP rear crasher

The entire powertrain has been re-developed as well. Effective 2014 the 120 km/h limit for re-using the recuperated energy on the front wheels is abolished. A new 230-hp MGU has become even lighter and more efficient. [13]

The electric flywheel energy storage system is new, too, and has a capacity of 600 kilojoules. Previously, seven recuperation zones of 500 kilojoules each, i.e., 3.5 megajoules per lap, applied at Le Mans. These zones have been eliminated. Every manufacturer can choose between 2, 4, 6 and 8 megajoules. The higher the class the greater the reduction of fossil energy, albeit the decrease is not proportional. Audi opts for the 2-megajoule class.

Audi Laser Light is introduced in the Audi R18 in 2014 (above). Fully covered brake rotors help keep temperatures and thus braking behavior at constant levels (below)

Tire width decreases from 16 to 14 inches and the total width of the race car from 2 to 1.90 meters. The smaller frontal area enhances overall aerodynamic drag

Development timeline

07/2012: Concept definition
10/2012: Initial wind tunnel trials
12/2012: Design of 4,200 single parts begins
03/2013: Component manufacturing
06/2013: Trials of slimmer tires on the Le Mans test day
06/2013: First dyno run for the V6 TDI 4.0
07/2013: Beginning of simulator tests
09/2013: Assembly of initial test mule (Chassis 401)
10/2013: Rollout at Le Castellet on October 8
12/2013: First photo published on December 8. Beginning of tests at Sebring
12/2013: World premiere at the Audi Sport Finale on December 18
04/2014: FIA WEC Silverstone racing premiere
06/2014: First victory (Le Mans 24 Hours)

"The idea was that, in total, everyone would have the same opportunity but that someone taking a greater risk, in other words switching to a higher hybrid class, should have a small resulting advantage," Wolfgang Ullrich recalls. "The intent was to reward the technical risk a little. And it was incredibly difficult. Everyone felt disadvantaged at one time or another. Whether that was really the case is debatable. But every three months there were discussions." [14]

Two other systems that Audi tests are chanceless: A compressed air hybrid that in overrun phases stores the air that has been compressed in three cylinders in an accumulator at around 30 bar and releases it again into the intake system during acceleration does not receive an approval. [15] Subsequently, "in weighing the risk potential," [16] the engineers exclude an electric turbocharger like the one in Formula One that Audi still announces in December 2013. [17]

The V6 TDI engine is completely new and merely its 120-degree bank angle and cylinder spacing are retained. Its displacement grows from 3.7 to four liters. An even larger volume would have required eight cylinders, which Audi wants to avoid. [18] Decisive for 2014 is the fact that the air restrictor is eliminated, that the permissible boost pressure increases from 2.5 to 4 bar, but the fuel quantity is limited. That shifts the focus to efficiency and not to higher injection pressures. "When we had an air-restricted engine, we had to try to make the maximum power out of it with no regard for fuel consumption," says engine developer Ulrich Baretzky. "Now we have an excess of air and then you make the combustion as efficient as it can physically be. You are running lambda values far beyond 1.0." [19]

Finally, the new regulations challenge the aerodynamicists to perform a pinpoint landing concerning the ratio between downforce and aerodynamic drag in order to comply with the targets for consumption and downforce. [20] Besides all the technology, the onus is on the drivers as well. Their driving style must be particularly efficient in order to precisely hit the consumption target. [21] In total, Audi on the way to victory manages using 22 percent less fuel at Le Mans than the year before. [22]

Audi leaves nothing to chance in steering wheel development either. Two dummies are used for testing the new ergonomic design and arrangement of the switches for 2014 (above).
A comparison of the steering wheels of the 1999 R8R and the 2013 R18 e-tron quattro shows how much progress has been made (below)

[13] Audi MediaInfo: Audi achieves pionieering feat with e-tron quattro four-wheel drive, March 9, 2014
[14] Transcript of interview with Dr. Wolfgang Ullrich on December 7, 2022
[15] Transcript of interview with Ulrich Baretzky on January 23, 2023 and internal argumentation of Audi Motorsports Communications: Topics of the weekend WEC test day Le Mans, June 4, 2013
[16] Audi Motorsport Communications Q&A hybrid system and engine power, dated March 4, 2014
[17] Audi MediaInfo: The next Audi R18 e-tron quattro, December 12, 2013
[18] Transcript of interview by Ian Bamsey with Ulrich Baretzky on June 12, 2014
[19] Ibid
[20] Audi MediaInfo: Audi develops sophisticated aerodynamics for Le Mans, May 13, 2014
[21] Audi MediaInfo: Efficiency of Audi drivers crucial in WEC, February 24, 2014
[22] Audi MediaInfo: Facts on Audi's 13th Le Mans victory, June 26, 2014

Audi presents the generation RP4 R18 during a warm-up in the blocked-off downtown area of Le Mans (above).
Three of the new race cars compete at the 24-hour race (below)

near the cathedral and leads all the way to the trackside paddock. Despite its low ride height Tom Kristensen boldly steers the sports prototype about eight kilometers through the city and on the steep entrances and exits in the paddock tunnel. To thank the police officers that escorted him on that drive, Tom Kristensen visits them at their station a year later. With the event, Audi brings back memories of the nearly forgotten tradition when the racers used to drive their race cars to Le Mans instead of having them hauled on a trailer. [23]

For the first time, the public gets to see the new color scheme of the R18 e-tron quattro that has become increasingly sophisticated over the years. Dirk van Braeckel, Design Manager Motorsport and Special Projects at Audi, explains: Silver emphasizes the racing successes scored in the past. White harmonizes well with silver, appears very light and stands for hybrid drive. The asymmetric utilization symbolizes the complexity of this powertrain technology, the contours are reminiscent of the graphics of conductive tracks. Black stands for lightweight design, red, as Audi's performance color, completes the look. The reflective styling is especially effective at night. [24] This effect is discernible on the cover of this book.

A season packed with debate

While Peugeot and Audi as the Le Mans protagonists with diesel powertrains until 2011 enjoyed an advantage the weighting has equalized since 2012 upon Peugeot's departure and Toyota's return with a gasoline engine. The 2014 season produces a preponderance on the part of the gasoline units because Porsche relies on that combustion principle as well. A complex chart puts diverse aspects in relation to each other for rating the race cars ("Equivalence of Technology"). They include the hybrid energy amount, the mass of the race car, the energy for gasoline and diesel engines per lap, the fuel tank volume, a fuel technology factor, plus a variable called "K factor" for the design-related higher weight of the diesel engine.

Two weeks before the first race the FIA WEC Endurance Committee changes the ratings. Fuel tank capacity and flow cross section for refueling are reduced for Audi but enlarged for Toyota and Porsche. [25] Following the season opener at Silverstone, Ulrich Baretzky in an interview with Autohebdo complains about the unequal treatment in several aspects, saying that the energy allocations between the classes for 2 and 6 megajoules are unfair. [26] The FIA and the WEC justify their actions at a press conference at Spa with detailed explanations of all individual aspects and intentions of the regulations. [27] In addition, Bernard Niclot, Technical Director of the FIA, takes a stand on the issue in the media. [28]

The atmosphere has been poisoned. The chemical redefinition of gasoline fuels spells further trouble. It does not result in a change to the amount of energy but it does change the knock limit, which promises to provide Porsche and Toyota with considerable thermodynamic advantages. Audi tests this gasoline in its own naturally aspirated V8 engine from the DTM and in a 1.6-liter Volkswagen turbo engine. The engineers arrive at the conclusion that it "is impossible to generate knocking." [29] Even before the new energy regulations for 2014 the idea of bringing the highly developed DTM powerplant to Le Mans as a customer engine emerges at Audi. [30] Because the

[23] Audi MediaInfo: Audi presents the new R18 in urban traffic at Le Mans, March 21, 2014
[24] Audi MediaInfo: Audi unveils the new R18 e-tron quattro, March 25, 2014
[25] Audi Motorsport Communications Q&A Rating of the Audi R18 e-tron quattro, April 9, 2014
[26] Romain Bernard: Technique Hybrides débridées, in Autohebdo, April 23, 2014, p. 42
[27] Equivalence of Technology LMP1. What is there behind the rules?, Presentation by the ACO, FIA and WEC, May 3, 2014
[28] Romain Bernard: La Joute des Joules, in Autohebdo, May 7, 2014, p. 26
[29] Ibid, p. 27
[30] Audi Motorsport Communications Q&A Statements concerning the utilization of DTM engines in LMP1 customer racing, November 10, 2013

Absolute fairness in engine allocation: Race engineers Kyle Wilson-Clarke (number 1) and Matthias Huber (number 3) with their colleague Leena Gade (number 2) after the drawing of lots for the individual powerplants

André Lotterer, Marcel Fässler, Benoît Tréluyer, Loïc Duval and Marco Bonanomi shown in relaxed pose at a PR commitment (above).
The new regulations limit the energy. Audi's e-tron quattro can use up to 30 percent or 6.16 liters per 100 kilometers less than the gasoline engines of Porsche and Toyota (left)

Marco Bonanomi, Lucas di Grassi, Oliver Jarvis, Tom Kristensen, reserve driver Marc Gené, Marcel Fässler, André Lotterer, Benoît Tréluyer and Filipe Albuquerque wish accident victim Loïc Duval a speedy recovery

Transmission designer Emil Schauer at the well-deserved Le Mans farewell (above).
Marc Gené welcomes his compatriot Fernando Alonso to the Audi garage (center).
Wolfgang Ullrich personally thanks the rescue squad for their work after Loïc Duval's accident (below)

assessment of all engines is always based on the respectively most efficient design in a class (gasoline or diesel), and Audi's engine in its own view is better than the Porsche and Toyota units, there would have been rating advantages. However, the envisioned collaboration with Neil Brown Engineering (NBE) and leasing of the powerplants by the Britons to the Rebellion LMP1 team never becomes a reality. [31]

At least one thing remains fair, though: to exclude any suspicion of unequal treatment within its own squad, Audi traditionally allocates its racing engines to the race engineers by the drawing of lots.

Every beginning is difficult

The beginning of the season is as rocky as the political road has been. In the season opener at Silverstone, Audi Sport Team Joest, after having set the fastest time in qualifying, suffers a total loss following crashes by Lucas di Grassi and Benoît Tréluyer on a wet track. At Spa, Audi clinches the runner-up's spot with Lucas di Grassi, Loïc Duval and Tom Kristensen. Following technical setbacks with a pulse generator and tire failure, Fässler/Lotterer/Tréluyer drop back to fifth position. Albuquerque and Bonanomi finish behind them. They are already testing the aerodynamic version for Le Mans that is not perfect for Spa. Audi uses the test day on June 1

From Thursday on, following the driver change from Duval to Gené, car number 1 bears the names of four drivers

to review driving styles in addition to setup work, tire wear and the final aerodynamic configuration. After all, the energy consumption targets put high demands on the drivers.

Shock on Wednesday

In free practice during the race week, car number 1 covers no more than 13 laps. In the Porsche Corners, at 270 km/h, Loïc Duval loses control of his car. There is no television footage of how the accident occurred. The R18 e-tron quattro crashes with its roof against the edge of a robust concrete wall. Consequently, the peak load at high speed is distributed to an extremely small area of the body shell, and parts of the CFRP structure collapse. A track safety camera films the wreckage for a short time. Despite the closed coupé shape of the race car

Duval's helmet is clearly visible. The Frenchman is admitted to a hospital with skin abrasions and stays overnight for observation. The next day – his 32nd birthday – he leaves Le Mans and returns to Geneva. Audi applies for permission to prepare a new car. It is based on the spare monocoque R18-415 that was previously on the grid at Silverstone as number 1. While qualifying is still in progress, race engineer Kyle Wilson-Clarke has chief mechanic Bastian Leiter and his colleagues prepare a new hybrid sports car. Despite the complex technology it is largely finished by Thursday morning. [32]

Reserve driver Marc Gené moves up into car number 1. The mechanics stick his name onto the cockpit as the fourth driver while retaining Duval's. The stewards accept the situation as a case of force majeure and still approve the change on Wednesday evening. [33] At the same time, that creates a vacancy

[31] Transcript of interview with Ulrich Baretzky on December 19, 2022

[32] Audi Motorsport Communications Q&A WEC: Accident of Loïc Duval at Le Mans, June 12, 2014

[33] The Stewards of the Meeting Decision No. 3, June 11, 2014

Oliver Jarvis and Wolfgang Ullrich comfort
Marco Bonanomi. A rival has torpedoed his
Audi during a rain shower

in the number 38 LMP2 race car. Gené has originally been planned as a regular driver for the Jota Sport team. Oliver Turvey replaces him on short notice.

Due to accidents, the first qualifying session is shortened to 50 minutes of real driving time instead of two hours; positions five and six claimed by the two Audi cars are not very conclusive. On Thursday, Oliver Jarvis secures the fifth spot on the grid for the number 3 Audi, André Lotterer in car number 2 is the sixth-fastest and Lucas di Grassi in number 1 is seventh.

An emotional roller-coaster

The 2014 Le Mans 24 Hours last 89 minutes for race engineer Matthias Huber and driver Marco Bonanomi. Filipe Albuquerque and Oliver Jarvis do not get to climb into the cockpit even once. On lap 26, Bonanomi on slicks brakes in rain on the Hunaudières straight. A GT participant in his Ferrari misjudges the situation and crashes into the R18 e-tron quattro that cannot continue racing after the accident. "I feel incredibly sorry, especially for my two teammates and the whole squad," says Bonanomi.

Number 3 drives into the night only in qualifying. After just 25 laps in the race, this Audi becomes the innocent victim of an accident

"Everybody gave everything for success for a whole year during the preparation – and now it's over for us so early. We had the potential to clinch a really good result." [34] The number 8 Toyota is involved in the accident as well but Nicolas Lapierre can continue racing.

Marc Gené, who has switched cars, knows the R18 e-tron quattro from tests but has to get used to driving under the new efficiency requirements on extremely short notice. When he gets out of the car after his first stint at 0.35 am, number 1 is in third position directly behind the sister car. [35] The team is impressed by the Spaniard's performances.

Up until the 219th lap, shortly before the end of the 14th hour of racing, the number 7 Toyota of Nakajima/Sarrazin/Wurz and the number 20 Porsche of Bernhard/Hartley/Webber take turns at the front of the field. Toyota achieves 203 leading laps in the process. However, the team admits having a problem maintaining the tire temperatures at night. [36] An unusual incident thwarts the idea of the Japanese to attack again when temperatures go up after sunrise. A cable harness leading to one of the FIA's onboard data monitoring systems causes a problem. Changing the harness would have cost just a few minutes but the cable melts before Kazuki Nakajima reaches the garage in the pit lane. The Japanese's car just stops. [37] Consequently, shortly before five in the morning, the time monitors show the number 2 Audi with Benoît Tréluyer at the wheel in the top spot for the first time.

Filipe Albuquerque is a Le Mans rookie in 2014 and after years in the DTM thoroughly enjoys the sports car discipline

However, the night does not go completely as planned for the four rings either. During the 13th hour of racing Tom Kristensen loses six minutes when he needs to have an injector changed shortly after three in the morning. About 38 minutes later a puncture forces him to pit again. He drops back to fourth position. [38] Porsche is meanwhile struggling with poor handling of car number 20 and braking issues of number 14. [39]

At 6.05 am, Audi is pleased about the one-two lead of Benoît Tréluyer in front of Lucas di Grassi for the first time. Yet the crack of dawn evolves into a crack of fortune when Marcel Fässler with a three-lap advantage is forced to head for the pits at 6.58 am. The power loss of his V6 TDI requires the turbocharger to be changed. The timing system measures

The many bright brains of the LMP project include telemetry engineer Emmanuel Gien, engine engineer Thibaut Meunier, aerodynamicist Jan Monchaux and engine engineer Thomas Weltert, among others

[34] Audi MediaInfo: Quotes following the retirement of the #3 Audi R18 e-tron quattro, June 14, 2014
[35] Audi MediaInfo: 24h Le Mans – Race Facts (Hour 10), June 15, 2014
[36] Gary Watkins: Audi masters the long game, in Autosport, June 19, 2014, p. 18
[37] Ibid, p. 19
[38] Audi MediaInfo: 24h Le Mans – Race Facts (Hour 13), June 15, 2014
[39] Gary Watkins: Audi masters the long game, in Autosport, June 19, 2014, p. 19

29 minutes and 29 seconds for the 253rd completed race lap before the car with a two-lap deficit returns to the track in third position again. In total, car number 2 loses five laps. For the actual change of the blazing hot turbocharger, the team measures 23 minutes and 18 seconds. [40] The sister car of Gené, di Grassi and Kristensen is now leading in front of the Porsche driven by Bernhard/Webber/Hartley and by 8.45 am extends its lead to as much as a full lap.

Marcel Fässler and André Lotterer meanwhile start fighting back and by the 19th hour have unlapped themselves once, in other words they are on the same race lap as the number 20 Porsche. The gap subsequently varies again due to individual pit stops. [41] André Lotterer continues to exert pressure, takes around five seconds per lap away from the car in front of him and sets a new fastest race lap in the process. At the front of the field, 20 hours into the race, Marc Gené and subsequently Tom Kristensen pull clear of their rival Porsche. Minutes later, car number 1 briefly stops after the first chicane. Yet even resetting the electronics is to no avail: the turbocharger on Tom Kristensen's car fails as well.

Lucas di Grassi succeeds Allan McNish in 2014. Shown in the background are Brad Kettler and Tom Kristensen

This time it takes Audi Sport Team Joest 17.36 minutes to change the unit. With a three-lap deficit the R18 e-tron quattro joins the race again in third position. [42]

As bitter as the setbacks are, they also show the strong team spirit that Wolfgang Ullrich has nurtured in his squad for many years: even in a situation of severe disappointment the drivers of one car do not begrudge their colleagues in the other car an unexpected chance for victory.

Ulrich Baretzky and his engineers soon realize that the VTG controller has failed but spend a lot of time looking for the cause. Abraded slides ultimately prove to be the root cause. Vibrations presumably produce this phenomenon. The problem is solved by isolating the parts by means of rubber elements. Ferdinand Piëch, who advocates on-site dismantling of the unit, which the engine experts refuse for reasons of precision in searching for the fault, insists. However, once dismantled, the described phenomenon cannot be detected with the naked eye. Only detailed analysis reveals the problem. Piëch responds by having three containers with laboratory equipment including microscopes hauled to Le Mans the following year enabling the team to troubleshoot on-site in case that should be necessary. [43]

Marc Gené switches from the Jota LMP2 cockpit to the Audi R18 during the race week. Engineer Kyle Wilson-Clarke is delighted about the Spaniard's performances (above).
The driver parade is a folk festival at Le Mans (below)

Flat-out to the finish line

With another – and now absolutely – fastest race lap 21 hours into the race, André Lotterer reduces the deficit to the leading Porsche to slightly more than one minute. Finally, on lap 340, the German in the Audi takes the top spot which he will not relinquish again on the remaining 40 laps. At the beginning of the 23rd hour, the number 20 Porsche retires so that Audi is now even running in front with two cars. The Toyota of Buemi/Davidson/Lapierre that due to the accident repair lost eight laps at the beginning finishes in third position. As a pleasant side note, Jota with Gené's replacement Oliver Turvey, Harry Tincknell and Simon Dolan makes the best out of the driver swap by winning the LMP2 class.

"It was a race of the kind you can only experience at Le Mans," comments Wolfgang Ullrich. "There were many incidents and none of the top cars made it across the distance without any problems. The decisive factors were that our Audi R18 e-tron quattro cars were able to drive consistently fast for 24 hours, our drivers made no mistakes and our squad responded properly and quickly to the issues that occurred. In Porsche and Toyota we had two really strong rivals who, as expected, did not make life easy for us. I always believed that, in spite of the particularly difficult prerequisites for us this year, we'd be able to succeed and that we've got the most efficient race car. [...]" [44]

A picture of symbolic value: Le Mans visitor Hannu Mikkola is Audi's first World Rally Champion in 1983 (pictured at right). In 2013, Allan McNish (left) together with his teammates Loïc Duval and Tom Kristensen clinches the last World Championship title for Audi in the WEC

[40] Audi MediaInfo: 24h Le Mans – Race Facts (Hour 17), June 15, 2014

[41] Audi MediaInfo: 24h Le Mans – Race Facts (Hour 19), June 15, 2014

[42] Audi MediaInfo: 24h Le Mans – Race Facts (Hour 21), June 15, 2014

[43] Transcript of interview with Ulrich Baretzky on December 19, 2022

[44] Audi MediaInfo: Triumph at Le Mans: Audi defeats Porsche and Toyota, June 15, 2014

Changeable weather challenges the team especially at the beginning of the race. Shown here is Lucas di Grassi on Saturday night shortly before the fifth hour of racing in front of Porsche driver Marc Lieb

After exiting the cockpit, André Lotterer hands number 2 over to his teammate Benoît Tréluyer

The media obviously enjoy the way the race is run. "A new high-tech era dawned with the 82nd running of the Le Mans 24 Hours at the weekend, yet this year's race had a decidedly old-school feel. This was a Le Mans where each and every factory LMP1 car encountered problems, where there were fightbacks galore and where the order continually reshuffled," writes Autosport. [45] auto motor und sport summarizes, "Not even the boldest Audi employees believed in a one-two win of their new R18 cars. But it turned out differently: once again, reliability was the key to success. Audi won despite turbo issues while the quick Toyota cars stumbled. Returnee Porsche cut a fine figure but was ultimately beaten below its potential." [46] L'Équipe comments, "Truly an AUDIssée: Even though the German team was not regarded as a favorite it managed to celebrate a one-two win at La Sarthe yesterday. But the battle against Toyota and Porsche was tough and undecided for a long time." [47]

What nobody knows at that time is that the fifth victory in a row and 13th in total is also Audi's last one at La Sarthe. The rate of victories has increased to 81.25 percent with it. Tom Kristensen, who quits at the end of the year, has been on the podium 14 times in 18 races, his nine victories included. For Marcel Fässler, André Lotterer and Benoît Tréluyer,

The third victory of André Lotterer, Benoît Tréluyer and Marcel Fässler's car number 2 is rather unexpected after a 23-minute repair on Sunday morning, but the sister car needs to have the turbocharger changed as well

this is the third success within four years – just like it is for their race engineer. "Leena Gade has a very large share in our success. She was always with us 150 percent. You need someone like that," Marcel Fässler still emphasizes today. [48]

The success in France is followed at the end of September by another victory scored by Fässler/Lotterer/Tréluyer on the race track at Austin. At that time, "Mr. Le Mans" Tom Kristensen is entertaining initial thoughts of retiring that he shares with Wolfgang Ullrich in Japan in October. [49] At Fuji, Shanghai and in Bahrain, Toyota wins three consecutive times, Porsche secures its first victory in the finale at São Paulo. In the end, Audi's Le Mans winners are the runners-up in the FIA WEC standings behind Toyota's Sébastien Buemi and Anthony Davidson.

After crossing the finish line, the winner traditionally makes a U-turn and in the opposite direction drives down the pit lane toward the podium through a crowd

[45] Gary Watkins: Audi masters the long game, in Autosport, June 19, 2014, p. 18
[46] Claus Mühlberger: Tortour de France, in auto motor und sport, June 26, 2014, p. 137
[47] Carole Capitaine: Une vraie AUDIssée, in L'Équipe, June 16, 2014, p. 2
[48] Transcript of interview with Marcel Fässler on November 15, 2022
[49] Transcript of interview with Tom Kristensen on December 6, 2022

German-German duel

In 2015, the nine Audi drivers are battling for victory for a long time at Le Mans but ultimately have to admit defeat to Porsche.

The Audi drivers in 2015: Marcel Fässler, André Lotterer and Benoît Tréluyer, Oliver Jarvis,
Loïc Duval and Lucas di Grassi, Filipe Albuquerque, Marco Bonanomi and René Rast (from left)

The FIA World Endurance Championship (WEC) with its highlight, Le Mans, is booming. Even the FIA is surprised by the success of the racing series. "Over the past three years the WEC has surpassed all our expectations in terms of growth, popularity, innovation and excitement," says President Jean Todt before the start of the season. [1] The field reflects that. With 14 cars, the 2015 LMP1 field is larger than ever before in the WEC. By the end of the LMP1 era in 2020, this record will never have been broken. A decisive reason is the technical regulations that offer ample freedom – even more than in Formula One. "This is a key factor of what endurance racing is all about and we are very happy to have provided a framework that has allowed technical innovation to be prominent," affirms Sir Lindsay Owen-Jones, President of the FIA Endurance Commission. [2]

Accordingly, the WEC that again encompasses eight rounds is attractive to manufacturers. New on the calendar is the Nürburgring that replaces São Paulo. As a result, the LMP1 race cars sporting the four rings have an appearance in Germany at the same venue for the first time since ALMS raced there in 2001. They must compete again with Toyota and Porsche, plus with newcomer Nissan.

Neuburg as a new location

Audi Sport tackles the season from a new headquarters. Instead of at a former supermarket in Ingolstadt, the racing department is now based

All 13 Le Mans winning cars are featured in the warm-up at Audi Sport in Neuburg

The complex of Audi Neuburg is opened in summer 2014 and covers 47 hectares

in Neuburg an der Donau, where in August 2014 a new high-tech complex is opened that is also home to the new Competence Center Motorsport. That makes a long-held dream of a modern location come true for Head of Sport Wolfgang Ullrich. During his first visit to the former customer team Champion in 1999 it was clear to the Austrian that Audi Sport needed a similarly modern infrastructure. "What I saw there was impressive," says Ullrich. [3] Now Audi Sport has an appropriate location as well. The modern complex of buildings with a total length of 300 meters and total width of 100 meters encompasses a workshop, a test bench building and a warehouse logistics hall as well as the prestigious main building with the development offices. [4] In addition, the area includes a track that can be used for initial rollouts.

[1] www.fia.com/news/wec-full-grids-2015, last retrieved on January 17, 2023
[2] Ibid
[3] Transcript of interview with Dr. Wolfgang Ullrich on December 8, 2022
[4] Audi MediaInfo: Audi opens high-tech complex in Neuburg an der Donau, August 30, 2014

Systematic work

The 2015 Audi R18 e-tron quattro is internally designated as RP5. It is based on the RP4 model for 2014 but clearly reflects further development in terms of energy amount and aerodynamics. "Even after the first tests our drivers confirmed that the reengineered race car feels like a new model," says Project Leader Chris Reinke. [5] Regarding energy recovery, Audi now chooses to move up from the smallest ERS class of up to 2 megajoules to the category of up to 4 megajoules. Therefore, the flywheel energy storage system in the cockpit has a capacity of up to 700 kilojoules – around 17 percent more than before. The electric motor for the front-wheel drive has been updated as well: It delivers more than 200 kW (272 hp), an increase of 30 kW (41 hp). However, according to the regulations, that entails a 2.5-percent reduction of available diesel fuel. The engine that has undergone detailed optimization now delivers 410 kW (558 hp), i.e., 21 additional horsepower. A new provision in the regulations limits the number of powerplants to five for the whole WEC season. While the monocoque has remained the same the modified front hood with front wings, wheel arches and a crash structure provides the sports car with a different look. It also requires a new crash test. Modified airflow through the side pods with new radiator arrangements for the engine and the hybrid system optimizes aerodynamic drag once again. The engine cover wraps around the V6 TDI even more tightly and clearly tapers off directly behind the cockpit. For the eight rounds of the FIA WEC, Audi develops two body versions. In combination with an optimized suspension and in close cooperation with tire partner Michelin, the performance of the sports prototype has been further improved. [6]

[5] Audi Communications Motorsport: Press kit Audi in the WEC 2015, p. 4
[6] Ibid p. 8 et seq

In the last year of its use at Audi, the flywheel energy storage system has a capacity of 700 kilojoules (left).
Modified aerodynamics defining the front give the RP5 a different look even though the monocoque stems from the RP4 (right)

Audi takes on the competition not only with an updated R18 but also with an adjusted driver line-up including five Le Mans winners and four world champions. Two R18 are regularly fielded at all WEC rounds plus a third one at Spa and at Le Mans. Marcel Fässler, André Lotterer and Benoît Tréluyer are working together for the sixth consecutive year; Loïc Duval and Lucas di Grassi, who are joined by Oliver Jarvis as a new regular driver following Tom Kristensen's retirement, form another team. The additional R18 is driven by Marco Bonanomi and Filipe Albuquerque, and René Rast is celebrating his LMP1 debut. The German won the 24-hour races at the Nürburgring and at Spa in the Audi R8 LMS the year before. Mike Rockenfeller is the reserve driver.

Just before the start: Joest's mechanics are pushing the Audi R18 of Loïc Duval, Oliver Jarvis and Lucas di Grassi onto the grid

Old and new rivals

For 2015, title defender Toyota continues to develop the successful TS040 Hybrid model, 80 percent of which is new. [7] Reorganizations have occurred in terms of personnel: Toyota Racing receives a new president, Toshio Sato, as well as changed driver teams. World champions Anthony Davidson and Sébastien Buemi share car number 1 with Kazuki Nakajima; Alex Wurz, Stéphane Sarrazin and Mike Conway are now sitting in the sister car. For the TS040, whose hybrid powertrain can recuperate six megajoules, Toyota publishes a system output of more than 1,000 horsepower. Even so, the season turns out to be a disappointment for the Japanese who do not score any victories.

Now Porsche is Audi's main rival. Even before the season opens, the Swabian brand bursts with self-confidence. Fritz Enzinger, Head of LMP1, states: "We're still a young team, but we finished our debut season with a race win in Brazil and expectations have increased accordingly. We have done intense preparation work for the start of the WEC." [8] Porsche retains the basic concept and name of the 2014-gen model but develops an all-new race car. [9] For the first time, it is homologated for the highest recuperation class with eight megajoules – as the only LMP1 model. Like Audi, Porsche is regularly entering two cars. The two regular squads consisting of Romain Dumas/

Impressive atmosphere: Not only Oliver Jarvis enjoys the traditional driver parade in the center of Le Mans

[7] Toyota press release: A New Era for the World Champions, March 26, 2015
[8] Porsche press release: Porsche Team heads to Silverstone full of energy, April 6, 2015
[9] Porsche press release: 2015 Porsche 919 Hybrid – proven base was extensively optimised, March 26, 2015

Diverse powertrain concepts

Unlike the LMP and LM-GTP rules at the beginning of Audi's campaign in 1999, the LMP1 regulations are standardized. Even so, they allow for ample diversity. 2015 is the season featuring four factory concepts with maximum differences. The Audi, Porsche, Nissan and Toyota race cars at a glance.

Audi R18 e-tron quattro

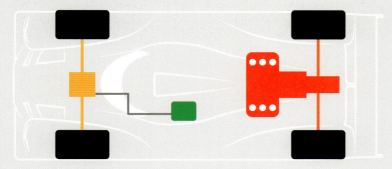

Audi is the only manufacturer in the field with a diesel engine. The four-liter V6 powerplant with a single turbocharger sits in front of the rear axle. For the 2015 season, the brand switches for the first time from the 2- to the 4-megajoule class. The kinetic energy is recovered and used on the front axle. As the only manufacturer to do so, Audi uses a flywheel system to store the energy.

Nissan GT-R LM Nismo

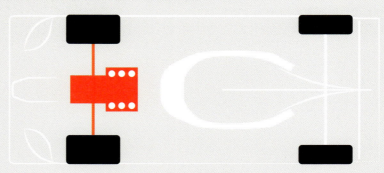

Nissan relies on front-wheel drive and a three-liter V6 biturbo gasoline engine. The intended hybrid system is not completed on time. The plan calls for kinetic energy recovery at the front axle, a twin flywheel energy storage system and feeding of the energy to the rear axle. Because no LMP1 brand is allowed to compete outside of the hybrid category Nissan has its car rated in the 2-MJ class.

Porsche 919 Hybrid

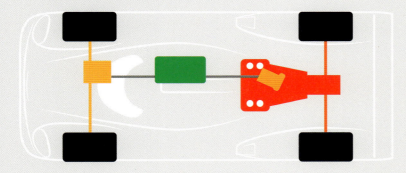

Porsche uses a two-liter V4 gasoline engine. It is installed lengthwise in front of the rear axle. Its exhaust gas drives not only a conventional turbocharger but also an electric generator. Together with the motor-generator unit at the front axle, it feeds a lithium-ion battery that supplies its energy again to the front axle. The 919 races in the 8-megajoule class.

Toyota TS040 Hybrid

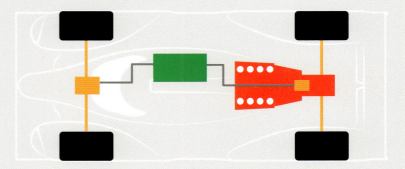

Toyota's powerplant is a 520-hp 3.7-liter mid-engine. The V8 gasoline unit is the only naturally aspirated engine in the LMP1 Hybrid field. One kinetic energy recuperation system each on the front and rear axle enables the Japanese race car to be rated in the 6-megajoule category. Toyota is the only manufacturer to use supercapacitors as an energy storage medium.

■ Internal combustion engine ■ Energy storage system ■ ERS system

The Fässler/Lotterer/Tréluyer squad clinches third place on the podium at Le Mans

Newcomer René Rast contests his only Le Mans race with Audi in 2015

Neel Jani/Marc Lieb and Timo Bernhard/Brendon Hartley/Mark Webber remain unchanged. At Spa and Le Mans, a third 919 is fielded. Formula One driver Nico Hülkenberg takes turns at its wheel with Earl Bamber and Nick Tandy.

Nissan is coming back to Le Mans. For the first time since 1999, Japan's second-oldest automobile manufacturer is returning to the top category of France's biggest auto race where Nissan debuted in 1986. The best result achieved to date has been third position in 1998. Over the past few years, the brand has consistently expanded its motorsport commitment. For instance, in 2008, Nissan started supporting junior talents worldwide in the GT Academy. In addition, Nissan has been involved in GT3 racing, as an engine supplier in the LMP2 and LMP3 classes and with two commitments in the Garage 56 class at Le Mans with its unusual models DeltaWing and the ZEOD RC that delivers the first all-electric lap in the warm-up at Le Mans in 2014. [10] The LMP1 program is announced in May 2014, at which time Andy Palmer, Chief Planning Officer at Nissan, proclaims his brand's aspiration to score victory [11] – something that, in retrospect, appears more like a slip of the tongue than a promise. The new LMP1 race car model, the GT-R LM Nismo, is unconventional due to its front engine and front-wheel drive. It is created in the United States and been tested since the end of 2014. The public gets to see the racer for the first time on February 1 in a Super Bowl halftime commercial break – an action with which Nissan reaches more than 100 million viewers worldwide. [12] At that time, the Japanese are still optimistically talking about a total output of more than 1,250 horsepower, more than 700 of which is supposed to come from the hybrid system. [13] Nissan cancels participations in the first WEC races at Silverstone and Spa though. On the Le Mans weekend, the immature car starts without energy recuperation. [14] As drivers for the three race cars, Motorsport Director Darren Cox signs a motley squad of ex-Formula One, previous Nissan GT and seasoned sports car racers. The team also includes former Audi driver Michael Krumm. At Le Mans, they are fighting in cars that in the race are more than 18 seconds short of the fastest lap. In qualifying, they miss the qualification criterion but are allowed to start at the end of the LMP field. After various problems, only one Nissan finishes at Le Mans but is not classified because it spends more than one third of the race in the garage. After Le Mans, Nissan does not compete in any other races and quietly ends the program in December. [15]

Also competing in the LMP1 field are two privateer teams: Rebellion Racing is fielding two R-One cars. The driver squad continues to include ex-Formula One driver Nick Heidfeld. The ByKolles team has also continued developing its LMP1 model P1/01 that in 2014 did not debut in the WEC until after Le Mans. It is driven by former Audi factory driver Pierre Kaffer, among others. In the race, neither team stands any chance against the factory squads. With a deficit of more than 60 laps, the two Rebellion cars finish in positions 18 and 23. The Kolles car is disqualified because the weight of one of its drivers is too light.

In addition to Audi, Toyota (left) and Porsche (right) compete in the LMP1 class

Promising WEC opener

For Audi, the season starts successfully. In both pre-Le Mans rounds, the brand from Ingolstadt proves unbeatable. Marcel Fässler/André Lotterer/Benoît Tréluyer win both the season opener at Silverstone in mid-April and round two at Spa in early May, where Audi tests the aerodynamic version with less down-force for the first time. By contrast, things go less than perfect for Loïc Duval and company: following collisions and minor technical issues, they clinch positions five and seven. In the third R18, Filipe Albuquerque/Marco Bonanomi/René Rast claim fifth place at Spa. When the teams set up camp at

Le Mans for the official test day at the end of May, Porsche sets the pace with three cars in the top four. Audi achieves positions three, five and six – within 1.9 seconds of the best time.

In the week of the race, the two German premium manufacturers determine events as well. In qualifying, Porsche again puts its cars at the top of the time sheets. Neel Jani at 3m16.887s clinches pole position, followed by Timo Bernhard and Nick Tandy in two other cars from Zuffenhausen. The Audi trio is led by Loïc Duval in fourth position. The best time

[10] www.autosport.com/wec/news/nissan-zeod-completes-first-all-electric-lap-of-le-mans-5052413/5052413/, last retrieved on January 18, 2023
[11] Nissan Leaflet Le Mans 24 Hours 2014
[12] Nissan press release: Nissan reveals Le Mans challenger during Super Bowl, February 1, 2015
[13] Nissan press kit Nissan GT-R LM Nismo, February 2015
[14] Gary Watkins: Nissan: What went wrong, in Autosport, June 18, 2015, p. 26 et seq
[15] www.autosport.com/wec/news/nissan-cans-lmp1-project-after-disastrous-le-mans-24-hours-4995313/4995313/, last retrieved on January 19, 2023

Shop talk: Jörg Zander (left), new Head of Technology at Audi Sport, and Chris Reinke, Head of LMP

Allan McNish remains a fascinating interview partner

set by the Frenchman, who is celebrating a promising comeback at Le Mans after his accident the year before: 3m19.866s. André Lotterer captures fifth on the grid, Filipe Albuquerque in the third R18 claims sixth. "As always, we didn't participate in the time chase because consistency is simply more important at Le Mans than a single fast lap is," Chris Reinke, Head of LMP, says afterwards and ventures a prediction: "Looking at the relative strengths, I'm sure that the first two thrilling WEC rounds at Silverstone and Spa provided a good taste of what the fans can expect here for 24 hours, starting on Saturday afternoon." [16]

Sister brands battling for seconds

Reinke is right. Even though Porsche is clearly faster than Audi in qualifying, the two brands battle each other on a par for a long time in the race. As early as on the starting lap, André Lotterer and Loïc Duval overtake the third Porsche. At the end of the first hour, they are in positions three and four behind Porsche drivers Bernhard and Jani, with mere deficits of 1.7 and 3.7 seconds. Two hours into the race Lotterer leads with a 2.4-second advantage over Bernhard. But about half an hour later, he has to make an unscheduled pit stop due to a puncture and drops back to fifth position. Shortly after that,

Loïc Duval in the number 8 R18 meets with even greater misfortune: at the end of a safety car period in the Indianapolis section, he runs up to several GT entrants that are not accelerating yet. The Frenchman has to avoid them by driving across the grass, touches another car and heavily crashes into the guard rails. The necessary repair costs one lap and causes number 8 to drop back to eighth position. Toward the end of the first quarter of the race, Fässler/Lotterer/Tréluyer fight back to second place again. Their deficit to the leading Porsche amounts to only 3.2 seconds anymore. Six hours into the race the two other Audi cars are in positions three with a twelve-second deficit and eight with a one-lap deficit. Eight hours into the race the top four, consisting two Audi and two Porsche cars, are within ten seconds of each other. Their positions keep changing, depending on the pitting strategy. The front runner now is the R18 driven by Albuquerque/Bonanomi/Rast. The close battle between the German rivals also fascinates the press: "Everyone yearns for the epic motor-racing fights of yesteryear in a way that often makes them fail to recognise when we are living through a period that future generations will look back upon with envy. The Porsche-versus-Audi battle is just that." [17]

During the night, the number 19 Porsche driven by Bamber/Hülkenberg/Tandy takes the lead and temporarily extends it again to more than one minute. However, at five on Sunday morning, Fässler/Lotterer/Tréluyer have narrowed the gap again to ten seconds. But then Audi encounters one problem after the other. Shortly before seven, Fässler has to have the rear cover changed and drops back to fifth position. The now best-placed number 9 Audi repeatedly encounters failures of the hybrid system and shortly before noon has to pit for seven minutes to have a front drive shaft changed. When number 7 loses additional time following a drive-through penalty imposed for disregarding a slow zone and two pit stops for a repair of the rear cover Audi has to give up all hopes of claiming another triumph. Bamber/Hülkenberg/Tandy score the 17th overall victory for the Porsche brand. The runner-up's spot goes to their brand colleagues Bernhard/Hartley/Webber. Fässler, Lotterer and Tréluyer clinch the 17th consecutive Le Mans podium for Audi. Loïc Duval, Lucas di Grassi and Oliver

The unusual Nissan GT-R LM Nismo with a front engine fails to impress

An accident following a safety car period costs
the number 8 Audi valuable time

Jarvis see the checkered flag in fourth position, and
Albuquerque/Bonanomi/Rast, after a strong race,
ultimately must settle for seventh.

That Audi in terms of pure speed would have had
every chance for victory is underscored by sport
auto's analysis: "In the average of the 100 fastest
race laps, the Porsche 919 Hybrid with car number
19 clocked a time of 3m20.209s. Only one LMP1
car was faster, the Audi R18 e-tron quattro number 7 driven by André Lotterer, Benoît Tréluyer and
Marcel Fässler: 3m20.051s – a paltry one and a
half tenths or 0.079 percent based on a lap time of
200 seconds." [18] Remarkable as well is the fact that
the six fastest race laps also go to Audi. [19] But none
of this can compensate for the time lost in the pit
lane. The winning car stops just under 34 minutes
while pitting 30 times, the Audi driven by Fässler/
Lotterer/Tréluyer about eight minutes longer while

Brand ambassador Tom Kristensen
presents "The Book" that was created
in collaboration with one of the
authors of this book

[16] Audi MediaInfo: WEC Le Mans Qualifying: Audi Sport quotes,
June 12, 2015
[17] Edd Straw: Porsche versus Audi is a battle for the ages, in
Autosport, June 18, 2015, p. 5
[18] Andrew Cotton, Marcus Schurig: Weiss gelacht, in sport auto,
August 2015, p. 133
[19] Serge Borgeaud: Summary Le Mans 2015, in Alain Bienvenu,
Christian Moity and Jean-Marc Teissedre: Le Mans 24 Hours 2015,
Antony: E-T-A-I 2015, p. 248

pitting 32 times. The problems with the rear cover have a major share in that: at seven in the morning, the repairs cost 6.56 minutes. When oil must be refilled around noon, the hood that has now been fastened with an adhesive has to be removed and attached again – which is why the stop takes 2.23 instead of some 1.20 minutes. Because the hood comes off again on the subsequent lap Tréluyer has to pit once again for 1.55 minutes. [20] "The cause was a problem with a fastener of the hoods," Wolfgang Ullrich reveals later. "That was never an issue before in any of the endurance tests. Arguably, it was a tolerance issue with the parts for the race weekend. That was hard to digest for us because that wasn't our style at all." [21] The two sister R18 cars, at 38 and 53 minutes respectively, spend

more time in the pit lane as well. [22] Accordingly, Ullrich sums up the race contritely: "That our Audi R18 e-tron quattro was absolutely competitive is a positive. Unfortunately, each of our three cars had at least one crucial incident. And when you're pitted against a strong rival like Porsche you can't afford that." [23]

[20] Transcript of interview with Dr. Wolfgang Ullrich on June 18, 2015
[21] Transcript of interview with Dr. Wolfgang Ullrich on December 8, 2022
[22] Alain Pernot: Audi trips up, in Alain Bienvenu, Christian Moity and Jean-Marc Teissedre: Le Mans 24 Hours 2015, Antony: E-T-A-I 2015, p. 248
[23] Audi MediaInfo: Le Mans: Audi fast but unfortunate, June 14, 2015

Filipe Albuquerque, Marco Bonanomi and René Rast have chances of victory up until Sunday noon

Rudolf Fuchs (pictured at right) is one of the four organizers of the Audi Sport Camp (left). Gerd Muthenthaller, Head of Audi Event Catering with responsibility for catering at the Audi hospitality lounges at Le Mans professionally helps in an emergency in 2000 (right)

An attraction year after year: The Audi Sport Camp at Le Mans

The Audi Sport Camp

For Romolo Liebchen, an engineer at Audi Sport who goes on to become the first Head of Audi Sport customer racing, there is something that is missing at Audi's first race at Le Mans in 1999: How can employees and suppliers that are not integrated in the team structure experience Le Mans on-site? Together with Traunstein beer brewer Theo Wochinger, Liebchen comes up with an idea that he starts organizing in 2000 together with employees Rudolf Fuchs, Jürgen Hofbauer and Maximilian Wüst. Initially, 270 people gather in an area of 3,000 square meters and subsequently 12,000 square meters are made available for half a thousand on the infield of the track. In addition to a parking place, sanitary facilities and cooking areas can be used for a service charge. On the Le Mans Fridays, a suckling pig barbecue is the highlight in the 10 x 30-meter marquee. "We of the race team always enjoyed getting together with the camp visitors even though taps were played for us at ten o'clock at night because we had to enter the race well rested," mechanic Thomas Bauch recalls. [24] Only in 2000, the consistently good organization needs to rely on professional help by Audi's caterer Gerd Muthenthaller. Audi's campground neighbors from the UK politely point out that the liquid manure tank of the Audi squad was overflowing into the British camp. The embarrassed organizers immediately solve the problem and invite the visitors from the island for a beer to make up for the mishap. They, however, do such damage to the beer supply that Muthenthaller has to help out with his stock. [25]

Tents, trailers, rarities such as the modified Audi 200 or motorhomes are used for sleeping at the Audi Sport Camp

[24] Transcript of interview with Thomas Bauch on October 28, 2022
[25] Kultbier, Tröte und Granitboden, in Donaukurier, June 20, 2006

Popular success: 62,000 spectators attend the
WEC premiere at the Nürburgring. The two
Audi R18 cars finish in third and fourth place there

Title race up until the finale

As a result of its one-two win in France, Porsche
takes the lead in the LMP1 manufacturers' classification from Audi. That is followed by an impressive
string of victories claimed by the Swabian brand that
goes on to win all other races of the season. In the
penultimate round at Shanghai, Porsche, on scoring
its fourth one-two of the year, secures the manufacturers' title early. The decision of the drivers' title is
marked by more suspense. Here, thanks to regular
podium finishes, Marcel Fässler, André Lotterer and
Benoît Tréluyer can keep the title race open until the
finale in Bahrain. Following the runner-up's spot in
the desert state, they miss it by only five points.
New driver world champions after four wins are the
Porsche squad of Timo Bernhard, Brendon Hartley
and Mark Webber.

At the WEC round in Japan, Mount
Fuji welcomes the Audi R18 cars

A hilarious
sense of humor

Every year at Le Mans, starting on Wednesday at 2 pm, Audi invites the media to a daily "Meet the Team" event at the hospitality lounge in the paddock. There is one face that is always present on those occasions: cartoonist Pierrick Chazeaud. The Frenchman from Nantes, who to some observers appears to have just emerged from one of his cartoons himself, names two things as his big passion: comics and motorsport. [26] In 1986, he discovers the Le Mans 24 Hours for himself. Ever since then, his illustrations have been published in daily papers such as Le Maine Libre or La Nouvelle République du Centre Ouest. Chazeaud takes his creations to the paddock in large folders that are several centimeters thick. Colorful subjects, powers of observation that are so important for cartoonists, particularly skillful portrayals of the many faces and good subject-matter knowledge define his cartoons: Emanuele Pirro, who is constantly in an upbeat mood, can be seen manically staring from the R8 cockpit, flanked by his German colleagues Marco Werner and Frank Biela. Leena Gade keeps appearing in the cartoons as well. As Miss "24 HRS Audi Sport" wearing a diadem made up of the four rings she wins the hearts of her three drivers, as "Queen Leena goes to Bentley" in 2016 the Audi squad sheds tears about her departure. Marco Bonanomi's distinctive nose inspires Chazeaud to drawing a nose that grows from the R18's monocoque. When Porsche returns to Le Mans in 2014 the cartoonist declares the facility at La Sarthe a "Family village." Although Audi says "Welcome back" to its sister brand a draw bridge rattles down and crushes the first arriving Porsche …

[26] www.pierrickchazeaud.com, last retrieved on January 14, 2023

Marco Werner, Emanuele Pirro and Frank Biela with a work by Pierrick Chazeaud (above).
The prominent artist with one of his cartoons next to Audi driver Benoît Tréluyer (below)

On December 16, 2016 employees gather in Neuburg with Audi's first and last Le Mans prototype to say goodbye

Farewell without flowers

With the new R18, Audi is hoping to be at the top again. Delays in the development set the team back, the withdrawal marks the end of a brilliant chapter of motorsport history.

The 2016 season evolves into Audi's most difficult one in LMP racing – in terms of technology and racing as well as in terms of sporting and corporate policy. And it ends in the brand's withdrawal. Delays occur in the process of building the new R18 race car. The model is fragile and a podium result at Le Mans is questionable for a long time. The prototype named RP6 develops its full potential only in the second half of the season. Politically, the LMP1 category is approaching a crossroads: should the high technology phase be continued or even intensified, like the ACO still announces at its press conference in June? Or are cost cuts and a realignment of the top category in endurance racing necessary? In terms of corporate policy, the diesel crisis has been casting a shadow on the entire Volkswagen Group since the end of 2015 but also affects the technological alignment of individual brands under Wolfsburg's umbrella. The TDI, of all engines, that Audi has been promoting with its LMP programs since 2006 comes under public pressure. [1]

[1] www.audi-mediacenter.com/de/publikationen/weitere/
umwelterklaerung-der-audi-ag-2022-audi-standort-ingolstadt-
der-audi-fertigung-muenchsmuenster-und-audi-neuburg-1134,
Aufarbeitung der Dieselkrise, p. 18, last retrieved on
February 2, 2023

A radical concept

The historically last R18, the RP6 model, is radically new. A slim nose and the new safety cell optimize airflow at the front end once again. The new monocoque calls for modified mounting points for the front axle. For the first time, Audi Sport uses single arms instead of A-arms (wishbones) at the front in order to improve kinematics. The linked suspension system (LSS) – a hydraulic link between the front and rear suspensions – enables passively generated optimal balance at all speeds. Active systems are prohibited. The R18 starts with ample rake, a concept known from Formula One where ground clearance at the rear is higher than at the front. As speed increases, downforce pushes the high rear closer to the ground. Via the hydraulic compensation the front axle can maintain a more constant distance level to the ground and is less dependent on load changes. The new proportions of the car force Audi to save space at the rear. That is achieved by a shorter transmission without a reverse gear. Even so, the car complies with the rule of having to be able to drive backwards – thanks to the hybrid system.

A new high-pressure central hydraulics unit replaces the electric actuators for the steering system, brakes, driveline and engine. For energy storage, Audi switches to a lithium-ion battery. It processes 6 megajoules – three times the amount in 2014 and 50 percent more than in 2015. The previous flywheel energy storage system guarantees high power density in smaller ERS classes. Switching to a higher class and the higher energy amount suggest changing the system. The MGU at the front axle delivers 350 kW (476 hp). In the rather short braking phases, it is allowed to have unlimited energy input but at Le Mans may only deliver 300 kW (408 hp) during acceleration. The higher the ERS class the lower the allocated amount of fuel. On balance, the 4-liter V6 uses 46.4 percent less energy than the first 2006-gen 5.5-liter V12 TDI. Even so, the R18 is ten to 15 seconds faster per lap. A lighter-weight turbocharger further enhances the efficiency of the engine that now delivers 378 kW (514 hp). In total, this results in nearly 1,000 horsepower of system output combining electric and ICE propulsion. [2]

[2] Audi Motorsport Communications: Basic information Audi in the WEC 2016

The slim nose of the Audi R18 Type RP6 accommodates complex technology for safety, the suspension and the powertrain in an extremely small space (above). For the first time, Audi uses a battery as the ERS energy storage system (below)

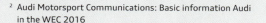

The new design achieves its first victory in the Spa 6 Hours in May

Three competitors

Following Nissan's withdrawal, Audi, Porsche and Toyota are left in the LMP1 class as they were before in 2014. Privateers Rebellion and ByKolles complete the LMP1 field. In the interest of limiting costs, the two German factories of the VW Group agree to reduce their lineups from three to two race cars. [3] Porsche, like the year before, relies on its driver trios Timo Bernhard/Mark Webber/Brendon Hartley and Romain Dumas/Neel Jani/Marc Lieb. Continuing to be signed at Toyota with no change are Sébastien Buemi/Anthony Davidson/Kazuki Nakajima and Mike Conway/Stéphane Sarrazin who are driving with Kamui Kobayashi following Alexander Wurz' retirement. Audi relies on Loïc Duval/Lucas di Grassi/Oliver Jarvis and for the seventh consecutive year on Marcel Fässler/André Lotterer/Benoît Tréluyer. René Rast is the reserve driver. Organizationally, Audi Sport assigns someone else to the role of Project Leader LMP after Chris Reinke has taken the reins of Audi Sport customer racing. Stefan Dreyer, previously Project Leader Racing Engine Operations and intimately familiar with endurance racing, assumes his new role after the Le Mans 24 Hours. Also, after that event, Erik Schuivens succeeds race engineer Leena Gade, who leaves Audi. [4]

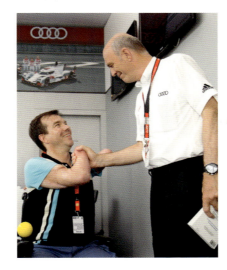

Wolfgang Ullrich with Frédéric Sausset (top left). Audi Sport supports the race of the quadruple amputee driver (above). The Frenchman shares the cockpit with Christophe Tinseau and Jean-Bernard Bouvet. All are wearing the four rings on their racing suits (left)

Part of the field as well is an exceptional trio that like Audi's six factory drivers is wearing the four rings on its racing suits. Frédéric Sausset, who had to have his arms and legs amputated after a bacterial infection, races in a specifically modified Morgan-Nissan based on an LMP2 model. He has prepared for the race in national endurance racing in France and in the European Le Mans Series. At Le Mans in 2016, he is on the grid as part of the Garage 56 project. [5] Audi Sport and Audi France support the project both non-materially and financially. Sausset and his teammates, Christophe Tinseau and Jean-Bernard Bouvet, put up a good fight. In the end, they can be proud of finishing the race and achieving position 38.

Ambitious concept

The technical innovations of the R18 include a lithium-ion high-voltage battery whose development is delayed. "We made exacting demands on the

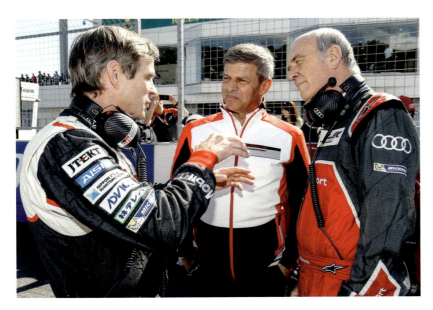

Pascal Vasselon, Technical Director of Toyota, Porsche's Head of Sport Fritz Enzinger and Head of Audi Sport Wolfgang Ullrich

[3] Audi Motorsport Communications Internal briefing booklet Le Mans 24 Hours, May 10, 2016
[4] Audi Motorsport Communications: Q&A personnel and current topics FIA WEC 2016 season opener, April 13, 2016
[5] https://srt41.com, last retrieved on February 2, 2023

Instagram
Now
24h 24heuresdumans
LE MANS Circuit des 24 Heures

♥ 18 190 616

For 2016, Audi reduces its driver lineup to Lucas di Grassi, Loïc Duval, Marcel Fässler, André Lotterer, Oliver Jarvis and Benoît Tréluyer

battery cells. They came from the United States and were intended only for military use," says Wolfgang Ullrich. "The delivery problems set us back not only with the software. We also needed the real battery for crash tests and other safety tests. That's why everything was delayed." [6] Marcel Fässler recalls today: "We had been planning for several thousand kilometers of testing at Sebring but completed only a fraction of that. The LSS suspension was so hard that my feet were hurting because they hit areas at the top and bottom of the monocoque. Afterwards André Lotterer got into the car and after a few laps said that it was undrivable. It had a lot of teething problems. Le Mans just came one or two months too early for us because the car was subsequently running better and better." [7]

When the Swiss and his teammates win the WEC opener at Silverstone in the middle of April many worries seem to have vanished into thin air, but the opposite is true: hours later, car number 7 is disqualified because the front skid block on the underfloor was worn by more than five millimeters and therefore too thin. [8] A defect in the linked suspension system is the root cause. Three weeks later, at Spa, Lucas di Grassi, Loïc Duval and Oliver Jarvis win in front of Porsche after Toyota has retired.

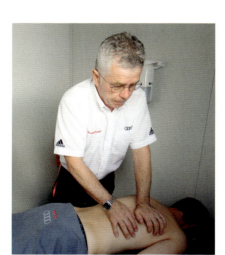

Physiotherapist Paul Bandus attends to the drivers throughout the entire Le Mans period (left).
Vincenzo Tota, shown here with physiotherapist Lena Nussbaumer, is the team's physician (above)

Stefan Dreyer, pictured on the right with Andreas Roos, Project Manager Operations, assumes leadership of the LMP project from Chris Reinke, who goes on to lead Audi Sport customer racing starting in 2016

Slow start at Le Mans

Yellow flags, so-called slow zones in which the participants must drive at reduced speed, several interruptions and plenty of rain: The race preparations of the teams at Le Mans in the qualifying sessions starting on Wednesday are anything but business as usual. The battle for the grid positions is decided as early as at the beginning of the first qualifying session on Wednesday night. After that, the lap times no longer improve. However, Audi Sport Team Joest is still working on both R18 cars at that time. André Lotterer subsequently sets the fifth-fastest lap, the sister car follows 43 thousandths of a second behind in sixth position. While Audi shares the third row on the grid with both cars, both Porsche cars are at the very front and Toyota locks out the second row. [9]

The race starts as laboriously as the week has begun. A heavy rain shower prompts race control to start the competition behind the safety car for the first time in the history of the event that has been held since 1923. Four-time Le Mans winner and Eurosport commentator Henri Pescarolo, who has experienced races in rain and fog, utters just one opinion about that: "Scandalous." [10] The competition is released only after 52 minutes.

Setbacks again and again

Meanwhile for Audi Sport Team Joest having taken the risk of an early tire change on a drying track after the race has been released pays off: André Lotterer is the first driver from the group of front runners to have slicks mounted at the beginning of the second hour. Loïc Duval follows a lap later. Lotterer cannot enjoy the lead resulting from this skillful tactical maneuver for very long though. At 4.19 pm, he has to pit to have the turbocharger changed. The reason is a housing that has not been manufactured with dimensional stability. [11]

After 20.40 minutes, the car, now driven by Benoît Tréluyer, returns to the track. A six-lap deficit causes

number 7 to drop to position 59. [12] By the sixth hour of racing Fässler, Lotterer and Tréluyer have fought back into the top ten.

The sister car battles with Porsche and Toyota for the top spots and in the early stage is running in third position. However, due to a door being changed before the end of the fifth hour of racing,

[6] Transcript of interview with Dr. Wolfgang Ullrich on December 7, 2022
[7] Transcript of interview with Marcel Fässler on November 15, 2022
[8] http://fiawec.alkamelsystems.com/noticeBoard. php?season=05_2016&evvent=01_Silverstone, last retrieved on February 2, 2023
[9] Audi MediaInfo: Both Audi cars on third row at Le Mans, June 17, 2016
[10] Gary Watkins: As wrong as rain, in Autosport, June 23, 2016, p. 13
[11] Transcript of interview with Ulrich Baretzky on December 19, 2022
[12] Audi Motorsport Communications: 24h Le Mans Hour 2, June 18, 2016

Car number 7 in front of the tradition-steeped Auberge des Hunaudières whose history dates to 1928

the best Audi loses two positions. Until shortly before 11 pm, both R18 are reeling off their laps when the mandatory illumination of the car numbers fails on both race cars. Changing the light on number 8 costs three minutes while the sister car in seventh position now has a total deficit of seven laps. [13] When Benoît Tréluyer shortly before midnight happens to drive through a gravel trap he has to have a new front hood installed. In the sister car, a puncture forces Loïc Duval to make an unscheduled stop shortly thereafter. Number 8 in fourth position is now two laps behind the front runner, Toyota. Fässler, too, has to have a blown tire changed in the eleventh hour of the race. Two hours later, he misses a braking point, can no longer engage any gears and drives fully electrically for a while. The transmission can be shifted regularly again only after that. [14]

In the following hours, both R18 consolidate positions four and five behind a Toyota, a Porsche and another Toyota. Only 17 hours into the race Audi manages to increase its pace. "We got it right at the test day and we thought we were happy with the balance, but come the race we had no grip," says Ralf Jüttner. [15] The tires pick up too much rubber. [16] Lap times improve only after the team manages to use the Michelin tires in the right operational window

Audi dealer Lecluse's guests enjoy a perfect view, here of car number 8 heading for the first Hunaudières chicane

again. After encountering vibrations, Audi Sport Team Joest, 19 hours into the race, changes the front and rear hoods on Marcel Fässler's car. In the 20th hour of racing the better of the two Audi R18 cars suffers a setback: Oliver Jarvis has to head for his crew at 10.41 am. The engineers detect a defect on the front right brake rotor that is causing further damage. Changing the entire quarter suspension costs the Brit 39.24 minutes. However, at the front end of the field, he does remain in fourth position with large gaps. To be on the safe side, the mechanics subsequently change the two front brake rotors on the other car in 9.29 minutes, Tréluyer maintains position five. [17]

Actor Brad Pitt visits Marcel Fässler at the Audi garage

[13] Audi Motorsport Communications: 24h Le Mans Hour 8, June 18, 2016
[14] Audi Motorsport Communications: 24h Le Mans Hour 13, June 19, 2016
[15] Gary Watkins: Porsche steals Toyota's race, in Autosport, June 23, 2016, p. 10
[16] Audi Motorsport Communications Q&A analysis of the Le Mans 24 Hours, July 12, 2016
[17] Audi Motorsport Communications: 24h Le Mans Hour 21, June 19, 2016

Well sorted

Races are also won in the garages – that is a true statement: Audi's 2011 winner, for instance, spends only 33.56 minutes being serviced. In the hybrid era, though, the race cars are more fragile and smaller fuel tank volumes require many pit stops. In 2016, the winning Porsche already stops for 38.08 minutes and Audi is forced to park even 1.13 hours due to defects on the third-placed car. In order to save every second during repairs, every – legal – trick matters. Instead of single parts, entire prefabricated assemblies such as quarter suspensions, i.e., suspensions with wishbones, drive shafts, pushrods, wheel carriers and pre-ventilated brakes, are stored in the garage tent behind the pits.

Audi started co-locating the requisite tools with the parts to be changed – brake rotors in this case – early on

"I created special tools and we thought about how to change the parts faster," Thomas Bauch recalls. "How might the design of assemblies be modified in order to change them faster? Our pit stop training was focused on accelerating processes as well." [18] The former Audi Sport mechanic relates that already at the beginning of the program, all spare parts have previously been installed in the car and run on the track once. That is the only way to ensure precision fit and functionality. The quick-change transmission in the R8 that was permitted before 2004 is even constantly pre-heated to ensure that it perfectly harmonizes with the hot engine. The team also always prepares small containers with parts including precisely the right tools. Despite such preparation, the mechanics' job during regular pit stops is extremely hard: the crew must resist the forces of wheelguns opening the wheel nuts at 1,000 Newton meters and closing them at 650 on the R8 and even at 850 Newton meters on the R10 TDI.

[18] Transcript of interview with Thomas Bauch on October 28, 2022

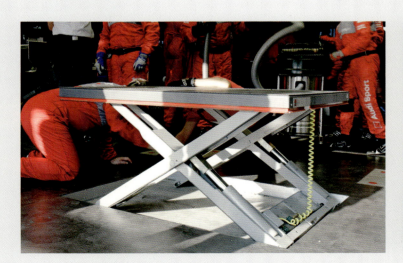

Audi Sport Team Joest experiments with repair lifts in the garage floor as early as in the days of the R10 TDI (far left). Prefabricated quarter suspensions make it easier to change them under time pressure (left)

Porsche clinches its second consecutive victory

Toyota has had to cope with what has arguably been the most unusual setback in Le Mans history one lap before the end on the start-finish straight while leading the race

Final act Hollywood-style

The number 8 Audi is in fourth position at the beginning of the last hour. With a deficit of 13 laps to the leading Toyota and nine to the third-placed car, chances are that Audi, for the first time in its Le Mans history, may miss a podium finish. Millions of TV viewers and the trackside crowd – including actor Brad Pitt who has visited Audi's garage – do not believe their eyes: Buemi/Davidson/Nakajima's Toyota that has been leading for 68 laps simply stops on the 383rd and penultimate lap on the start and finish straight, right at the level of the Toyota pit perch. On their 18th attempt, the Japanese are once again

deprived of victory. As a result, six years after having set his distance record for Audi, Romain Dumas together with his Porsche teammates Neel Jani and Marc Lieb crosses the finish line as the unexpected winner. Because Toyota cannot repair the defect in time and thus fails to comply with a time requirement in the regulations car number 5 completely drops out of the classification. That is the only reason why Lucas di Grassi and his teammates move up to third position, followed by their sister car.

"The cars were fragile," says Leena Gade looking back. "The R18 was very complex. And when it wasn't working it was just one system affected another system

An idea
with potential

Audi designs a form of mobility for the future in which green electricity plays a key role. It can supply not only the electric motors in the e-tron models but is also the driving force behind some of the Audi e-fuels: climate-friendly alternative fuels for internal combustion engines. Audi produces petroleum-independent fuels that bind as much CO_2 during their production process as they release again during combustion. They are called Audi e-gas, Audi e-diesel, Audi e-gasoline and Audi e-ethanol. [19]

Therefore, the company in 2013 opens the Audi e-gas plant in Werlte, in the northern German Emsland district. Using wind power, the site produces the Audi e-gas from water and carbon dioxide. In the first stage, the plant uses the renewable electricity for splitting water into oxygen and hydrogen. The hydrogen in the medium term can also serve as fuel for fuel cell cars. In the second process stage, synthetic methane, is produced by the reaction of hydrogen with CO_2 that is provided by the exhaust gas flow from a neighboring organic waste biogas plant. Chemically, it is nearly identical to fossil natural gas and can be distributed to CNG filling stations through the natural gas network. [20]

Audi Sport wants to use that idea for contesting Le Mans in 2016 in a CO_2-neutral way. The plan is to compensate for the CO_2 emissions caused by the production of Shell's Le Mans diesel fuel in Qatar. However, in view of the diesel crisis and highly sensitive public awareness concerning offsetting arrangements for reporting purposes, the management board does not give the plan the green light. [21]

[19] www.audi-mediacenter.com/en/presskits/audi-e-fuels-5119, last retrieved on February 1, 2023
[20] www.audi-mediacenter.com/de/audi-future-performance-days-2015-5097/die-audi-e-fuels-5104, last retrieved on August 12, 2022
[21] Transcript of interview with Ulrich Baretzky on January 23, 2023

Audi e-gas project

Wind energy
Electric power generated from renewable sources provides the basis for the Audi e-gas project

Power grid
The wind energy is fed into the public grid

Gas network
The e-gas is stored in the public gas network and therefore can also supply households and industry with energy from renewable sources

Electrolysis
The electrolyzer that operates with wind power splits water into oxygen and hydrogen

CO_2

Methanation
Hydrogen reacts with carbon dioxide in a methanation system. The result is e-gas (synthetic natural gas)

CNG filling station
The increasing share of e-gas promotes climate-friendly long-distance mobility

Audi e-gas plant

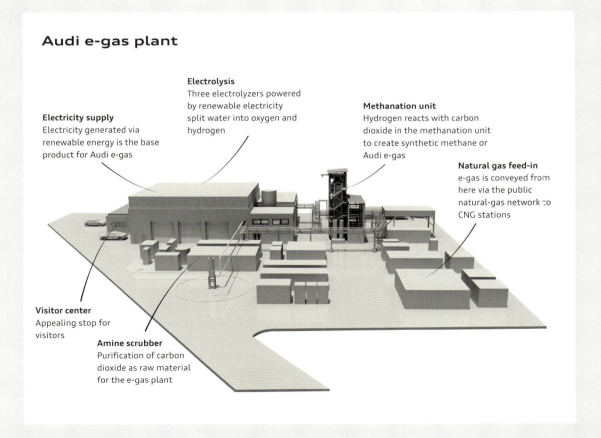

Electricity supply
Electricity generated via renewable energy is the base product for Audi e-gas

Electrolysis
Three electrolyzers powered by renewable electricity split water into oxygen and hydrogen

Methanation unit
Hydrogen reacts with carbon dioxide in the methanation unit to create synthetic methane or Audi e-gas

Natural gas feed-in
e-gas is conveyed from here via the public natural-gas network to CNG stations

Visitor center
Appealing stop for visitors

Amine scrubber
Purification of carbon dioxide as raw material for the e-gas plant

Electric future

When the Le Mans project ends in 2016 the era of electrification in motorsport at Audi is already in its fifth year. But that does not mean that the technological journey into the electric age has ended – on the contrary. By entering FIA Formula E Audi not only fields a battery-electric vehicle (BEV) for the first time. The single-seater contesting the 2017/18 season uses the motor-generator unit (MGU) that on the R18 sits on the electrified front axle. For 2021, its final Formula E season, Audi Sport develops the completely new MGU05 including an inverter with 97-percent efficiency in all relevant driving conditions. [22] It drives not only the Audi e-tron FE07 to success. When the brand begins it Dakar Rally development program in 2021 it uses three of these units: one MGU drives the front and one the rear axle. A third one is part of the energy converter that charges the high-voltage battery for the electric powertrain as needed. [23] Thus, a technology transfer takes place also between those projects.

[22] www.audi-mediacenter.com/en/audi-in-formula-e-2021-13376, last retrieved on February 14, 2023

[23] www.audi-mediacenter.com/en/audi-at-the-dakar-rally-13989, last retrieved on February 14, 2023

Audi continues pursuing the pathway of electrification in motorsport in FIA Formula E (above).
The Audi RS Q e-tron for the Dakar Rally also has an electric drive (right)

affected another system. As race engineers, we were just managing a bit here and managing a bit there. We were just trying to keep the car running." [24]

Decision-making stage

After the checkered flag has fallen at La Sarthe things become complicated. "Could such a disappointment jeopardize the brand's future in endurance racing?" Before the race day has ended L'Équipe confronts Audi's Head of Sport with that question directly. "One thing is certain. Going home with such a result is not very pleasant. Nobody is happy. We'll see in the next few days. But in sports you should never forget that there are days when nothing is going

For the first time since 2013, Marcel Fässler, André Lotterer and Benoît Tréluyer are not on podium

right and you've got to stay motivated to do better next time," Wolfgang Ullrich responds. [25] In the same issue of the French sports paper, Audi's marketing department places an ad that says, "364 days to go. Audi Sport congratulates Porsche on winning the most prestigious endurance race and Toyota on the competition. We thank our teams for their exceptional performances and our fans for their support. We look forward to participating again next year. Even faster."

The ambivalence of these messages is matched by the ambivalence of the sport as a whole: the race cars are highly efficient but also extremely complex, no longer as reliable as before and extremely expensive. From today's view, the plans for 2018

that the ACO announces during the Le Mans week appear almost bizarre: the ERS categories are supposed to be extended by a 10-megajoule top class, the number of permissible energy recuperation systems to increase from two to three. At the same time, the allocation of gasoline and diesel is planned to drop by eight percent respectively. [26] As we know today, the LMP1 category does not have a long future anymore. In 2021, the lower-cost Hypercars encompassing the Le Mans Hypercar (LMH) and Le Mans Daytona h (LMDh) versions replace the former top division. [27]

In terms of racing, the second half of the season clearly points upward for Audi. At the Nürburgring, Duval/di Grassi/Jarvis record a runner-up's spot in

[24] Transcript of interview with Leena Gade on December 13, 2022
[25] Carole Capitaine: Audi, le plein de soucis, in L'Équipe, June 20, 2016, p. 48
[26] 24h Le Mans Informations Presse: L'Automobile Club de l'Ouest présente ses nouveautés 2016 et les règlements à venir, June 16, p. 9
[27] www.fiawec.com/en/classes/32, last retrieved on February 2, 2023

The many farewell gifts include this cartoon presented to Wolfgang Ulrich at the finale by Sheik Salman bin Isa Al Khalifa, the director of the race track in Bahrain

front of their teammates; Lotterer and Fässler in the absence of Tréluyer who was injured in a bicycle accident subsequently finish runners-up in Mexico. At Austin and at Fuji, Duval/di Grassi/Jarvis are runners-up again.

End of the LMP program

Ten days after the race in Japan, it is announced: "Audi with new motorsport strategy: Formula E instead of WEC." [28] The company talks about a strategic realignment. "We're going to contest the race for the future on electric power," states the Management Board before the manufacturer enters the all-electric Formula E racing series.

Following disappointing positions five and six in round eight of the season at Shanghai, Audi crowns

its commitment with a worthy finish at Bahrain: Although Porsche and Toyota are battling for the manufacturers' championship title di Grassi/Duval/Jarvis as new runners-up in the world championship together with Fässler/Lotterer/Tréluyer celebrate a dominant one-two win with an advantage of more than one minute over Porsche. Two weeks after the new course was set at Audi, Volkswagen decides to end its rally program, and a year later, Porsche leaves the FIA WEC and Le Mans as well.

"Honestly, I've got to say that for a very long time I was still optimistic that we would be able to do the next year for sure or else we would not have continued the development of the new car without any limitations," Wolfgang Ullrich says today, looking back. "Ultimately, the decision to quit came as a surprise for me too even though I repeatedly attended management board meetings. I realized that something had to have happened from the Group's side. A sizable part of the budget for the development of the next-gen car was already spent. And our bosses knew that. When that decision was made anyhow it must have been driven by something that I couldn't affect with my arguments. Having to tell the team was painful. They were in the process of getting the best LMP car off the ground that we had ever made." [29]

Internally, Audi justifies the decision with the greatest transformation phase in the company's history and excessive burdens. "The diesel issue has accelerated our decision," says a response to query. [30]

The ending after 107 sports car victories including 13 successes at Le Mans is emotional. In Bahrain, tears of joy about victory blend with those of regret about the end of the LMP program. At a farewell event in Neuburg in December, journalists are provided with a last opportunity to test the R18 on the track. Audi parts with the sports car program in dignified style. A heyday in the marque's motorsport history has ended.

[28] Audi MediaInfo: Audi with new motorsport strategy: Formula E instead of WEC, October 26, 2016
[29] Transcript of interview with Dr. Wolfgang Ullrich on December 7, 2022
[30] Audi Motorsport Communications Q&A: Audi with new motorsport strategy: Formula E instead of WEC, October 26, 2016

Competitor Toyota says goodbye with a gesture of good sportsmanship

Just like the whole squad says Cheerio! Audi's PR team led by LMP manager Eva-Maria Veith (center row, fourth from left) is farewelled by the FIA WEC PR team headed by press spokeswoman Fiona Miller (center row, fifth from left)

Bidding farewell with a one-two win: In Bahrain, Audi is leaving the LMP stage after 18 years

The phantom

The public never gets to see the R18 that was planned for 2017 because it does not exist as a real race car. However, models in various scales provide an impression.

This is what the R18 for 2017 would have looked like. The wind tunnel model reveals many details

Although the race car that is internally named RP7 has been designed Audi cancels all orders with its suppliers when the management board puts an end to the LMP program in October 2016. A considerable part of the development budget has already been invested. "I was an optimist for a very long time; otherwise, we would not have unstintingly continued the development," Wolfgang Ullrich recalls. "The decision came as a surprise to me, too, even though I repeatedly attended board meetings." [1]

[1] Transcript of interview with Dr. Wolfgang Ullrich on December 7, 2022

Extreme flow: The air ducted through the front end – shown here along the left front wheel – gives an inkling of the aerodynamicists' radical thinking

The photographs in this chapter show two models: a 60-percent scale model for the wind tunnel to develop the car's aerodynamics and a smaller model for visualizing the planned wrap. Just like the RP2 and RP3 as well as the RP4 and RP5 versions before it shared the same monocoque as a basis, the RP7 builds on the RP6. The designers have set their sights on aerodynamics and packaging for 2017, attempting to compensate for further restrictions imposed by the regulations. The new rules prescribe 65 instead of 50 millimeters of ride height, which reduces downforce. A lateral "exclusion zone" in the wheel arch serves to improve flow inclination in yaw angles to prevent the race cars from lifting off when they start spinning. In addition, the ACO reduces the dimensions of the rear diffusor in length and height with the objective of reducing downforce by an additional 20 to 25 percent.

Radical aerodynamics

To implement the car's aerodynamics, the engineers led by Jörg Zander have optimized the arrangement of the radiators in the tightly tailored side pods. The coolant, the charge air and the low-temperature fluid for the hybrid system circulate inside these radiators. The 120-degree V6 TDI engine, whose main

features date back to 2011, is provided with individual, optimized details. They include a new turbocharger and the next-generation engine control unit. The MS 24.11 evolution has higher processing power.

The hybrid powertrain that was fundamentally redeveloped for 2016 is retained for 2017. Audi continues using the compact MGU for the extremely slim front end. The slender nose provides the aerodynamicists with the necessary freedom to optimize air ducting and to thereby maximize the available energy when the air hits the aero platform. The lithium-ion battery located to the left of the driver is retained for 2017 as well. With the RP7 model, Audi intends to continue racing in the ERS class with 6 megajoules of energy for the track at Le Mans. By contrast, the RP8 planned for 2018 is designed for the class of up to 8 megajoules. For that purpose, the developers intend to install a second hybrid system on the rear axle, but the development will never progress to that point. [2]

Audi develops innovative ideas for ideally ducting the air toward the aero platform (above). This is what the livery for 2017 would have looked like (right)

[2] Information provided by developer Axel Löffler on August 31, 2022

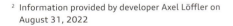

The heavily tapered tail releases the air to the outside after it has flowed through the car (far left). For 2017, a battery-electric drive system is planned again (left)

Transfer
in both directions

When in 1998 Audi is forced to give up quattro all-wheel drive in racing, the threat of "Vorsprung durch Technik" becoming invisible looms. In reality, it will start flourishing again, in the LMP age.

In 2014, Audi's laser light debuts in the R8 LMX, and in the same year also at Le Mans

With Le Mans, Audi evolves into a key contender in the sports car segment. The first R8 is derived from the 2003 Le Mans quattro concept car (left). The second generation pioneers the use of CFRP as structural components, shown here on the R8 Spyder (above)

Whether in rallying, at Pikes Peak, in circuit racing in America, in the DTM or in Super Touring Car events: Since 1981, quattro all-wheel drive has always been on board with Audi in motorsport. It not only improves driving dynamics and leads to victories and titles but the successes in motorsport can also be transferred to the production side of the house. In the first four decades since 1980 alone, Audi produces about 10.5 million models with four driven wheels. [1] The new driveline enables the brand to introduce increasingly more powerful engines as one of the stepping stones to the premium class in which Audi causes a paradigm shift: competitors feel that they must follow suit, and all-wheel drive has been available in the lineup of all premium brands ever since.

quattro: From symbol to ban

In motorsport, the task is becoming increasingly difficult from discipline to discipline. While at first quattro naturally has a bonus on dirt roads in rallying, the traction-related advantages clearly decrease on the tarmac in circuit racing due to higher friction coefficients. Moreover, during the course of the years, Audi can use less and less power. From over 700 horsepower in the Audi 90 fielded in the IMSA GTO to about 470 horsepower in the DTM, it drops to mere-

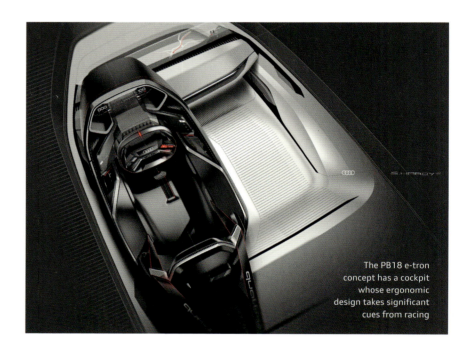

The PB18 e-tron concept has a cockpit whose ergonomic design takes significant cues from racing

ly 300 horsepower in Super Touring Car racing. Even so, Audi Sport designs the A4 quattro so efficiently that it can convert its traction advantage into victories and titles despite low output and higher weight. The dominance of the four driven wheels ultimately leads to a ban in FIA circuit racing from 1998 on. With the sports prototypes at Le Mans, all-wheel drive is irrelevant. "When we went to Le Mans, one of the things that were painful for us, was having to give up the link between our top-caliber motorsport activities and all-wheel drive that we previously always had," admits former Head of Sport Wolfgang Ullrich in retrospect. [2]

Arrival in the sports car segment

However, Audi Sport does not have to wait long before shining again with new technological concepts. Its entry to the category of sports prototypes and initial victories at Le Mans have suddenly made the former brand of automobiles for middle-class citizens a credible contender in the sports car segment. When in September 2003 the Le Mans quattro concept debuts at the Frankfurt International Motor Show IAA, the audience gets a foretaste of the sporty future. [3] Just three years later, customers can order the road-going sports car Audi R8 that has directly evolved from the concept. Besides the

name of the legendary Le Mans race car, it has adopted many features from racing, from the double wishbone suspension to lightweight design to the mid-mounted engine. The second generation of this model range that is introduced in 2015 already has a Multimaterial Space Frame, combining aluminum with carbon fiber reinforced plastic (CFRP), the material that is of vital importance in constructing the Le Mans prototypes. The center tunnel, the rear wall and the B-pillars are made of it. Together, they form the car's high-strength, extremely torsion-resistant backbone. Not every concept from AUDI AG becomes a reality like the Le Mans quattro but the endurance race remains a source of inspiration. The PB18 e-tron is presented two years after the end of the Le Mans program at the Pebble Beach Automotive Week in Monterey, California. Not only the similarity of the name suggests the kinship. Audi makes explicit reference to the technology genes of the R18 e-tron

[1] www.audi-mediacenter.com/en/40-years-of-quattro-the-all-conquering-technology-from-audi-12598/four-rings-four-wheel-drive-40-years-of-quattro-12599, last retrieved on February 15, 2022

[2] Transcript of interview with Dr. Wolfgang Ullrich on December 7, 2022

[3] www.audi-mediacenter.com/en/audi-le-mans-quattro-3411, last retrieved on February 15, 2022

At Laguna Seca, California, in 2018, Audi unveils the PB18 e-tron as a puristic sports car of the future

On the R18, Audi switches to full-LED headlights. Eight modules per unit illuminate the track better than ever before

Matrix LED headlights with Audi laser light

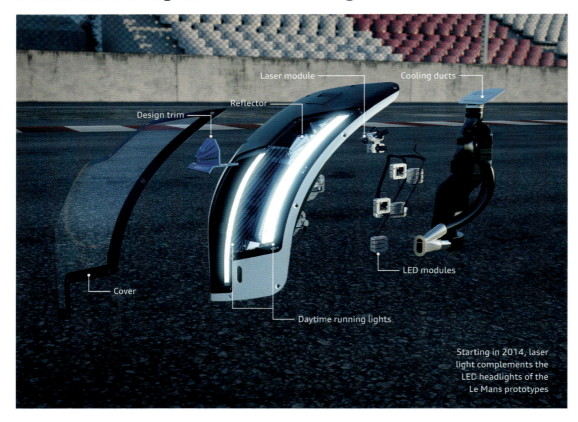

Laser module

Cooling ducts

Reflector

Design trim

LED modules

Cover

Daytime running lights

Starting in 2014, laser light complements the LED headlights of the Le Mans prototypes

quattro LMP1 race car such as the double wishbone suspension with a push-rod system at the front and pull-rod operation at the rear. [4] The monocoque shell that is slidable sideways inside the cockpit and provides for by-wire operation of the steering and pedal systems instead of using mechanical controls promises particular sophistication.

Lighting inspirations for the future

In addition to such fundamental inspirations, there are far more links between motorsport and production technology in the Le Mans era. Audi first uses modern LED technology in 2006 as daytime running lights on the R10 TDI. On the R15 TDI, the light diodes additionally function as the high beam. The modules have been adopted directly from the production Audi R8 that is the world's first automobile with full LED headlights at that time. When the Audi R18 TDI contests its first Le Mans race with full-LED headlights in 2011, the drivers are thrilled by the illumination of the racetrack. The eight LED modules per headlight consume less energy for this purpose than before and increase the light range from 482 to 836 meters, i.e., by 73 percent. During the day, five of the eight main diodes generate a low beam, and in high beam mode at night, all eight elements are active. The color temperature of 5,500 kelvins is similar to that of daylight, thus reducing driver fatigue. Plus, the circumferential light strip, which serves as a turn signal among other things, switches to a color allocated to the car's number when the driver enters the pit lane. As a result, the mechanics can identify their car from a distance and summon it to the right parking place. At about the same time, ten NEDC measurement cycles with the Audi A6 reveal that the new lighting technology helps avoid roughly one gram of carbon dioxide emissions per driven kilometer. In that case, the LED headlights consume only 80 watts instead of the 135 watts of halogen units. [5] Matrix-beam technology is introduced in the race car as well, enabling a kind of cornering light by activating, deactivating or dimming individual modules. Thanks to glare-free high beams, lane light, orientation light and marking light using the new digital matrix-LED headlights, Audi customers travel clearly safer and more comfortably on the road.

Digital matrix LED headlights

 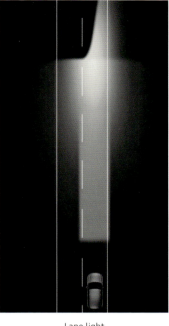  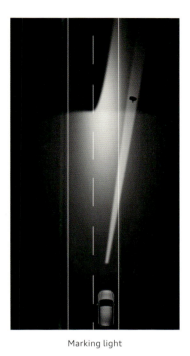

Glare-free high beam   Lane light   Orientation light   Marking light

In 2014, Audi uses a combination of LED and laser light. The laser enables a far more homogeneous and precise spread in front of the car. In January, at CES 2014 in Las Vegas, Audi concurrently presents the Audi Sport quattro laserlight concept and a frontal section of the new Audi R18 e-tron quattro including the headlights. Audi only retrofits the previous R18 with matrix LED technology whereas the engineers integrate matrix-beam and laser diodes in the new generation right from the beginning, thus enabling further optimization of the intelligent cornering light. Depending on the car's position on the race-track, it illuminates a corner even before the driver turns in. "I've never had such good light on a race car as on the new R18," enthuses Marcel Fässler. "It's

4 www.audi-mediacenter.com/en/press-releases/world-premiere-at-pebble-beach-the-audi-pb18-e-tron-concept-car-10599, last retrieved on February 15, 2022
5 Audi MediaInfo Magazine: Motorsport and Production: Audi Le Mans Prototypes 1999–2013, 2013, p. 31

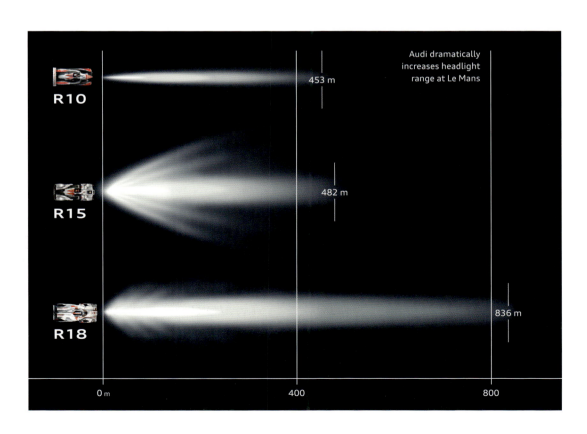

TDI engines set standards at Le Mans particularly in the area of high-pressure injection technology

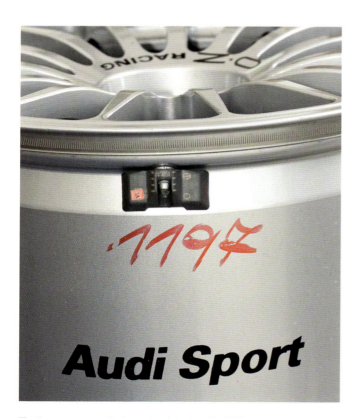

The tire pressure monitoring system introduced in 2001 uses production-level sensor technology

even clearly better than last year. I wouldn't call this just one step forward, but three. The laser light is brighter, more concentrated and more precise. For example, you can see the apex of a corner much better with it." [6] The motorsport team explicitly takes advantage of its close cooperation with the Technical Development division at AUDI AG that helps with components and know-how from development projects, for example. The brand's customers benefit from the new technology as well. In 2014, the Audi R8 LMX is the first model equipped with laser light that soon becomes an option in other model ranges as well. To this day, Audi has been consistently expanding its position as a leading manufacturer in this area for the benefit of its customers thanks to digitization and other innovations. [7]

From tire pressure to the engine

Even the early chapters of Le Mans history provide examples of technology transfer. When, in April 2001, Michele Alboreto, due to a puncture caused by foreign object debris (FOD), dies in a test at the Lausitzring, Audi is already working on a tire pressure monitoring system (TPMS). For Le Mans, it is fully fit for use. The technology for it stems from production. "The technical coordination of using it in each tire was a difficult task," Wolfgang Ullrich recalls. "The system had to understand where which tires are mounted and with which sensors the wheels are equipped. That was extremely complex, not visible to the public and, even so, placed a massive burden on the team. But all of us were unanimously in favor of it and implemented it. As the system continued to evolve, things became easier." [8]

2001 also marks the debut of FSI technology. Gasoline direct injection is already a topic of interest in the Super Touring Car years but the availability of the still rare injector prototypes on the suppliers' side of the house is not guaranteed. The subject receives a new boost in sports prototypes. In 1999, the first cylinder heads are already designed for future direct injection, and in January 2000, the actual work begins. [9] At the Vienna Engine Symposium in June 2000, Volkswagen's Chairman of the Management Board Ferdinand Piëch announces direct injection as the way forward. [10] In 2001, the racing engine debuts at Jarama and shortly afterward wins at Le Mans. A basic decision in favor of a homogeneous mixture formation instead of a stratified charge marks the project's beginning. The intake ports generate a tumble in order to maximize the homogeneity of the charge by means of the controlled air movement with a corresponding injection valve. This principle is subsequently fed into mass production, enabling driving pleasure, sportiness and ten to twelve percent less consumption in the typically used power ranges. [11] Since the technology asserts itself in the Group the reduced consumption has effects on a worldwide scale in millions of vehicles.

While in the case of the gasoline engine racing technology inspires the production vehicle developers, it is the other way around with the TDI engine

in the Le Mans project – at least in the beginning. Since 1989 Audi has been producing TDI engines for road-going vehicles. "It was very important that, after the FSI, we'd come up with a technology for Le Mans again that, via Le Mans, would then be brought to the world in a new positioning effort," says Wolfgang Ullrich. "And at that time, the diesel engine accounted for an extremely large share of cars sold in the Group and at Audi. Plus, the diesel practically ticked all the boxes. The only thing it was slightly lacking was the 'sporty touch,' so we saw the opportunity to change that. And we succeeded. That was also always a very supportive reason we could state vis-à-vis the management board." [12]

[6] Audi MediaInfo: Laser light assists Audi drivers at Le Mans, January 20, 2014
[7] www.audi-mediacenter.com/en/press-releases/how-audis-light-digitization-is-pointing-the-way-toward-the-future-14624, last retrieved on February 15, 2022
[8] Transcript of interview with Dr. Wolfgang Ullrich on December 7, 2022
[9] Transcript of interview with Ulrich Baretzky on December 19, 2022
[10] Automobil-Wirtschaft 2-2000, June 7, 2000
[11] Ulrich Baretzky, Wolfgang Hatz, Dr. Wolfgang Ullrich: Rennsport bei Audi – Impulse für die Serienentwicklung am Beispiel FSI, presentation without location and year, p. 7
[12] Transcript of interview with Dr. Wolfgang Ullrich on December 7, 2022

As Head of Engine Development at Audi Sport, Ulrich Baretzky, in 2001, introduces FSI direct injection and, in 2006, TDI technology at Le Mans

When Audi unveils the camera-based digital rearview mirror with an AMOLED display in the R18 (both pictures above) it appears like a message from the future. By now, the camera-based mirror helps save energy in the e-tron production models (below)

During the preparation of the racing engine Ulrich Baretzky consults with the diesel development department of the Technical Development division. For the first time, a one-cylinder unit for testing a variety of parameters is also created at the beginning of the racing project. However, the production V12 TDI that is concurrently in preparation clearly differs from the racing version because it only has 60-degree cylinder bank angles in order to enable its installation in the passenger car from the bottom. The racing engine has 90-degree bank angles in view of the center of gravity and stiffness. Even so, the simultaneousness of the development does have an advantage: The motorsport team's attempt to keep their concept under wraps for as long as possible is successful. Whenever a rumor emerges, they refer to the twelve-cylinder unit for consumers that is in fact in the making. "Nothing was leaked to the outside world even though the whole Neckarsulm site knew about it. I'm still proud of those people today," Baretzky recalls. [13] With the progress achieved in the following years, the injection pressure limit of 2,000 bar is soon exceeded. Subsequently, the corresponding levels in the production units follow suit. The utilization of variable turbine geometry starting in 2009, however, catches up with a step that has long become routine business on the production side of the house, but which in motorsport, at temperatures of 1,000 degrees centigrade, reaches limits from which road-going passenger cars are far away. When the regulations start reducing displacement by one third in 2011, Audi Sport pursues the path of downsizing, which exactly matches the objectives for lowering emissions of production vehicles.

Lessons learned from aerodynamics

Last but not least, a look at aerodynamics reveals amazing parallels as well. When Audi, in 2012, introduces a digital rearview mirror, the primary reason is to enhance vision. The closed cockpits obstruct the driver's external field of vision. A roof-mounted, miniaturized rearview camera transmits its signals to a display in the interior of the R18. However, instead of the common LCD displays with LED backlighting, Audi uses an active-matrix OLED display

Audi e-tron Sportback 55 quattro

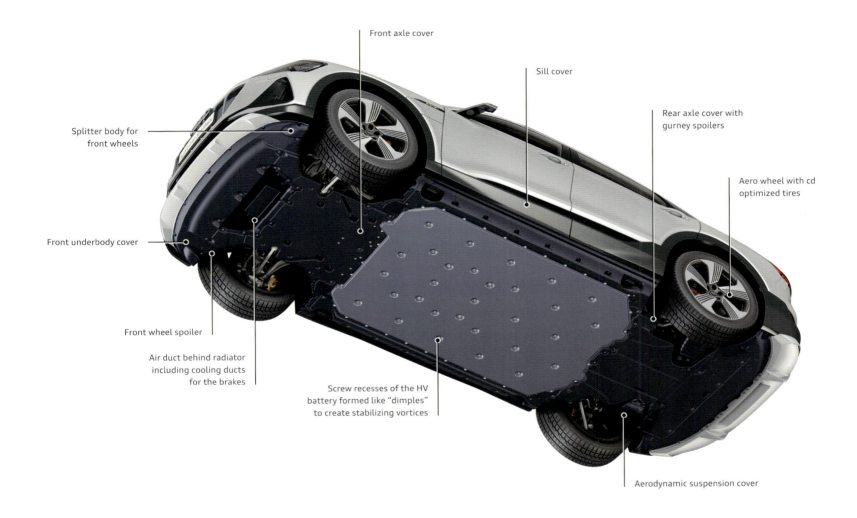

Front axle cover

Sill cover

Rear axle cover with
gurney spoilers

Splitter body for
front wheels

Aero wheel with cd
optimized tires

Front underbody cover

Front wheel spoiler

Air duct behind radiator
including cooling ducts
for the brakes

Screw recesses of the HV
battery formed like "dimples"
to create stabilizing vortices

Aerodynamic suspension cover

(AMOLED). In it, the organic materials used are luminous themselves and do not require backlighting. The displays are thinner and of lighter weight, deliver high contrast and good color accuracy, and operate with switching times of just a few milliseconds. Even at 330 km/h in real-time transmission, they achieve a totally fluid image flow. [14] In Audi's current e-tron models, the camera, compared to out-side mirrors, decreases the frontal area and thus demonstrably reduces aerodynamic drag. As a result, it contributes to optimizing aerodynamics and increasing range – a key factor in electric mobility. Another principle, which is invisible on the road but extremely effective, is directly modeled after its counterpart in motorsport as well: the planked underfloor helps enhance airflow and therefore extend range.

[13] Transcript of interview with Ulrich Baretzky on December 19, 2022
[14] Audi MediaInfo Magazine: Motorsport and Production. e-tron quattro, 2012, p. 62

Audi Sport from the media's perspective

The assessment of the Le Mans era and its many facets is not intended to be solely up to the two authors of this book. Various international media professionals agreed to express their independent views of the Audi sports car program at the 24-hour race.

Stéphane Barbé, French journalist, born in 1960. Covered the 24 Hours of Le Mans 34 times, initially as a young reporter having started in 1976 and 1977, and then, from 1986 to 2021, as a journalist for L'Automobile Magazine and, especially, for L'Equipe

Stéphane Barbé

The Frenchest of all foreign race teams

For a French journalist, it was a blessing that Audi Sport selected drivers such as Romain Dumas, Loïc Duval und Benoît Tréluyer, and thanks to their French-speaking teammates André Lotterer and Marcel Fässler, even more so. A fantastic trio! Because, even though everyone in this environment was able to converse in English, it's always easier to engage in exchanges in your native language. For greater nuance and precision in speech, better background with reference to explanations, and

easier-to-grasp descriptors that a journalist appreciates. With Romain, Benoît and Loïc, we managed to build a sound relationship of trust to better understand the world of Audi Sport, for exciting interviews for the newspaper L'Equipe and for very comprehensive articles. That enabled us to explain to our readers the challenges and mode of operation of a major race like the Le Mans 24 Hours or the World Endurance Championship WEC.

These close ties were, no doubt, very visible because they also made the relationship with all the other drivers of the team easier: Tom Kristensen, though less familiar with the French language and I even less with the Danish language. Dindo Capello, who spoke English, too, but once, amused, recited a French nursery rhyme from his school in Italy – I think it was about a delivery van and a little bell that could be used for honking. And, of course, Emanuele Pirro, who on the podium of the 24-hour race communicated with the audience: his wonderful Italian accent was simply enchanting. And, finally, there was the outstanding French that Dr. Ullrich practiced. He knew how to play with that: when he spoke in the language of Molière, we were immediately softer on him with his little secrets as Head of Sport. Thanks to all of them, the press events of the Audi Sport team were always a pleasure.

In this very Francophile atmosphere, which gave the fierce battle against the Pescarolo prototypes or the Peugeot 908 a particularly respectful character, I mustn't forget my friend Allan McNish. I'd very much appreciated our relationship since Formula 3000 in the nineteen-nineties, especially during his much-noted time with the DAMS race team of the late Jean-Paul Driot. That's where the Scotsman learned the French language and subsequently perfected it when he took up residence in Monaco. Following a series of interviews that he had given in French before the Le Mans 24 Hours, he started the conversation with me by saying, "For you it's going to be in English!" Thanks, my old friend.

Christian Borel

2011: The year of the grail!

My debut at Le Mans dates to 1967, the "race of the century," according to experts. Naturally, it was the last century in which I had the good fortune to see the car of the century (still the 20th century) in action: the Porsche 917! But how the French novelist Bernard Clavel writes in his book "Victoire au Mans:" "What I got to know at Le Mans is a very simple thing: life."

I would add: encounters, some of them unlikely, all of them friendly. People you enjoy meeting once a year at Quinconce des Jacobins or trackside; drivers, journalists, many anonymous people, plus the mechanics that the media forget. The people that find their rewards in sweat and oil! A victory at Le Mans is reserved to just a handful of chosen ones, but for them, it's already a victory when their car sees the checkered flag or continues its hellish race after a long break.

In 1982, at the Monte Carlo Rally, I came to know Audi Sport. A team led by Roland Gumpert with Stig Blomqvist, Hannu Mikkola and Michèle Mouton. With its all-wheel drive, Audi turned the World Championship upside down. The end of the last century then saw the big leap to the marathon around the clock at Le Mans, and this time, the face of endurance racing was fundamentally changed. Everything is changing. For us journalists and photographers, the age of communication begins. With all its deficits and benefits: the lack of spontaneity of the drivers who, more often than not, reel off the lessons they've learned, is the main weakness. Other than that, everything's almost perfect.

In addition to the brand's numerous triumphs, Audi, in 2011, gave us the grail that the Swiss fans of the 24-hour race at Le Mans were still lacking: victory. At the end of 2007, together with five colleagues, we published the first volume of "Les Suisses au Mans." We were desperate because, despite 123 appearances since 1923, no one had ever

Christian Borel, born in 1950, reported about the Le Mans 24 Hours 47 times from 1967 to 2017. He wrote for L'Impartial (Swiss daily paper), La Revue Automobile (French version), Pole Position (Canada), and since 2007, the volumes "Les Suisses au Mans" together with five co-authors and as the publisher

stood on the top step of the podium. Second places, group victories, index victories, one pole position ... but no winner across the distance! At 1500 hours 2 minutes and a few seconds, on Sunday, June 12, Marcel Fässler closed that gap together with Benoît Tréluyer and André Lotterer. The event did not begin well for Audi because they lost two cars before midnight. And it ended in a sprint. Arguably, one of the brand's sweetest victories. For us Swiss, it was the most fantastic one. The team repeated this feat the following year, and in 2014, with the same success.

Thank you to that fantastic winning machine, in which the unplannable is planned. At the top of the hierarchy are the continually available Dr. Wolfgang Ullrich, the engine genius Ulrich Baretzky, Leena Gade, the car's engineer, and the dozens of managers, mechanics and assistants.

Carole Capitaine

At the 1999 Le Mans 24 Hours, an edition that is shaped by the participation of numerous global manufacturers, Audi already stands out even though they're not yet in contention for victory. The team competed at La Sarthe with two kinds of prototypes, a closed Audi R8C and an open Audi R8R. Why is that so? Because the brand with the rings, which despite its collaboration with the seasoned Joest Racing team was new in endurance racing, was not sure whether one or the other would have an advantage on a track as special as that of Le Mans. In front of everyone's eyes – competitors, organizers, journalists – Audi acknowledges its questions as well as its financial means – and does so without complexes.

Without complexes! That's what I as a French journalist take away from Audi's successful adventure at the Le Mans 24 Hours. "Sans complexe" means not presumptuous or arrogant. Without complexes means unwavering commitment, intense passion for competition.

Carole Capitaine, born in 1972, longtime journalist at L'Equipe, the French daily sports paper for which she reported about the Le Mans 24 Hours from 1998 to 2016

Dr. Ullrich and his teams always respected their rivals without giving them a break (!). Dr. Ullrich and his teams always respected their partners while demanding quality and performance of them. The structure soon became a winning machine scoring success. The legend starts writing itself, with women and men that stick together, with drivers, engineers and mechanics that listen to each other and truly work together.

Without complexes, Audi introduces the direct-injection engine, the diesel engine and the hybrid powertrain into the races and wins … with Tom Kristensen sets the record for the most winner's trophies for a driver, which is nine, or the longest distance covered during a 24-hour race, of more than 5,410 km, in 2010. Aside from the successes, the dizzying statistics, the design of the prototypes, the organization of the team and the character of some of its poster boys and girls, the picture or pictures that Audi has stamped on my memory talk about the unfiltered passion for racing. In the pits, live during the 24-hour race, in the films produced by Audi and in the words of the officials and drivers, the race and everything it stands for – competition, risk, defeat, fear, accident, fatigue, concentration, strain, industrial challenge – was always highlighted, sublimated, and portrayed without complexes.

As a result, Audi, in its communication with the general public, was able to share snapshots of victories as well as documents of defeats, of anxiety, of stress, of the horrible accidents at Le Mans in which, for example, Allan McNish, Mike Rockenfeller or Loïc Duval were involved … All emotions of the competition were always shared regardless of whether they were very positive or much less positive. In 2009, following the defeat against Peugeot, Audi treated itself to a campaign in the media, especially in L'Equipe, to congratulate the winner and to emphasize that this new experience, the one of losing, was not to its taste. Who would dare communicate a defeat? Audi! And without any complexes.

Andrew Cotton

The secret to Audi's success in endurance racing was its unwavering commitment under the direction of Motorsport Director, Dr Wolfgang Ullrich. Following Audi's debut at Le Mans in 1999 most of the other manufacturers had stopped their programmes, including Mercedes, Toyota and Nissan. However, against expectations Audi stayed, facing the likes of BMW, Cadillac, Bentley, Peugeot, Toyota and Porsche during its 17-year era in prototype racing.

Dr Ullrich had a vision, one that would ensure that Audi's name became indelibly linked to Le Mans. Audi used its endurance racing platform to introduce technology that was relevant to production cars, including direct fuel injection, an aluminium diesel engine and a flywheel hybrid system. Never was there an engine failure on track and rarely were cars retired from races due to mechanical failure.

What was also remarkable was Audi's commitment to its drivers. They were expected to be great, but Audi turned them from drivers into brand ambassadors. Tom Kristensen won seven of his nine Le Mans titles with Audi, but others such as Emanuele Pirro, Frank Biela, Rinaldo Capello and Allan McNish represented Audi for many years as part of the family. They were valued assets, and they repaid that faith with some extraordinary races. The wins at Le Mans in 2008 and 2011 will be spoken about for many years due to the manner in which they were won. Against strong opposition from Peugeot, Audi triumphed, in 2008 thanks to an aggressive strategy by long-time partners Audi Sport Team Joest and its lead race engineer Howden Haynes, and in 2011 thanks to some remarkable driving from Benoît Tréluyer (who could forget THAT overtake on Sunday morning!), Marcel Fässler and André Lotterer, who set fastest lap of the race with a punctured rear tyre.

The R8 was an almost perfect racing car in factory and customer hands. Teams such as Veloqx, Goh and Champion were able to take big wins with the car around the world. Audi encouraged its importers to run the cars, such as Audi UK, Audi Japan and Audi North America which further developed Audi's global family.

Andrew Cotton, born in 1974, is editor of Racecar Engineering and writes for sport auto and Motorsport aktuell magazines. He has been working in sports car racing since 1995 and has been on the ground at Le Mans from 1995 to 1997 and every year since 1999. His father, Michael, was at Le Mans as a spectator in 1963, '65 and '67, and started working there a year later. He quit in 2008, saying that he would never witness a better race, so he missed out on 2011...

Graham Goodwin

The R8R featured the first carbon chassis that Audi had built, and at first the management was not sure that it could be done in Germany. Such technology was not yet commonplace but, in the UK, racing technology norfolk did have the expertise. Therefore, Audi commissioned them to also build a car, the closed-cockpit R8C. It was commissioned too late to be fully developed for the 1999 race and the R8R was ultimately chosen to take Audi forward. Dr Ullrich preferred the open-topped car. There were politics behind the scenes of course, but the Austrian was convinced that the spectators needed to see the drivers at work and to identify them by their crash helmets.

The Bentley Speed 8 that came in 2001–2003 featured an Audi-based engine and many accuse Bentley of running the Audi with a roof. However, Bentley's Speed 8 of 2003 was far advanced compared to the R8 and much of its technology, including telemetry system and gearbox was adopted by Audi into its diesel R10 programme. The R10 TDI was a car that transformed the perception of diesel as a sporting fuel, and it succeeded particularly in the US. Despite regulations that limited their potential, the diesels were dominant until the hybrid era truly began in 2014. Audi was there first, with the R18 e-tron quattro in 2012, although the hybrid wasn't fully developed at that stage and was not powerful enough to make a difference.

Audi stayed faithful to diesel to the end of its programme, and many were sad to see it leave. Audi still had so much more to give, and as it was loyal to endurance racing, many in endurance racing developed a lasting affection for Audi.

Audi's arrival on the scene in sports prototype racing saw the game moved on very considerably. That manifested itself in engineering innovation in both engine and aerodynamic design, a level of serviceability for the R8 that left the competition gasping in their wake, and a level of superiority over the competition that saw the car successively reeled in by the rule makers to give the rest a chance!

And no sooner had the rulebook and the competition closed the gap on the all-conquering, five times Le Mans-winning R8, then Audi simply changed gear again. The step forwards this time though was perhaps even more significant. The history-making R10 TDI brought with it a revolution in endurance racing, an era where the astonishing torque of modern turbo-diesel technology would reign unchallenged for half a decade.

Three more Le Mans wins came for the R10 as Audi faced off a worthy adversary in Peugeot, the French factory worked to overcome the Audi dominance in the shorter races, but failed all but once to deliver the biggest crown of them all at Le Mans! That era saw the relatively short reign of the radical, but perhaps not handsome R15, the initial car deemed an aero step too far by the powers-that-be, but a revised version taking on and beating Peugeot yet again in 2010!

And then 2011 and the R18, a series of Audis that would straddle yet another new era, this time for hybrid technology with Audi starting the history of the FIA World Endurance Championship as they had completed the Le Mans Series years, as winners.

Graham Goodwin, born in 1964, is a renowned authority on endurance racing. In 1995, he was at Le Mans for the first time, and since 2002, he has been working as editor and partner of the Dailysportscar website. His range of activities also encompass television and radio, for instance as a colour commentator in the FIA World Endurance Championship (WEC)

Twice World Champions as a manufacturer and a team, and yet more racing legends in mechanical and human form came as 2012 saw hybrid technology become the stunning norm, the flick of the switch to an era of outlandish performance and astonishing battles.

By the time the programme was ended, in the views of many somewhat prematurely, Audi had scored 13 wins in the Le Mans 24 Hours in just 18 years (with the 2003 Bentley also powered by an Audi turbo V8).

The Audi programme changed sportscar racing forever. The cars were legends, and many of the drivers too – 15 drivers won at Le Mans at the wheel of an Audi – and no fewer than nine of them did so more than once!

The level of preparation and excellence of the Audis saw seismic shifts right across the sport, and the pace and reliability of Audi and their challengers set records time after time after time.

And whilst the cars showcased an array of emerging technology, much of it with now familiar nomenclature: TFSI, TDI, e-tron quattro, they also proved to be just as effective in pushing customers to the showrooms as the Audi brand emerged from the shadows to establish a market presence for sporting and stylish road cars that it retains to this day.

As one pressroom colleague said to me more than once: "There are two sorts of people in this room – those that have already bought an Audi, and those that want to!"

Gary Watkins

When the Audi R8 crossed the line to take victory in the 2000 Sebring 12 Hours, we knew we had witnessed the debut of a rather special racing car. The sportscar world immediately installed Audi and the R8 as favourites for the Le Mans 24 Hours just three months later, but no one could have envisaged the success the LMP car would go on to enjoy over such a protracted period. Nor that it would change the face of our branch of the sport.

The legacy of the R8 stretches far beyond its five Le Mans victories, six drivers' and manufacturers' title doubles in the American Le Mans Series, and 60-plus wins over six and a half seasons, and the reputations it helped make, nine-time Le Mans winner Tom

Kristensen's included. It didn't so much as move the goalposts in endurance racing, as pick them up and then plonk them down on another playing field. Endurance races became flat-out sprints in the R8 era. The car could be driven hard and fast over a full 24 hours, and if it did break, it could most likely be repaired in double-quick time. Who can forget two R8s limping back to the pits after going off on oil at Le Mans in 2004 and then rapidly returning to the fray? The crashed Audi Sport UK Team Veloqx entry could be put back together, though the driver, Allan McNish, couldn't. He had to sit the race out as his car came home a delayed fifth.

The super-fast changes of the complete rear end were a key to the famed serviceability of the R8. The backhanded compliment paid to the car and its designers was a rule change that outlawed the practice. The R8 also set new standards for safety. The Formula 1-style head-restraint, previously unseen in sportscars, inspired another rule change. They subsequently became mandatory on prototypes under Le Mans rules.

The R8 did have a negative effect on sportscar racing, however. The argument that the R8 didn't face the kind of opposition as, say, that other great of endurance racing, Porsche's 956/962, isn't entirely fair. The Audi triumphed over rivals from Cadillac, Chrysler, Panoz, MG and, in America only, BMW. But it is true that Audi armed with such an effective machine as the R8 frightened off opposition. Cadillac admitted that it quit the scene because it couldn't compete on fuel mileage with the direct-injection FSI version introduced in 2001.

It's not difficult to put your finger on the secret of the R8's success. Just talk to the drivers who raced the car, and to a man they will tell you that it was an easy car to drive. It was quickly honed into a machine with few if any vices. It was easy for teams to run, as well. It came with a manual, which if you followed made the R8 the ultimate plug and play racing car.

Gary Watkins, born in 1967, grew up within earshot of the racetrack at Brands Hatch. He joined motorsport in 1976 when James Hunt was occupying the front and back pages of the newspapers, has been a journalist since 1989 and, since 1990, has missed only one edition of the Le Mans 24 Hours. He is known as a journalist of Autosport magazine but publishes in Motor Sport, Racer, Autoweek, Autocar and Autocourse as well

Driver parade

Without the many drivers competing at Le Mans with Audi between 1999 and 2016 the impressive results in the 24-hour race would not have been possible. Brief portraits of all factory drivers and race winners

Christian Abt
Born on May 8, 1967

Christian Abt initially contests single-seater and subsequently touring car races for ABT Sportsline. He celebrates numerous successes with the Audi A4 and benefits from his technical knowledge in the process. The German Super Touring Car title in 1999 is a career highlight. Following a season as a factory driver in 1998, Audi includes him in the sports car project as a test driver. In 1999 and 2000, Abt has the chance to race at Le Mans, once in the R8C and once in the R8, in which he achieves a podium finish. After eight seasons in the DTM, he stays with Audi and as a driver and team principal wins the ADAC GT Masters with the R8 LMS several times.

Laurent Aiello
Born on May 23, 1969

In 1998, Laurent Aiello with Allan McNish and Stéphane Ortelli wins Le Mans for Porsche. At the premiere of the Audi R8R in 1999, he achieves fourth position. In 2000, he finishes runner-up with McNish and Ortelli, a result he repeats in 2001. The Frenchman clinches his biggest success with the R8 in March 2001 as the winner at Sebring. Subsequently, he focuses on the DTM. In 2002, the hobby DJ wins this championship in the Abt-Audi TT-R following previous title wins in France, in the German Super Touring Car Cup and in the UK. Later, Aiello ventures the leap into jet skiing where he becomes world champion in his category.

Michele Alboreto
Born on December 23, 1956
Died on April 25, 2001

Michele Alboreto is at Le Mans for Audi as early as in 1999. The Italian, the 1997 winner at La Sarthe in the Joest TWR Porsche, is truly a stroke of luck for Audi Sport. Thanks to his calm nature and huge experience from nearly 200 Formula One races, the five-time Grand Prix winner and 1985 Formula One championship runner-up has a major share in the team's steeply rising learning curve. With Audi, Alboreto wins twice, both times in the United States: in 2000, in Petit Le Mans at Road Atlanta and in 2001, in the Sebring 12 Hours. The fatal test accident at the Lausitzring in 2001 ends his dream of a Le Mans victory with Audi.

Filipe Albuquerque

Born on June 13, 1985

In 2010, the Portuguese paves his way for promotion on winning in the Race of Champions and finishing runner-up in the Italian GT Championship. Audi enters him in the DTM for three years and in 2014, he switches to an LMP cockpit. At Le Mans, his R18 fails to finish. In 2015, Albuquerque, Bonanomi and Rast are on course for a podium for a long time. A technical issue causes them to drop back to seventh position. After a GT3 program in 2016, the Iberian leaves the brand with the four rings. In 2020, he wins the LMP2 class at Le Mans, in the WEC and in the ELMS. In the IMSA series in 2021 and 2022, he is the overall runner-up and wins the Daytona 24 Hours twice.

Seiji Ara

Born on May 5, 1975

Seiji Ara, besides JJ Lehto, is one of two non-factory drivers to clinch a victory with Audi at Le Mans. In 2004, he achieves that feat together with Dindo Capello and Tom Kristensen in an R8 fielded by his long-time supporter Kazumichi Goh. After beginnings in the Japanese Volkswagen Cup and races in the United States, he moves all the way up into the Super GT series in his native Japan, a series that he is still contesting today. Supported by Goh, Ara in 2001 debuts in an LMP Chrysler at Le Mans, followed by three races in the Goh Audi. In 2004, he triumphs with the R8 not only in the iconic 24-hour race but also clinches several podiums in the LMS.

Frank Biela

Born on August 2, 1964

Frank Biela drives for Audi for the first time in 1991 and in a V8 quattro immediately wins the DTM. Super Touring Car titles follow in France, the UK and in the FIA World Cup. The reliable German is one of the first drivers for the Le Mans project. As an excellent test driver, he is often the first one behind the wheel of a new Audi race car. In 2000, he scores the brand's premiere victory, achieves the hat-trick in 2002 and in 2006/07, adds the first diesel victories to his tally. With a total of five successes, he is the best German driver in the iconic event. Following his sports car career, he serves as a development driver of the Audi R8 LMS.

Timo Bernhard

Born on February 24, 1981

Timo Bernhard and Romain Dumas repeatedly beat the Audi R10 TDI in an LMP2 Porsche in America from 2006 to 2008. When that program ends after three years Wolfgang Ullrich borrows both drivers until 2012. Bernhard wins in the legendary 2010 edition of Le Mans. In 2012, he misses a fourth participation after a test accident at Sebring. From 2013 on, Bernhard is one of Audi's fiercest rivals at Porsche. In 2015, he snatches the world championship title from the R18 trio of Fässler/Lotterer/Tréluyer with a five-point advantage. In 2017, world championship title and Le Mans victory number two follow.

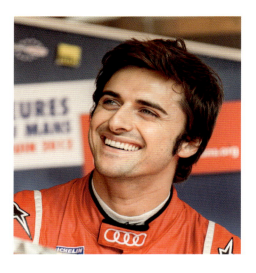

Marco Bonanomi
Born on March 12, 1985

In 2010, Bonanomi drives an Audi for the first time in Italian GT racing, becomes championship runner-up with Filipe Albuquerque and in 2011, wins the title. Meanwhile he has also become an Audi LMP test driver. In 2012, the Italian completes Audi's one-two-three result in his first Le Mans appearance together with Jarvis and Rockenfeller. The following year he focuses on the development and gets to drive at Le Mans only on the test day. Following the DNF in 2014, Bonanomi, in 2015, is on course for a podium for a long time but drops back. Two years later, the Italian returns to La Sarthe once again with the Kolles team but does not see the checkered flag.

Lucas di Grassi
Born on August 11, 1984

Lucas di Grassi wins the 2005 Grand Prix in Macau, finishes the 2007 GP2 Series runner-up and races in Formula One in 2010. He starts driving for Audi in 2012 in his native São Paulo. Following a podium finish, he is allowed to race at Le Mans a year later and clinches third position. Di Grassi in 2014 moves up into the regular WEC driver squad as the successor of World Champion Allan McNish, who has stepped down. The runner-up's spot is his best result at Le Mans. A third podium finish follows in 2016. In Audi's WEC farewell year, he wins twice and becomes world championship runner-up. In Formula E, he wins the champion's title in 2016/17.

Dindo Capello
Born on June 17,1964

Following his Super Touring Car years and the 1996 title win with Audi, Dindo Capello is also part of the LMP project from day one. On its debut at Sebring, he clinches third position but is out of luck at Le Mans for years. Fourth position in 1999 is followed by third, second and second again. He does not win until 2003 – in a Bentley. The following year the dream of a Le Mans victory with Audi comes true for the valued team player. A third triumph follows in 2008 in an Audi R10 TDI. By 2012 he achieves four more podium finishes in France with Tom Kristensen and Allan McNish. Capello clinches three pole positions, more than any other Audi driver.

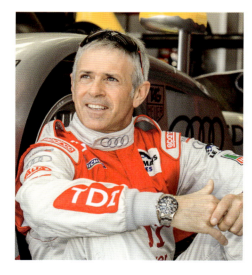

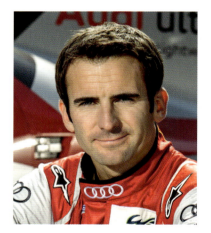

Romain Dumas
Born on December 14, 1977

Romain Dumas contests circuit, rally and hillclimb events. As the second driver on loan from Porsche besides Timo Bernhard, he competes at Le Mans four times for Audi from 2009 to 2012 and in 2010 celebrates the victory and a distance record. With his regular brand, Porsche, he is successful for a second time, in 2016. The same year he is celebrated as WEC champion. At the Nürburgring and at Spa, Dumas wins six other 24-hour races. Class wins in the World Rally Championship, several victories in the legendary Pikes Peak hillclimb and numerous participations in the Dakar Rally underscore the versatility of the Swiss resident.

Loïc Duval
Born on June 12, 1982

In a Peugeot, of all cars, Loïc Duval in 2011 recommends himself for a slot at Audi. Following victory at Sebring and fifth place at Le Mans in a privateer Oreca, Audi signs him starting in 2012. The Frenchman shows strong performances and in 2013 as Dindo Capello's successor joins Tom Kristensen and Allan McNish's car. In his first full season with Audi, he clinches pole and first place at Le Mans, plus two other WEC wins and the world championship title. In 2016, he achieves another podium finish at La Sarthe with Audi, plus the runner-up's spot in the WEC. Subsequently, in 2017 and 2018, he races for the four rings in the DTM.

Marcel Fässler
Born on May 27, 1976

After the Swiss in the wake of the financial crisis in 2009 comes within a whisker of an ALMS program with Audi, he is signed as a regular driver for 2010. Together with André Lotterer and Benoît Tréluyer he forms a successful trio until 2016 that harmonizes perfectly, wins at Le Mans three times and is world champion in 2012. That makes Fässler the first Swiss

to win at La Sarthe. Despite those successes Fässler, whose first career steps take place in the La Filière race driver school in France, always remains modest and finds the Alps to be the perfect haven of tranquility for himself and his family.

Mattias Ekström
Born on July 14, 1978

Mattias Ekström at Le Mans? The Swede never races there in reality but in 2007 is on standby for a long time. Only a few days before the race it is clear that Tom Kristensen after his serious DTM accident at Hockenheim will compete at Le Mans after all. Previously, on the Le Mans test day, Ekström had familiarized himself with the Audi R10 TDI and the track. It is his only excursion into the sports prototypes scene. Aside from that, he demonstrates his versatility with touring car titles back home and in the DTM in 2004 and 2007 and the World Rallycross Championship title in 2016. Since 2022, he has been competing for Audi in the Dakar Rally.

Marc Gené
Born on March 29, 1974

Marc Gené achieves his best Le Mans result with Audi as a reserve driver: Following Loïc Duval's accident in qualifying in 2014, he clinches the runner-up's spot together with Tom Kristensen and Lucas di Grassi. As early as in 2012, Gené – standing in for injured Timo Bernhard – on clinching the WEC victory at Spa is off to a strong start at Audi. Previously, from 1999 to 2004, the Spaniard contests Formula One and is subsequently a Ferrari test driver. Concurrently, in 2009, he clinches overall victory at Le Mans with Peugeot. Gené's older brother, Jordi, in 1996 is one of seven drivers to win a touring car title for Audi.

Johnny Herbert
Born on June 25, 1964

Besides Michele Alboreto the Englishman is one of two Grand Prix winners at Audi. A strong year in the ALMS with Champion Racing recommends him for a factory cockpit. In 2002, he wins in the debut at Sebring. In 2002, 2003 with Bentley and in 2004, he is runner-up at Le Mans, just barely missing a second victory after 1991 in a Mazda with rotary engine. Just three years earlier, in 1988, his career is at risk when he has a serious Formula 3000 accident at Brands Hatch. He makes it into Formula One anyhow and goes on to win three races – two of them in Michael Schumacher's world champion's year of 1995 as his teammate.

Oliver Jarvis
Born on January 9, 1984

Starting in 2008, Jarvis competes for Audi for four years in the DTM but occasionally ventures into the world of prototypes. In 2009, he debuts in the Kolles R10 in the Asian Le Mans Series, and in 2010 at Le Mans. From 2012 to 2014, he races in the third factory car at La Sarthe and clinches third position twice. At Sebring in 2013, the Englishman even scores victory. In 2015, his dream of becoming a regular Audi driver finally comes true. In 2016, he achieves two WEC victories and another third-place finish at Le Mans. Following the withdrawal of the Ingolstadt-based brand, Jarvis celebrates success particularly in the IMSA series. In 2022, he wins the top category, DPI, there.

Stefan Johansson
Born on September 8, 1956

Three times Stefan Johansson contests Le Mans in an Audi; following the retirements in 1999 and 2001, he finishes on podium in 2003 with Champion Racing. He celebrates his biggest success in an Audi R8 in 2001 on winning the title in the European Le Mans Series – dual-hatting as Team Principal and driver. In Formula One, the Swede achieves podium results with the top-flight teams of Ferrari and McLaren. After four years in the Champ Car series, Johansson switches to sports cars where he scores the Le Mans victory in 1997. Today, the go-getting northerner is the manager of various race drivers.

Pierre Kaffer
Born on November 7, 1976

Following title wins in Formula Ford and Formula Opel, Pierre Kaffer contests five seasons in German Formula 3 from 1997 to 2001, winning twelve races. After two years in the Porsche Cup, he wins at Sebring in the first race as an Audi factory driver in a Veloqx-R8. Kaffer subsequently triumphs also at the Nürburgring and finishes Le Mans in fifth position. In 2005 and 2006, Kaffer races for Audi in the DTM and subsequently contests GT and sports car races. As a driver of Audi Sport customer racing, he is the only former Le Mans factory driver to still have an Audi driver agreement at the copy deadline.

Tom Kristensen
Born on July 7, 1967

Tom Kristensen wins his Le Mans debut in 1997 in a Joest TWR Porsche. Eight more victories follow, all of them with Audi except for the Bentley triumph in 2003. Plus, he claims two second and three third places. Since 1923 nobody else has been as successful at La Sarthe as the fitness fanatic who also wins the 2001 ALMS and the 2013 WEC titles for Audi. The Dane, who acts practically without making any mistakes, has perfect intuition for Le Mans. The secret of his success is the "5P principle" of the former gearbox mechanic Michel Picard: "Proper preparation prevents poor performance." He also lets his teammates benefit from his experience. Until his retirement at the end of 2014, endurance racing is his true destiny even though he is also successful in single-seater and touring car racing.

Michael Krumm
Born on March 19, 1970

Michael Krumm joins Audi for Le Mans 2002. In Germany he has been almost forgotten because, except for one season in the Super Touring Car championship, he has been racing almost exclusively in Japan since 1994 with great success in single-seater, touring car or GT events. In his only race in the R8, he immediately achieves third position at Le Mans. It is his best result in seven participations – mostly in Nissan's employ. In 2009, Krumm briefly returns in an Audi, in the ELMS at the wheel of a privately fielded R10. His biggest international success is the 2011 win of the FIA GT1 World Championship with Lucas Luhr.

JJ Lehto
Born on January 31, 1966

His real name is Jyrki Järvilehto but at the recommendation of his manager, Keke Rosberg, the northerner just calls himself JJ Lehto. Following several seasons in the F1 midfield, the top-flight Benetton team signs him for 1994. Following a serious test accident, he finds a new home with sports cars and in 1995 wins at Le Mans for the first time. Subsequently, he is promoted to the role of factory driver at BMW and Cadillac and from 2003 on, he is a regular driver of an R8 entered by Champion Racing. Another Le Mans victory, in 2005, is a highlight. That makes him the only victorious non-factory driver of an Audi besides Seiji Ara.

André Lotterer
Born on November 19, 1981

After his career has begun to stall in Europe, André Lotterer goes to Japan in 2003 and becomes a star. Even so, Europe continues to appeal to the German who grew up in Belgium. As a pay driver, he races at Le Mans in 2009 in a privateer Audi R10 of the Kolles team. He delivers such a strong performance that Audi signs him in 2010. Three Le Mans triumphs, eight further WEC victories and a World Championship title follow – all of them together with Marcel Fässler and Benoît Tréluyer. In 2014, the car enthusiast, whose classic car collection includes an Audi Sport quattro, fulfills his dream of racing in Formula One at Spa.

Lucas Luhr
Born on July 22, 1979

In his first season for Audi in 2007, Lucas Luhr contests a program in the DTM and with sports cars. From 2008 on, he focuses on the latter. The best result at Le Mans is fourth place, in 2008. By clinching the title in the American Le Mans Series with Marco Werner the same year he proves his class. In the brand's GT3 program, he scores endurance racing successes such as the runner-up's spot at the R8 LMS' debut in the 2009 Nürburgring 24 Hours. After his time with Audi, he wins the FIA GT1 World Championship in 2011 and the ALMS in 2012 and 2013.

Perry McCarthy
Born on March 3, 1961

Briton Perry McCarthy personifies the fate of someone who has been born under an unlucky star. In his biography, "Flat out, flat broke," he describes his failed Formula One career. Yet where McCarthy shows up everyone laughs – including him laughing about himself. He works on oil rigs to finance his way into motorsport. As an Audi factory driver, he finishes fifth at Sebring in 1999 but retires in the R8C at Le Mans. In 2003, he returns to the cockpit of an R8 with Audi Sport UK. Sixth position at Sebring and fourth on the test day are followed by a DNF in the race when teammate Frank Biela runs out of gasoline.

Allan McNish
Born on December 29, 1969

Allan McNish discovers his love of sports cars late and wins Le Mans with Porsche in 1998. The Scot celebrates his biggest successes with Audi: ALMS Champion in 2000, 2006 and 2007, WEC Champion in 2013, 29 race victories including Le Mans in 2008 and 2013. Even though he is just 1.65 meters tall, McNish is a giant in cars, impressing particularly with his fighting spirit. Following various test roles in Formula One, he can catch a whiff of racing air for one season there in 2002. As brand ambassador and Formula E Team Principal, McNish stays with Audi even years after the end of his active career in 2013.

Yvan Muller
Born on August 16, 1969

Together with Mattias Ekström the Frenchman is an exceptional case: Audi nominates him for Le Mans but he does not drive. Following years in single-seaters, Muller switches to touring cars in 1994. He becomes French champion in just his second year and is signed by Audi. He goes on to race in the Audi A4 in Italy, Germany and the UK for three years. His preference of a car with a roof over the Audi R8R on short notice leads to a touring car title in the UK and four others in the World Championship. In addition, Muller wins the French ice racing series Trophée Andros ten times.

Stéphane Ortelli
Born on March 30, 1970

In 1999, Stéphane Ortelli switches to Audi as last year's Le Mans winner, but retires in the R8C. The next year is better: runner-up in the R8 with Allan McNish and Laurent Aiello. That result is

followed by two titles with Porsche in the FIA GT series and an overall victory in the Spa 24 Hours before the Monégasque returns to Le Mans in an Oreca Audi in 2005 and finishes in fourth position. At Silverstone, he clinches his only victory with Audi. In 2007, he wins the GT1 class in the Le Mans Series. In 2012, he decides the Blancpain Endurance Series and in 2013, the FIA GT Series, in his favor, both times in an Audi R8 LMS.

Christian Pescatori
Born on December 1, 1971

Christian Pescatori in 2001 replaces Michele Alboreto at Audi. He finishes Le Mans runner-up twice and Sebring as the overall winner. With titles in Formula 3 and Formula 3000, the driver from Brescia attracts attention to his talent early. However due to lack of sponsors, he does not make it into Formula One and switches to sports cars. With Scuderia Italia, he debuts at Le Mans in 1997 and goes on to score successes in the Ferrari 333 SP sports prototype. Following his brief Audi career, he races two more times at Le Mans with Scuderia Italia. In 2017, he returns to La Sarthe as Sport Director of an LMP2 team.

Philipp Peter
Born on April 6, 1969

The Viennese with an Austrian and a Swiss passport contests only two sports prototype races for Audi: in 2002, he finishes Le Mans in third position and in 2003, he wins at Sebring. As early as in Super Touring Car racing, he competes with Audi: in 1995, he wins the privateer drivers' classification in the German Super Touring Car Cup that earns him an Audi factory agreement for 1995 and 1996. Peter rewards the brand with a victory and podium finishes. Two years in the Indy Lights series in the United States follow before Peter in 2000 finishes second in the Sports Racing World Cup. In 2014, after 25 years and 400 races, he retires.

Emanuele Pirro
Born on January 12, 1962

Emanuele Pirro joins Audi in 1994 as a former Formula One racer. He clinches two titles in Italy and one in Germany for the brand from Ingolstadt. The Italian takes third position at Audi's Le Mans debut in 1999. It marks the beginning of a string of nine personal podium finishes – a record for this race. He achieves the hat-trick of victories from 2000 to 2002 and the first diesel successes in 2006 and 2007. Pirro is one of the regular drivers in the ALMS as well and in 2001 and 2005 wins the drivers' titles. Following his Audi career, Pirro returns to Le Mans once more with a privateer team in 2010.

Alexandre Premat
Born on April 5, 1982

Alexandre Premat brings a runner-up's finish from the Formula 3 Euro Series, a victory in the Formula 3 GP in Macau and third place in the GP2 series to the squad when he starts a dual program in the DTM and in sports car racing with Audi in 2007. Position four in an Audi R10 TDI in 2008 is his best result at Le Mans. The same year he secures the title in the European Le Mans Series. Following his time with Audi, he starts contesting sports car races in 2011 with privateer teams, is on the grid in the Supercars Championship in Australia and together with Shane van Gisbergen wins the Enduro Cup there in 2016.

René Rast
Born on October 26, 1986

René Rast passes through many stages in motorsport in the Volkswagen Group: he wins the Volkswagen Polo Cup, is runner-up in the Seat Supercopa and clinches titles in the Porsche Carrera Cup and in the Porsche Supercup. Afterwards, the German is promoted to GT3 racing where he wins the ADAC GT Masters and

the 24-hour races at the Nürburgring and at Spa in an Audi R8 LMS in 2014. He is promoted to the Audi R18 but misses a podium finish twice at his races in 2015. Subsequently, the situation improves for him in the DTM where he becomes the 2017, 2019 and 2020 champion in the Audi RS 5 DTM.

Mike Rockenfeller
Born on October 31, 1983

Mike Rockenfeller joins Audi from Porsche in 2007 and retires at his Le Mans debut due to an accident. In the following year, Rockenfeller makes up for that by winning the LMS title. In 2010, he sets a distance record with Timo Bernhard and Romain Dumas on clinching victory at Le Mans. Following an accident in 2011 in which he was not at fault, he returns in 2012 and finishes on the podium again. He subsequently focuses on the DTM in which he competes from 2007 to 2019. With success: in 2013, Rockenfeller crowns himself champion. Other highlights in his career are victories in the 24-hour races at Daytona and at the Nürburgring.

Didier Theys
Born on October 19, 1956

Didier Theys is 43 years old when Audi gives him an opportunity on making its sports car debut. The Belgian residing in the United States has previously won the Daytona 24 Hours and the Sebring 12 Hours in 1998. He joins the brand from Ingolstadt based on a recommendation by the Belgian Audi Club. Shortly before Le Mans 1999, he

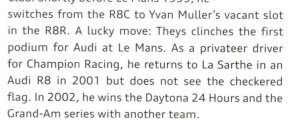

switches from the R8C to Yvan Muller's vacant slot in the R8R. A lucky move: Theys clinches the first podium for Audi at Le Mans. As a privateer driver for Champion Racing, he returns to La Sarthe in an Audi R8 in 2001 but does not see the checkered flag. In 2002, he wins the Daytona 24 Hours and the Grand-Am series with another team.

Benoît Tréluyer
Born on December 7, 1976

Like André Lotterer, Benoît Tréluyer spends a large part of his career in Japan. In 2001, he wins Formula 3, in 2006, Formula Nippon and in 2008, the Super GT series. Following races at Le Mans for Henri Pescarolo, Audi signs him in 2010. With Lotterer and Marcel Fässler, he immediately finishes Le Mans runner-up. In 2011, 2012 and 2014, the trio mounts the top step of the podium and in 2012 wins the inaugural WEC season. Three runner-up spots in the championship follow. After Audi's withdrawal, Tréluyer develops tires for Formula E, among other things.

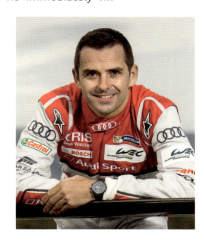

Marco Werner
Born on April 27, 1966

Audi is a stroke of luck for Marco Werner: through no fault of his own, Werner's career has often seen more lows than highs when he is given an opportunity in an Audi R8 in 2002 and finishes Le Mans in third position. In 2003 and 2004, he wins the American Le Mans Series and starting in 2005, he prevails three times in a row in the Le Mans 24 Hours as well. In 2008, he secures a third ALMS title before his sports car career with Audi ends after 2009. One private start in Le Mans follows. Afterwards he is a sought-after coach in the Audi race experience and GT3 race driver. In addition, he passes on his knowledge as a mentor in the Audi Sport TT Cup.

Andy Wallace
Born on February 19, 1961

Only 22 drivers in the 99-year history up to 2022 achieve the feat of clinching overall victory on making their debut. They include Andy Wallace in 1988. Up until his last race in 2010, the Englishman competes there on 21 occasions and finishes on podium three more times. In 1999, Audi Sport UK signs him for the debut of the R8C but Wallace and company do not finish. The driver from Oxford spends a large part of his career in the United States. He wins three times in the Daytona 24 Hours and twice in the Sebring 12 Hours. At Champion Racing, he starts driving a privateer R8 in the ALMS in 2001.

James Weaver
Born on March 4, 1955

James Weaver is one of the most successful sports car drivers when Audi signs him in 1999 for Le Mans in the R8C. It is his twelfth and last participation there. Weaver contests Le Mans for the factory teams of Mazda, Nissan, Porsche and Panoz, among others. He celebrates his biggest success in 1985 on finishing overall runner-up in a Porsche 962. The Brit spends many years of his career in North America where he clinches 40 overall or class victories, driving for Dyson Racing for 20 years in total. Weaver celebrates successes in Europe as well and in 1996 wins the BPR series in a McLaren.

Anecdotes

You know everything about Audi at Le Mans now that you've read this book? Well, some of the stories presented at the end may still contain a surprise here and there.

Regulation and freedom

The Technical Stewards of the ACO refuse to approve the Audi R18 e-tron quattro in scrutineering: The car does not comply with the prescribed length of the rear overhang measured from the center of the wheel. Audi Sport performs another dimensional check and must admit the mistake. Is it a true-to-size issue with a supplier part? However, for that to be the case, the measured tolerances are too large. Finally, the engineers realize that the suspension kinematics allows such freedom of adjustment that, due to the extremely long wishbones in the LMP1 sports car, the center of the wheel can clearly shift. The alleged issue of dimensional compliance is resolved by merely changing the suspension settings.

Humans and hardware

At the beginning of the 2000s: The Nikasil plating of the cylinder bores on the Audi R8 keeps dissolving, and the engine developers are desperate. The plating procedure provides for an external contractor to subject the crankcase to a bath process, followed by etching in acid and cleaning. Afterward, the Nikasil plating must be applied quickly in a time-controlled process to prevent oxidation of the sensitive surfaces. The engineers spend a lot of time looking for the root cause of the damage, testing materials and machines. Ultimately, it turns out that an employee regularly uses the acid procedure for a cigarette break, which extends the etching job accordingly and causes the Nikasil plating to subsequently dissolve.

From 2012 onward, the Audi R18 e-tron quattro requires a dedicated cooling circuit for the hybrid system. The high-temperature circuit for the engine radiators and its low-temperature counterpart for the hybrid system are, of course, separated but integrated in a closely connected radiator system. Engineers keep noticing that the two different liquids mix, identifying corrosion as the root cause. But why does a brand-new radiator corrode? Audi Sport investigates this question for a long time but only AUDI AG's quality inspection team finds the answer: Before Audi Sport is provided with its own track facilities in Neuburg in 2015 the engineers use a nearby military airfield for short post-preparation roll-outs of the race cars. It turns out that the runways there are sprayed with salt in winter to keep them ice-free. The salt crystals subsequently cause the radiators to corrode.

Paris

Audi Motorsport Press Spokesman Jürgen Pippig is on the verge of despair before the R10 presentation in Paris (see p. 110). Only a handwritten letter softens up the city fathers at the eleventh hour. The local government approves the event but requires Audi to take care of closing off the area in question on its own. A private-sector services provider assists by performing this official duty using a fleet of Audi A8 cars. The presentation in the presence of the management board has been saved.

The four-liter V8 engine from Neckarsulm lasts 24 hours in 2003, powering the Bentley Speed 8 to victory. The subsequent officially approved parade down Champs Élysées takes place, as the reader may guess, without the area being closed off. Derek Bell has to stop at every red light, keeps the engine running and mumbles something about 120 or 130 degrees on the radio. While more than 70 percent full throttle at Le Mans doesn't faze the winning powerplant, urban traffic does: the engine fails miserably.

Mismatched

The quick-connect coupler on the rear end of the Audi R8 is regarded as a technical stroke of genius. Audi develops fixed plug-in connector modules grouping various connectors and thus excluding mix-ups for quick-connect assemblies only in later years. On the R8, the mechanics still need to connect hydraulic and pneumatic ports individually. Because the systems have identical quick-release devices many a mix-up that has occurred in the heat of the moment remains undetected – at first. Race driver Perry McCarthy is flabbergasted when he hits the gas pedal again after the rear end of his car was changed. Instead of moving forward, the R8 lifts in the pit lane: the rising pressure in the oil circuit has caused the air jacks to extend via the misconnected pneumatic system.

Track test

May 4, 2003, pre-test at Le Mans: Press Spokesman Peter Oberndorfer has convinced Head of Sport Wolfgang Ullrich to provide former Le Mans winner Paul Frère with an opportunity to test the R8 on the race track. Nota bene, Frère is 86 years old, and the time window approved by the organizers on the test day is very short. The idea is for Audi's photographer Bodo Kräling, who provided most of the pictures for this book, to do his job in a prone position from the trunk and through the open tailgate of a preceding Audi RS 6 Avant. So far so good – up until the first chicane. The Audi handles the curbs in racing style, and the digital camera gives up its ghost. The sporting result is that Frère requires 4m01.590s for one lap on that day, just roughly 20 seconds less than the current factory drivers. He's as fast as the best GT race drivers. The photographic result is a single static photograph that was shot in advance; that's it. At the wheel of the RS 6 was Reinhold Joest.

The costliest glue

In 2015, only five engines per season are allowed in the FIA WEC. The powerplants are sealed inside the race cars. On June 13, in a post-warm-up check, the inspectors discover missing seals on the number 7 Audi R18 that ultimately finishes in third position. A case of attempted fraud in order to use an additional engine? That would be a serious incident. The stewards admit that changing an engine in the short space of time before the race starts can hardly be accomplished. Even so, they must act in accordance with the rules and law, resulting in a penalty of 50,000 euros. The human root cause: Audi has no fraudulent intent whatsoever. Out of a false sense of thrift, an employee has used a glue for the seals that has long surpassed its shelf life. Consequently, Audi Sport is not allowed to use the invalidly sealed engines any longer, which results in an unscheduled endurance test: Fässler/Lotterer/Tréluyer use only two instead of five engines in the full 2015 WEC season far beyond their defined mileages – without any problems.

Snow in August

As far back as in 1998, Audi, with an early evolution of the R8C, wishes people a "Happy Journey to Le Mans," in Christmas greetings featuring simple artwork. Following the brand's first victory, the artwork becomes more elaborate. However, in 2000, the virtual world of advertising hasn't reached today's level yet. Real-world photographs are desired, photo compositions are possible to a limited extent and renderings are greetings from the future. For a Christmas poster picture, an advertising agency stages a complex idea. In August 2000, Audi Sport mechanic Thomas Bauch drives the number 8 R8 across the track at Le Mans as Santa Claus in full Christmas regalia. In tedious repro work, the two race cars with different wraps pursuing the R8 are derived from it. The white flakes are not produced by photo retouching but are decorative snowflakes. The stuffed reindeers the crew have taken to the site are arranged in various seats until multiple exposures create the impression of a large crowd of animal spectators. Following this massive production effort, Audi ultimately extends best wishes for Restful Holidays and a Happy New Year.

Facts and figures

An overview of the technical data of Audi's Le Mans prototypes, race results at Le Mans and standings in worldwide racing series from 1999 to 2016.

Audi R8C (1999)

Audi R8R (1999)

Vehicle

	Audi R8C (1999)	Audi R8R (1999)
Vehicle type	Le Mans GT Prototype (LM-GTP)	Le Mans Prototype (LM-P)
Monocoque	Carbon fiber (development partner rtn); crash structure ACO and FIA approved; steel rollcage	Carbon fiber, crash structure ACO and FIA approved, steel rollcage front and rear
Bodywork	Carbon fiber	Carbon fiber

Engine

Engine	V8, 90 degree cylinder angle, 4 valves per cylinder, DOHC, 2 Garrett turbo chargers, to comply with the regulations 2 x 33.9 mm air restrictors and boost pressure restriction to 1.87 bars absolute	V8, 90 degree cylinder angle, 4 valves per cylinder, DOHC, 2 Garrett turbo chargers, to comply with the regulations 2 x 33.2 mm air restrictors and boost pressure restriction to 1.67 bars absolute
Engine management	Bosch MS 2.8	Bosch MS 2.8
Engine lubrication	Dry sump, Shell	Dry sump, Shell
Displacement	3,600 ccm	3,600 ccm
Output	More than 441 kW / 600 hp	More than 404 kW / 550 hp
Torque	More than 650 Nm	More than 600 Nm

Transmission

Transmission	Rear wheel drive	Rear wheel drive
Clutch	CFRP clutch	CFRP clutch
Gearbox	Sequential 6-speed sports gearbox, partner Ricardo	Sequential 6-speed sports gearbox, partner Ricardo
Differential	Multiple-disc limited-slip differential	Multiple-disc limited-slip differential
Driveshafts	Constant velocity tripod plunge-joint driveshafts	Constant velocity tripod plunge-joint driveshafts

Suspension/steering/brakes

Steering	Mechanical rack and pinion steering, no power steering	Mechanical rack and pinion power steering
Suspension	Independent suspension at front and rear, double wishbone suspension, pushrod system with horizontal spring/damper unit, adjustable gas-filled shock absorbers	Independent suspension at front and rear, double wishbone suspension, pushrod system with horizontal spring/damper unit, adjustable gas-filled shock absorbers
Brakes	Hydraulic dual-circuit brake system, monobloc light-alloy brake calipers, ventilated carbon fiber brake discs at front and rear, brake balance continuously adjustable by driver	Hydraulic dual-circuit brake system, monobloc light-alloy brake calipers, ventilated carbon fiber brake discs at front and rear, brake balance continuously adjustable by driver
Rims	O.Z. forged magnesium wheels Front: 12.25 x 18 inches, rear: 13 x 18 inches	O.Z. forged magnesium wheels Front: 13 x 18 inches, rear: 14.5 x 18 inches
Tires	Michelin Radial Front: 29/65-18, rear: 31/71-18	Michelin Radial Front: 32/65-18, rear: 36/71-18

Weight/dimensions

Length	4,800 mm	4,650 mm
Width	2,000 mm	2,000 mm
Height	980 mm	1,080 mm
Minimum weight	900 kgs	900 kgs
Fuel tank capacity	90 liters	90 liters

Audi R8 (2000–2006) | Audi R10 TDI (2006–2008)

Vehicle

	Audi R8 (2000–2006)	Audi R10 TDI (2006–2008)
Vehicle type	Le Mans Prototype (LMP, LMP 900 from 2001, LM P1 from 2005)	Le Mans Prototype (LM P1)
Monocoque	Carbon fiber, crash structure ACO and FIA approved. CFC rollbars front and rear, carbon fiber body	Carbon-fiber composite construction with aluminum honeycomb core, tested in accordance with the strict FIA crash and safety standards

Engine

Engine	V8, 90 degree cylinder angle, 4 valves per cylinder, DOHC, 2 Garrett turbo chargers, to comply with the regulations 2 x 32.4 mm (from 2000), 30.7 mm (from 2003), 29.9 mm (Le Mans/LMES 2005) air restrictors and boost pressure restriction to 1.67 bars absolute, direct fuel injection FSI (from 2001)	V12, 90 degree cylinder angle, 4 valves per cylinder, DOHC, 2 Garrett turbo chargers, 2 x 39.9 mm engine-air intake restrictors (defined by regulations) and maximum turbo pressure of 2.94 bar absolute, diesel direct injection TDI, stressed aluminum crankcase, 2 Dow Automotive diesel particle filters
Engine management	Bosch MS 2.8 (2000), MS 2.9 (from 2001)	Bosch MS14
Engine lubrication	Dry sump, Shell	Dry sump, Shell
Displacement	3,600 ccm	5,500 ccm
Output	448 kW / 610 hp (from 2000), 404 kW / 550 hp (2003), 382 kW / 520 hp (Le Mans/LMES 2005), 404 kW / 550 hp (ALMS 2005)	More than 478 kW / 650 hp
Torque	700 Nm (2000), 750 Nm (2001), more than 700 Nm (from 2002)	More than 1,100 Nm

Transmission

Transmission	Rear wheel drive	Rear wheel drive, traction control (ASR)
Clutch	CFRP clutch	CFRP clutch
Gearbox	Sequential 6-speed sports gearbox, partner Ricardo	Pneumatically-actuated sequential 5-speed race gearbox, partner Xtrac
Differential	Multiple-disc limited-slip differential	Viscous-mechanical locking differential
Driveshafts	Constant velocity tripod plunge-joint driveshafts	Constant velocity tripod plunge-joint driveshafts

Suspension/steering/brakes

Steering	Rack and pinion power steering	Electrically assisted rack and pinion power steering
Suspension	Independent suspension at front and rear, double-wishbone suspension, pushrod system with spring/damper unit, adjustable gas-filled shock absorbers	Independent front and rear double-wishbone suspension, pushrod-system with torsion bars and adjustable dampers
Brakes	Hydraulic dual-circuit brake system, monobloc light-alloy brake calipers, ventilated carbon fiber brake discs at front and rear, brake balance continuously adjustable by driver	Hydraulic dual-circuit braking system, monobloc light-alloy brake calipers, ventilated carbon fiber brake discs front and rear, brake balance continuously adjustable by driver
Rims	O.Z. forged magnesium wheels Front: 13.5 x 18 inches, rear: 14.5 x 18 inches	O.Z. forged magnesium wheels Front: 13 x 18 inches, rear: 14.5 x 18 inches
Tires	Michelin Radial Front: 33/65-18, rear: 36/71-18 (from 2000), 37/71-18 (from 2002)	Michelin Radial Front: 33/68-18, rear: 37/71-18

Weight/dimensions

Length	4,650 mm	4,650 mm
Width	2,000 mm	2,000 mm
Height	1,080 mm	1,030 mm
Minimum weight	900 kgs, 950 kgs (Le Mans/LMES 2005), 935 kgs (ALMS 2006)	925 kgs (from 2006), 900 kgs (2008)
Fuel tank capacity	90 liters (from 2000), 80 liters (Le Mans/LMES 2005)	90 liters (2006), 81 liters (from 2007) Shell V-Power Diesel

Audi R15 TDI / R15 plus (2009–2010) Audi R18 TDI (2011) – RP1

Vehicle

	Audi R15 TDI / R15 plus (2009–2010)	Audi R18 TDI (2011) – RP1
Vehicle type	Le Mans Prototype (LM P1)	Le Mans Prototype (LM P1)
Monocoque	Composite-fiber design from carbon-fiber with aluminum honeycomb, tested in accordance with the strict FIA crash and safety standards	Carbon-fiber composite design incorporating aluminum honeycomb core, tested in accordance with the strict FIA crash and safety standards
Battery for electrical system	Lithium ion battery	Lithium ion battery

Engine

Engine	V10, 90 degree cylinder angle, 4 valves per cylinder, DOHC, 2 Garrett VTG turbochargers, 2 x 37.9 mm (2009), 2 x 37,5 (2010) engine air-intake restrictors (stipulated by regulations) and maximum turbo pressure of 2.75 bar (2009), 2.59 bar (2010) absolute, diesel direct injection TDI, fully stressed aluminum crankcase, 2 Dow Automotive diesel particle filters	V6, 120 degree cylinder angle, 4 valves per cylinder, DOHC, 1 Garrett VTG turbocharger, 1 x 47.5 mm diameter intake air restrictor (stipulated by regulations), turbo boost pressure restricted to 3.0 bar absolute, diesel direct injection TDI, full stressed aluminum crankcase, diesel particle filter
Engine management	Bosch MS14	Bosch MS14
Engine lubrication	Dry sump, Shell	Dry sump, Castrol
Displacement	5,500 ccm	3,700 ccm
Output	More than 441 kW / 600 hp (2009), 440 kW / 598 hp (2010)	More than 397 kW / 540 hp
Torque	More than 1,050 Nm	More than 900 Nm

Transmission

Transmission	Rear wheel drive, traction control (ASR)	Rear wheel drive, traction control (ASR)
Clutch	CFRP clutch	CFRP clutch
Gearbox	Sequential, pneumatically operated 5-gear sport gearbox, partner Xtrac	Sequential, electrically activated 6-speed sport gearbox, partner Xtrac
Differential	Limited slip differential	Limited slip differential
Driveshafts	Constant velocity tripod plunge-joint driveshafts	Constant velocity tripod plunge-joint driveshafts

Suspension/steering/brakes

Steering	Electrically assisted rack and pinion power steering	Electrically assisted rack and pinion power steering
Suspension	Independent front and rear double wishbone suspension, pushrod system with torsion bars and adjustable dampers	Independent suspension with double wishbones all-round, pushrod system with torsion bars and adjustable dampers
Brakes	Hydraulic dual-circuit braking system, monobloc light alloy brake calipers, ventilated carbon-fiber brake discs front and rear, brake balance continuously adjustable by driver	Hydraulic dual circuit braking system, monobloc light-alloy brake calipers, ventilated carbon-fiber brake discs front and rear, brake balance continuously adjustable by driver
Rims	O.Z. forged magnesium wheels Front: 13.5 x 18 inches, rear: 14.5 x 18 inches	O.Z. forged magnesium wheels Front: 14.75 x 18 inches, rear: 14.5 x 18 inches
Tires	Michelin Radial Front: 33/68-18, rear: 37/71-18	Michelin Radial Front: 360/710-18, rear: 370/710-18

Weight/dimensions

Length	4,650 mm	4,650 mm
Width	2,000 mm	2,000 mm
Height	1,030 mm	1,030 mm
Minimum weight	900 kgs (beginning of 2009 season), 930 kgs (from Le Mans 2009)	900 kgs
Fuel tank capacity	81 liters (Shell V-Power Diesel)	65 liters

	Audi R18 e-tron quattro / ultra **(2012–2013) – RP2/RP3**	**Audi R18 e-tron quattro** **(2014–2015) – RP4/RP5**
Vehicle		
Vehicle type	Le Mans Prototype (LMP1)	Le Mans Prototype (LMP1)
Monocoque	Carbon-fiber composite with aluminum honeycomb, tested in accordance with the strict FIA crash and safety standards	Composite fiber construction of carbon fibers with aluminum honeycomb core and Zylon side panels, tested in accordance with the strict FIA crash and safety standards, rear CFRP crasher
Battery for electrical system	Lithium ion battery	Lithium ion battery
Engine		
Engine	V6, 120 degree cylinder angle, 4 valves per cylinder, DOHC, 1 Garrett VTG turbocharger, mandatory engine air intake restrictor of 1 x 45.8 mm (2012), 45.1 mm (2013) and turbo boost pressure limited to 2.8 bar absolute, diesel direct injection TDI, fully stressed aluminum crankcase	V6, 120 degree cylinder angle, 4 valves per cylinder, DOHC, 1 Garrett VTG turbocharger, diesel direct injection TDI, fully stressed aluminum crankcase
Engine management	Bosch MS24	
Engine lubrication	Dry sump, Castrol	
Displacement	3,700 ccm	4,000 ccm
Output	More than 375 kW / 510 hp (2012), more than 360 kW / 490 hp (2013)	More than 395 kW / 537 hp (2014), more than 410 kW / 558 hp (2015)
Torque	More than 850 Nm	More than 800 Nm (2014), more than 850 Nm (2015)
Hybrid system*		
Type of accumulator	Electric flywheel accumulator, usable storage capacity 500 KJ, WHP	Electric flywheel accumulator, WHP, usable storage capacity more than 600 KJ (2014), more than 700 KJ (2015)
Motor Generator Unit (MGU)	MGU on the front axle, water cooled with integrated power electronics, 2 x 75 kW (2012), 2 x 80 kW (2013)	MGU on the front axle, water cooled with integrated power electronics, more than 170 kW (2014), more than 200 kW (2015)
Energy class	7 braking zones of 500 KJ each, valid for Le Mans circuit	ERS 2 MJ (2014), ERS 4 MJ (2015), valid for Le Mans circuit
Transmission		
Transmission	Rear wheel drive, traction control (ASR), four-wheel drive e-tron quattro from 120 km/h*	Rear wheel drive, traction control (ASR), four-wheel drive e-tron quattro in hybrid mode
Clutch	CFRP clutch	CFRP clutch
Gearbox	Sequential, electrically activated 6-speed racing gearbox	Sequential, electrically activated 7-speed racing gearbox
Differential	Limited-slip rear differential	Limited-slip rear differential
Transmission housing	CFRP with titanium inserts	CFRP with titanium inserts
Driveshafts	Constant velocity tripod plunge-joint driveshafts	Constant velocity tripod plunge-joint driveshafts
Suspension/steering/brakes		
Steering	Electrically assisted rack and pinion power steering	Electrically assisted rack and pinion power steering
Suspension	Front and rear double wishbone independent suspension, front pushrod system and rear pullrod system with adjustable dampers	Front and rear double wishbone independent suspension, front pushrod system and rear pullrod system with adjustable dampers, twin wheel tethers per wheel
Brakes	Hydraulic dual circuit brake system, monobloc light alloy brake calipers, ventilated carbon disc brakes front and rear, brake balance continuously adjustable by driver	Hydraulic dual circuit brake system, monobloc light alloy brake calipers, ventilated carbon fiber disc brakes front and rear
Rims	O.Z. forged magnesium wheels	O.Z. forged magnesium wheels
Tires	Michelin Radial Front: 360/710-18, rear: 370/710-18	Michelin Radial Front: 31/71-18, rear: 31/71-18
Weight/dimensions		
Length	4,650 mm	4,650 mm
Width	2,000 mm	1,900 mm
Height	1,030 mm	1,050 mm
Minimum weight	900 kgs (2012), 915 kgs (2013)	870 kgs
Fuel tank capacity	58*, 60 liters	54.3 liters (2014), 54.2 liters (2015)

*Different specification for R18 e-tron quattro

Audi R18 (2016) – RP6

Vehicle

Vehicle type	Le Mans Prototype (LMP1)
Monocoque	Composite fiber construction of carbon fibers with aluminum honeycomb core and Zylon side panels, tested in accordance with the strict FIA crash and safety standards, front and rear CFRP crashers
Battery for electrical system	Lithium ion battery

Engine

Engine	V6, 120 degree cylinder angle, 4 valves per cylinder, DOHC, 1 Garrett VTG turbocharger, diesel direct injection TDI, fully stressed aluminum crankcase
Displacement	4,000 ccm
Output	More than 378 kW / 514 hp
Torque	More than 850 Nm

Hybrid system

Type of accumulator	Electrochemical due to lithium-ion battery, usable storage capacity more than 2 MJ
Motor Generator Unit (MGU)	MGU on the front axle, integrated limited slip differential. Low-temperature cooling circuit for MGU, integrated power electronics and energy storage. MGU output: more than 350 kW for recuperation/boost (300 kW for boost at Le Mans)
Energy class	ERS 6 MJ, valid for Le Mans circuit

Transmission

Transmission	Rear wheel drive, traction control (ASR), e-tron quattro four-wheel drive in hybrid mode
Clutch	CFRP clutch
Gearbox	Sequential 6-speed racing transmission
Differential	Limited slip differential rear
Transmission housing	CFRP with titanium inserts
Driveshafts	Constant velocity tripod plunge-joint driveshafts

Suspension/steering/brakes

Steering	Rack and pinion power steering
Suspension	Front and rear independent suspension on upper and lower wishbones, pushrod system at the front axle and pullrod system at the rear axle with adjustable dampers, two wheel tethers per wheel
Brakes	Hydraulic dual-circuit brake system, monobloc light alloy brake calipers, ventilated carbon fiber disc brakes front and rear
Rims	O.Z. forged magnesium wheels
Tires	Michelin Radial Front: 31/71-18, rear: 31/71-18

Weight/dimensions

Length	4,650 mm
Width	1,900 mm
Height	1,050 mm
Minimum weight	875 kgs
Fuel tank capacity	49.9 liters

24h Le Mans 1999

Position	Number	Class	Drivers	Car	Team	Lap time (minutes)
1	1	LMGTP	Martin Brundle/Emmanuel Collard/Vincenzo Sospiri	Toyota	Toyota Motorsports	3.29,930
2	2	LMGTP	Thierry Boutsen/Ralf Kelleners/Allan McNish	Toyota	Toyota Motorsports	3.30,801
3	3	LMP	Tom Kristensen/JJ Lehto/Jörg Müller	BMW	BMW Motorsport	3.31,209
4	6	LMGTP	Pedro Lamy/Franck Lagorce/Bernd Schneider	Mercedes	AMG-Mercedes	3.31,541
5	12	LMP	Eric Bernard/David Brabham/Butch Leitzinger	Panoz	Panoz Motor Sports	3.33,711
6	15	LMP	Yannick Dalmas/Pierluigi Martini/Joachim Winkelhock	BMW	BMW Motorsport	3.33,931
7	5	LMGTP	Christophe Bouchut/Peter Dumbreck/Nick Heidfeld	Mercedes	AMG-Mercedes	3.34,138
8	3	LMGTP	Ukyo Katayama/Toshio Suzuki/Keiichi Tsuchiya	Toyota	Toyota Motorsports	3.34,755
9	7	LMP	Laurent Aiello/Michele Alboreto/Dindo Capello	Audi R8R	Audi Sport Team Joest	3.34,891
10	4	LMGTP	Jean-Marc Gounon/Marcel Tiemann/Mark Webber	Mercedes	AMG-Mercedes	3.35,301
11	8	LMP	Frank Biela/Emanuele Pirro/Didier Theys	Audi R8R	Audi Sport Team Joest	3.35,371
20	10	LMGTP	Perry McCarthy/Andy Wallace/James Weaver	Audi R8C	Audi Sport UK	3.42,155
23	9	LMGTP	Christian Abt/Stefan Johansson/Stéphane Ortelli	Audi R8C	Audi Sport UK	3.45,202

Race June 12/13

Position	Number	Class	Drivers	Car	Team	Laps/Gap/Reason for DNF
1	15	LMP	Yannick Dalmas/Pierluigi Martini/Joachim Winkelhock	BMW	BMW Motorsport	365 laps
2	3	LMGTP	Ukyo Katayama/Toshio Suzuki/Keiichi Tsuchiya	Toyota	Toyota Motorsports	−1 lap
3	8	LMP	Frank Biela/Emanuele Pirro/Didier Theys	Audi R8R	Audi Sport Team Joest	−5 laps
4	7	LMP	Laurent Aiello/Michele Alboreto/Dindo Capello	Audi R8R	Audi Sport Team Joest	−19 laps
5	18	LMP	Bill Auberlen/Thomas Bscher/Stever Soper	BMW	Price + Bscher DPR	−20 laps
6	13	LMP	Alex Caffi/Andrea Montermini/Mimmo Schiattarella	Courage Nissan	Courage Competition	−23 laps
7	12	LMP	Eric Bernard/David Brabham/Butch Leitzinger	Panoz	Panoz Motor Sports	−29 laps
8	21	LMP	Didier Cottaz/Fredrik Ekblom/Marc Goossens	Courage Nissan	Nissan Motorsports	−31 laps
9	14	LMP	Michel Ferté/Patrice Gay/Henri Pescarolo	Courage Porsche	Pescarolo Promotion Racing Team	−38 laps
10	51	LMGTS	Olivier Beretta/Dominique Dupuy/Karl Wendlinger	Chrysler	Viper Team Oreca	−40 laps
DNF	10	LMGTP	Perry McCarthy/Andy Wallace/James Weaver	Audi R8C	Audi Sport UK	lap 199 transmission
DNF	9	LMGTP	Christian Abt/Stefan Johansson/Stéphane Ortelli	Audi R8C	Audi Sport UK	lap 56 differential

American Le Mans Series 1999

Prototype Drivers

Position	Drivers	Car	Team	Points
1	Elliott Forbes-Robinson	Riley & Scott-Ford	Dyson Racing Team	141
2	Eric Bernard/David Brabham	Panoz	Panoz Motor Sports	135
3	JJ Lehto	BMW	BMW Motorsport	123
12	Stefan Johansson	Audi R8R/Ferrari	Audi Sport Team Joest/Doran Matthews Racing	81
40	Michele Alboreto/Dindo Capello	Audi R8R	Audi Sport Team Joest	24
46	Frank Biela/Perry McCarthy/Emanuele Pirro	Audi R8R	Audi Sport Team Joest	20

Prototype Manufacturers

Position	Manufacturer	Points
1	Panoz	149
2	BMW	147
3	Ferrari	122
5	Audi	24

Prototype Teams

Position	Team	Points
1	Panoz Motor Sports	149
2	BMW Motorsport	147
3	Dyson Racing Team	139
15	Audi Sport Team Joest	24

24h Le Mans 2000

Qualifying June 14/15

Position	Number	Class	Drivers	Car	Team	Lap time (minutes)
1	9	LMP900	Laurent Aiello/Allan McNish/Stéphane Ortelli	Audi R8	Audi Sport Team Joest	3.36,124
2	8	LMP900	Frank Biela/Tom Kristensen/Emanuele Pirro	Audi R8	Audi Sport Team Joest	3.36,650
3	7	LMP900	Christian Abt/Michele Alboreto/Dindo Capello	Audi R8	Audi Sport Team Joest	3.37,086
4	11	LMP900	Mario Andretti/David Brabham/Jan Magnussen	Panoz	Panoz Motor Sports	3.39,156
5	21	LMP900	Emanuele Naspetti/Didier de Radigues/Mimmo Schiattarella	Lola Ford	Team Rafanelli	3.39,651
6	17	LMP900	Didier Cottaz/Philippe Gache/Gary Formato	Courage Judd	SMG	3.39,917
7	24	LMP900	Stefan Johansson/Jim Matthews/Guy Smith	Reynard Judd	Johansson Matthews Racing	3.40,124
8	12	LMP900	Hiroki Katoh/Johnny O'Connell/Pierre-Henri Raphanel	Panoz	Panoz Motor Sports	3.41,359
9	3	LMP900	Eric Bernard/Emmanuel Collard/Franck Montagny	Cadillac	DAMS	3.42,616
10	20	LMP900	Tom Coronel/Peter Kox/Jan Lammers	Lola Ford	Konrad Motorsport	3.43,188

Race June 17/18

Position	Number	Class	Drivers	Car	Team	Laps/Gap/Reason for DNF
1	8	LMP900	Frank Biela/Tom Kristensen/Emanuele Pirro	Audi R8	Audi Sport Team Joest	368 laps
2	9	LMP900	Laurent Aiello/Allan McNish/Stéphane Ortelli	Audi R8	Audi Sport Team Joest	−1 lap
3	7	LMP900	Christian Abt/Michele Alboreto/Dindo Capello	Audi R8	Audi Sport Team Joest	−3 laps
4	16	LMP900	Sébastien Bourdais/Emmanuel Clérico/Olivier Grouillard	Courage Peugeot	Pescarolo Sport	−24 laps
5	12	LMP900	Hiroki Katoh/Johnny O'Connell/Pierre-Henri Raphanel	Panoz	Panoz Motor Sports	−26 laps
6	23	LMP900	Masahiko Kageyama/Masami Kageyama/Toshio Suzuki	Panoz	TV Asahi Team Dragon	−28 laps
7	51	LMGTS	Olivier Beretta/Dominique Dupuy/Karl Wendlinger	Chrysler	Viper Team Oreca	−35 laps
8	22	LMP900	Akira Iida/Masahiko Kondo/Keiichi Tsuchiya	Panoz	TV Asahi Team Dragon	−38 laps
9	53	LMGTS	Ni Amorim/Anthony Beltoise/David Donohue	Chrysler	Viper Team Oreca	−40 laps
10	64	LMGTS	Kelly Collins/Franck Fréon/Andy Pilgrim	Corvette	Corvette Racing	−41 laps

American Le Mans Series 2000

Prototype Drivers

Position	Drivers	Car	Team	Points
1	Allan McNish	Audi R8	Audi Sport North America	270
2	Dindo Capello	Audi R8	Audi Sport North America	257
3	Emanuele Pirro	Audi R8	Audi Sport North America	232
4	Frank Biela	Audi R8	Audi Sport North America	231
24	Tom Kristensen	Audi R8	Audi Sport North America	58
27	Michele Alboreto	Audi R8	Audi Sport North America	44

Prototype Chassis Manufacturers

Position	Manufacturer	Points
1	Audi	264
2	BMW	217
3	Panoz	208

Prototype Engine Manufacturers

Position	Manufacturer	Points
1	Audi	264
2	BMW	217
3	Elan Power Products	208

Prototype Teams

Position	Team	Points
1	Audi Sport North America	264
2	BMW Motorsport	219
3	Panoz Motor Sports	208

24h Le Mans 2001

Qualifying June 13/14

Position	Number	Class	Drivers	Car	Team	Lap time (minutes)
1	2	LMP900	Laurent Aiello/Dindo Capello/Christian Pescatori	Audi R8	Audi Sport North America	3.32,429
2	1	LMP900	Frank Biela/Tom Kristensen/Emanuele Pirro	Audi R8	Audi Sport Team Joest	3.32,458
3	3	LMP900	Johnny Herbert/Ralf Kelleners/Didier Theys	Audi R8	Champion Racing	3.34,349
4	9	LMP900	Donny Crevels/Val Hillebrand/Jan Lammers	Dome Judd	Racing for Holland	3.34,838
5	4	LMP900	Tom Coronel/Stefan Johansson/Patrick Lemarié	Audi R8	Johansson Motorsport	3.35,128
6	16	LMP900	Olivier Beretta/Pedro Lamy/Karl Wendlinger	Chrysler	Team PlayStation	3.36,155
7	7	LMGTP	Martin Brundle/Stéphane Ortelli/Guy Smith	Bentley	Team Bentley	3.36,535
8	5	LMP900	Eric Bernard/Emmanuel Collard/Marc Goossens	Cadillac	DAMS	3.37,402
9	8	LMGTP	Butch Leitzinger/Eric van de Poele/Andy Wallace	Bentley	Team Bentley	3.37,408
10	19	LMP900	Anthony Beltoise/Philippe Gache/Jérôme Policand	Courage Judd	SMG	3.38,746

Race June 16/17

Position	Number	Class	Drivers	Car	Team	Laps/Gap/Reason for DNF
1	1	LMP900	Frank Biela/Tom Kristensen/Emanuele Pirro	Audi R8	Audi Sport Team Joest	321 laps
2	2	LMP900	Laurent Aiello/Dindo Capello/Christian Pescatori	Audi R8	Audi Sport North America	−1 lap
3	8	LMGTP	Butch Leitzinger/Eric van de Poele/Andy Wallace	Bentley	Team Bentley	−15 laps
4	16	LMP900	Olivier Beretta/Pedro Lamy/Karl Wendlinger	Chrysler	Team PlayStation	−23 laps
5	38	LMP675	Jean-Denis Délétraz/Pascal Fabre/Jordi Gené	Reynard Volkswagen	ROC Auto	−37 laps
6	83	LMGT	Fabio Babini/Luca Drudi/Gabrio Rosa	Porsche	Seikel Motorsport	−38 laps
7	77	LMGT	Romain Dumas/Philippe Haezebrouck/Gunnar Jeannette	Porsche	Freisinger Motorsport	−39 laps
8	63	LMGTS	Ron Fellows/Johnny O'Connell/Scott Pruett	Corvette	Corvette Racing	−43 laps
9	75	LMGT	Michel Neugarten/Thierry Perrier/Nigel Smith	Porsche	Perspective Racing	−46 laps
10	80	LMGT	Jean-Luc Chéreau/Sébastien Dumez/Patrice Goueslard	Porsche	Larbre Compétition	−47 laps
DNF	3	LMP900	Johnny Herbert/Ralf Kelleners/Didier Theys	Audi R8	Champion Racing	lap 82 clutch
DNF	4	LMP900	Tom Coronel/Stefan Johansson/Patrick Lemarié	Audi R8	Johansson Motorsport	lap 36 electrics

American Le Mans Series 2001

LMP900 Drivers

Position	Drivers	Car	Team	Points
1	Emanuele Pirro	Audi R8	Audi Sport North America	202
2	Frank Biela	Audi R8	Audi Sport North America	198
3	Dindo Capello	Audi R8	Audi Sport North America	175
4	Tom Kristensen	Audi R8	Audi Sport North America	161
6	Andy Wallace	Audi R8	Champion Racing	153
8	Johnny Herbert	Audi R8	Champion Racing	113
9	Stefan Johansson	Audi R8	Johansson Motorsport	89
18	Patrick Lemarié	Audi R8	Johansson Motorsport	46
19	Guy Smith	Audi R8	Johansson Motorsport	42
20	Dorsey Schroeder	Audi R8	Champion Racing	41
22	Laurent Aiello/Michele Alboreto	Audi R8	Audi Sport North America	31
27	Ralf Kelleners	Audi R8	Champion Racing	24

LMP900 Chassis Manufacturers

Position	Manufacturer	Points
1	Audi	206
2	Panoz	162
3	Cadillac	86

LMP900 Engine Manufacturers

Position	Manufacturer	Points
1	Audi	206
2	Elan Power Products	162
3	Northstar	86

LMP900 Teams

Position	Team	Points
1	Audi Sport North America	206
2	Panoz Motor Sports	162
3	Champion Racing	151
4	Johansson Motorsport	86

European Le Mans Series 2001

LMP900 Drivers

Position	Drivers	Car	Team	Points
1	Stefan Johansson	Audi R8	Johansson Motorsport	123
2	Dindo Capello	Audi R8	Audi Sport North America	84
3	Tom Kristensen	Audi R8	Audi Sport North America	82
4	Patrick Lemarié	Audi R8	Johansson Motorsport	80
5	Frank Biela/Emanuele Pirro	Audi R8	Audi Sport North America	76
9	Guy Smith	Audi R8	Johansson Motorsport	61
14	Tom Coronel	Audi R8	Johansson Motorsport	28

LMP900 Teams

Position	Team	Points
1	Johansson Motorsport	115
2	Audi Sport North America	80
3	Pescarolo Sport	65

24h Le Mans 2002

Qualifying June 12/13

Position	Number	Class	Drivers	Car	Team	Lap time (minutes)
1	2	LMP900	Dindo Capello/Johnny Herbert/Christian Pescatori	Audi R8	Audi Sport North America	3.29,905
2	1	LMP900	Frank Biela/Tom Kristensen/Emanuele Pirro	Audi R8	Audi Sport Team Joest	3.30,219
3	3	LMP900	Michael Krumm/Philipp Peter/Marco Werner	Audi R8	Audi Sport Team Joest	3.30,801
4	14	LMP900	Nicolas Minassian/Franck Montagny/Stéphane Sarrazin	Dallara Judd	PlayStation Team Oreca	3.31,828
5	16	LMP900	Tom Coronel/Val Hillebrand/Jan Lammers	Dome Judd	Racing for Holland	3.32,734
6	27	LMP675	Julian Bailey/Mark Blundell/Kevin McGarrity	MG Lola	MG Sport & Racing	3.33,254
7	15	LMP900	Olivier Beretta/Erik Comas/Pedro Lamy	Dallara Judd	PlayStation Team Oreca	3.33,403
8	7	LMP900	Eric Bernard/Emmanuel Collard/JJ Lehto	Cadillac	Team Cadillac	3.33,569
9	11	LMP900	David Brabham/Bryan Herta/Jan Magnussen	Panoz	Panoz Motor Sports	3.34,824
10	6	LMP900	Max Angelelli/Wayne Taylor/Christophe Tinseau	Cadillac	Team Cadillac	3.35,042
15	5	LMP900	Seiji Ara/Yannick Dalmas/Hiroki Katoh	Audi R8	Audi Sport Japan Team Goh	3.38,129

Race June 15/16

Position	Number	Class	Drivers	Car	Team	Laps/Gap/Reason for DNF
1	1	LMP900	Frank Biela/Tom Kristensen/Emanuele Pirro	Audi R8	Audi Sport Team Joest	375 laps
2	2	LMP900	Dindo Capello/Johnny Herbert/Christian Pescatori	Audi R8	Audi Sport North America	−1 lap
3	3	LMP900	Michael Krumm/Philipp Peter/Marco Werner	Audi R8	Audi Sport Team Joest	−3 laps
4	8	LMGTP	Butch Leitzinger/Eric van de Poele/Andy Wallace	Bentley	Team Bentley	−13 laps
5	15	LMP900	Olivier Beretta/Erik Comas/Pedro Lamy	Dallara Judd	PlayStation Team Oreca	−16 laps
6	14	LMP900	Nicolas Minassian/Franck Montagny/Stéphane Sarrazin	Dallara Judd	PlayStation Team Oreca	−16 laps
7	5	LMP900	Seiji Ara/Yannick Dalmas/Hiroki Katoh	Audi R8	Audi Sport Japan Team Goh	−17 laps
8	16	LMP900	Tom Coronel/Val Hillebrand/Jan Lammers	Dome Judd	Racing for Holland	−24 laps
9	6	LMP900	Max Angelelli/Wayne Taylor/Christophe Tinseau	Cadillac	Team Cadillac	−30 laps
10	17	LMP900	Jean-Christophe Boullion/Sébastien Bourdais/Franck Lagorce	Courage Peugeot	Pescarolo Sport	−32 laps

American Le Mans Series 2002

LMP900 Drivers

Position	Drivers	Car	Team	Points
1	Tom Kristensen	Audi R8	Audi Sport North America/Champion Racing	232
2	Dindo Capello	Audi R8	Audi Sport North America	230
3	Frank Biela	Audi R8	Audi Sport North America	209
4	Johnny Herbert	Audi R8	Audi Sport North America/Champion Racing	206
	Emanuele Pirro	Audi R8	Audi Sport North America	206
8	Stefan Johansson	Audi R8	Champion Racing	175
31	Christian Pescatori	Audi R8	Audi Sport North America	30
32	Jan Lammers	Audi R8	Champion Racing	27
33	Andy Wallace	Audi R8	Champion Racing	26

LMP900 Chassis Manufacturers

Position	Manufacturer	Points
1	Audi	252
2	Panoz	188
3	Lola	121

LMP900 Engine Manufacturers

Position	Manufacturer	Points
1	Audi	252
2	Elan Power Products	192
3	Judd	141

LMP900 Teams

Position	Team	Points
1	Audi Sport North America	243
2	Champion Racing	195
3	Panoz Motor Sports	186

24h Le Mans 2003

Qualifying June 11/12

Position	Number	Class	Drivers	Car	Team	Lap time (minutes)
1	7	LMGTP	Dindo Capello/Tom Kristensen/Guy Smith	Bentley	Team Bentley	3.32,843
2	8	LMGTP	Mark Blundell/David Brabham/Johnny Herbert	Bentley	Team Bentley	3.35,098
3	10	LMP900	Frank Biela/Perry McCarthy/Mika Salo	Audi R8	Audi Sport UK	3.35,745
4	15	LMP900	John Bosch/Jan Lammers/Andy Wallace	Dome Judd	Racing for Holland	3.36,156
5	5	LMP900	Seiji Ara/Jan Magnussen/Marco Werner	Audi R8	Audi Sport Japan Team Goh	3.36,418
6	6	LMP900	Stefan Johansson/JJ Lehto/Emanuele Pirro	Audi R8	Champion Racing	3.36,857
7	4	LMP900	Marc Goossens/Jim Matthews/Christophe Tinseau	Riley & Scott Ford	Riley & Scott Racing	3.37,476
8	16	LMP900	Beppe Gabbiani/Tristan Gommendy/Felipe Ortiz	Dome Judd	Racing for Holland	3.38,058
9	13	LMP900	Jonathan Cochet/Jean-Marc Gounon/Stéphane Grégoire	Courage Judd	Courage Competition	3.40,400
10	11	LMP900	Olivier Beretta/Gunnar Jeannette/Max Papis	Panoz	JML Team Panoz	3.40,766

Race June 14/15

Position	Number	Class	Drivers	Car	Team	Laps/Gap/Reason for DNF
1	7	LMGTP	Dindo Capello/Tom Kristensen/Guy Smith	Bentley	Team Bentley	377 laps
2	8	LMGTP	Mark Blundell/David Brabham/Johnny Herbert	Bentley	Team Bentley	–2 laps
3	6	LMP900	Stefan Johansson/JJ Lehto/Emanuele Pirro	Audi R8	Champion Racing	–5 laps
4	5	LMP900	Seiji Ara/Jan Magnussen/Marco Werner	Audi R8	Audi Sport Japan Team Goh	–7 laps
5	11	LMP900	Olivier Beretta/Gunnar Jeannette/Max Papis	Panoz	JML Team Panoz	–17 laps
6	15	LMP900	John Bosch/Jan Lammers/Andy Wallace	Dome Judd	Racing for Holland	–17 laps
7	13	LMP900	Jonathan Cochet/Jean-Marc Gounon/Stéphane Grégoire	Courage Judd	Courage Competition	–17 laps
8	17	LMP900	Jean-Christophe Boullion/Franck Lagorce/Stéphane Sarrazin	Courage Peugeot	Pescarolo Sport	–21 laps
9	18	LMP900	Soheil Ayari/Eric Helary/Nicolas Minassian	Courage Peugeot	Pescarolo Sport	–25 laps
10	88	GTS	Jamie Davies/Tomáš Enge/Peter Kox	Ferrari	Veloqx Prodrive Racing	–41 laps
DNF	10	LMP900	Frank Biela/Perry McCarthy/Mika Salo	Audi R8	Audi Sport UK	lap 29 lack of fuel

American Le Mans Series 2003

LMP900 Drivers

Position	Drivers	Car	Team	Points
1	Frank Biela/Marco Werner	Audi R8	Infineon Team Joest	170
2	JJ Lehto	Audi R8	ADT Champion Racing	163
3	Johnny Herbert	Bentley/Audi R8	Team Bentley/ADT Champion Racing	160
12	Philipp Peter	Audi R8	Infineon Team Joest	26
15	Emanuele Pirro/Stefan Johansson	Audi R8	ADT Champion Racing	22
20	Jonny Kane/Perry McCarthy/Mika Salo	Audi R8	Audi Sport UK	12

LMP900 Chassis Manufacturers

Position	Manufacturer	Points
1	Audi	192
2	Panoz	130
3	Riley & Scott	64

LMP900 Engine Manufacturers

Position	Manufacturer	Points
1	Audi	192
2	Elan Power Products	130
3	Lincoln	60

LMP900 Teams

Position	Manufacturer	Points
1	Infineon Team Joest	170
2	Champion Racing	163
3	JML Team Panoz	130
8	Audi Sport UK	12

FIA Sportscar Championship 2003

SR1 Drivers

Position	Drivers	Car	Team	Points
1	John Bosch/Jan Lammers	Dome Judd	Racing for Holland	44
2	Beppe Gabbiani/Felipe Ortiz	Dome Judd	Racing for Holland	36
3	Hayanari Shimoda	DBA Zytek	RN Motorsport	26
5	Seiji Ara/Tom Kristensen	Audi R8	Audi Team Goh for Belgium	20

SR1 Constructors

Position	Manufacturer	Points
1	Dome	62
2	Courage	34
3	DBA	26
4	Audi	20

SR1 Teams

Position	Team	Points
1	Racing for Holland	62
2	Pescarolo Sport	34
3	RN Motorsport	26
4	Audi Team Goh for Belgium	20

24h Le Mans 2004

Qualifying June 09/10

Position	Number	Class	Drivers	Car	Team	Lap time (minutes)
1	88	LMP1	Jamie Davies/Johnny Herbert/Guy Smith	Audi R8	Audi Sport UK Team Veloqx	3.32,838
2	8	LMP1	Frank Biela/Pierre Kaffer/Allan McNish	Audi R8	Audi Sport UK Team Veloqx	3.33,233
3	22	LMP1	David Brabham/Hayanari Shimoda/Andy Wallace	Zytek	Zytek Engineering	3.33,923
4	5	LMP1	Seiji Ara/Dindo Capello/Tom Kristensen	Audi R8	Audi Sport Japan Team Goh	3.34,038
5	17	LMP1	Sébastien Bourdais/Emmanuel Collard/Nicolas Minassian	Pescarolo Judd	Pescarolo Sport	3.34,252
6	2	LMP1	JJ Lehto/Emanuele Pirro/Marco Werner	Audi R8	Champion Racing	3.34,927
7	9	LMP1	Ryo Fukuda/Ryo Michigami/Hiroki Katoh	Dome Mugen	Kondo Racing	3.36,285
8	15	LMP1	Chris Dyson/Jan Lammers/Katsutomo Kaneishi	Dome Judd	Racing for Holland	3.36,353
9	6	LMP1	Martin Short/Rob Barff/João Barbosa	Dallara Judd	Rollcentre Racing	3.39,260
10	16	LMP1	Tom Coronel/Ralph Firman/Justin Wilson	Dome Judd	Racing for Holland	3.40,261

Race June 12/13

Position	Number	Class	Drivers	Car	Team	Laps/Gap/Reason for DNF
1	5	LMP1	Seiji Ara/Dindo Capello/Tom Kristensen	Audi R8	Audi Sport Japan Team Goh	379 laps
2	88	LMP1	Jamie Davies/Johnny Herbert/Guy Smith	Audi R8	Audi Sport UK Team Veloqx	+41,354 seconds
3	2	LMP1	JJ Lehto/Emanuele Pirro/Marco Werner	Audi R8	Champion Racing	−11 laps
4	18	LMP1	Soheil Ayari/Erik Comas/Benoît Tréluyer	Pescarolo Judd	Pescarolo Sport	−18 laps
5	8	LMP1	Frank Biela/Pierre Kaffer/Allan McNish	Audi R8	Audi Sport UK Team Veloqx	−29 laps
6	64	GTS	Olivier Beretta/Oliver Gavin/Jan Magnussen	Corvette	Corvette Racing	−34 laps
7	15	LMP1	Chris Dyson/Jan Lammers/Katsutomo Kaneishi	Dome Judd	Racing for Holland	−38 laps
8	63	GTS	Ron Fellows/Johnny O'Connell/Max Papis	Corvette	Corvette Racing	−45 laps
9	65	GTS	Colin McRae/Rickard Rydell/Darren Turner	Ferrari	Prodrive Racing	−50 laps
10	90	GT	Jörg Bergmeister/Patrick Long/Sascha Maassen	Porsche	White Lightning Racing	−52 laps

American Le Mans Series 2004

P1 Drivers

Position	Drivers	Car	Team	Points
1	JJ Lehto/Marco Werner	Audi R8	ADT Champion Racing	183
2	Butch Leitzinger/James Weaver	Lola Aer	Dyson Racing Team	111
3	Andy Wallace	Lola Aer	Dyson Racing Team	101
5	Pierre Kaffer	Audi R8	Audi Sport UK Team Veloqx/ADT Champion Racing	71
6	Johnny Herbert	Audi R8	Audi Sport UK Team Veloqx/ADT Champion Racing	64
7	Frank Biela/Allan McNish	Audi R8	Audi Sport UK Team Veloqx	26
9	Emanuele Pirro	Audi R8	ADT Champion Racing	22
10	Jamie Davies/Guy Smith	Audi R8	Audi Sport UK Team Veloqx	19

P1 Chassis Manufacturers

Position	Manufacturer	Points
1	Audi	191
2	Lola	149
3	Dallara	16

P1 Engine Manufacturers

Position	Manufacturer	Points
1	Audi	191
2	Aer	133
3	Judd	32

P1 Teams

Position	Team	Points
1	ADT Champion Racing	183
2	Dyson Racing Team	133
3	Intersport Racing	25

Le Mans Endurance Series 2004

LMP1 Drivers

Position	Drivers	Car	Team	Points
1	Jamie Davies/Johnny Herbert	Audi R8	Audi UK/Veloqx	34
2	Pierre Kaffer/Allan McNish	Audi R8	Audi UK/Veloqx	28
3	Seiji Ara/Dindo Capello	Audi R8	Team Goh	27
17	Tom Kristensen	Audi R8	Team Goh	6

LMP1 Teams

Position	Team	Car	Points
1	Audi UK/Veloqx	Audi #88	34
2	Audi UK/Veloqx	Audi #8	28
3	Team Goh	Audi #5	27

24h Le Mans 2005

Qualifying June 15/16

Position	Number	Class	Drivers	Car	Team	Lap time (minutes)
1	16	LMP1	Jean-Christophe Boullion/Emmanuel Collard/Erik Comas	Pescarolo Judd	Pescarolo Sport	3.34,715
2	17	LMP1	Soheil Ayari/Eric Helary/Sébastien Loeb	Pescarolo Judd	Pescarolo Sport	3.35,555
3	2	LMP1	Frank Biela/Emanuele Pirro/Allan McNish	Audi R8	Champion Racing	3.37,795
4	5	LMP1	Seiji Ara/Ryo Michigami/Katsutomo Kaneishi	Dome Mugen	Jim Gainer International	3.38,094
5	4	LMP1	Jean-Marc Gounon/Franck Montagny/Stéphane Ortelli	Audi R8	Audi PlayStation Oreca	3.38,929
6	13	LMP1	Jonathan Cochet/Bruce Jouanny/Shinji Nakano	Courage Judd	Courage Competition	3.38,735
7	7	LMP1	Jamie Campbell-Walter/Nicolas Minassian/Andy Wallace	DBA Judd	Creation Autosportif	3.38,929
8	3	LMP1	Tom Kristensen/JJ Lehto/Marco Werner	Audi R8	Champion Racing	3.38,988
9	18	LMP1	João Barbosa/Vanina Ickx/Martin Short	Dallara Judd	Rollcentre Racing	3.39,643
10	9	LMP1	Sam Hignett/Haruki Kurosawa/John Stack	Zytek	Team Jota Zytek	3.41,177

Race June 18/19

Position	Number	Class	Drivers	Car	Team	Laps/Gap/Reason for DNF
1	3	LMP1	Tom Kristensen/JJ Lehto/Marco Werner	Audi R8	Champion Racing	370 laps
2	16	LMP1	Jean-Christophe Boullion/Emmanuel Collard/Eric Comas	Pescarolo Judd	Pescarolo Sport	–2 laps
3	2	LMP1	Frank Biela/Emanuele Pirro/Allan McNish	Audi R8	Champion Racing	–6 laps
4	4	LMP1	Jean-Marc Gounon/Franck Montagny/Stéphane Ortelli	Audi R8	Audi PlayStation Oreca	–8 laps
5	64	GT1	Olivier Beretta/Oliver Gavin/Jan Magnussen	Corvette	Corvette Racing	–21 laps
6	63	GT1	Ron Fellows/Johnny O'Connell/Max Papis	Corvette	Corvette Racing	–23 laps
7	10	LMP1	John Bosch/Elton Julian/Jan Lammers	Dome Judd	Racing for Holland	–24 laps
8	12	LMP1	Alexander Frei/Dominik Schwager/Christian Vann	Courage Judd	Courage Competition	–31 laps
9	59	GT1	David Brabham/Stéphane Sarrazin/Darren Turner	Aston Martin	Aston Martin Racing	–37 laps
10	71	GT2	Leo Hindery/Marc Lieb/Mike Rockenfeller	Porsche	Alex Job Racing	–38 laps

American Le Mans Series 2005

P1 Drivers

Position	Drivers	Car	Team	Points
1	Frank Biela/Emanuele Pirro	Audi R8	ADT Champion Racing	182
2	Chris Dyson	Lola Aer	Dyson Racing Team	154
3	JJ Lehto/Marco Werner	Audi R8	ADT Champion Racing	148
9	Tom Kristensen	Audi R8	ADT Champion Racing	26
10	Allan McNish	Audi R8	ADT Champion Racing	22

P1 Team

Position	Team	Points
1	ADT Champion Racing	200
2	Dyson Racing Team	174

P1 Chassis

Position	Manufacturer	Points
1	Audi	200
2	Lola	174
3	Riley & Scott	45

P1 Engine

Position	Manufacturer	Points
1	Audi	200
2	Aer	174
3	Elan	45

Le Mans Endurance Series 2005

LM P1 Drivers

Position	Drivers	Car	Team	Points
1	Jean-Christophe Boullion/Emmanuel Collard	Pescarolo Judd	Pescarolo Sport	34
2	Hayanari Shimoda	Zytek	Zytek Motorsport	32
3	Stéphane Ortelli/Allan McNish	Audi R8	Audi PlayStation Team Oreca	26

LM P1 Teams

Position	Team	Points
1	Pescarolo Sport	34
2	Zytek Motorsport	32
3	Audi PlayStation Team Oreca	26

24h Le Mans 2006

Position	Number	Class	Drivers	Car	Team	Lap time (minutes)
1	7	LMP1	Dindo Capello/Tom Kristensen/Allan McNish	Audi R10 TDI	Audi Sport Team Joest	3.30,466
2	8	LMP1	Frank Biela/Emanuele Pirro/Marco Werner	Audi R10 TDI	Audi Sport Team Joest	3.30,584
3	16	LMP1	Emmanuel Collard/Erik Comas/Nicolas Minassian	Pescarolo Judd	Pescarolo Sport	3.32,584
4	17	LMP1	Eric Helary/Sébastien Loeb/Franck Montagny	Pescarolo Judd	Pescarolo Sport	3.32,990
5	13	LMP1	Jean-Marc Gounon/Haruki Kurosawa/Shinji Nakano	Courage Mugen	Courage Competition	3.34,120
6	14	LMP1	Stefan Johansson/Jan Lammers/Alex Yoong	Dome Judd	Racing for Holland	3.34,864
7	9	LMP1	Jamie Campbell-Walter/Beppe Gabbiani/Felipe Ortiz	Creation Judd	Creation Autosportif	3.36,459
8	2	LMP1	Philip Andersen/Casper Elgaard/John Nielsen	Zytek	Zytek Engineering	3.39,252
9	5	LMP1	Marcel Fässler/Philipp Peter/Harold Primat	Courage Judd	Swiss Spirit	3.40,182
10	12	LMP1	Alexander Frei/Gregor Fisken/Sam Hancock	Courage Mugen	Courage Competition	3.40,443

Position	Number	Class	Drivers	Car	Team	Laps/Gap/Reason for DNF
1	8	LMP1	Frank Biela/Emanuele Pirro/Marco Werner	Audi R10 TDI	Audi Sport Team Joest	380 laps
2	17	LMP1	Eric Helary/Sébastien Loeb/Franck Montagny	Pescarolo Judd	Pescarolo Sport	−4 laps
3	7	LMP1	Dindo Capello/Tom Kristensen/Allan McNish	Audi R10 TDI	Audi Sport Team Joest	−13 laps
4	64	LMGT1	Olivier Beretta/Oliver Gavin/Jan Magnussen	Corvette	Corvette Racing	−25 laps
5	16	LMP1	Emmanuel Collard/Eric Comas/Nicolas Minassian	Pescarolo Judd	Pescarolo Sport	−28 laps
6	007	LMGT1	Tomáš Enge/Andrea Piccini/Darren Turner	Aston Martin	Aston Martin Racing	−30 laps
7	72	LMGT1	Luc Alphand/Patrice Goueslard/Jerôme Policand	Corvette	Alphand Aventures	−34 laps
8	25	LMP2	Thomas Erdos/Mike Newton/Andy Wallace	MG Lola	RML	−37 laps
9	62	LMGT1	David Brabham/Antonio Garcia/Nelson Piquet	Aston Martin	Russian Age Racing	−37 laps
10	009	LMGT1	Pedro Lamy/Stéphane Ortelli/Stéphane Sarrazin	Aston Martin	Aston Martin Racing	−38 laps

American Le Mans Series 2006

P1 Drivers

Position	Drivers	Car	Team	Points
1	Dindo Capello/Allan McNish	Audi R10 TDI	Audi Sport North America	204
2	James Weaver	Lola Aer	Dyson Racing Team	119
3	Butch Leitzinger	Lola Aer	Dyson Racing Team	106
4	Frank Biela/Emanuele Pirro	Audi R10 TDI	Audi Sport North America	99
13	Tom Kristensen	Audi R10 TDI	Audi Sport North America	26
18	Marco Werner	Audi R10 TDI	Audi Sport North America	14

P1 Team

Position	Team	Points
1	Audi Sport North America	215
2	Dyson Racing Team	125
3	Autocon Motorsports	60

P1 Chassis

Position	Manufacturer	Points
1	Audi	215
2	Lola	160
3	Zytek	33

P1 Engine

Position	Manufacturer	Points
1	Audi	215
2	Aer	160
3	Zytek	33

24h Le Mans 2007

Position	Number	Class	Drivers	Car	Team	Lap time (minutes)
1	8	LMP1	Sébastien Bourdais/Pedro Lamy/Stéphane Sarrazin	Peugeot	Team Peugeot Total	3.26,344
2	2	LMP1	Dindo Capello/Tom Kristensen/Allan McNish	Audi R10 TDI	Audi Sport North America	3.26,916
3	7	LMP1	Marc Gené/Nicolas Minassian/Jacques Villeneuve	Peugeot	Team Peugeot Total	3.27,724
4	1	LMP1	Frank Biela/Emanuele Pirro/Marco Werner	Audi R10 TDI	Audi Sport North America	3.28,301
5	3	LMP1	Lucas Luhr/Alexandre Premat/Mike Rockenfeller	Audi R10 TDI	Audi Sport Team Joest	3.29,736
6	16	LMP1	Jean-Christophe Boullion/Emmanuel Collard/Romain Dumas	Pescarolo Judd	Pescarolo Sport	3.33,590
7	13	LMP1	Jean-Marc Gounon/Stefan Johansson/Guillaume Moreau	Courage Aer	Courage Competition	3.35,171
8	18	LMP1	João Barbosa/Stuart Hall/Martin Short	Pescarolo Judd	Rollcentre Racing	3.35,559
9	14	LMP1	Jeroen Bleekemolen/David Hart/Jan Lammers	Dome Judd	Racing for Holland	3.35,660
10	9	LMP1	Jamie Campbell-Walter/Shinji Nakano/Felipe Ortiz	Creation Judd	Creation Autosportif	3.36,279

Race June 16/17

Position	Number	Class	Drivers	Car	Team	Laps/Gap/Reason for DNF
1	1	LMP1	Frank Biela/Emanuele Pirro/Marco Werner	Audi R10 TDI	Audi Sport North America	369 laps
2	8	LMP1	Sébastien Bourdais/Pedro Lamy/Stéphane Sarrazin	Peugeot	Team Peugeot Total	–10 laps
3	16	LMP1	Jean-Christophe Boullion/Emmanuel Collard/Romain Dumas	Pescarolo Judd	Pescarolo Sport	–11 laps
4	18	LMP1	João Barbosa/Stuart Hall/Martin Short	Pescarolo Judd	Rollcentre Racing	–22 laps
5	009	LMGT1	David Brabham/Rickard Rydell/Darren Turner	Aston Martin	Aston Martin Racing	–26 laps
6	63	LMGT1	Ron Fellows/Jan Magnussen/Johnny O'Connell	Corvette	Corvette Racing	–27 laps
7	008	LMGT1	Christophe Bouchut/Casper Elgaard/Fabrizio Gollin	Aston Martin	AMR Larbre Competition	–28 laps
8	15	LMP1	Jan Charouz/Stefan Mücke/Alex Yoong	Lola Judd	Charouz Racing	–31 laps
9	007	LMGT1	Tomáš Enge/Johnny Herbert/Peter Kox	Aston Martin	Aston Martin Racing	–32 laps
10	54	LMGT1	Jean-Philippe Belloc/Laurent Groppi/Nicolas Prost	Saleen	Team Oreca	–32 laps
DNF	2	LMP1	Dindo Capello/Tom Kristensen/Allan McNish	Audi R10 TDI	Audi Sport North America	lap 263 lost wheel
DNF	3	LMP1	Lucas Luhr/Alexandre Premat/Mike Rockenfeller	Audi R10 TDI	Audi Sport Team Joest	lap 24 accident

American Le Mans Series 2007

P1 Drivers

Position	Drivers	Car	Team	Points
1	Dindo Capello/Allan McNish	Audi R10 TDI	Audi Sport North America	246
2	Marco Werner	Audi R10 TDI	Audi Sport North America	210
3	Emanuele Pirro	Audi R10 TDI	Audi Sport North America	175
12	Frank Biela	Audi R10 TDI	Audi Sport North America	26
14	Tom Kristensen	Audi R10 TDI	Audi Sport North America	22
15	Mike Rockenfeller	Audi R10 TDI	Audi Sport North America	19
16	Lucas Luhr	Audi R10 TDI	Audi Sport North America	16

P1 Team

Position	Team	Points
1	Audi Sport North America	258
2	Autocon Motorsports	99
3	Intersport Racing	95

P1 Chassis

Position	Manufacturer	Points
1	Audi	258
2	Creation	161
3	Lola	98

P1 Engine

Position	Manufacturer	Points
1	Audi	258
2	Judd	161
3	Aer	98

24h Le Mans 2008

Qualifying June 11/12

Position	Number	Class	Drivers	Car	Team	Lap time (minutes)
1	8	LMP1	Pedro Lamy/Stéphane Sarrazin/Alexander Wurz	Peugeot	Team Peugeot Total	3.18,513
2	9	LMP1	Christian Klien/Franck Montagny/Ricardo Zonta	Peugeot	Peugeot Sport Total	3.18,682
3	7	LMP1	Marc Gené/Nicolas Minassian/Jacques Villeneuve	Peugeot	Team Peugeot Total	3.20,451
4	2	LMP1	Dindo Capello/Tom Kristensen/Allan McNish	Audi R10 TDI	Audi Sport North America	3.23,847
5	3	LMP1	Lucas Luhr/Alexandre Premat/Mike Rockenfeller	Audi R10 TDI	Audi Sport Team Joest	3.24,287
6	10	LMP1	Jan Charouz/Tomáš Enge/Stefan Mücke	Lola Aston Martin	Charouz Racing System	3.25,158
7	1	LMP1	Frank Biela/Emanuele Pirro/Marco Werner	Audi R10 TDI	Audi Sport North America	3.25,289
8	11	LMP1	Daisuke Ito/Tatsuya Kataoka/Yuji Tachikawa	Dome Judd	Dome Racing Team	3.26,928
9	16	LMP1	Jean-Christophe Boullion/Emmanuel Collard/Romain Dumas	Pescarolo Judd	Pescarolo Sport	3.28,533
10	5	LMP1	Soheil Ayari/Loïc Duval/Laurent Groppi	Courage-Oreca Judd	Team Oreca Matmut	3.30,490

Race June 14/15

Position	Number	Class	Drivers	Car	Team	Laps/Gap/Reason for DNF
1	2	LMP1	Dindo Capello/Tom Kristensen/Allan McNish	Audi R10 TDI	Audi Sport North America	381 laps
2	7	LMP1	Marc Gené/Nicolas Minassian/Jacques Villeneuve	Peugeot	Team Peugeot Total	+4.31,094 minutes
3	9	LMP1	Christian Klien/Franck Montagny/Ricardo Zonta	Peugeot	Peugeot Sport Total	–2 laps
4	3	LMP1	Lucas Luhr/Alexandre Premat/Mike Rockenfeller	Audi R10 TDI	Audi Sport Team Joest	–7 laps
5	8	LMP1	Pedro Lamy/Stéphane Sarrazin/Alexander Wurz	Peugeot	Team Peugeot Total	–13 laps
6	1	LMP1	Frank Biela/Emanuele Pirro/Marco Werner	Audi R10 TDI	Audi Sport North America	–14 laps
7	17	LMP1	Harold Primat/Christophe Tinseau/Benoît Tréluyer	Pescarolo Judd	Pescarolo Sport	–19 laps
8	5	LMP1	Soheil Ayari/Loïc Duval/Laurent Groppi	Courage-Oreca Judd	Team Oreca Matmut	–24 laps
9	10	LMP1	Jan Charouz/Tomáš Enge/Stefan Mücke	Lola Aston Martin	Charouz Racing System	–27 laps
10	34	LMP2	Jeroen Bleekemolen/Pieter van Merkstijn/Jos Verstappen	Porsche	Van Merkstijn Motorsport	–27 laps

American Le Mans Series 2008

P1 Drivers

Position	Drivers	Car	Team	Points
1	Lucas Luhr/Marco Werner	Audi R10 TDI	Audi Sport North America	219
2	Emanuele Pirro	Audi R10 TDI	Audi Sport North America	156
3	Richard Berry	Lola Aer	Intersport Racing	106
5	Dindo Capello	Audi R10 TDI	Audi Sport North America	102
6	Allan McNish	Audi R10 TDI	Audi Sport North America	60
8	Frank Biela	Audi R10 TDI	Audi Sport North America	42
10	Tom Kristensen	Audi R10 TDI	Audi Sport North America	30
12	Mike Rockenfeller	Audi R10 TDI	Audi Sport North America	26
13	Marcel Fässler	Audi R10 TDI	Audi Sport North America	21
13	Christijan Albers	Audi R10 TDI	Audi Sport North America	21

P1 Team

Position	Team	Points
1	Audi Sport North America	230
2	Intersport Racing	129
3	Autocon Motorsports	41

P1 Chassis

Position	Manufacturer	Points
1	Audi	230
2	Lola	129
3	Creation	56

P1 Engine

Position	Manufacturer	Points
1	Audi	230
2	Aer	129
3	Peugeot	46

Le Mans Series 2008

LM P1 Drivers

Position	Drivers	Car	Team	Points
1	Alexandre Premat/Mike Rockenfeller	Audi R10 TDI	Audi Sport Team Joest	35
2	Marc Gené/Nicolas Minassian	Peugeot	Team Peugeot Total	32
3	Dindo Capello/Allan McNish	Audi R10 TDI	Audi Sport Team Joest	27

LM P1 Manufacturers

Position	Manufacturer	Points
1	Audi	62
2	Peugeot	53
3	Pescarolo	31

LM P1 Teams

Position	Team	Car	Points
1	Audi Sport Team Joest #2	Audi R10 TDI	35
2	Team Peugeot Total #7	Peugeot	32
3	Audi Sport Team Joest #1	Audi R10 TDI	27

24h Le Mans 2009

Qualifying June 10/11

Position	Number	Class	Drivers	Car	Team	Lap time (minutes)
1	8	LMP1	Sébastien Bourdais/Franck Montagny/Stéphane Sarrazin	Peugeot	Team Peugeot Total	3.22,888
2	1	LMP1	Dindo Capello/Tom Kristensen/Allan McNish	Audi R15 TDI	Audi Sport Team Joest	3.23,650
3	7	LMP1	Christian Klien/Pedro Lamy/Nicolas Minassian	Peugeot	Team Peugeot Total	3.24,860
4	17	LMP1	Jean-Christophe Boullion/Simon Pagenaud/Benoît Tréluyer	Peugeot	Pescarolo Sport	3.25,062
5	9	LMP1	David Brabham/Marc Gené/Alexander Wurz	Peugeot	Peugeot Sport Total	3.25,252
6	2	LMP1	Lucas Luhr/Mike Rockenfeller/Marco Werner	Audi R15 TDI	Audi Sport North America	3.25,780
7	3	LMP1	Timo Bernhard/Romain Dumas/Alexandre Premat	Audi R15 TDI	Audi Sport Team Joest	3.27,106
8	007	LMP1	Jan Charouz/Tomáš Enge/Stefan Mücke	Lola Aston Martin	AMR Eastern Europe	3.27,180
9	008	LMP1	Anthony Davidson/Darren Turner/Jos Verstappen	Lola Aston Martin	Aston Martin Racing	3.27,704
10	13	LMP1	Andrea Belicchi/Neel Jani/Nicolas Prost	Lola Judd	Speedy Racing Sebah	3.28,134
13	15	LMP1	Christijan Albers/Christian Bakkerud/Giorgio Mondini	Audi R10 TDI	Kolles	3.31,192
14	14	LMP1	Narain Karthikeyan/André Lotterer/Charles Zwolsman	Audi R10 TDI	Kolles	3.31,548

Race June 13/14

Position	Number	Class	Drivers	Car	Team	Laps/Gap/Reason for DNF
1	9	LMP1	David Brabham/Marc Gené/Alexander Wurz	Peugeot	Peugeot Sport Total	382 laps
2	8	LMP1	Sébastien Bourdais/Franck Montagny/Stéphane Sarrazin	Peugeot	Team Peugeot Total	–1 lap
3	1	LMP1	Dindo Capello/Tom Kristensen/Allan McNish	Audi R15 TDI	Audi Sport Team Joest	–6 laps
4	007	LMP1	Jan Charouz/Tomáš Enge/Stefan Mücke	Lola Aston Martin	AMR Eastern Europe	–9 laps
5	11	LMP1	Soheil Ayari/Nicolas Lapierre/Olivier Panis	Oreca Aim	Team Oreca Matmut Aim	–12 laps
6	7	LMP1	Christian Klien/Pedro Lamy/Nicolas Minassian	Peugeot	Team Peugeot Total	–13 laps
7	14	LMP1	Narain Karthikeyan/André Lotterer/Charles Zwolsman	Audi R10 TDI	Kolles	–13 laps
8	16	LMP1	João Barbosa/Bruce Jouanny/Christophe Tinseau	Pescarolo Judd	Pescarolo Sport	–14 laps
9	15	LMP1	Christijan Albers/Christian Bakkerud/Giorgio Mondini	Audi R10 TDI	Kolles	–22 laps
10	31	LMP2	Emmanuel Collard/Casper Elgaard/Kristian Poulsen	Porsche	Team Essex	–25 laps
17	3	LMP1	Timo Bernhard/Romain Dumas/Alexandre Premat	Audi R15 TDI	Audi Sport Team Joest	–49 laps
DNF	2	LMP1	Lucas Luhr/Mike Rockenfeller/Marco Werner	Audi R15 TDI	Audi Sport North America	lap 105 accident

American Le Mans Series 2009

P1 Drivers

Position	Drivers	Car	Team	Points
1	David Brabham/Scott Sharp	Acura	Patrón Highcroft Racing	179
2	Gil de Ferran/Simon Pagenaud	Acura	De Ferran Motorsports	162
3	Jon Field/Clint Field	Lola Aer	Intersport Racing	116
6	Dindo Capello/Allan McNish	Audi R15 TDI	Audi Sport Team Joest	53
9	Lucas Luhr/Marco Werner	Audi R15 TDI	Audi Sport North America	43
13	Tom Kristensen	Audi R15 TDI	Audi Sport Team Joest	30
15	Mike Rockenfeller	Audi R15 TDI	Audi Sport North America	23

P1 Chassis

Position	Manufacturer	Points
1	Acura	199
2	Lola	123
3	Ginetta-Zytek	58
5	Audi	53

P1 Engine

Position	Manufacturer	Points
1	Acura	199
2	Aer	123
3	Zytek	58
5	Audi	53

Le Mans Series 2009

LM P1 Drivers

Position	Drivers	Car	Team	Points
1	Jan Charouz/Tomáš Enge/Stefan Mücke	Lola Aston Martin	Aston Martin Racing	39
2	Jean-Christophe Boullion/Christophe Tinseau	Pescarolo Judd	Pescarolo Sport	26
3	Nicolas Lapierre/Olivier Panis	Oreca Aim	Team Oreca Matmut Aim	22
9	Andy Meyrick/Charles Zwolsman	Audi R10 TDI	Kolles	12
11	Narain Karthikeyan	Audi R10 TDI	Kolles	11
15	Christijan Albers/Christian Bakkerud	Audi R10 TDI	Kolles	6
19	Giorgio Mondini	Audi R10 TDI	Kolles	2
20	Michael Krumm	Audi R10 TDI	Kolles	1

LM P1 Manufacturers

Position	Manufacturer	Points
1	Lola Aston Martin	65
2	Oreca Aim	34
3	Pescarolo Judd	29
4	Audi	18

LM P1 Teams

Position	Team	Car	Points
1	Aston Martin Racing	Lola Aston Martin	39
2	Pescarolo Sport	Pescarolo Judd	26
3	Team Oreca Matmut Aim	Oreca Aim	23
7	Kolles #14	Audi R10 TDI	12
11	Kolles #15	Audi R10 TDI	6

Asian Le Mans Series 2009

LM P1 Teams

Position	Team	Car	Points
1	Sora Racing	Pescarolo Judd	18
2	Aston Martin Racing	Lola Aston Martin	15
3	Team Oreca Matmut Aim	Oreca Aim	14
4	Kolles #15	Audi R10 TDI	10
6	Kolles #14	Audi R10 TDI	7

24h Le Mans 2010

Qualifying June 09/10

Position	Number	Class	Drivers	Car	Team	Lap time (minutes)
1	3	LMP1	Sébastien Bourdais/Pedro Lamy/Simon Pagenaud	Peugeot	Peugeot Sport Total	3.19,711
2	1	LMP1	Anthony Davidson/Marc Gené/Alexander Wurz	Peugeot	Team Peugeot Total	3.20,317
3	2	LMP1	Nicolas Minassian/Franck Montagny/Stéphane Sarrazin	Peugeot	Team Peugeot Total	3.20,325
4	4	LMP1	Loïc Duval/Nicolas Lapierre/Olivier Panis	Peugeot	Team Oreca Matmut	3.21,192
5	9	LMP1	Timo Bernhard/Romain Dumas/Mike Rockenfeller	Audi R15 TDI	Audi Sport North America	3.21,981
6	7	LMP1	Dindo Capello/Tom Kristensen/Allan McNish	Audi R15 TDI	Audi Sport Team Joest	3.22,176
7	8	LMP1	Marcel Fässler/André Lotterer/Benoît Tréluyer	Audi R15 TDI	Audi Sport Team Joest	3.23,605
8	007	LMP1	Adrian Fernandez/Stefan Mücke/Harold Primat	Lola Aston Martin	Aston Martin Racing	3.26,680
9	009	LMP1	Juan Barazi/Sam Hancock/Darren Turner	Lola Aston Martin	Aston Martin Racing	3.26,747
10	6	LMP1	Didier André/Soheil Ayari/Andy Meyrick	Oreca Aim	Aim Team Oreca Matmut	3.29,506
12	14	LMP1	Christophe Bouchut/Manuel Rodrigues/Scott Tucker	Audi R10 TDI	Kolles	3.30,907
13	15	LMP1	Christijan Albers/Christian Bakkerud/Oliver Jarvis	Audi R10 TDI	Kolles	3.31,661

Race June 12/13

Position	Number	Class	Drivers	Car	Team	Laps/Gap/Reason for DNF
1	9	LMP1	Timo Bernhard/Romain Dumas/Mike Rockenfeller	Audi R15 TDI	Audi Sport North America	397 laps
2	8	LMP1	Marcel Fässler/André Lotterer/Benoît Tréluyer	Audi R15 TDI	Audi Sport Team Joest	–1 lap
3	7	LMP1	Dindo Capello/Tom Kristensen/Allan McNish	Audi R15 TDI	Audi Sport Team Joest	–3 laps
4	6	LMP1	Didier André/Soheil Ayari/Andy Meyrick	Oreca Aim	Aim Team Oreca Matmut	–28 laps
5	42	LMP2	Jonny Kane/Nick Leventis/Danny Watts	HPD Honda	Strakka Racing	–30 laps
6	007	LMP1	Adrian Fernandez/Stefan Mücke/Harold Primat	Lola Aston Martin	Aston Martin Racing	–32 laps
7	35	LMP2	Jan Charouz/Matthieu Lahaye/Guillaume Moreau	Pescarolo Judd	Oak Racing	–36 laps
8	25	LMP2	Thomas Erdos/Mike Newton/Andy Wallace	Lola HPD	RML	–39 laps
9	24	LMP2	Richard Hein/Jacques Nicolet/Jean-François Yvon	Pescarolo Judd	Oak Racing	–56 laps
10	41	LMP2	Gary Chalandon/Tim Greaves/Karim Ojjeh	Ginetta Zytek	Team Bruichladdich	–56 laps
DNF	14	LMP1	Christophe Bouchut/Manuel Rodrigues/Scott Tucker	Audi R10 TDI	Kolles	lap 332 accident
DNF	15	LMP1	Christijan Albers/Christian Bakkerud/Oliver Jarvis	Audi R10 TDI	Kolles	lap 183 transmission

Intercontinental Le Mans Cup 2010

LM P1 Teams

Position	Team	Car	Points
1	Peugeot Sport Total	Peugeot	118
2	Audi Sport Team Joest	Audi R15 TDI	101
3	Drayson Racing	Lola Judd	32

LM P1 Manufacturers

Position	Manufacturer	Points
1	Peugeot	140
2	Audi	101

24h Le Mans 2011

Qualifying June 08/09

Position	Number	Class	Drivers	Car	Team	Lap time (minutes)
1	2	LMP1	Marcel Fässler/André Lotterer/Benoît Tréluyer	Audi R18 TDI	Audi Sport Team Joest	3.25,738
2	1	LMP1	Timo Bernhard/Romain Dumas/Mike Rockenfeller	Audi R18 TDI	Audi Sport Team Joest	3.25,799
3	9	LMP1	Sébastien Bourdais/Pedro Lamy/Simon Pagenaud	Peugeot	Team Peugeot Total	3.26,010
4	8	LMP1	Nicolas Minassian/Franck Montagny/Stéphane Sarrazin	Peugeot	Peugeot Sport Total	3.26,156
5	3	LMP1	Dindo Capello/Tom Kristensen/Allan McNish	Audi R18 TDI	Audi Sport North America	3.26,165
6	7	LMP1	Anthony Davidson/Marc Gené/Alexander Wurz	Peugeot	Peugeot Sport Total	3.26,272
7	10	LMP1	Loïc Duval/Nicolas Lapierre/Olivier Panis	Peugeot	Team Oreca Matmut	3.30,084
8	12	LMP1	Jeroen Bleekemolen/Neel Jani/Nicolas Prost	Lola Toyota	Rebellion Racing	3.32,883
9	16	LMP1	Emmanuel Collard/Julien Jousse/Christophe Tinseau	Pescarolo Judd	Pescarolo Team	3.33,066
10	13	LMP1	Andrea Belicchi/Jean-Christophe Boullion/Guy Smith	Lola Toyota	Rebellion Racing	3.34,573

Race June 11/12

Position	Number	Class	Drivers	Car	Team	Laps/Gap/Reason for DNF
1	2	LMP1	Marcel Fässler/André Lotterer/Benoît Tréluyer	Audi R18 TDI	Audi Sport Team Joest	355 laps
2	9	LMP1	Sébastien Bourdais/Pedro Lamy/Simon Pagenaud	Peugeot	Team Peugeot Total	+13,854 seconds
3	8	LMP1	Nicolas Minassian/Franck Montagny/Stéphane Sarrazin	Peugeot	Peugeot Sport Total	–2 laps
4	7	LMP1	Anthony Davidson/Marc Gené/Alexander Wurz	Peugeot	Peugeot Sport Total	–4 laps
5	10	LMP1	Loïc Duval/Nicolas Lapierre/Olivier Panis	Peugeot	Team Oreca Matmut	–16 laps
6	12	LMP1	Jeroen Bleekemolen/Neel Jani/Nicolas Prost	Lola Toyota	Rebellion Racing	–17 laps
7	22	LMP1	Vanina Ickx/Bas Leinders/Maxime Martin	Lola Aston Martin	Kronos Racing	–27 laps
8	41	LMP2	Tom Kimber-Smith/Olivier Lombard/Karim Ojjeh	Zytek Nissan	Greaves Motorsport	–29 laps
9	26	LMP2	Soheil Ayari/Franck Mailleux/Lucas Ordoñez	Oreca Nissan	Signatech Nissan	–35 laps
10	33	LMP2	João Barbosa/Christophe Bouchut/Scott Tucker	Lola Honda	Level 5 Motorsports	–36 laps
DNF	1	LMP1	Timo Bernhard/Romain Dumas/Mike Rockenfeller	Audi R18 TDI	Audi Sport Team Joest	lap 117 accident
DNF	3	LMP1	Dindo Capello/Tom Kristensen/Allan McNish	Audi R18 TDI	Audi Sport Team Joest	lap 15 accident

Intercontinental Le Mans Cup 2011

LM P1 Teams

Position	Team	Car	Points
1	Peugeot Sport Total	Peugeot	113
2	Audi Sport Team Joest	Audi R15 TDI/Audi R18 TDI	85
3	Rebellion Racing	Lola Toyota	50

LM P1 Manufacturers

Position	Manufacturer	Points
1	Peugeot	211
2	Audi	119

24h Le Mans 2012

Qualifying June 13/14

Position	Number	Class	Drivers	Car	Team	Lap time (minutes)
1	1	LMP1	Marcel Fässler/André Lotterer/Benoît Tréluyer	Audi R18 e-tron quattro	Audi Sport Team Joest	3.23,787
2	3	LMP1	Romain Dumas/Loïc Duval/Marc Gené	Audi R18 ultra	Audi Sport Team Joest	3.24,078
3	8	LMP1	Sébastien Buemi/Anthony Davidson/Stéphane Sarrazin	Toyota	Toyota Racing	3.24,842
4	2	LMP1	Dindo Capello/Tom Kristensen/Allan McNish	Audi R18 e-tron quattro	Audi Sport Team Joest	3.25,433
5	7	LMP1	Nicolas Lapierre/Kazuki Nakajima/Alexander Wurz	Toyota	Toyota Racing	3.25,488
6	4	LMP1	Marco Bonanomi/Oliver Jarvis/Mike Rockenfeller	Audi R18 ultra	Audi Sport North America	3.26,420
7	21	LMP1	Jonny Kane/Nick Leventis/Danny Watts	HPD Honda	Strakka Racing	3.29,622
8	12	LMP1	Nick Heidfeld/Neel Jani/Nicolas Prost	Lola Toyota	Rebellion Racing	3.29,837
9	13	LMP1	Andrea Belicchi/Jeroen Bleekemolen/Harold Primat	Lola Toyota	Rebellion Racing	3.31,866
10	17	LMP1	Seiji Ara/Sébastien Bourdais/Nicolas Minassian	Dome Judd	Pescarolo Team	3.33,066

Race June 16/17

Position	Number	Class	Drivers	Car	Team	Laps/Gap/Reason for DNF
1	1	LMP1	Marcel Fässler/André Lotterer/Benoît Tréluyer	Audi R18 e-tron quattro	Audi Sport Team Joest	378 laps
2	2	LMP1	Dindo Capello/Tom Kristensen/Allan McNish	Audi R18 e-tron quattro	Audi Sport Team Joest	–1 lap
3	4	LMP1	Marco Bonanomi/Oliver Jarvis/Mike Rockenfeller	Audi R18 ultra	Audi Sport North America	–3 laps
4	12	LMP1	Nick Heidfeld/Neel Jani/Nicolas Prost	Lola Toyota	Rebellion Racing	–11 laps
5	3	LMP1	Romain Dumas/Loïc Duval/Marc Gené	Audi R18 ultra	Audi Sport Team Joest	–12 laps
6	22	LMP1	David Brabham/Karun Chandhok/Peter Dumbreck	HPD Honda	JRM	–21 laps
7	44	LMP2	Ryan Dalziel/Enzo Potolicchio/Tom Kimber-Smith	HPD Honda	Starworks Motorsport	–24 laps
8	46	LMP2	Mathias Beche/Pierre Thiriet/Christophe Tinseau	Oreca Nissan	Thiriet by TDS Racing	–25 laps
9	49	LMP2	Soheil Ayari/Luis Perez-Companc/Pierre Kaffer	Oreca Nissan	Pecom Racing	–26 laps
10	26	LMP2	Nelson Panciatici/Pierre Ragues/Roman Rusinov	Oreca Nissan	Signatech Nissan	–27 laps

FIA World Endurance Championship 2012

Position	Drivers	Car	Team	Points
	World Endurance Drivers			
1	Marcel Fässler/André Lotterer/Benoît Tréluyer	Audi R18 TDI/R18 e-tron quattro	Audi Sport Team Joest	172.5
2	Tom Kristensen/Allan McNish	Audi R18 TDI/R18 e-tron quattro/R18 ultra	Audi Sport Team Joest	159
3	Nicolas Lapierre/Alexander Wurz	Toyota	Toyota Racing	96
5	Dindo Capello	Audi R18 TDI/R18 e-tron quattro	Audi Sport Team Joest	77
6	Romain Dumas/Loïc Duval	Audi R18 TDI/R18 ultra	Audi Sport Team Joest	67
11	Marc Gené	Audi R18 ultra	Audi Sport Team Joest	49
21	Timo Bernhard	Audi R18 TDI	Audi Sport Team Joest	18
22	Lucas di Grassi	Audi R18 ultra	Audi Sport Team Joest	15

LMP1 Manufacturers World Championship

Position	Manufacturer	Points
1	Audi	173
2	Toyota	96

24h Le Mans 2013

Qualifying June 19/20

Position	Number	Class	Drivers	Car	Team	Lap time (minutes)
1	2	LMP1	Loïc Duval/Tom Kristensen/Allan McNish	Audi R18 e-tron quattro	Audi Sport Team Joest	3.22,349
2	1	LMP1	Marcel Fässler/André Lotterer/Benoît Tréluyer	Audi R18 e-tron quattro	Audi Sport Team Joest	3.23,696
3	3	LMP1	Marc Gené/Lucas di Grassi/Oliver Jarvis	Audi R18 e-tron quattro	Audi Sport Team Joest	3.24,341
4	8	LMP1	Sébastien Buemi/Anthony Davidson/Stéphane Sarrazin	Toyota	Toyota Racing	3.26,654
5	7	LMP1	Nicolas Lapierre/Kazuki Nakajima/Alexander Wurz	Toyota	Toyota Racing	3.26,676
6	12	LMP1	Nick Heidfeld/Neel Jani/Nicolas Prost	Lola Toyota	Rebellion Racing	3.28,935
7	13	LMP1	Mathias Beche/Andrea Belicchi/Congfu Cheng	Lola Toyota	Rebellion Racing	3.32,167
8	21	LMP1	Jonny Kane/Nick Leventis/Danny Watts	HPD Honda	Strakka Racing	3.36,547
9	24	LMP2	Alex Brundle/David Heinemeier Hansson/Olivier Pla	Morgan Nissan	Oak Racing	3.38,621
10	26	LMP2	Mike Conway/John Martin/Roman Rusinov	Oreca Nissan	G-Drive Racing	3.39,535

Race June 22/23

Position	Number	Class	Drivers	Car	Team	Laps/Gap/Reason for DNF
1	2	LMP1	Loïc Duval/Tom Kristensen/Allan McNish	Audi R18 e-tron quattro	Audi Sport Team Joest	348 laps
2	8	LMP1	Sébastien Buemi/Anthony Davidson/Stéphane Sarrazin	Toyota	Toyota Racing	–1 lap
3	3	LMP1	Marc Gené/Lucas di Grassi/Oliver Jarvis	Audi R18 e-tron quattro	Audi Sport Team Joest	–1 lap
4	7	LMP1	Nicolas Lapierre/Kazuki Nakajima/Alexander Wurz	Toyota	Toyota Racing	–7 laps
5	1	LMP1	Marcel Fässler/André Lotterer/Benoît Tréluyer	Audi R18 e-tron quattro	Audi Sport Team Joest	–10 laps
6	21	LMP1	Jonny Kane/Nick Leventis/Danny Watts	HPD Honda	Strakka Racing	–16 laps
7	35	LMP2	Bertrand Baguette/Ricardo Gonzalez/Martin Plowman	Morgan Nissan	Oak Racing	–19 laps
8	24	LMP2	Alex Brundle/David Heinemeier Hansson/Olivier Pla	Morgan Nissan	Oak Racing	–20 laps
9	42	LMP2	Michael Krumm/Jann Mardenborough/Lucas Ordoñez	Zytek Nissan	Greaves Motorsport	–21 laps
10	49	LMP2	Pierre Kaffer/Nicolas Minassian/Luis Perez-Companc	Oreca Nissan	Pecom Racing	–23 laps

FIA World Endurance Championship 2013

Position	Drivers	Car	Team	Points
	World Endurance Drivers			
1	Loïc Duval/Tom Kristensen/Allan McNish	Audi R18 e-tron quattro	Audi Sport Team Joest	162
2	Marcel Fässler/André Lotterer/Benoît Tréluyer	Audi R18 e-tron quattro	Audi Sport Team Joest	149.25
3	Sébastien Buemi/Anthony Davidson/Stephane Sarrazin	Toyota	Toyota Racing	106.25
9	Marc Gené/Lucas di Grassi/Oliver Jarvis	Audi R18 e-tron quattro	Audi Sport Team Joest	45

World Endurance Manufacturers

Position	Manufacturer	Points
1	Audi	207
2	Toyota	142.5

24h Le Mans 2014

Qualifying June 11/12

Position	Number	Class	Drivers	Car	Team	Lap time (minutes)
1	7	LMP1 H	Kazuki Nakajima/Stéphane Sarrazin/Alexander Wurz	Toyota	Toyota Racing	3.21,789
2	14	LMP1 H	Romain Dumas/Neel Jani/Marc Lieb	Porsche	Porsche Team	3.22,146
3	8	LMP1 H	Sébastien Buemi/Anthony Davidson/Nicolas Lapierre	Toyota	Toyota Racing	3.22,523
4	20	LMP1 H	Timo Bernhard/Brendon Hartley/Mark Webber	Porsche	Porsche Team	3.22,908
5	3	LMP1 H	Filipe Albuquerque/Marco Bonanomi/Oliver Jarvis	Audi	Audi Sport Team Joest	3.23,271
6	2	LMP1 H	Marcel Fässler/André Lotterer/Benoît Tréluyer	Audi	Audi Sport Team Joest	3.24,276
7	1	LMP1 H	Marc Gené/Lucas di Grassi/Tom Kristensen	Audi	Audi Sport Team Joest	3.25,814
8	12	LMP1 L	Mathias Beche/Nick Heidfeld/Nicolas Prost	Rebellion Toyota	Rebellion Racing	3.29,763
9	13	LMP1 L	Andrea Belicchi/Dominik Kraihamer/Fabio Leimer	Rebellion Toyota	Rebellion Racing	3.31,608
10	46	LMP2	Ludovic Badey/Tristan Gommendy/Pierre Thiriet	Ligier Nissan	Thiriet by TDS Racing	3.37,609

Race June 14/15

Position	Number	Class	Drivers	Car	Team	Laps/Gap/Reason for DNF
1	2	LMP1 H	Marcel Fässler/André Lotterer/Benoît Tréluyer	Audi R18 e-tron quattro	Audi Sport Team Joest	379 laps
2	1	LMP1 H	Marc Gené/Lucas di Grassi/Tom Kristensen	Audi R18 e-tron quattro	Audi Sport Team Joest	–3 laps
3	8	LMP1 H	Sébastien Buemi/Anthony Davidson/Nicolas Lapierre	Toyota	Toyota Racing	–5 laps
4	12	LMP1 L	Mathias Beche/Nick Heidfeld/Nicolas Prost	Rebellion Toyota	Rebellion Racing	–19 laps
5	38	LMP2	Simon Dolan/Harry Tincknell/Oliver Turvey	Zytek Nissan	Jota Sport	–23 laps
6	46	LMP2	Ludovic Badey/Tristan Gommendy/Pierre Thiriet	Ligier Nissan	Thiriet by TDS Racing	–24 laps
7	36	LMP2	Paul-Loup Chatin/Nelson Panciatici/Oliver Webb	Alpine Nissan	Signatech Alpine	–24 laps
8	24	LMP2	Vincent Capillaire/Jan Charouz/René Rast	Oreca Nissan	Sébastien Loeb Racing	–25 laps
9	35	LMP2	Alex Brundle/Jann Mardenborough/Mark Shulzhitskiy	Ligier Nissan	Oak Racing	–25 laps
10	43	LMP2	Romain Brandela/Gary Hirsch/Christian Klien	Morgan Judd	Newblood by Morand Racing	–27 laps
DNF	3	LMP1 H	Filipe Albuquerque/Marco Bonanomi/Oliver Jarvis	Audi R18 e-tron quattro	Audi Sport Team Joest	lap 26 accident

FIA World Endurance Championship 2014

World Endurance Drivers

Position	Drivers	Car	Team	Points
1	Sébastien Buemi/Anthony Davidson	Toyota	Toyota Racing	166
2	Marcel Fässler/André Lotterer/Benoît Tréluyer	Audi R18 e-tron quattro	Audi Sport Team Joest	127
3	Romain Dumas/Neel Jani/Marc Lieb	Porsche	Porsche Team	117
4	Lucas di Grassi/Tom Kristensen	Audi R18 e-tron quattro	Audi Sport Team Joest	117
7	Loïc Duval	Audi R18 e-tron quattro	Audi Sport Team Joest	81
12	Marc Gené	Audi R18 e-tron quattro	Audi Sport Team Joest	36
22	Filipe Albuquerque/Marco Bonanomi	Audi R18 e-tron quattro	Audi Sport Team Joest	8

World Endurance Manufacturers

Position	Manufacturer	Points
1	Toyota	289
2	Audi	244
3	Porsche	193

24h Le Mans 2015

Qualifying June 10/11

Position	Number	Class	Drivers	Car	Team	Lap time (minutes)
1	18	LMP1 H	Romain Dumas/Neel Jani/Marc Lieb	Porsche	Porsche Team	3.16,887
2	17	LMP1 H	Timo Bernhard/Brendon Hartley/Mark Webber	Porsche	Porsche Team	3.17,767
3	19	LMP1 H	Earl Bamber/Nico Hülkenberg/Nick Tandy	Porsche	Porsche Team	3.18,862
4	8	LMP1 H	Loïc Duval/Lucas di Grassi/Oliver Jarvis	Audi R18 e-tron quattro	Audi Sport Team Joest	3.19,866
5	7	LMP1 H	Marcel Fässler/André Lotterer/Benoît Tréluyer	Audi R18 e-tron quattro	Audi Sport Team Joest	3.20,561
6	9	LMP1 H	Filipe Albuquerque/Marco Bonanomi/René Rast	Audi R18 e-tron quattro	Audi Sport Team Joest	3.20,997
7	2	LMP1 H	Mike Conway/Stéphane Sarrazin/Alexander Wurz	Toyota	Toyota Racing	3.23,543
8	1	LMP1 H	Sébastien Buemi/Anthony Davidson/Kazuki Nakajima	Toyota	Toyota Racing	3.23,767
9	12	LMP1	Mathias Beche/Nick Heidfeld/Nicolas Prost	Rebellion Aer	Rebellion Racing	3.26,874
10	13	LMP1	Daniel Abt/Alexandre Imperatori/Dominik Kraihamer	Rebellion Aer	Rebellion Racing	3.28,930

Race June 13/14

Position	Number	Class	Drivers	Car	Team	Laps/Gap/Reason for DNF
1	19	LMP1 H	Earl Bamber/Nico Hülkenberg/Nick Tandy	Porsche	Porsche Team	395 laps
2	17	LMP1 H	Timo Bernhard/Brendon Hartley/Mark Webber	Porsche	Porsche Team	–1 lap
3	7	LMP1 H	Marcel Fässler/André Lotterer/Benoît Tréluyer	Audi R18 e-tron quattro	Audi Sport Team Joest	–2 laps
4	8	LMP1 H	Loïc Duval/Lucas di Grassi/Oliver Jarvis	Audi R18 e-tron quattro	Audi Sport Team Joest	–3 laps
5	18	LMP1 H	Romain Dumas/Neel Jani/Marc Lieb	Porsche	Porsche Team	–4 laps
6	2	LMP1 H	Mike Conway/Stéphane Sarrazin/Alexander Wurz	Toyota	Toyota Racing	–8 laps
7	9	LMP1 H	Filipe Albuquerque/Marco Bonanomi/René Rast	Audi R18 e-tron quattro	Audi Sport Team Joest	–8 laps
8	1	LMP1 H	Sébastien Buemi/Anthony Davidson/Kazuki Nakajima	Toyota	Toyota Racing	–9 laps
9	47	LMP2	Richard Bradley/Matthew Howson/Nicolas Lapierre	Oreca Nissan	KCMG	–37 laps
10	38	LMP2	Simon Dolan/Mitch Evans/Oliver Turvey	Gibson Nissan	Jota Sport	–37 laps

FIA World Endurance Championship 2015

World Endurance Drivers

Position	Drivers	Car	Team	Points
1	Timo Bernhard/Brendon Hartley/Mark Webber	Porsche	Porsche Team	166
2	Marcel Fässler/André Lotterer/Benoît Tréluyer	Audi R18 e-tron quattro	Audi Sport Team Joest	161
3	Romain Dumas/Neel Jani/Marc Lieb	Porsche	Porsche Team	138.5
4	Loïc Duval/Lucas di Grassi/Oliver Jarvis	Audi R18 e-tron quattro	Audi Sport Team Joest	99
12	Filipe Albuquerque/Marco Bonanomi/René Rast	Audi R18 e-tron quattro	Audi Sport Team Joest	24

World Endurance Manufacturers

Position	Manufacturer	Points
1	Porsche	344
2	Audi	264
3	Toyota	164
4	Nissan	0

24h Le Mans 2016

Qualifying June 15/16

Position	Number	Class	Drivers	Car	Team	Lap time (minutes)
1	2	LMP1 H	Romain Dumas/Neel Jani/Marc Lieb	Porsche	Porsche Team	3.19,733
2	1	LMP1 H	Timo Bernhard/Brendon Hartley/Mark Webber	Porsche	Porsche Team	3.20,203
3	6	LMP1 H	Michael Conway/Kamui Kobayashi/Stéphane Sarrazin	Toyota	Toyota Gazoo Racing	3.20,737
4	5	LMP1 H	Sébastien Buemi/Anthony Davidson/Kazuki Nakajima	Toyota	Toyota Gazoo Racing	3.21,903
5	7	LMP1 H	Marcel Fässler/André Lotterer/Benoît Tréluyer	Audi R18	Audi Sport Team Joest	3.22,780
6	8	LMP1 H	Loïc Duval/Lucas di Grassi/Oliver Jarvis	Audi R18	Audi Sport Team Joest	3.22,823
7	13	LMP1	Alexancre Imperatori/Dominik Kraihamer/Mathéo Tuscher	Rebellion Aer	Rebellion Racing	3.26,586
8	12	LMP1	Nick Heidfeld/Nelson Piquet/Nicolas Prost	Rebellion Aer	Rebellion Racing	3.27,348
9	4	LMP1	Pierre Kaffer/Simon Trummer/Oliver Webb	CLM Aer	ByKolles Racing Team	3.34,168
10	26	LMP2	René Rast/Roman Rusinov/Will Stevens	Oreca Nissan	G-Drive Racing	3.36,605

Race June 18/19

Position	Number	Class	Drivers	Car	Team	Laps/Gap/Reason for DNF
1	2	LMP1 H	Romain Dumas/Neel Jani/Marc Lieb	Porsche	Porsche Team	384 laps
2	6	LMP1 H	Michael Conway/Kamui Kobayashi/Stéphane Sarrazin	Toyota	Toyota Gazoo Racing	–3 laps
3	8	LMP1 H	Loïc Duval/Lucas di Grassi/Oliver Jarvis	Audi R18	Audi Sport Team Joest	–12 laps
4	7	LMP1 H	Marcel Fässler/André Lotterer/Benoît Tréluyer	Audi R18	Audi Sport Team Joest	–17 laps
5	36	LMP2	Gustavo Menezes/Nicolas Lapierre/Stéphane Richelmi	Alpine Nissan	Signatech Alpine	–27 laps
6	26	LMP2	René Rast/Roman Rusinov/Will Stevens	Oreca Nissan	G-Drive Racing	–27 laps
7	37	LMP2	Kirill Ladygin/Vitaly Petrov/Victor Shaytar	BR Nissan	SMP Racing	–31 laps
8	42	LMP2	Jonny Kane/Nick Leventis/Danny Watts	Gibson Nissan	Strakka Racing	–33 laps
9	33	LMP2	Nick de Bruijn/Tristan Gommendy/Pu Junjin	Oreca Nissan	Eurasia Motorsport	–36 laps
10	41	LMP2	Nathanaël Berthon/Julien Canal/Memo Rojas	Ligier Nissan	Greaves Motorsport	–36 laps

FIA World Endurance Championship 2016

World Endurance Drivers

Position	Drivers	Car	Team	Points
1	Romain Dumas/Neel Jani/Marc Lieb	Porsche	Porsche Team	160
2	Loïc Duval/Lucas di Grassi/Oliver Jarvis	Audi R18	Audi Sport Team Joest	147.5
3	Mike Conway/Kamui Kobayashi/Stéphane Sarrazin	Toyota	Toyota Gazoo Racing	145
5	Marcel Fässler/André Lotterer	Audi R18	Audi Sport Team Joest	104
6	Benoît Tréluyer	Audi R18	Audi Sport Team Joest	70

World Endurance Manufacturers

Position	Manufacturer	Points
1	Porsche	324
2	Audi	266
3	Toyota	229

Textual sources

Newspapers and magazines

- AutoBild
- auto motor und sport
- Auto Zeitung
- Autohebdo
- Automobil-Wirtschaft
- Automobiltechnische Zeitschrift (ATZ)
- Autosport
- Donaukurier
- Edgar Middle East Magazine
- L'Equipe
- Heilbronner Stimme
- Kölnische Rundschau
- Le Mans Series & Sportscar Racer
- mot
- Motor Sport
- Motorsport aktuell
- Motorsport Guide
- Programme Officiel 24h Le Mans
- PS report
- Race Tech International
- Race Tech Magazine
- Racecar Engineering
- Racer
- revvv
- sport auto
- Trackstar – Das Audi-Motorsportmagazin

Online

- https://au.motorsport.com
- https://newsroom.porsche.com
- https://newsroom.toyota.eu
- https://panoz.com
- https://srt41.com
- https://thecoastalstar.com
- www.24h-lemans.com
- www.acisport.it
- www.auto-motor-und-sport.de
- www.audi-mediacenter.com
- www.autonewsinfo.com
- www.autosport.com
- www.bentleymotors.com
- www.championracing.net
- www.dailysportscar.com
- www.facebook.com/PeterStevensDesign
- www.fia.com
- www.fiawec.com
- www.gibsontech.co.uk
- www.goethe.de
- www.gulfoilltd.com
- www.ladepeche.fr
- www.michel-vaillant.de
- www.motorsport-total.com
- www.motorsportmagazine.com
- www.pierrickchazeaud.com
- www.press.bmwgroup.com
- www.racecar-engineering.com
- www.roadandtrack.com
- www.speedweek.com
- www.totalenergies24hours.com
- www.toyota-media.de
- www.volkswagen-newsroom.com

Monographs and compendiums

- James Baker: American Le Mans Series Yearbook 2000. Teddington: Haymarket Autosport Publications, 2001
- Alain Bienvenu, Christian Moity, Jean-Marc Teissedre: Le Mans 24 Hours 2011, Waterloo: Apach, 2011
- Alain Bienvenu, Christian Moity, Jean-Marc Teissedre: Le Mans 24 Hours 2013, Antony: E-T-A-I, 2013
- Alain Bienvenu, Christian Moity, Jean-Marc Teissedre: Le Mans 24 Hours 2015, Antony: E-T-A-I, 2015
- Charles-Henri Bonnet: Winning Spirit since 1980, Kortenberg: Motion Motorsports, 2017
- Christian Borel, Mario Luini, Gérard Vallat, Benoît Wyder, Jean-Marie Wyder: Les Suisses au Mans 2009, Couvet: turbo éditions, 2009
- Christian Borel, Mario Luini, Gérard Vallat, Benoît Wyder, Jean-Marie Wyder: Die Schweizer in Le Mans 2011, Saint-Sulpice: turbo éditions, 2011
- Christian Borel, Mario Luini, Gérard Vallat, Benoît Wyder, Jean-Marie Wyder: Les Suisses au Mans 2012, Saint-Sulpice: turbo éditions, 2012
- Christian Borel, Mario Luini, Gérard Vallat, Benoît Wyder, Jean-Marie Wyder: Les Suisses au Mans 2013, Saint-Sulpice: turbo éditions, 2013
- Michael Cotton, Alfredo Filippone, Oliver Loisy: Le Mans Endurance Series Yearbook 2005, St. Cyr-au-Mont: Apollo Publishing, undated
- Carlo Demand, Paul Simsa: Die Gordon-Bennett-Rennen 1900–1905, Stuttgart: Motorbuch-Verlag, 1987
- Pierre Dieudonné: Never stop Challenging! Mazda's Conquest of Le Mans, Waterloo: Apach, 2011
- Thomas Erdmann, Ralf Friese, Peter Kirchberg, Ralph Plagmann: Vier Ringe: Die Audi Geschichte, Bielefeld: Delius Klasing, 2009
- Wilfried Feldenkirchen: Unternehmenspolitische Aspekte in der Geschichte des Motorsports bei der Daimler-Benz AG, in Wilfried Feldenkirchen, Armin Herrmann, Harry Niemann: Wissenschaftliche Schriftenreihe des DaimlerChrysler Konzernarchivs Band 5 – Geschichte des Rennsports, Bielefeld: Delius Klasing, 2002
- Nils Finderup: Tom K & Le Mans. Forlaget Finsen, no location, 2003
- Nils Finderup: Tom Kristensen. We are the Champions, Forlaget Finsen, no location, 2005
- Jörg Thomas Födisch, Jost Nesshöver, Rainer Rossbach, Harold Schwarz: Porsche 917: Die Helden, die Sieger, der Mythos, Cologne: Verlag Reinhard Klein, 2006

- Connie Goudinoff: Mazda Motorsports, Osceola: Motorbooks International, 1992

- Peter Higham: The Guinness Book of International Motor Racing, London: Guinness World Records Limited/Motorbooks International, 1995

- Peter Hofmann: Hybridfahrzeuge. Vienna: Springer-Verlag, 2014

- François Hurel: Alpine au Mans, Nîmes: Editions du Palmier, 2002

- Tom Kristensen, Lars Krone: Tom Kristensen – The Book, no location, no publisher, 2015

- Christian Moity, Jean-Marc Tesseidre: 24 Heures du Mans 1923–1992, Tome 1. Besançon/Le Mans: Editions d'Art J. P. Barthelemy/Automobile Club de l'Ouest, 1992

- Christian Moity, Jean-Marc Teissedre: 2000 Le Mans 24 Hours, Brussels: GSN Publishing, 2000

- Christian Moity, Jean-Marc Teissedre: 2001 Le Mans 24 Hours, Brussels: GSN Publishing, 2001

- Christian Moity, Jean-Marc Teissedre: 2005 Le Mans 24 Hours, Waterloo: Apach Publishing, 2005

- Michael Pfadenhauer: Aerodynamikentwicklung im Rennsport am Beispiel Audi R8, in Michael Bargende, Jochen Wiedemann (Hrsg.): Kraftfahrwesen und Verbrennungsmotoren, Renningen: expert verlag, 2001

- Mathias Pfaffel: Vom selbständigen Unternehmen zum integrierten Konzernstandort. Die AUDI NSU AUTO UNION AG in Neckarsulm 1969–1984, Stuttgart: Franz Steiner Verlag, 2019

- Peter Schäffner: The Story of a Champion. Timo Bernhard, Duisburg: Gruppe C Motorsport Verlag, 2015

- Tony Southgate: From drawing board to chequered flag, Croydon: Motor Racing Publications, 2010

- Quentin Spurring: Le Mans. The official history of the world's greatest Motor race 1949–59, Sparkford: Haynes Publishing, 2011

- Jean-Marc Teissedre: The Quest for Le Mans, Paris: EPA Publishing, 2009

- David Tremayne: Champion Racing. A little bit of magic, Phoenix: David Bull Publishing, 2014

- Patrice Vergès: Des DB aux Matra. No location, Drivers, 2005

- Thomas Voigt: Audi A4. DTM Champion 2004. Ingolstadt: AUDI AG, 2004

- Thomas Voigt: Audi R8. Born to win, Ingolstadt: AUDI AG, 2006

- Thomas Voigt: Rocky der Rennfahrer, Hamburg: Adrenalin Verlag, 2014

- Ian Wagstaff: Audi R8, Dorchester: Veloce Publishing, 2011

- Alexander von Wegner: 30 years of Audi Sport, Ingolstadt: AUDI AG, 2010

- Othmar Wickenheiser: Audi Design: Automobildesign von 1965 bis zur Gegenwart. Bielefeld: Delius Klasing, 2015

Exhibition catalog

- Sarthe, terre des pionniers. Centenaire des vols de Wilbur Wright au Mans 1908–2008, Le Mans: Archives départementales de la Sarthe, 2008

AUDI AG publications

- Audi Express 1, June 10, 1999

- Audi Express 3, June 12, 1999

- Audi Express 4, June 13, 1999

- Audi Express 1, June 16, 2006

- Audi Express 1, June 20, 2006

- Audi 2006 Annual Report

- Audi 2011 Annual Report

- Audi 2012 Annual Report

- Audi Communications: Press kit Audi. Vorsprung. 100. Mut, 2009

- Audi Motorsport Communications: Press kit Le Mans 1999

- Audi Motorsport Communications: Press kit Audi at Le Mans 2000

- Audi Motorsport Communications: Booklet Audi Press Information Le Mans 2002

- Audi Motorsport Communications: Booklet Motorsport Media Info 2003

- Audi Motorsport Communications: Booklet Le Mans 2006

- Audi Motorsport Communications: Booklet 24h Le Mans 2008

- Audi Motorsport Communications: Press kit Audi in Motorsport 2008/2009

- Audi Motorsport Communications: Booklet Audi R15 TDI 2010

- Audi Motorsport Communications: Booklet Audi sports prototypes 2011

- Audi Motorsport Communications: Booklet Audi sports prototypes 2012

- Audi Motorsport Communications: Booklet Audi sports prototypes 2013

- Audi Motorsport Communications: Booklet Audi sports prototypes 2014

- Audi Motorsport Communications: Press kit Audi in the 2015 WEC

- Audi Motorsport Communications: Basic information Audi in the 2016 WEC

- Audi MediaInfo Magazine: Motorsport and Production, 2011

- Audi MediaInfo Magazine: Motorsport and Production. e-tron quattro, 2012

- Audi MediaInfo Magazine: Motorsport and Production. Audi Le Mans Prototypes 1999–2013, 2013

- Audi MediaInfo

- Encounter. The Audi Technology Magazine 01/2011

- Encounter. The Audi Technology Magazine 01/2012

AUDI AG internal papers and presentations

- Audi Motorsport Communications Q&A

- Audi Motorsport Communications Internal briefing booklet Le Mans 24 Hours

- Entwicklungsprozess Audi Sport – Trends, working paper by Dr. Martin Mühlmeier (undated)

- Internal argumentation of Audi Motorsport Communications: Topics of the weekend

- Internal report Howden Haynes: Le Mans 2008 Race Week Chassis R10T-204

- Le Mans 2011 Race Statistics, internal source Audi Sport

- Leichtbau – Die Audi Kernkompetenz, internal presentation of the I/VS-21 department, 2011

- Comparison of consumption. Contemporary data, internal document (undated)

- Ulrich Baretzky, Wolfgang Hatz, Dr. Wolfgang Ullrich: Rennsport bei Audi – Impulse für die Serienentwicklung am Beispiel FSI, presentation (undated)

- A. S. Mantzel: Rennbericht über Rennen Le Mans am 15./16. Juni 1963, correspondence, June 18, 1963

- Karl-Friedrich Trübsbach: Vorbericht Les 24 Heures du Mans am 15./16. Juni 1963, internal document of the Sport Support Department VI-35 dated June 7, 1963

- Dr. Wolfgang Ullrich: Audi – der Sieger von Le Mans, presentation on ÖVK event, May 11, 2004

Miscellaneous publications

- 24h Le Mans Press Information

- ACO Press Information

- Audi Sport Japan Team Goh press release

- BMW Group Corporate Communications

- Champion Racing press release

- Johansson Motorsport team information

- Michelin Formel 1 & Motorsport News

- Nissan Leaflet Le Mans 24 Hours

- Nissan press releases and press kits

- Oreca press releases and press kits

- Peugeot press releases and press kits

- Porsche Press Information

- Team Bentley Press release

- Team Goh International Press kit

- Toyota Press release

- Volkswagen Annual Report 2007

- Volkswagen Motorsport Information

Research manuscripts and interview transcripts

- Authors' research manuscript, May 10, 2012

- Authors' research manuscript, November 9, 2012

- Transcript of interview with Ulrich Baretzky on December 19, 2022

- Transcript of interview with Ulrich Baretzky on January 23, 2023

- Transcript of interview with Ulrich Baretzky by Ian Bamsey on June 12, 2014

- Transcript of interview with Dieter Basche on October 28, 2022

- Transcript of interview with Thomas Bauch on October 28, 2022

- Transcript of interview with Dindo Capello on November 24, 2022

- Transcript of interview with Pierre Dieudonné on July 29, 2022

- Transcript of interview with Marcel Fässler on November 15, 2022

- Transcript of interview with Leena Gade on December 13, 2022

- Transcript of interview with Ralf Jüttner on November 17, 2022

- Transcript of interview with Andreas Köppen on October 27, 2022

- Transcript of interview with Tom Kristensen on December 6, 2022

- Transcript of interview with Allan McNish on April 11, 2015

- Transcript of interview with Dr. Franz-Josef Paefgen on October 27, 2022

- Transcript of interview with Torsten Robbens on August 23, 2022

- Transcript of interview with Dr. Wolfgang Ullrich on March 31, 2009

- Transcript of interview with Dr. Wolfgang Ullrich on April 30, 2012

- Transcript of interview with Dr. Wolfgang Ullrich by Yumiko Kaijima on May 20, 2012

- Transcript of interview with Dr. Wolfgang Ullrich on June 20, 2012

- Transcript of interview with Dr. Wolfgang Ullrich on June 18, 2015

- Transcript of interview with Dr. Wolfgang Ullrich on December 7/8, 2022

- Transcript Interview Timo Witt, October 27, 2022

List of image sources

ACO 220
Adrenal Media/Gabi Tomescu 260
Aston Martin Racing 152
AUDI AG 13, 20, 22, 23, 24, 26–45, 50, 52, 54–57, 60, 62, 66, 67, 74, 75, 80, 82, 92, 93, 95, 97, 105–109, 113, 114, 122, 126, 143, 146, 153, 170, 174, 175, 185, 190, 192, 193, 194, 215, 219, 236, 257, 258, 267–271, 274, 275, 288, 287, 290–293, 295
AUDI AG/Klaus Nagel 53, 55, 56, 58/59, 61, 63–66, 69–73, 76, 272, 284–285, 291
AUDI AG/Thomas Kittel 135
AUDI AG/Daniel Wollstein 114
Audi Motorsport Communications/Ferdi Kräling Motorsport-Bild GmbH 3, 6–7, 8–12, 15, 17–19, 25, 26, 28, 47, 49, 51–53, 57, 60, 61–63, 67, 69–72, 77, 80–83, 110, 112–122, 124–135, 136–144, 147, 148–159, 160–169, 171–173, 175–188, 190–191, 193, 195–197, 199–212, 214, 216–219, 221–235, 237, 238, 240–261, 265, 270, 272–274, 279, 282–296
Audi Motorsport Communications/Michael Kunkel 236, 250, 258, 262–265
Pascal Aunai 254
Autocar, via www.imago-images.de 22
Bentley 11, 87–89
BMW 17
BTZ 46/47
John Brooks 51
Chrysler Corporation 198
Ferrari 12
Graton Editeur 130, 131
Hoch Zwei/Thomas Suer 198
Bernhard Huber 268
Jaguar 12, 17
Burkhard Kasan 146
Daniel Koebe 195
LAT Photographic 138
Regis Lefebure 48, 77–79, 84, 91, 92, 94–97, 99–105, 288
David Lister 85
David Lord 280
Mazda 14
Nissan 15, 242
Oreca/Bernard Bakalian 103
Panoz 198
Peugeot Sport/DPPI 152, 167
Peugeot Sport 138, 198
Porsche AG 16, 53, 162, 198, 218, 251
Privat 7, 29, 277, 295
Renault 10
Gunter Stachon Photography 213
Toyota Deutschland 198
Toyota Gazoo Racing 189, 197, 209, 218, 241, 251
Turbopress/Christian Borel 62
Turbopress/Audrey Perriard 278
Volkswagen Motorsport/DPPI 123
Volkswagen Motorsport/Ferdi Kräling Motorsport-Bild GmbH 145
Volkswagen 29, 123

Publishing details

Publisher
Auto Union GmbH
Auto-Union-Straße 1
85057 Ingolstadt
www.audi.de/tradition

Authors
Lars Krone
Alexander von Wegner

Copy Editors
David Feist
Dr. Mathias Pfaffel

Translation
Helga Oberländer

Layout
Speedpool GmbH, Hamburg

Printed by
L.E.G.O. – Legatoria Editoriale Giovanni Olivotto, Vicenza
Printed in Italy 2023

Delius Klasing Verlag
Siekerwall 21, 33602 Bielefeld
Phone +49 521 / 559-0
Fax +49 521 / 559-115
info@delius-klasing.de
www.delius-klasing.de

**Bibliographical Information
of the German National Library**
The German National Library catalogs
this publication in the German
National Bibliography;
detailed bibliographic information
can be found on the Internet
website: http://dnb.dnb.de.

1st edition
ISBN 978-3-667-12653-5

© Auto Union GmbH
April 2023

MIX
Paper | Supporting
responsible forestry
FSC® C023419